The Choice
Is Always Ours

Revised and Abridged

The Choice Is Always Ours

The Classic Anthology on the Spiritual Way

editor

Dorothy Berkley Phillips,

coeditors

Elizabeth Boyden Howes

Lucille M. Nixon,

1817

Harper & Row, Publishers, San Francisco

New York, Grand Rapids, Philadelphia, St. Louis
London, Singapore, Sydney, Tokyo, Toronto

An 82-page Study Guide for use with *The Choice Is Always Ours* is available from the Guild for Psychological Studies, 2230 Divisadero Street, San Francisco, California 94115. Please send $4.50 per copy ordered, plus $1.50 for postage and handling.

FIRST HARPER AND ROW PAPERBACK EDITION PUBLISHED IN 1989

Library of Congress Cataloging-in-Publication Data

The Choice Is Always Ours.

1. Spiritual life. I. Phillips, Dorothy Berkley,
1906– . II. Howes, Elizabeth Boyden, 1907–
III. Nixon, Lucille M., 1908–1963.
BL624.C4753 1989 291.4′4 88-45660
ISBN 0-06-066549-1

89 90 91 92 93 FAIR 10 9 8 7 6 5 4 3 2

In gratitude to
Carl Gustav Jung
Fritz Kunkel
Henry Burton Sharman

and to
Sheila Moon
who has through the years given of her literary and poetic gifts to help weave this book into an artistic whole.

PERSONAL ACKNOWLEDGMENTS

As the last of the three editors of this book, I would like to dedicate this new edition to:

Dorothy Berkley Phillips, the main editor and central figure behind this unique achievement. In a real sense it was her "offspring," and she tended and cared for it. Because Dorothy was a semi-invalid most of her adult life, she had the time to meet its demands. It is fitting that I should be writing this acknowledgment on the third anniversary of her death.

The idea of this book originated from our dialogue with one another on the implications of the study done together in the summer of 1930 in a seminar given by Dr. Henry Burton Sharman on *The Records of the Life of Jesus*. The inspiration for the book and the general format (division into three sections) came from insights into that material. The dialogue and deep relationship with Dorothy I treasure as central to my life and to my religious contribution, reflected in the seminars offered the year around by the Guild for Psychological Studies in San Francisco. They offer people the opportunity to search the depth and meaning of "the mosaic of human insight" into the Way as expressed here in this book.

Lucille Nixon (1909–1963), as the third editor, gave years of cooperation on this book and deep and trustworthy friendship.

I wish to express deep gratitude to the long list of people (seventy-five) who did much of the initial reading of the first edition of this book. In addition, there were many others who provided criticism and assistance with subsequent editions. It is impossible to list them all. I would like to make special note of the contributions of Florence Little, who handled all the permissions and library research, and of Luella Sibbald, who worked on the Index.

Finally, I am aware, as was Dorothy Phillips, of all the individuals who through the years profoundly influenced the thinking of us as editors. They have proved to be determining factors in whatever insights and truths are to be found in this book. Even profound gratitude does not fully acknowledge their gift.

Elizabeth Boyden Howes
Berkeley, California
August 15, 1988

ACKNOWLEDGMENT FOR PERMISSION TO PUBLISH

Grateful acknowledgment is made to the following for permission to reprint selections from the works indicated below. Any inadvertent errors or omissions in this list will be corrected in future editions after notification to the editors.

ABINGDON PRESS: From *The Springs of Creative Living* by Rollo May, copyright renewal 1968 by Rollo May, used by permission of Abingdon Press; from *Victorious Living* by E. Stanley Jones, copyright renewal 1964 by E. Stanley Jones, used by permission of Abingdon Press; from *Ways of Praying* by Muriel Lester, used by permission of Abingdon Press.

THE ANALYTICAL PSYCHOLOGY CLUB OF NEW YORK, INC.: Article by Tao Strong in *Bulletin of the Analytical Psychology Club of New York*, 1957.

GEORGE ALLEN AND UNWIN, LTD. (London): *Mysticism and Logic* by Bertrand Russell, 1929; *Towards Democracy* by Edward Carpenter, 1922.

BEACON PRESS: *Beyond God the Father* by Mary Daly, copyright 1973 by Mary Daly.

BAILLERE, TINDALL AND COX (London): *Mythology of the Soul* by H. G. Baynes, 1940.

JOHN ELOF BOODIN: *Cosmic Evolution* by John Elof Boodin, copyright 1925 by John Elof Boodin.

CAMBRIDGE UNIVERSITY PRESS (New York): *New Pathways in Science* by Sir Arthur Eddington, copyright 1935 by The Macmillan Company; *The Nature of the Physical World* by Sir Arthur Eddington, copyright 1928, 1935 by The Macmillan Company; *Devotions upon Emergent Occasions* by John Donne (Sparrow ed.).

CHATTO AND WINDUS AND JOANNA FIELD (Mrs. Marion Milner): *A Life of One's Own* by Joanna Field, copyright 1934 by Joanna Field.

CLARENDON PRESS (Oxford): *The Dhammapada*, in *Sacred Books of the East*, trans. F. Max Müller, 1881; *The Discourses and Manual of Epictetus*, trans. P. E. Matheson.

STANWOOD COBB: Poem in *Patterns in Jade* by Wu Ming Fu, published by Avalon Press, 1935.

WILLIAM CLEVELAND, JR., Editor, *Inward Light:* Selections by Richard Gregg, William Penn and Rufus Jones.

DIVISION OF CHRISTIAN EDUCATION OF THE NATIONAL COUNCIL OF CHURCHES OF CHRIST IN THE U.S.A.: *The Holy Bible,* Revised Standard Version, copyright 1946, 1952 by the Division of Christian Education of the National Council of the Churches of Christ in the U.S.A.

HOWARD E. COLLIER, *and The Guild of Pastoral Psychology* (London): *The Place of Worship in Modern Medicine* by Howard E. Collier, 1944.

COLUMBIA UNIVERSITY PRESS: *Rainer Maria Rilke Poems,* trans. Jessie Lemont, 1943.

JOHN DAY AND COMPANY and INTEXT PRESS: *The Way of Life according to Lao-tzu,* trans. Witter Bynner, copyright © 1944 by Witter Bynner; *The Discovery of India* by Jahwaharlal Nehru, copyright © 1946, John Day Company.

DEVIN-ADAIR COMPANY: *Conversations with Artists* by Selden Rodman, copyright © 1957 by Devin-Adair Co.

DOUBLEDAY AND COMPANY INC.: Excerpt from *America Is Hard to Find* by Daniel Berrigan, copyright © 1972 by Daniel Berrigan, reprinted by permission of Doubleday and Company, Inc.

E. P. DUTTON AND COMPANY: *The Republic of Plato,* trans. A. D. Lindsay, 1950; *The Life of Prayer* by Friedrich von Hugel; *Concerning the Inner Life* by Evelyn Underhill, 1926.

FORDHAM UNIVERSITY PRESS: *Still-Point* by William Johnston, copyright 1970, Fordham University Press.

GERRY, PEGGY BAUM: Selection from *Bulletin of the Analytical Psychology Club of Los Angeles.*

MRS. A. C. W. GRAHAM (Aelfrido Catherine Tillyard): *Spiritual Exercises and Their Results* by Aelfrida Catherine Tillyard.

DWIGHT GODDARD ESTATE: *Lao-tzu's Tao and Wu-wei,* trans. Bhikshu Wai-dau and Dwight Goddard.

GOLDEN QUILL PRESS and Sheila Moon for *Joseph's Son* by Sheila Moon, copyright 1972 by Golden Quill Press.

GROVE PRESS, INC.: *The Spirit of Zen,* copyright © 1958 by Alan Watts, reprinted by permission of Grove Press, Inc.

GUILD FOR PSYCHOLOGICAL STUDIES (San Francisco): . . . *And a Time to Die* by Mark Pelgrin, edited by Sheila Moon and Elizabeth B. Howes.

HARCOURT, BRACE, JOVANOVICH, INC.: From *Murder in the Cathedral* by T. S. Eliot, copyright 1935 by Harcourt, Brace, Jovanovich, renewed, 1963 by T. S. Eliot, reprinted by permission of the publishers; from *No Man Is an Island* by Thomas Merton, copyright © 1955 by the Abbey of Our Lady of Gesthemane, reprinted by permission of Harcourt, Brace, Jovanovich, Inc.; *Proving of Psyche* by Hugh L'Anson Fausett; *The Social Substance of Religion* by Gerald Heard; from *The Little Prince* by Antoine de Saint-Exupéry, trans. Katherine Woods, copyright 1943, 1971 by Harcourt, Brace, Jovanovich, Inc. and reprinted with their permission; from choruses from "The Rock" in *Collected Poems* 1909–1962 by T.S. Eliot, copyright 1936, Harcourt, Brace, Jovanovich, Inc. and copyright 1963, 1964 by T.S. Eliot; from *Four Quartets,* copyright 1942, 1943 by T.S. Eliot, renewed 1970 by Esme Eliot, reprinted by permission of Harcourt, Brace, Jovanovich, Inc.

HARPER AND ROW, PUBLISHERS: *The Perennial Philosophy* by Aldous Huxley, copyright 1945 by Aldous Huxley; *Purity of Heart* by Sören Kierkegaard, trans. Douglas Steere, copyright 1938 by Harper and Row; *The Interpretation of Christian Ethics* by Reinhold Niebuhr, copyright 1935 by Harper and Row, Publishers, Inc.; *The Spiritual Life* by Evelyn Underhill, copyright 1955 by Harper and Row; *A Testament of Devotion* by Thomas Kelly, copyright 1941 by Harper and Row; *Meister Eckhart,* trans. Raymond B. Blakney, copyright 1941 by Harper and Row; "Cicadas" from *The Collected Poetry of Aldous Huxley* (1971) edited by Donald Watt; *Why We Can't Wait* by Martin Luther King, copyright 1963 by Martin Luther King, Jr., by permission of Harper and Row, Publishers, Inc.; *Kagawa* by William Axling, copyright 1946 by Harper and Row; *The Growth of Religion* by Henry Nelson Wieman and Walter Marshall Horton, copyright 1938 by Harper and Row; *Paulus* by Rollo May, copyright 1973 by Rollo May, by permission of Harper and Row, Publishers, Inc.; *Time to Spare* by Douglas Steere, copyright 1949 by Harper and Row, Publishers, Inc.; *God* by John Middleton Murry, 1929; *Hymn of the Universe* by Teilhard de Chardin, copyright 1965, Harper and Row and William Collier's Sons Company Ltd. (London), used with permission of Harper and Row; *The Creed of Christ,* copyright 1940 by Gerald Heard; *Pain, Sex and Time,* copyright 1939 by Gerald Heard; *A Preface to Prayer,* copyright © 1954 by Gerald Heard.

HENRY HOLT AND CO., INC.: *The Religious Situation* by Paul Tillich, trans. H. Richard Niebuhr, copyright 1932 by Henry Holt and Co., Inc.; and George Allen and Unwin, Ltd. (London).

HOUGHTON MIFFLIN CO.: *The Edge of the Sea* by Rachel Carson, copyright © 1955 by Rachel Carson; *The Dance of Life* by Havelock Ellis, copyright 1923 by Havelock Ellis.

ELIZABETH BOYDEN HOWES: *Intersection and Beyond,* Guild for Psychological Studies, 2230 Divisadero St., San Francisco, Ca. 94115, copyright Elizabeth Boyden Howes.

HUNTER, ALLAN, *Three Trumpets Sound,* copyright 1939 by International Committee of the Y.W.C.A.

MRS. LAURA A. HUXLEY for *Meditation on Grace* by Aldous Huxley.

JONATHAN CAPE, LTD. (London), and John Middleton Murry: *To the Unknown God* by John Middleton Murry, 1930.

ALFRED A. KNOPF, INC.: *Buddhist Meditations* by Grace Constant Lounsbery, copyright 1935 by Alfred A. Knopf, Inc.; sayings from Abba Dorotheus, reprinted from *Tertium Organum* by P. D. Ouspensky, copyright 1922 by Claud Bragdon; *The Singing Wilderness* by Sigurd F. Olson, copyright © 1956 by Sigurd F. Olson; and John Middleton Murry: *The Journal of Katherine Mansfield,* copyright 1927 by Alfred A. Knopf, Inc.; *Markings* by Dag Hammarskjold, trans. Leif Sjoberg and W. H. Auden, copyright 1964 by Alfred A. Knopf, Inc. and Faber and Faber, Ltd., foreword copyright, W. H. Auden.

F. LAFITTE-AXON: *The Dance of Life,* copyright 1923, permission of F. Lafitte-Axon.

LITTLE, BROWN AND CO.: "A Death Blow is a Life Blow to Some" from *The Poems of Emily Dickinson,* ed. Martha Dickinson Bianchi and Alfred Leete Hampon, and Atlantic Monthly Press: *John Woolman: American Quaker* by Janet Payne Whitney, copyright 1942 by Janet Payne Whitney.

LONGMANS, GREEN & CO., LTD. (London): *Personal Religion and the Life of Devotion* by William R. Inge, 1924.

LONGMANS, GREEN & CO., INC. (New York): *The In-*

ward Vision by R. H. J. Steuart; *The Hidden Life of the Soul* by Jean Nicholas Grou, ed. William Hutchings; *The Spiritual Letters of Archbishop Fénelon,* trans. H. L. Sidney Lear, 1909; Lecomte du Noüy, *Human Destiny,* copyright 1947 by Longmans, Green & Co., Inc.; and Eleanor Bertine: *Human Relationships* by Eleanor Bertine, copyright © by Eleanor Bertine. All reprinted with special permission of David McKay, Publisher.

MACMILLAN & CO., LTD. (London): *Spiritual Reformers of the Sixteenth and Seventeenth Centuries* by Rufus Jones, 1914; *Theologia Germanica,* trans. Susanna Winkworth, 1907; *The Avatars* by George W. Russell, 1933.

MACMILLAN PUBLISHING COMPANY (New York): *Religion in the Making* by Alfred North Whitehead, copyright 1926 by Macmillan Publishing Company, Inc., renewed 1954 by Evelyn Whitehead; *Beyond Personality* by C. S. Lewis 1945; from *Mere Christianity* by C. S. Lewis, reprinted with permission of Macmillan Publishing Company, copyright 1943, 1945, 1952.

METHUEN & CO., LTD. (London): and Executrix of Evelyn Underhill's Estate, *Mysticism* by Evelyn Underhill, 1911; and Vyvyan Holland and the Philosophical Press, *De Profundis* by Oscar Wilde, copyright 1951 by Vyvyan Holland.

SHEILA MOON: "Solstice" by Sheila Moon, 1958.

EDWARD MORGAN for permission to publish "Give Freedom" from *Your Own Path* by Elise Morgan.

WILLIAM MORROW AND CO., INC.: and Gerald Heard, *The Third Morality* by Gerald Heard, copyright 1937 by Gerald Heard; and Laurens Van der Post: *The Dark Eye in Africa* by Laurens Van der Post, copyright © 1955 by Laurens Van der Post.

NEW DIRECTIONS: Henry Miller, *The Wisdom of the Heart,* copyright 1941 by New Directions Publishing Corporation, reprinted by permission of New Directions Publishing Corporation; Thomas Merton, *Zen and the Birds of Appetite,* copyright © 1968 by The Abbey of Gethsemene, Inc., reprinted by permission of New Directions Publishing Corporation.

W. W. NORTON & CO., INC.: *The Neurotic Personality of Our Time* by Karen Horney, copyright 1937, 1968 by W. W. Norton & Co.; *Letters to a Young Poet* by Rainer Maria Rilke, rev. ed. copyright 1954 by W. W. Norton & Co., Inc.; *Studies in Analytical Psychology* by Gerhard Adler, copyright 1948 by W. W. Norton & Co., Inc.

OXFORD UNIVERSITY PRESS (New York): *These Hurrying Years* by Gerald Heard, copyright 1934 by Gerald Heard; *A Study of History* by Arnold J. Toynbee, abridgment by D. C. Somervell, 2 vols., copyright 1946, 1957 by Oxford University Press. (Work published by Oxford University Press on behalf of Royal Institute of International Affairs.)

OXFORD UNIVERSITY PRESS (London): *Christian Discourses* by Sören Kierkegaard, trans. Walter Lowrie, 1939; *Studies in Keats* by John Middleton Murry, 1930; *English Revised Version of the Bible,* 1881.

PANTHEON BOOKS, INC.: *Charles Peguy,* Vol. I, trans. Ann and Julian Green, copyright by Pantheon Books, Inc.; and Anne Morrow Lindbergh: *Gift from the Sea* by Anne Morrow Lindbergh, copyright © 1955 by Anne Morrow Lindbergh; *Memories, Dreams, Reflections* by C. G. Jung, ed. by Aniela Jaffé, trans. Richard and Clara Winston, copyright 1961, 1962, 1963 by Random House.

PENDLE HILL PAMPHLETS: *A Sense of Living* by Mildred Tonge, copyright © 1954 by Pendle Hill; *Art and Faith* by Fritz Eichenberg, copyright 1952 by Fritz Eichenberg.

PETER PAUPER PRESS: Two poems, *Japanese Haiku,* copyright 1955, 1956 by Peter Pauper Press.

SWAMI PAVITRANANDA: *Karma-Yoga* by Swami Vivekananda, 1938.

GWYNNE PETICOLAS: Lecture "Art for Non-Professionals" by Sherry Peticolas.

H. S. L. POLAK, Executor of the Estate of C. F. Andrews, and The Macmillan Company: *Mahatma Gandhi's Ideas* by C. F. Andrews, 1930.

M. GONTRIN De PONCINS: *Kabloona* by M. Gontrin de Poncins, copyright 1941 by M. Gontrin de Poncins.

SWAMI PRABHAVANANDA: *Vedic Philosophy and Religion,* published by Sri Ramakrishna Math, 1950.

PRENTICE HALL: *Reason and Emotion* by John Macmurray, copyright 1936 by John Macmurray, permission by Prentice Hall.

PRINCETON UNIVERSITY PRESS: *Myths and Symbols in Indian Art and Civilization* by Heinrich Zimmer, Bollingen Series VI (copyright 1946 by Bollingen Foundation), reprinted by permission of Princeton University Press; *Works of Love* by Sören Kierkegaard, trans. David F. Swenson, copyright 1946 by Princeton University Press; *THE COLLECTED WORKS OF C. G. JUNG*, ed. by G. Adler, M. Fordham, W. McGuire, and H. Read, trans. by R.F.C. Hull, Bollingen Series XX, vol. 7, *Two Essays on Analytical Psychology* (copyright 1953 & © 1966 by Bollingen Foundation); vol. 8, *The Structure and Dynamics of the Psyche* (copyright © 1960 by Bollingen Foundation and © 1969 by Princeton University Press); vol. 9i, *The Archetypes and the Collective Unconscious* (copyright © 1959 & 1969 by Bollingen Foundation); vol. 10, *Civilization in Transition* (copyright © 1964 by Bollingen Foundation); vol. 11 *Psychology and Religion: West and East* (copyright © 1958 by Bollingen Foundation & © 1969 by Princeton University Press); vol. 12, *Psychology and Alchemy* (copyright 1953 & © 1968 by Bollingen Foundation); vol. 13, *Alchemical Studies* (copyright © 1968 by Bollingen Foundation); vol. 16, *The Practice of Psychotherapy* (copyright 1954 and © 1966 by Bollingen Foundation); vol. 17, *The Development of Personality,* copyright 1954 by Bollingen Foundation; all reprinted by permission of Princeton University Press.

G. P. PUTNAM'S SONS and C. G. JUNG FOUNDATION FOR ANALYTICAL PSYCHOLOGY for *Depth Psychology and the New Ethic* by Erich Neumann, copyright © 1969 by Hodder and Stoughton Ltd. and C. G. Jung Foundation for Analytical Psychology; *Woman's Mysteries* by M. Esther Harding, copyright © 1971 by C. G. Jung Foundation for Analytical Psychology; *The Way of All Women* by M. Esther Harding, copyright 1933, 1954 by M. Esther Harding.

RANDOM HOUSE, INC.: *The Golden Mean of Tzeze* and *The Book of Tao,* quoted in *Wisdom of China and India,* ed. Lin Yutang, copyright 1942 by Random House; and W. H. Auden: *For the Time Being* by W. H. Auden, copyright 1944 by W. H. Auden.

RAMAKRISHNA-VIVEKANANDA CENTER: *Raja-Yoga* by Swami Vivekananda, copyright 1933 by Ramakrishna-Vivekananda Center.

ROUTLEDGE & KEGAN PAUL (London): *Experiment in*

Depth by P. W. Martin, copyright 1955 by Pantheon Books.

DANE RUDHYAR: *I Charge You* from *Of Vibrancy and Peace* by Dane Rudhyar, copyright by Dane Rudhyar, used with permission.

RUSSELL & VOLKENING, INC. and MAY SARTON: "Santos: New Mexico" from *The Lion and the Rose* by May Sarton, copyright 1948 by May Sarton.

CHARLES SCRIBNER'S SONS: *Discerning the Signs of the Times* by Reinhold Niebuhr, copyright 1946 by Charles Scribner's Sons; *How Character Develops* by Fritz Kunkel, copyright 1940 by Charles Scribner's Sons and *In Search of Maturity* by Fritz Kunkel, copyright by Charles Scribner's Sons, both reprinted with permission of Charles Scribner's Sons; *The New Being* by Paul Tillich, copyright 1955, reprinted with permission of Charles Scribner's Sons; *Principles of Christian Theology* by John Macquarrie, copyright 1966, reprinted with permission of Charles Scribner's Sons.

SHEED AND WARD: From *Progress Through Mental Prayer* by Edward Leen, published by Sheed and Ward, Inc.; from *The Spiritual Letters of Dom John Chapman,* by Dom Roger Huddleston, 1944, published by Sheed and Ward, Inc.

SIMON AND SCHUSTER, INC. and Joshua Loth Liebman: *Peace of Mind* by Joshua Loth Liebman, copyright 1946 by Joshua Loth Liebman; *Year's End* by Josephine Johnson, copyright 1937 by Josephine Johnson; "September" from *Winter Orchard* by Josephine Johnson, copyright 1935 by Josephine Johnson; *Report to Greco* by Nikos Kazantzakis, English trans. copyright 1965 by Simon and Schuster, original Greek language edition . . . by Helen N. Kazantzakis.

SOCIETY FOR THE PROMOTION OF CHRISTIAN KNOWLEDGE (London): *The Art of Mental Prayer* by Bede Frost, 1932.

DOUGLAS STEERE for permission to quote from *Prayer and Worship.*

STUDENT CHRISTIAN MOVEMENT PRESS (London) and John Macmurray: *Creative Society* by John Macmurray, copyright 1938 by John Macmurray.

MRS. FRANCES TEMPLE: *The Hope of a New World* by William Temple.

ROSE TERLIN: *Prayer and Christian Living* by Rose Terlin.

UNIVERSITY OF CHICAGO PRESS: *Bhagavad-Gita,* trans. A. Ryder, copyright 1929 by the University of Chicago; *The Complete Bible — An American Translation* by J. M. Powis Smith and Edgar J. Goodspeed, copyright 1935 by the University of Chicago; *The Prayers of Kierkegaard* by Sören Kierkegaard, trans. Perry D. Le Fevre, copyright 1956 by the University of Chicago.

STANFORD UNIVERSITY PRESS: Portion of a "Prayer of a Navajo Medicine Man," adapted with permission from *The Pollen Path* by Margaret Schevill Link, with the permission of the publishers, Stanford University Press, copyright © 1956 by the Board of Trustees of the Leland Stanford Junior University.

UNITED CHURCH HERALD: *Prayer for Growing Old* by Harold Kohn, used by permission.

THE VEDANTA CENTRE: *Bhagavad-Gita,* trans. by Swami Paramananda.

VIKING PRESS: *The Letters of D. H. Lawrence,* ed. Aldous Huxley, 1932 by Estate of D. H. Lawrence, copyright 1932 by Estate of D. H. Lawrence.

VLASTOS, GREGORY: *The Religious Way; The Religious Person in the World Today; Christian Faith and Democracy,* all used with permission of Gregory Vlastos.

IVES WASHBURN, INC.: *Let's Be Normal* by Fritz Kunkel, copyright 1929 by Ives Washburn, Inc.; and *God Helps Those* by Fritz Kunkel, copyright 1931 by Ives Washburn, Inc.

EDA LOU WALTON: trans. "Blackfeet War Song" from *Dawn Boy* by Eda Lou Walton.

PEGOT WARING: "Speak with Granite Tongues," an essay by Pegot Waring.

JOHN M. WATKINS (London): *The Cloud of Unknowing,* ed. Evelyn Underhill, 1912, 1934.

FRANCES G. WICKES: *The Inner World of Man* by Frances G. Wickes, copyright 1938, 1948 by Frances G. Wickes; "The Creative Process," published in *Spring,* copyright 1948 by The Analytical Psychology Club of New York; and Appleton-Century-Crofts, Inc.: *The Inner World of Childhood* by Frances G. Wickes, copyright 1927 by Appleton-Century-Crofts, Inc.

HENRY NELSON WIEMAN: *The Issues of Life,* 1930, and

Methods of Private Religious Living, 1929, by Henry Nelson Wieman.

MISS TONI WOLFF AND THE GUILD OF PASTORAL PSYCHOLOGY (London): Selections from lecture, "Christianity Within" by Toni Wolff.

NATIONAL BOARD OF THE YOUNG WOMEN'S CHRISTIAN ASSOCIATION OF THE U.S.A.: *Christian Faith and Social Action* by Rose Terlin, 1940.

WESTMINSTER PRESS: *Man the Choicemaker* by Elizabeth Boyden Howes and Sheila Moon, copyright © 1973, The Westminster Press.

YALE UNIVERSITY PRESS: *A Common Faith* by John Dewey, copyright 1934 by Yale University Press; *The Meaning of God in Human Experience* by W. E. Hocking, copyright 1912 by Yale University Press; *The Psychology of Jung* by Jolande Jacobi, trans. K. W. Bash, 1943; *A Philosophical Study of Mysticism* by Charles A. Bennett, copyright 1923 by Yale University Press.

EDITOR'S NOTE

Throughout this anthology the use of a single asterisk (*) at the end of a selection indicates that the material has been abridged. Two asterisks (**) appear following selections in which the quoted material has been slightly rearranged.

The choice is always ours. Then, let me choose
The longest art, the hard Promethean way
Cherishingly to tend and feed and fan
That inward fire, whose small precarious flame,
Kindled or quenched, creates
The noble or the ignoble men we are,
The worlds we live in and the very fates,
Our bright or muddy star.

ALDOUS HUXLEY

Contents

General Introduction

This anthology presents a mosaic of human insight. It has as its central theme a "Way" which all men seek, few find, few enter, and still fewer progressively follow, though it proffers the means by which man's most fundamental longing can be realized.

Deep in the psychic structure of every individual there is an urge for the kind of fulfillment which will yield meaning, joy and creativity. Men and women, consciously or unconsciously, desire to obtain the insight whereby they can resolve their own personal turbulences, achieve an organic interdependence with other human beings and gain a sense of the end for which they were created. For some individuals this longing becomes so heightened that they penetrate to a perception of the Way to its achievement. Around the life and teachings of a few of these have grown the world's great religions. Unfortunately the accumulation of belief and rigid dogma too often served to conceal the path which they had discovered. It is with the original insights and convictions of these individuals and with those who follow them in point of time that we are herein concerned. However, because there is interest in discovering the furthest reaches in the universality of the Way, and in presenting it stripped of nonessentials, the book is not limited to religious literature, but extends to other fields wherein the same process is discoverable.

If measured by events, the years between the first edition of this book and the present edition cover an incredible span of time—forty years, 1948–1988. The world's outer shell—of space, of time, of the distance between man and man—has been broken open by the fearful pace of the technological thrust. Man, "that scratcher at the crack in creation,"[1] looks through into a different kind of universe in which he can no longer project responsibility onto remote outer causes because he is in the midst of them, and they surround him and are part of him. His history, his technology, and now the threatened rape of his earth have confronted him with himself. History and technology and the earth's needs have become Hounds of Heaven[2] peering back at man through creation's crack. And there is nowhere else to go except inward for a solution to the outer dilemmas. The two faces of life—outer and inner—must be seen as inseparable and eternally interdependent.

[1]*JB,* a play by Archibald MacLeish.

[2]*The Hound of Heaven,* a poem by Francis Thompson.

We must choose, with a globe-circling intensity, between construction and total destruction. The atomic age passed in a night of time into the hydrogen age—and on into the incomprehensible *now* almost before we could draw a breath. This Hound of Heaven moves within the smallest infinite energy components of the atom and into the immeasurable galaxies of space. The force of the centrifugal rush into outer dimensions with no balancing inner movement has threatened the cohesion of the meaning of man. The human personality is exposed to psychological fragmentation, and a characteristic psychic pressure sets in. We try to escape this Hound of Heaven in every conceivable way, frequently through mental illness or the use of drugs, but no one really can escape the effect of the intensification of issues. We are, and will continue to be, forced to count the inevitable cost—unless and until we turn toward a counterbalancing process.

Perhaps the human extremity is not only God's opportunity but our opportunity—our chance to choose to search for the meaning and purpose of our own lives and thus for the life of the world; our chance to turn and see that the outer relates to the inner, and that the answer has as much to do with ourselves as individuals as it has to do with ourselves as members of the race. In the face of this enormity of forces and challenges, what are we tending to do? We seem to be trying to keep ourselves as unconscious as possible and have succeeded with remarkable versatility. A desperate kind of escapism has become pervasive—contributing to the development of a spurious sort of religion which puts in the foreground of human purposes the false gods of success, happiness, peace, security, certainty.

Is it not a travesty of our destiny as human beings that we, endowed with the capacity to grapple not only with "nature" and its elements but also with our own nature, should so hide from the very essence of our greatness? And in our attempt to escape the kind of struggle and suffering that is meaningful and rewarding we are rushing toward an ever more terrible and meaningless suffering. "It is a remarkable fact," writes Dr. Jung, "that in their hedonistic aims, materialism and a certain species of 'joyful' Christianity join. [Yet] the symbolic prototype of Christ's early life ended, not in complacent bliss, but on the cross."[3] One is reminded of a passage in T.S. Eliot's *Murder in the Cathedral,* taken from the

[3]C. G. Jung, *The Practice of Psychotherapy,* pp. 199–200 (Princeton University Press).

last sermon delivered by the Archbishop four days before he was martyred: "Reflect now, how our Lord Himself spoke of Peace. He said to His disciples, 'My peace I leave with you, my peace I give unto you.' Did He mean peace as we think of it: the kingdom of England at peace with its neighbors, the barons at peace with the King, the householder counting over his peaceful gains, the swept hearth, his best wine for a friend at the table, his wife singing to the children? Those men, His disciples, knew no such things: they went forth to journey afar, to suffer by land and sea, to know torture, imprisonment, to suffer death by martyrdom. What then did He mean? If you ask that, remember then that He said also, 'Not as the world gives, give I unto you.' So then, He gave to His disciples peace, but not peace as the world gives."

What is this different kind of peace? What way leads to its counterbalancing source? The urgency of these questions makes *The Choice Is Always Ours,* we believe, even more contemporary today than when it was first published. For in order to find the Ground of his own being and to be rooted in this Ground, out of which grows the other kind of peace, man must become a partaker and a participator in life in its ultimate meaning. This book, since it is wholly concerned with the Way to this meaning, still stands on the frontier of man's deepest need.

The changes made by the editors in the various editions always emphasized the paradoxical nature of the Way to Life. New material has not been added to this edition, but when it happened earlier, it was always to provide additional clues regarding many religious and psychological processes and how they contribute to following the Way.

In spite of wide variance in emphasis and diversity in expression, significant agreements are discovered in the writings and recorded sayings of men and women from all eras and disciplines. One such agreement concerns the nature of man's basic desire. Selections presenting this central motivating factor form the opening aspect of Chapter I, entitled "The Search for the Way." Another area of agreement concerns itself with the answer to the question: "How can man actualize this basic desire?" and "What conditions are required for its fulfillment?" Material formulating these conditions and their implications composes the major portion of Part One.

There is also concurrence in the idea that this Way is one of progression, "not a state, but a walk," leading through several stages. In order to overcome obstacles and to accelerate the rate of progress, special training is indicated—a training which reaches beyond this conscious self to the unconscious where are rooted the habit patterns needing transformation. The principal methods which are found to be effective in assisting this reconditioning process are described in Part Two, "The Techniques."

Another agreement has to do with outcomes resulting in the lives of those who progressively follow the Way. It is found that no particular "set" of outcomes can be expected to occur uniformly in all persons, but rather that they can be foreseen to vary in degree and kind according to individual temperament, background, and stage of clarification. There is essential and convincing agreement that all results at every stage of the Way are releasing of the real and expanding self, as opposed to the false and constricting self. They are Life-giving.

In summary, distinctions are made in the three parts of this book between that which motivates man to seek fullness of life; that which leads him to the true goal; the methods by which he progressively achieves fulfillment, and the outcomes of his search.

The four main areas of agreement forming the structure of this anthology rest on a minimal philosophic premise, i.e., that there exists an ultimate Reality that is by nature both transcendent and immanent. The immanent aspect, "this something of God in man," traces its ancestry to early Hindu sources, thence to the Socratic movement in philosophy, and on to the teaching of Jesus. Since then it has been variously expressed as: "the deep center," "the ground of the soul," "the inward Voice," "the Real Self," "the inner Vocation," "that something which binds us to the deeper processes of consciousness," "that potentiality of an extension of consciousness," *et cetera*. An appendix on "The Object of Devotion" was designed as an integral part of this book.

This leads to a striking observation: Whatever the approach, and however complicated the philosophical, psychological or theological superstructure erected upon it, the essentials of the Way whereby the suprapersonal reality becomes transformingly effective in the individual life are found to be virtually identical and universal.

Because the arrangement in Parts One and Two is a sequential one the reader will find it to his advantage to proceed through these sections in their present order, choosing those selections in each aspect, as he goes along, which are most meaningful to him. Since variety of approach was one of the goals of the research, it is not expected that all selections will have a like appeal for all readers.

Perhaps it is well to point out that the reader can expect to find some terms which suffer from semantic confusion—a confusion which is inevitable when many fields dealing with the same phenomena are in the process of drawing closer together. Most of this confusion corrects itself when the book, especially Part One, is read in sequence with attention to footnotes and editors' linking statements which are designed to illuminate the text. Even so, there are several words which should be mentioned specifically. They are "ego," "egocentricity," and "self." The terms "ego" and "self" (especially as in "self-love" and "selfishness") will be found used by some writers as synonymous with "egocentricity" (see pp. 100–109), and thus as something partial, false, rigid, and to be eliminated. Others, particularly psychologists, use "ego" to denote a positive core of personality giving the individual structure and solidity (see Wolff selection, p. 83). It is suggested that the term "ego" be considered as the conscious willing factor, a sort of focal point of consciousness (Jung), and that egocentricity (Kunkel), or "ego-defensiveness" (Fromm), or "self" as in "self-will" (the mystics) be considered as the negative and destructive state of partialness (neurotic inflation or deflation) wherein the "ego" attempts to become the exclusive center of the whole personality, indeed, of the whole world.

It was with increasing humility the editors pursued this work. Now, more than ever, it is believed, and evidence seems to warrant it, that a compilation of this kind may be even more needed when the human inner conflict, as tragic evidence of his unfulfilled nature, has perpetrated on the world crisis after crisis. This book speaks to those who seek the cultivation of an inner life that expresses itself creatively in personal and social manifestations.

PART ONE

The Way

I give you the end of a golden string;
Only wind it into a ball,
It will lead you in at Heaven's gate—
Built in Jerusalem's wall. WILLIAM BLAKE

Let not the authority of the writer offend thee whether he be of great or small learning; but let the love of pure truth draw thee to read. THOMAS À KEMPIS

CONTENTS

Part One

CHAPTER I

The Search and the Finding

Do you not seek a light, ye who are surrounded by darkness? THE DHAMMAPADA

Whosoever shall seek to save his life shall lose it; and whosoever shall lose his life shall preserve it.
JESUS OF NAZARETH

Never to have seen the truth is better than to have seen it and not to have acted upon it.
ANONYMOUS

The Search for the Way

"There is one great and universal wish of mankind expressed in all religions, in all art and philosophy, and in all human life; *the wish to pass beyond himself as he now is.*"[1]

In this statement we find one expression on the part of man of a persistent desire continuing throughout the centuries for a fulfillment which brings to actuality the capacities and capabilities that are truly his own nature but which lie dormant. This search has been conceived of and expressed in an infinite number of ways within the fields of religion, philosophy, psychology, art, literature, and those other fields which concern themselves with dynamic life processes. At its core has been the consciousness that man could and wanted to live with an orientation toward all persons and events such as would give his life a sense of meaning, of purpose, of reality, and of eternity.

This desire is the underlying motive for the search, the

---

[1]Beatrice Hinkle, *The Re-creating of the Individual* (Harcourt, Brace, 1923).

finding, and the actuation of the religious way of life as defined in this book.—Ed.

As a Great Cry

Blowing through heaven and earth, and in our hearts and the heart of every living thing, is a gigantic breath—a great Cry—which we call God. Plant life wished to continue its motionless sleep next to stagnant waters, but the Cry leaped up within it and violently shook its roots: "Away, let go of the earth, walk!" Had the tree been able to think and judge, it would have cried, "I don't want to. What are you urging me to do! You are demanding the impossible!" But the Cry, without pity, kept shaking its roots and shouting, "Away, let go of the earth, walk!"

It shouted in this way for thousands of eons; and lo! as a result of desire and struggle, life escaped the motionless tree and was liberated.

Animals appeared—worms—making themselves at home in water and mud. "We're just fine here," they said. "We have peace and security; we're not budging!"

But the terrible Cry hammered itself pitilessly into their loins. "Leave the mud, stand up, give birth to your betters!"

"We don't want to! We can't!"

"You can't, but I can. Stand up!"

And lo! after thousands of eons, man emerged, trembling on his still unsolid legs.

The human being is a centaur; his equine hoofs are planted in the ground, but his body from breast to head is worked on and tormented by the merciless Cry. He has been fighting, again for thousands of eons, to draw himself, like a sword, out of his animalistic scabbard. He is also fighting—this is his new struggle—to draw himself out of his human scabbard. Man calls in despair, "Where can I go? I have reached the pinnacle, beyond is the abyss." And the Cry answers, "I am beyond. Stand up!" All things are centaurs. If this were not the case, the world would rot into inertness and sterility.

Nikos Kazantzakis, 1885–1957, Greek writer.
Report to Greco.

As a Surging Purpose

We all know that there are regions of the human spirit untrammeled by the world of physics. In the mystic sense of the creation around us, in the expression of art, in a yearning towards God, the soul grows upward and finds fulfilment of something implanted in its nature. The sanction for this development is within us, a striving born of our consciousness or an inner light proceeding from a greater power than ours. Science can scarcely question this sanction, for the pursuit of science springs from a striving which the mind is impelled to follow, a questioning that will not be suppressed. Whether in the intellectual pursuits of science or in the mystical pursuits of the spirit, the light beckons ahead and the purpose surging in our natures responds.

Sir Arthur Eddington, 1882–1944.
English physicist, astronomer.
The Nature of the Physical World.

As a Desire for Orientation

Psychologists well know that the deepest element of human happiness is embodied in the idea of movement toward something; movement in the "right" direction; and all of the devices of therapeutic psychiatry are really only shoves and pushes and suggestions intended to help a mind find its particular right direction of movement. Continued observations of this basic dynamic nature of happiness, especially in clinical psychological practice, leads almost inevitably to the conclusion that deeper and more fundamental than sexuality, deeper than the craving for social power, deeper even than the desire for possessions, there is a still more generalized and more universal craving in the human make-up. *It is the craving for knowledge of the right direction— or orientation.*

This craving is not quite so obvious as the other patterns of human desire, because it is more general, deeper, and the positive and negative feeling-tones it engenders are not locally felt, hence come less often to a specific attention focus. Yet every system of philosophy, whether called religious or not, is at bottom a human attempt to satisfy the craving to be pointed in the right direction.

William H. Sheldon, M.D., 1899–1963. American psychologist.
Psychology and the Promethean Will.

As the Intent of Nature

Know that, by nature, every creature seeks to become like God. Nature's intent is neither food nor drink nor clothing, nor comfort, nor anything else in which God is left out. Whether you like it or not, whether you know it or not, secretly nature seeks, hunts, tries to ferret out the track on which God may be found.*

Meister Johannes Eckhart, 1260–1327.
German scholar, mystic.
Meister Eckhart. Trans. R. Blakney.

As the Quest of Consciousness

No one is born a new being. He bears in his psyche the imprint of past generations. He is a combination of ancestral units from which a new being must be fused, yet he also bears within him an essential germ, a potential of a unique individual value. The discovery of this unique essence and its development is the quest of consciousness.

Frances G. Wickes, 1875–1970. American psychotherapist.
The Inner World of Man.

For Thou hast created us for Thyself, and our heart cannot be quieted till it may find repose in Thee.

Saint Augustine, 354–430. Latin church father.
Confessions. Trans. W. Watts.

As a Mystical Aspiration

The religious spirit is in us. It preceded the religions, and their task as well as that of the prophets, of the initiated, consists of releasing, directing, and developing it. This mystical aspiration is an essentially human trait. It slumbers at the bottom of our souls awaiting the event, or

---

*The use of a single asterisk in this anthology indicates an abridgment of material.—Ed.

the man capable, in the manner of an enzyme, of transforming it into true mysticism, into faith.

Lecomte du Noüy, 1883–1947. French biophysicist.
Human Destiny.

As an Intrinsic Longing for Unity

We do not understand, but somehow we are part of a creative destiny, reaching backward and forward to infinity—a destiny that reveals itself, though dimly, in our striving, in our love, our thought, our appreciation. We are the fruition of a process that stretches back to star-dust. We are material in the hands of the Genius of the universe for a still larger destiny that we cannot see in the everlasting rhythm of worlds. Nothing happens but what somehow counts in the creative architecture of things. We fail and fall by the way, yet redeeming grace fashions us anew and eliminates our failures in the larger pattern. The pangs of pain, of failure, in this mortal lot, are the birth-throes of transition to better things. We are separated for a time by the indifference of space and by our blindness which particularizes and isolates us. But in us is the longing for unity. We are impelled by a hidden instinct to reunion with the parts of the larger heart of the universe.

John Elof Boodin, 1869–1950. American philosopher.
Cosmic Evolution.

As the Desire for Intentional Living

Life does not need comfort, when it can be offered meaning, nor pleasure, when it can be shown purpose. Reveal what is the purpose of existence and how he may attain it—the steps he must take—and man will go forward again hardily, happily, knowing that he has found what he must have—intentional living—and knowing that an effort, which takes all his energy because it is worth his full and constant concentration, is the only life deserving the devotion, satisfying the nature and developing the potentialities of a self-conscious being.

Anonymous.

As the Desire for Oneness with the Universe

Ask yourself what you would wish, if God would grant you the fulfillment of your one deepest request. And what do you think other people would wish for? Very soon you would discover that there are layers of desire and the deeper desire often contradicts the more superficial one. We need a careful explanation and definition of the more general wishes to be happy or good or a child of God. Moreover, there are unconscious goals which control our behavior in contradition to our conscious evaluation. One may wish to be humble, in order to be acknowledged by the Lord as the most humble and best of all His servants. —If we could be perfectly honest and transparent, what would we find to be the deepest and most central need of the human being?

The first answer would be: it is the desire to exist. But then our ideas, and our emotions, too, split into two opposite directions. On one hand, existence means to be, as we are, to persist; and the deepest desire becomes self-preservation. Then the greatest danger is change, commitment, giving up oneself. On the other hand we discover—or at least we could discover, if we were able to see reality as it is—that persistence without change is death, is nothing, is just what we are afraid of. But the second desire, the deeper one, tells us that we should renounce our self-preservation, we should not try to be like Olympic gods, above time but in time, above change in everlasting youth, and emptiness. This deep desire tells us to face reality, to be as human as possible, and that means going through time, through change, through death, keeping nothing, not even our life, giving everything, even our own will, being poor in spirit, being one with the universe, with our darkest enemy and with God. That is what we wish for most whether we know it or not.

Fritz Kunkel, M.D., 1889–1956. American psychiatrist.
Written for this anthology.

As the Sense of Being Sought by "Another"

One is not likely to describe easily or reliably the underlying motivations that have led him to the religious life. It is too easy to read back into past situations and experiences what one sees very clearly at the present time. Somehow it seems that there never was a time when I was not religious, though there certainly have been times when I have felt strong revulsions against certain forms of religious behavior and practice. One thing that has frequently been present is the desire to see and know myself as I really am. Another has been the longing to achieve serenity and inner integrity where there was much that was chaotic and broken. More important has been the urgency of a moral imperative which through the years has come insistently and persistently to place life under radical tensions.

But in looking over my past experience, I cannot resist the conviction that it has not been primarily my seeking and searching that has been important, but rather the awareness of *being sought and found* by Another. It is possible that I am reading certain present attitudes into my past; somehow or other the thought that a purposive, personal, active Reality has gone forth to meet me tends to dominate my thought more and more. In my best moments it is most natural to think of a Living God who has 'invaded' the chaos and confusion of life to give it strength and vitality and hope. It is He who 'fashions' and 'creates' and 'finds,' and thus *gives* existence. It is He who 'speaks' and reveals His will, and sets life before its imperative. The sense of moral obligation is His commanding, and my response is the will to obey or disobey.

The language of the Bible seems to express my own experience best of all. Moses' characteristic responses to the divine impulsions, Elijah's forlornness before the mountain cave, Amos' encounter with Amaziah the priest, Isaiah's dilemma in a national crisis, Jeremiah in the presence of the collapse of his world, Second Isaiah's sense of mission, Jesus' vision as He comes out of the baptismal waters—these situations have an authenticity about them which seems not merely personally convincing but almost universally recognizable. And I suppose that the influence of the Bible as a Scripture wrought from the heart of the world's life has accounted largely for many of my attitudes and the forms in which experience has been clothed. But paralleled with the appreciation of the Bible has come some understanding and appreciation of history, first of all the history of the Semitic East, but also the history of our own modern times.

But whatever the underlying psychological forces that have been at play, for me religion has simply been a necessity. Indeed, it has been the only real possibility. Other ways seem to have led to dead ends. In the only kind of world I have ever known, and in the kind of world that historical records reveal to me, relative loyalties are not enough. Hebrew Christian faith places life in a context of dynamic meaning and cosmic support; it kindles living by placing it under absolute commands which are adequately expressed in the Old and New Testaments; it provides a goal in the fullness and richness of its conception of the Sovereign Rule of God.*

James Muilenburg, 1896—1974 American theologian.
Written for this anthology.

As the Fountain of Spirit

As rivers have their source in some far off fountain, so the human spirit has its source. To find his fountain of spirit is to learn the secret of heaven and earth.

Lao-tzu, sixth century B.C. Chinese philosopher.
Tao-Teh, King. Trans. Bhikshu Wai-dau and D. Goddard.

The Finding of the Way

"Why," it may be asked, "if all men have within them the desire for fulfillment, do so few find it?" While many speculative answers[2] could be given, a practical approach[3] to the question involves consideration of some of the widespread misconceptions of the Way.

One set of misconceptions arises from mistaking *outcomes* of the way for the Way itself. Often the resultant half-truths tragically mislead the seeker. Some of these half-truths say that the Way is "living for others"; or following the Golden Rule; or living according to certain high principles and ideals; or imitating the virtues of the saints (instead of seeking to discover the source of their life quality); or giving oneself to a philanthropic cause. These are, in a sense, *what the Way is not.* They are "outer" or imitative, or ends of a process, rather than "inner," and creative,

---

[2]The question points to philosophic speculations into the nature of man and of the universe and may be unanswerable in its profoundest sense.

[3]Also see Chap. III under "Obstacles to Progression."

and means to an end. The importance of discrimination here cannot be overemphasized.

Another major misconception comes from identifying the Way with specific cosmological ideas and beliefs. It is essential that the way, as described herein, be understood as the Religious Way, as differentiated from the Way of any specific religion. In this compilation an attempt is made to present material which cuts through the accumulation of dogmas and creeds in order to reveal the Way in high relief —to set it forth so that it will be seen as an inexorable law involving all of life. In doing this there has been no intention of riding roughly over the significant variations in belief and symbol which characterize specific religious faiths.

It would have been valuable to examine the divergences in tradition but limitations of time and space precluded such a wide range of endeavor. Those variations indigenous to the period wherein they had their inception, and those which have been retained as appropriate to modern culture, undoubtedly had and have high value as aids to spiritual progress. The difficulty arises when, instead of being given a minor position, such variations assume first place. Then they obscure the Way and frequently prevent needed enlargements of *viewpoint*. Vital symbols appropriate to both culture and personality are, of course, always needed by mankind; they must be seized upon wherever they appear if they implement the Way. In our time the emergence of such symbols has become an urgent need.

The idea that the Way to fullness of life is an easy one is probably the most insidious of all misconceptions. Were it true, most of mankind might already have chosen it, since the need is so pressing and universal. But the process of finding and following this Way is arduous and long, because it requires a basic reorientation of the entire personality, in both its known and unknown, its conscious and unconscious aspects. It requires patience, perseverance and a great and steady openness to whatever comes.

The research for this book led first to the earliest known accounts of those in whom there was unmistakable evidence of truly enlightened living. The impact of these lives on their contemporaries and the authoritative nature of their teaching have caused their words and the reports of their lives to be designated as Sacred Literature. In these accounts were discovered clues to the way by which each had become free in spirit. Two major conditions were outlined representing the negative and positive aspects of a single process. The negative emphasis was found reiterated over and over in all the accounts as a paradoxical law. Positively emphasized, it appeared over and over as a commandment. In the teaching of Jesus both aspects received what we consider their most lucid description. Jesus' expression of the paradox appears in Luke 17:33—"Whosoever shall lose his life shall preserve it," and the commandment in Luke 10:27, "Thou shalt love the Lord thy God with all thy heart, and with all thy soul, and with all thy strength, and with all thy mind."

The major portion of Part One is made up of a pattern of statements presenting this Way and its far-reaching implications in both their negative and positive aspects.

The search was not limited to the earliest accounts but was extended to include the writings of other "authentics" who followed in point of time, and whose writings further illumined the conditions of the Way. Selections from recent and contemporary sources were also sought. We believe they serve the special function of bringing the precious insights closer to our understanding through their modern terminology, while at the same time adding to those insights through the means of newly available psychological knowledge into the nature of human conduct—knowledge such as is represented by the several psychological systems.

In describing the Way it seemed best to start with the negative emphasis thus presenting some of the most succinct and ultimate of all expressions—those in paradoxical form. In them it is seen as an inexorable law, the fulfillment of which determines the difference between life and death in every area of life. Though some expressions of the paradox have become dulled by familiarity, its truth is inescapable, and its relevancy in a world faced by atomic power becomes ever more desperately urgent.

The great paradox is "the golden string" which threads its way through this entire compilation—forming the underlying theme.—Ed.

Paradoxical Statements of the Way

Whosoever shall seek to save his life shall lose it; and whosoever shall lose his life shall find it.

Jesus of Nazareth.
New Testament (Luke 17:33).

He who humbles himself shall be saved;
He who bends shall be made straight;
He who empties himself shall be filled.

Laotzu, sixth century B.C. Chinese philosopher.
Tao-Teh-King.

Oh, let the self exalt itself,
Not sink itself below:
Self[4] is the only friend of self,
And self Self's only foe.
For self, when it subdues itself,
Befriends itself. And so
When it eludes self-conquest, is
Its own and only foe.

So calm, so self-subdued, the Self
Has an unshaken base
Through pain and pleasure, cold and heat,
Through honor and disgrace.

The "New Testament" of Hindu Scriptures, first century B.C.
Bhagavad-Gita. Trans. A. W. Ryder.

In Nature

And the more he [the individual] studies Nature, the more he will discover that death is not opposed to life, or

[4] The Way rests on the basic assumption that there are two centers within the personality structure: (1) the center of consciousness known as the "ego," the conscious willing factor, and frequently referred to as the "self," or the "seeming self"; and, (2) that central point of the total personality, both conscious and unconscious, often designated as the "Self," the "Christ within," the "Real-Self," the "Creative Center."—(See pp. 83–128, 452–453).

Whenever the ego (or self) becomes inflated and thus egocentric (pp. 27, 28, 103, 109), mistaking itself for the totality, it becomes the "foe" of itself as well as the "foe" of the "Self."—Ed.

decay to growth, but that they are mutually dependent; that just as the seed will only grow if the outer mass of it decays and thus generates the germ of life in its midst, so the individual can only complete his being through absorbing the creative energy released by the continuous death of his private self and its exclusive appetites.

The intimate dependence of growth on decomposition in the physical world may seem at first to bear but remotely upon the processes of the spiritual world. But the more we study the chemistry of the body, the more kindred it appears to the chemistry of the soul. That we must give, for example, if we are to receive, is not a rule, as is so often supposed, in defiance of Nature. Rather all the processes of Nature reflect its unconscious action. Life could sustain its being in no other way. And the same is true of the law, that in dying we live and in living, die.

Those, therefore, who no longer feel instinctively the subtle ties which knit together the diverse forces of Nature's energy and no longer obey instinctively her laws can only cease to be alien to the earth on which they dwell and at cross-purposes with life even in their yearning for some heavenly home, by rediscovering these ties rationally as a prelude to re-experiencing them imaginatively.

Hugh l'Anson Fausset, 1895–1965. English critic, poet.
Proving of Psyche.

The seed that is to grow
  must lose itself as seed;
And they that creep
  may graduate through
chrysalis to wings.

Wilt thou then, O mortal,
  cling to husks which
  falsely seem to you
    the self?

Wu Ming Fu, Chinese poet, philosopher.
Patterns in Jade.

In Art

It is because the artist loses himself in the reality of that which he describes or depicts or reveals, because of his individual self-effacement, that his work is a spontaneous expression of himself. That is one meaning of the penetrating saying of Jesus: "He that saveth his life shall lose it, and he that loseth his life shall save it." Personal spontaneity is always objective, always in terms of the independent reality of an object which absorbs us. There is no other self-expression possible. If we block the avenues of the outpouring of self, if we withdraw from the reality of the world, if we allow our actions to be subjectively determined by mere instincts and habits, following our inclinations, we do not express ourselves, we frustrate our own self-expression, surrender our freedom and suffocate all creative spontaneity. The artist does not act by impulse, still less by the compulsion of rules, but by the nature of the reality which he apprehends. By doing this he becomes free and his action becomes a self-expression. In no other way can self-expression be achieved. In particular it cannot be achieved by will or purpose. The man of iron will is always the man who cannot be spontaneous, who cannot act in terms of reality, who cannot be free.

John Macmurray, 1891–19—. Scottish professor of philosophy.
Reason and Emotion.

In Science

[Indeed] it may be said that every individual science sets about its task by the explicit renunciation of the egocentric and anthropocentric standpoint. In the earlier stages of human thought mankind turned its attention exclusively to the impressions received through the senses, and primitive man made himself and his own interests the center of his system of reasoning. As long as he remained bound within the limits of this method of treating his environment it was impossible for him to make any approach toward real scientific knowledge. His first advance in this knowledge was accomplished only after he had taken leave of his own immediate interests. At a later stage he succeeded in abandoning the idea that the planet whereon he lives is the central point of the universe. Then he took up the more modest position of keeping as far as possible in the background, so as not to intrude his own idiosyncrasies and personal ideas between himself and his observations of natural phenomena. It was only at this stage that the outer world of nature began to unveil its mystery to him, and at the same time to furnish him with means which . . . he could never have discovered if he had continued looking for them in the candlelight of his own egocentric interests. The progress of science is an excellent illustration of the truth of the paradox that man must lose his soul before he can find it.*

Max Planck, 1858–1947. German mathematical physicist.
Where Is Science Going? Trans. J. Murphy.

A death blow is a life blow to some
Who, till they died, did not alive become;
Who, had they lived, had died, but when
They died, vitality begun.

Emily Dickinson, 1830–1886. American poet.

In Man's Psychic Life

The problem of releasing our powers is the problem of both mastering and submitting to the process of becoming a person. A submission that is also a mastering! Here is the paradox of rationality in a finite and growing being. A sort of dialectic is involved: self-affirmation, followed by self-denial, and then realization that this denial of self is in reality a higher and fuller affirmation of self-hood.

George Albert Coe, 1862–1951. American educator, author.
Motives of Men.

It is only to be expected that for many people who have false ideas about themselves the [process of psychotherapy] is a veritable torture. For, in accordance with the old mystical saying, "Give up what thou hast, then shalt thou receive!" they are called upon to abandon all their cherished illusions in order that something deeper, fairer, and more embracing may arise within them.**

Carl G. Jung, M.D., 1875–1961. Swiss psychiatrist.
Two Essays on Analytical Psychology. Trans. R.F.C. Hull.

For the garden is the only place there is, but you will not
find it

**The use of two asterisks in this anthology indicates material is slightly rearranged.—Ed.

Until you have looked for it everywhere and found nowhere that is not a desert;
The miracle is the only thing that happens, but to you it will not be apparent,
Until all events have been studied and nothing happens that you cannot explain;
And life is the destiny you are bound to refuse until you have consented to die.

W. H. Auden, 1907–1973. English poet.
For the Time Being.

Die and Become.
Till thou hast learned this
Thou art but a dull guest
On this dark planet.

Johann Wolfgang von Goethe, 1749–1832.
German philosopher, poet.
Selige Sehnsucht.

God Speaks

It is innocence that is full and experience that is empty.
It is innocence that wins and experience that loses.
It is innocence that is young and experience that is old.
It is innocence that grows and experience that wanes.
It is innocence that is born and experience that dies.
It is innocence that knows and experience that does not know.
It is the child who is full and the man who is empty,
Empty as an empty gourd and as an empty barrel:
That is what I do with that experience of yours.
Now then, children, go to school.
And you men, go to the school of life.
Go and learn
How to unlearn.

Charles Péguy, 1873–1913. French writer.
Innocence and Experience. Trans. A. and J. Green.

In History

If history reveals anything it is that dissolution and growth have been aspects of the same phenomenon. Growth has not occurred anywhere without involving dissolution. Every major cultural change throughout history has involved this two-fold process of death and emergence.*

Bernard Eugene Meland, 1899–.
American philosopher, professor of religion.
From an article in *The Personalist.*

In the "World Body"

Neither in the world of nations, nor in the world of the nation, will all individuals sacrifice their interests. They cannot do it. It is impossible. They have not reached that stage of ethical development. But there is a handful of individuals—hundreds, thousands, maybe hundreds of thousands who have reached it. They have learned, or begun to conjecture, that the moment is come when they must sacrifice their *all.* At first slowly, then with slowly increasing speed, then in the last hundred years with a truly sickening acceleration, first the nation, then the world of nations has become one *body.* The vast world is one Man. And that one Man is sick, as individual men, time out of mind, have been sick; he is divided within him. There is unconscious growth below; the mind above is fixed. The pangs of rebirth are at hand. He dreams of better things, he desires better things; but how to achieve them he does not know. The World Man now longs, as the individual man has longed, time after time, for newness of life. And the answer to the World Man is the same answer that was given to the individual men two thousand years ago: "He that loseth his life, the same shall save it."

John Middleton Murry, 1889–1957. English author, critic.

General Statements of the Way

The paradoxical expressions of the Way stress the negative requirement for becoming free in spirit. They point to the necessary "losing of life," "dying to self," i.e., the "leave-taking of egocentric goals,"—a dedicating of the "I" whereby Ultimate Reality[5]—the "Ground of the Soul"—the "not I"—becomes transformingly effective in the individual life.

---

[5]See appendix, pp. 439–467.

The following selections not only amplify this "negative" aspect; they also include the other half of the process—that positive transaction wherein the will and its choices are transferred from the direction of the ego-driven, limited self to the direction of a real and uniquely individual, yet transpersonal Self. The ego must give over its autonomy for a larger purpose. It must relate to (but not identify with) a new Center. This action has been called "commitment," or "fidelity," or "plastic responsiveness." It completes "the emptying and the filling" conditions of the Life-giving process.

Because of the misconceptions concerning the Way, nothing seemed more difficult to find stated in lucid terms. Most general statements were in the often narrow framework of institutionalized beliefs. Those finally selected were chosen because of a singular freedom in this regard. Even so, they will be seen to vary in philosophical bases and terminology. They range from the minimal humanistic approach (Dewey) to the mystical approach (Eckhart). The reader who finds this variety confusing or burdensome, rather than clarifying and convincing, will do well on first reading to disregard all except the selections which are meaningful to him. Other readers will, by holding their focus on the centrality of the process, come to see behind the differences to that oneness which infuses the whole with its spirit.—Ed.

The Way as Turning

Such macrocosmic motes
as drift and spin in black space
beyond our remaining hills
are of less moment than how
turning enters a man,
how a slow year comes alone
to a man, to Man,
warming himself under Orion.
Universes may be bright or dead,
may have lived and ended
in incandescence, in cold snow,
be going mute through time
flowing interminably into itself;

and man be time's absurd King,
coloring his Kingdom with himself,
trying to outwit brevity with fire.
Whether he goes or does not go
beyond orbits of day-night-day
to some similar earth, if he is lost
he will be lost, here or there.
And if he turns, can learn
to wrestle his desire another way,
can face it around to see its eyes,
here or there, why then he will turn.
Those other places—hanging stars
or canyons of the sea—are not so wise.

* * *

There are a few who, during spans
of historied man's harvest,
have risked a fuller fruit, have
plunged to blind ground
and left behind the rasping years.
True was their descent, asked
by itself only, plumb line straight,
smashing at midnight
in a bright bloody river of seed.
Such men have turned, have lent
their flesh to needs of earth,
to life wanting birth and tomorrow.
They are wanderers. They bear questions
fresh with asking and desire
toward always a farther garden.
They come from nowhere, their home
is sorrow, their eyes hear gold
and their ears see dreams. They
yearn for points of fire unborn,
above each abyss they brood light
and follow smallest gleam on feet
burning with love. What is this
they do? What breach in our walls
comes with their coming, to let
into our prison the smell of sun
and grass? Their existence tells
itself to ours through the crack.

One such was Jesus the Jew, bearing
his hours on his back,—pedlar
of choices and fisher for God.
Let him pass.*

Sheila Moon, contemporary Jungian analyst and poet.
Joseph's Son.

The Way as a Hidden Treasure

There was once a pious rabbi, Eisik of Cracow, capital of Poland, who had a dream in which a voice told him to go to far off Prague, where under the great bridge to the royal castle he would discover a hidden treasure. This same commanding dream was repeated twice. He finally decided to go—making the long journey by foot. On arriving in Prague he found the bridge; but as there were sentinels posted there day and night, he did not venture to dig. However, day after day he returned and loitered around unostentatiously trying to study the situation. Finally he attracted the attention of one of the guards. "Have you lost anything, my good man," he asked. The rabbi told him of his dream. The officer laughed and exclaimed, "You poor man—to have worn out a pair of shoes traveling all this way only because of a dream! Why I had a foolish dream once. A voice commanded me to go to Cracow and search for the home of a rabbi Eisik, son of Jekel, where I would find a great treasure buried in a dirty corner behind the stove. Imagine believing in such a dream," and he laughed again. Rabbi Eisik bowing politely bid the officer farewell. He then hurried back to Cracow. There he dug under the neglected corner behind his stove and found the treasure—thus putting an end to his poverty.[6]

* * *

In commenting on this tale Heinrich Zimmer writes: "Now the real treasure, to end our misery and trials, is never far away; it is not to be sought in any distant region;

[6] This tale first appeared in Khassechscher Bücher by Martin Buber. It has appeared in various versions since.

it lies buried in the innermost recess of our own home, that is to say, our own being. And it lies behind the stove, the life-and-warmth-giving center of the structure of our existence, our heart of hearts—if we could only dig. But there is the odd and persistent fact that it is only after a faithful journey to a distant region, a foreign country, a strange land, that the meaning of the inner voice that is to guide our quest can be revealed to us.[7]

The Way as "Steps" to Real Simplicity

In the world when people call anyone simple they generally mean a foolish, ignorant, credulous person. But real simplicity, so far from being foolish, is almost sublime. All good men like and admire it, are conscious of sinning against it, observe it in others, and know what it involves, and yet they could not precisely define it. I should say that simplicity is an uprightness of soul which prevents self-consciousness. It is not the same as sincerity, which is a much humbler virtue. Many people are sincere who are not simple; they say nothing but what they believe to be true, and do not aim at appearing anything but what they are; but are forever thinking about themselves, weighing their every word and thought, and dwelling upon themselves, in apprehension of having done too much or too little. These people are sincere, but they are not simple; they are not at their ease with others, or others with them; there is nothing easy, frank, unrestrained, or natural about them; one feels one would like less admirable people better, who are not so stiff.

To be absorbed in the world around, and never turn a thought within, as is the blind condition of some who are carried away by what is present and tangible, is one extreme as opposed to simplicity. And to be self-absorbed in everything, whether it be duty to God or man, is the other extreme, which makes a person wise in his own conceits—reserved, self-conscious, uneasy at the least thing which disturbs his inward self-complacency. Such false wisdom, in spite of its solemnity, is hardly less vain and foolish than the folly of those who plunge headlong into worldly plea-

[7]*Myths and Symbols in Indian Art and Civilization* (Paperback, 1946—Harper and Row).

sure. The one is intoxicated by his outer surroundings, the other by what he believes himself to be doing inwardly; but both are in a state of intoxication, and the last is a worse state than the first, because it seems to be wise, though it is not really, and so people do not try to be cured. Real simplicity lies in a *juste milieu,* equally free from thoughtlessness and affectation, in which the soul is not overwhelmed by externals so as to be unable to reflect, nor yet given up to the endless refinements which self-consciousness induces. That soul which looks where it is going, without losing time arguing over every step, or looking back perpetually, possesses true simplicity.

Verily such simplicity is a great treasure! How shall we attain to it? I would give all I possess for it; it is the costly pearl of Holy Scripture.

The first step is for the soul so to put away outward things and look within as to know its own real interests; so far all is right and natural; thus much is only a wise self-love which seeks to avoid the intoxication of the world.

In the next step the soul must add the contemplation of God, Whom it fears, to that of self. This is a faint approach to the real wisdom, but the soul is still greatly self-absorbed· it is not satisfied with fearing God; it wants to be certain that it does fear Him, and fears lest it fear Him not, going round in a perpetual circle of self-consciousness. All this restless dwelling in self is very far from the peace and freedom of real love; but that is yet in the distance—the soul must needs go through a season of trial, and were it suddenly plunged into a state of rest, it would not know how to use it.

The third step is that, ceasing from a restless self-contemplation, the soul begins to dwell upon God instead, and by degrees forgets itself in Him—it becomes full of Him and ceases to feed upon self. Such a soul is not blinded to its own faults or indifferent to its own errors; it is more conscious of them than ever, and increased light shows them in plainer form, but this self-knowledge comes from God, and therefore it is not restless or uneasy.

But, you will ask, how can I help being constantly self-engrossed when a crowd of anxious thoughts disturb me and set me ill at ease? I only ask that which is in your own power. If you are steadfast in resisting them whenever you become conscious of their existence, by degrees you will get free, but do not hunt them out with the notion of conquering them. A continual attempt to repress thoughts of self and self-interest is practically continual self-consciousness, which will only distract you from the duties incumbent on you and deprive you of the sense of God's Presence.

The great thing is to resign all your interests and pleasures and comfort and fame to God. He who unreservedly accepts whatever God may give him in this world—humiliation, trouble, and trial from within or from without—had made a great step towards self-victory; he will not dread praise or censure, he will not be sensitive; or if he finds himself wincing, he will deal so cavalierly with his sensitiveness that it will soon die away. Such full resignation and unfeigned acquiescence is true liberty, and hence arises perfect simplicity. Blessed indeed are they who are no longer their own, but have given themselves wholly to God!*

François Fénelon, 1651–1715.
French Archbishop of Cambray.
Letters to Women. Trans. H. L. Lear.

The Way as Voluntary Change of Will

What are the *attitudes* that lend deep and enduring support to the processes of living? I have, for example, used the words "adjustment" and "orientation." What do they signify?

While the words "accommodation," "adaptation," and "adjustment" are frequently employed as synonyms, attitudes exist that are so different that for the sake of clear thought they should be discriminated. There are conditions we meet that cannot be changed. If they are particular and limited, we modify our own particular attitudes in accordance with them. Thus we accommodate ourselves to changes in weather, alterations in income when we have no other recourse. When the external conditions are lasting we become inured, habituated, or as the process is now called, conditioned. The two main traits of this attitude, which I should like to call accommodation, are that it affects *particular* modes of conduct, not the entire self, and that the process is mainly *passive*. It may, however, become general and then it becomes fatalistic resignation or submission. There are other attitudes toward the environment that are also particular but that are more active. We re-act against conditions and endeavor to change them to meet our wants and demands. Plays in a foreign language are "adapted" to meet the demands of an American audience. A house is rebuilt to suit changed conditions of the household; the telephone is invented to serve the demands for speedy communication at a distance; dry soils are irrigated so that they may bear abundant crops. Instead of accommodating ourselves to conditions, we modify conditions so that they will be accommodated to our wants and purposes. This process may be called adaptation.

Now both of these processes are often called by the more general name of adjustment. But there are also changes in ourselves in relation to the world in which we live and are much more inclusive and deep-seated. They relate not to this and that want in relation to this and that condition of our surroundings, but pertain to our being in its entirety. Because of their scope, this modification of ourselves is enduring. It lasts through any amount of vicissitude of circumstances, internal and external. There is a composing and harmonizing of the various elements of our being such that, in spite of changes in the special conditions that surround us, these conditions are also arranged; settled, in relation to us. This attitude includes a note of submission. But it is voluntary, not externally imposed; and as voluntary it is something more than a mere Stoical resolution to endure unperturbed throughout the buffetings of fortune. It is more outgoing, more ready and glad, than the latter attitude, and it is more active than the former. And in calling it voluntary, it is not meant that it depends upon a particular resolve or volition. It is a change of will conceived as the organic plenitude of our being, rather than any special change in will.*

John Dewey, 1859–1952. American philosopher, educator.
A Common Faith.

The Way as Total Responsiveness to the Best in Each Situation

This religious way of living is different from every other found among men. It differs from that of the moral idealist. The idealist picks out of each situation whatever will promote his ideal. All the rest he ignores or fights or tolerates.

He is blind to all the abundance that overflows or conflicts with his ideal. Over against the idealist stands the man of uninhibited desire. His way of living differs from that of the religious just as much as does that of the idealist, but at the opposite extreme. He picks out of the riches of each situation whatever will satisfy his specific desires, but all the rest flows over him unappreciated and unapprehended. The religious man on the other hand, in contradistinction from both of these, explores sensitively and reverently for the emerging new meanings in each situation, the while holding his desires and ideals in control as experimental instruments to be used in guiding him into the situation where they are bound to be transcended or submerged by the richness of value which he cannot possibly apprehend before he experiences it in the full concreteness of consummatory synthesis.

The steps by which one achieves this way of religious living[8] cannot be taken once and for all. They constitute a practice that is repeated again and again. This life is the faith that saves the world. It serves both the needs of individual personality and of society in the only ways which can enable this age to escape destruction.

This spontaneity of free and full and plastic responsiveness down to the deepest level of the organization of the psycho-physical organism is the prime condition for all mental health. The psychological desperation of our time is shown in all the multiple forms of mental illness and derangement of personality which are increasing steadily and amounting to madness in many cases. The religious way does surely protect from these mental ills. A glance at some of the major sources of the derangements of personality will make this plain. Men suffer these psychic ills when they struggle to do what is impossible and cannot resign themselves to the inevitable; when they strive to maintain a certain view of themselves in the face of incoming evidence to the contrary; when they cannot relinquish some desire in the face of a conscience or society that condemns. But all these disorganizing conditions fade out and disappear when the total personality becomes plastic; when it becomes free-

[8]These steps Dr. Wieman designates as propulsion, crisis, decision, release, specification and fellowship. For a description of each step see pp. 299–307 of *The Growth of Religion*. It was impossible to abridge these pages sufficiently to include here.—Ed.

ly and fully responsible to the best possible in each situation; when it finds in the full flood of circumstance the riches of laughter, or tragedy, and of fulfillment, but does not cling to the impossible and does not demand that any fixed desire or fixed ideal be satisfied.*

Henry Nelson Wieman,[9] 1884–1973.
American philosopher, theologian, educator.
The Growth of Religion.

The Way as Commitment

Of the many half-truths floating about in sermons and articles today I know few so misleading as this: "Religion is life." It is misleading just because it is not obviously false. It contains important truths. For one thing, it says this: Religion, wherever it exists, spreads over the whole of life. One cannot take it up as one takes up golf—by giving it a couple of afternoons a week. That kind of amateur religion is not religion. Religion is either the whole of one's life, or else it is not religion, no matter how much fuss is made over it. This is true, and dangerously true. "Religion is life," so understood, cuts with condemnation. To all those who want religion, but want it "in its place," that is, apart from their business, their politics, their luxuries or their conveniences, or anything else, this says, "My good friend, what you call your 'religion' is something or other, but you had better find its name and call it by its name; don't call it religion."

Religion can never be lived except with one's whole life, and what cannot be humanly lived is not religion or any concern of religion. So far "religion is life" makes sense. But how much farther? Does it hint at the all-important fact that religion is not any kind of life, but a difficult and exacting way to which many are called but few chosen? Does it suggest just what it is that marks off religion from all the other kinds of lives that have been lived and can be lived—the life of the dilettante or of the egotist or the cynic or the romantic, or of the healthy cabbage? Jesus told Nicodemus, "You must be born again." He told the rich young ruler, "Sell all you have," and the disciples, "He who

[9]Part I by Walter Marshall Horton, Part II by Henry Nelson Wieman.

would save his life must lose it." Could you have guessed any of these things from "religion is life"? Where is the way of the cross, the demand for decision, the necessity for absolute loyalty? Something slips between the fingers of this plausible generality and this something is commitment.

Commitment is all-important in our understanding of religion because it expresses clearly, as "life" does not, this fact: Religion is a relationship. This may sound like a truism. Yet even a truism is significant when it is denied. Every kind of subjectivism is such a denial. Nothing is so attractive to the tired sophisticate as the call to leave awhile the world that is too much with him and retreat to a place of stillness within his own soul. That there is such a place is an exciting discovery, and so is the art of finding it, steering safely to it, and avoiding the dangerous turmoils of the world of outer fact or the world of the inner self, both full of confusion and strife. To explore this middle ground of introspection and reverie, and flavor its precarious peace, is an engrossing adventure, especially when it is dignified with the name of religion.

To such religious romanticism the word "commitment" brings a rude corrective. It reminds one inescapably of the essential thing in religion—God. It is easy to forget God when one is most concerned about one's inner experiences. It is not so easy to forget Him when one is concerned about commitment. One can give oneself only to something which is there, which can be observed, understood and obeyed; to something which makes demands and holds out promises and obligations. It warns against subjectivity. One's own subjectivity can hide God from one just as much as the pressure of work or the hypocrisies of polite society.

If one is not clear about God, one will always tend to shy away toward something more accessible, like one's own conscious states. To talk about commitment brings one face to face with the question of God, so that one cannot dodge it. . . .[10]

[Any] cosmic reach in our description of God must not distract our attention from the specific human focus within which our experiences of the good are most intense and most decisive. It is here most of all that we know God as a daily fact. We have tried the ways of ambition, of self-

[10]See the Appendix. "The Object of Devotion," for the author's idea of God—pp. 447–449.—Ed.

aggrandizement, of aggressive opportunism, and we have seen the kind of flimsy success to which they lead, we have tasted the bitter poisons they generate, we have known the conflict, the disgust, the inner division, the outer isolation that follow in their wake. We have also tried in some small measure the other way, and known that every man and woman must have love; that there is no life or peace without love; only strife, waste, madness, destruction, death. There is that in life which makes it necessary that men should find the way of truth, of understanding, of justice, or else destroy themselves and each other. You have not seen it? You cannot move a step but you stumble into it; it is in the structure of your world; you cannot live a day or an hour without saying either yes or no to it, without finding life through it or death without it.

Even a faint glimpse of this reality brings you back to yourself. Whither do you move? With it or without it? The alternatives are simple—terrifyingly simple and clear. To compromise in this matter is to decide; to waver is to decide; to postpone and evade decision is to decide; to hide the matter is to decide. There is no escape. You must say yes, or no. There are a thousand ways of saying no; one way of saying yes; and no way of saying anything else.*–**

Gregory Vlastos, 1909–. American professor of philosophy.
The Religious Way.

The Way as Willing One Thing

Purity of heart is to will one thing, but to will one thing could not mean to will the world's pleasure and what belongs to it, even if a person only named one thing as his choice, since this one thing was one only by a deception. Nor could willing one thing mean willing it in the vain sense of mere bigness which only to a man in a state of giddiness appears to be one. *For in truth to will one thing a man must will the Good.* On the other hand, as for each act of willing the Good which does not will it in truth, it must be declared to be double-mindedness. Then there is a type of double-mindedness that in a more powerful and active sort of inner coherence seems to will the Good, but deceptively wills something else. It wills the Good for the sake of reward, out of fear of punishment, or as a form of self-assertion. But there is another kind of double-mindedness that wills the Good in a kind of sincerity, but only wills it 'to a certain degree.' If, then, a man in truth wills the Good, then *he must be willing to do all for it or he must be willing to suffer all for it.*

Let us first consider: the willingness to do all for the Good. All—yet will not this talk easily exceed all bounds, if all is named? Will it not become an impossibility to master all the differences included under the term "all," and as a result will the talk not become vague, since the Good can demand the most different things of different people? It can sometimes demand that a man leave his esteemed calling and put on lowliness, that he give away all his possessions to the poor, that he shall not even dare to bury his father. Again it can demand of others that they shall assume the power and the dignity that are offered them, that they shall take over the working power of wealth, that they shall bury the father, and that perhaps a large part of their lives shall be consecrated to faithfulness which is to be faithful over the little to this extent, that their own life has no claims of its own, but rather is faithful to the memory of a departed one. Now let us not multiply confusion and distraction in a host of individual details. For these also remind us of the struggle of pettiness for preference, where one person thinks that by doing one thing he is doing more for the Good than another who does something else. For if both in relation to the demand do all, then they do equally much. And if neither of them does all, then they do equally little. Instead of multiplying details, let us simplify this all into its essential unity and likeness by saying that to will to do all is: in the commitment to will to be and to remain loyal to the Good. Because the commitment is just the committing of all, just as it is also that which is essentially one thing. No one believes that this is a long-drawn-out affair. On the contrary, from the standpoint of eternity, if I dare say so, it is this abbreviating of all life's fractions (for eternity's length is the true abbreviation) that frees life of all its difficulties, and it is through deciding to will to be and to remain loyal to the Good that so much time is gained. For that which absorbs men's time when they complain about the lack of time is irresoluteness, distraction, half thoughts, half resolutions, indecisiveness, great moments—great moments. It was because of these that we said: to be and to remain loyal to, so that the commitment should not be confused with the extravagance of an expansive moment. The person, who in decisiveness wills to be and to remain loyal to the Good, can find time for all possible things. No, he cannot do that. But neither does he need to do that, for he wills only one thing, and just on that account he will not have to do all possible things, and so he finds ample time for the Good.

So now let us talk of doing all, and speak of the men who, in this or that way, are assigned to the external world as to a stage. It makes no difference at all, God be praised, how great or how small the task may be. All the ruinous quarreling and comparison which swells up and injures, which sighs and envies, the Eternal does not recognize. Its claim rests equally on each, the greatest who has ever lived, and the most insignificant. Yes, the sun's rays do not shine with more equality on the peasant's hut and the ruler's palace, than the equality with which the Eternal looks down upon the highest and the lowest. The demand upon each is exactly the same: to be willing to do all. If this be fulfilled then the Good bestows its blessing equally upon each one who makes and remains loyal to his commitment.*–**

Sören Kierkegaard, 1813–1855. Danish philosopher.
Purity of Heart. Trans. Douglas Steere.

The Way as Denying of Self-Will

People say: "Alas, sir, but I would prefer to stand well with God, to have the devotion and the divine calm of some people." Or they say: "It will never do if I cannot be here or there and do thus and so. I must get away—or go into a cloister or a cell."

The truth is that you yourself are at fault in all this or no one else. It is pure self-will. Whether you realize it or not, there can be no restlessness unless it come from self-will, although not every person understands this. This is what I mean: people fly from this to seek that—these places, these people, these manners, those purposes, that activity—but they should not blame ways or things for thwarting them. When you are thwarted, it is your own attitude that is out of order.

Begin, therefore, first with self and forget yourself! If you do not first get away from self, then whatever else you get away from you will still find obstacles and restlessness. People look in vain for peace, who seek it in the world outside, in places, people, ways, activities, or in world-flight, poverty and humiliation, whatever the avenue or degree; for there is no peace this way. They are looking in the wrong direction, and the longer they look the less they find what they are looking for.

* * *

There is no way of making a person true unless he gives up his own will. In fact, apart from complete surrender of the will, there is no traffic with God. But if it did happen that we gave up completely and dared to put off everything, physical and spiritual, for God's sake—then we should have done all and not before.

Such people are rare. Aware of it or not, people have wanted to have the "great" experiences; they want it in this form, or they want that good thing; and this is nothing but self-will. Yield completely to God and then be satisfied, whatever he does with his own.

* * * * * *

We must learn always to find and procure the advantage of God. For God does not give gifts, nor did he ever give one, so that man might keep it and take satisfaction in it; but all were given—all he ever gave on earth or in heaven—that he might give this one more: himself. . . . Therefore I say that we must learn to look through every gift and every event to God and never be content with the thing itself. There is no stopping place in this life—no, nor was there ever one for any man, no matter how far along his way he'd gone. This above all, then, be ready at all times for the gifts of God and always for new ones.*

Meister Johannes Eckhart, 1260–1327.
German scholar, mystic.
Meister Eckhart. Trans. R. Blakney.

The Way as Conscious Fidelity to "Inner Vocation"[11]

The achievement of personality means nothing less than the optimum development of the whole individual human being. It is impossible to foresee the endless variety of conditions that have to be fulfilled. A whole lifetime, in all its biological, social, and spiritual aspects, is needed. Personality is the supreme realization of the innate idiosyncrasy of a living being. It is an act of high courage flung in the face of life, the absolute affirmation of all that constitutes the individual, the most successful adaptation to the universal conditions of existence coupled with the greatest possible freedom for self-determination. To educate a man to *this* seems to me no light matter. It is surely the hardest task the modern mind has set itself. And it is dangerous too . . . as dangerous as the bold and hazardous undertaking of nature to let women bear children. . . .

Just as the child must develop in order to be educated, so the personality must begin to sprout before it can be trained. And this is where the danger begins. For we are handling something unpredictable, we do not know how and in what direction the budding personality will develop, and we have learned enough of nature and the world to be somewhat chary of both. On top of that, we were brought up in the Christian belief that human nature is intrinsically evil. But even those who no longer adhere to the Christian teaching are by nature mistrustful and not a little frightened of the possibilities lurking in the subterranean chambers of their being. Even enlightened psychologists like Freud give us an extremely unpleasant picture of what lies slumbering in the depths of the human psyche. So it is rather a bold venture to put in a good word for the development of personality. . . . "Anything might happen," people say. Or they dish up the old, feebleminded objection to "individualism." But individualism is not and never has been a natural development; it is nothing but an unnatural usurpation, a freakish, impertinent pose that proves its hol-

[11]See Chap. VII, pp. 167–186, in *The Development of Personality,* Vol. 17 of *Collected Works* by Carl G. Jung, for a further discussion of this "Way" which the author most frequently terms "the process of individuation." This selection is of necessity an abridgment of the text.—Ed.

lowness by crumpling up before the least obstacle. What we have in mind is something very different. . . .

. . . The development of personality means fidelity to the law of one's own being. . . . Fidelity to the law of one's own being is a trust in this law, a loyal perseverance and confident hope; in short, an attitude such as a religious man should have towards God. It can now be seen how portentous is the dilemma that emerges from behind our problem: personality can never develop unless the individual chooses his own way, consciously and with moral deliberation. Not only the causal motive—necessity—but conscious moral decision must lend its strength to the process of building the personality. If the first is lacking, then the alleged development is a mere acrobatics of the will; if the second, it will get stuck in unconscious automatism. But a man can make a moral decision to go on his own way only if he holds that way to be the best. If any other way were held to be better, then he would live and develop that other personality instead of his own. The other ways are conventionalities of a moral, social, political, philosophical, or religious nature. The fact that the conventions always flourish in one form or another only proves that the vast majority of mankind do not choose their own way, but convention, and consequently develop not themselves but a method and a collective mode of life at the cost of their own wholeness.[12]

To develop one's own personality is indeed an unpopular undertaking, a deviation that is highly uncongenial to the herd. . . . Small wonder then, that from earliest times only the chosen few have embarked upon this strange adventure. Had they all been fools, we could safely dismiss them as mentally "private" persons who have no claim on our interest. But, unfortunately, these personalities are as a rule the legendary heroes of mankind, the very ones who are looked

---

[12]Just as the psychic and social life of mankind at the primitive level is exclusively a group life with a high degree of unconsciousness among the individuals composing it, so the historical process of development that comes afterwards is in the main collective and will doubtless remain so. That is why I believe convention to be a collective necessity. It is a stopgap and not an ideal, either in the moral or in the religious sense, for submission to it always means renouncing one's wholeness and running away from the final consequences of one's own being.

up to, loved, and worshipped, the true sons of God whose names perish not. They are the flower and the fruit, the ever fertile seeds of the tree of humanity. . . . They towered up like mountain peaks above the mass that still clung to its collective fears, its beliefs, laws, and systems, and boldly chose their own way. To the man in the street it has always seemed miraculous that anyone should turn aside from the beaten track with its known destinations, and strike out on the steep and narrow path leading into the unknown. Hence it was always believed that such a man, if not actually crazy, was possessed by a daemon or a god. . . .

What is it, in the end, that induces a man to go his own way and to rise out of unconscious identity with the mass as out of a swathing mist? Not necessity, for necessity comes to many, and they all take refuge in convention. Not moral decision, for nine times out of ten we decide for convention likewise. What is it, then, that inexorably tips the scales in favor of the *extraordinary?*

It is what is commonly called *vocation*: an irrational factor that destines a man to emancipate himself from the herd and from its well-worn paths. True personality is always a vocation and puts its trust in it as in God, despite its being, as the ordinary man would say, only a personal feeling. But vocation acts like a law of God from which there is no escape. The fact that many a man who goes his own way ends in ruin means nothing to one who has a vocation. . . . Anyone with a vocation hears the voice of the inner man: he is *called*. That is why the legends say that he possesses a private daemon who counsels him and whose mandates he must obey. The best known example of this is Faust, and an historical instance is provided by the daemon of Socrates. . . . The original meaning of "to have a vocation" is "to be addressed by a voice." The clearest examples of this are to be found in the avowals of the Old Testament prophets. . . .

Vocation, or the feeling of it, is not, however, the prerogative of great personalities; it is also appropriate to the small ones all the way down to the "midget" personalities, but as the size decreases the voice becomes more and more muffled and unconscious . . . until finally it merges indistinguishably with the surrounding society, thus surrendering its own wholeness and dissolving into the wholeness of the group. In the place of the inner voice there is the voice of the group with its conventions, and vocation is replaced by collective necessities. . . .

. . . [Likewise] to become a personality is not the absolute prerogative of the genius, for a man may be a genius without being a personality. In so far as every individual has the law of his life inborn in him, it is theoretically possible for any man to follow this law and so become a personality, that is, to achieve wholeness. . . . Only the man who can consciously assent to the power of the inner voice becomes a personality; but if he succumbs to it he will be swept away by the blind flux of psychic events and destroyed. That is the great and liberating thing about any genuine personality: he voluntarily sacrifices himself to his vocation, and consciously translates into his own individual reality what would only lead to ruin if it were lived unconsciously by the group.

One of the most shining examples of the meaning of personality that history has preserved for us is the life of Christ. . . . Obeying the inner call of his vocation, Jesus voluntarily exposed himself [in the Temptations] to the assaults of the imperialistic madness that filled everyone, conqueror and conquered alike. In this way he recognized the nature of the objective psyche which had plunged the whole world into misery and had begotten a yearning for salvation that found expression even in the pagan poets. Far from suppressing or allowing himself to be suppressed by this psychic onslaught, he let it act on him consciously, and assimilated it. Thus was world-conquering Caesarism transformed into spiritual kingship, and the Roman Empire into the universal kingdom of God that was not of this world. While the whole Jewish nation was expecting an imperialistically minded and politically active hero as a Messiah, Jesus fulfilled the Messianic mission not so much for his own nation as for the whole Roman world, and pointed out to humanity the old truth that where force rules there is no love, and where love reigns force does not count. The religion of love was the exact psychological counterpart to the Roman devil-worship of power.

The example of Christianity is perhaps the best illustration of my previous abstract argument. This apparently unique life became a sacred symbol because it is the psychological prototype of the only meaningful life, that is, of a life that strives for the individual realization—absolute and unconditional—of its own particular law. Well may we exclaim with Tertullian: *anima naturaliter christiana!*

The deification of Jesus, as also of the Buddha, is not surprising, for it affords a striking example of the enormous valuation that humanity places upon these hero figures and hence upon the ideal of personality. . . . The ideal of personality is one of the ineradicable needs of the human soul.

. . . Just as the great personality acts upon society to liberate, to redeem, to transform, and to heal, so the birth of personality in oneself has a therapeutic effect. It is as if a river that had run to waste in sluggish side-streams and marshes suddenly found its way back to its proper bed, or as if a stone lying on a germinating seed were lifted away so that the shoot could begin its natural growth.*–**

Carl G. Jung, M.D., 1875–1961. Swiss psychiatrist.
The Development of Personality. Trans. R. F. C. Hull.

The Way as Openness to the "New Creation"

For neither circumcision counts for anything nor uncircumcision, but a new creation. Galatians 6:15.

If I were asked to sum up the Christian message for our time in two words, I would say with Paul: It is the message of a "New Creation." We have read something of the New Creation in Paul's second letter to the Corinthians. Let me repeat one of his sentences in the words of an exact translation: "If anyone is in union with Christ he is a new being; the old state of things has passed away; there is a new state of things." Christianity is the message of the New Creation, the New Being, the New Reality which has appeared with the appearance of Jesus who for this reason, and just for this reason, is called the Christ. . . .

We all live in the old state of things, and the question asked of us by our text is whether we *also* participate in the new state of things. . . . We have known ourselves in our old being, and we shall ask ourselves in this hour whether we also have experienced something of a New Being in ourselves.

What is this New Being? Paul answers first by saying what it is *not*. It is neither circumcision, or uncircumcision, he says. For Paul and for the readers of his letter this meant something very definite. It meant that neither to be a Jew nor to be a pagan is ultimately important; that only one thing counts, namely, the union with Him in whom the New Reality is present. Circumcision or uncircumcision—what does that mean for us? It can also mean something very definite, but at the same time something very universal. It means that no religion as such produces the New Being. Circumcision is a religious rite, observed by the Jews; sacrifices are religious rites, observed by the pagans; baptism is a religious rite, observed by the Christians. All these rites do not matter—only a New Creation. And since these rites stand, in the words of Paul, for the whole religion to which they belong, we can say: No religion matters—only a new state of things. . . . There are the great religions beside Christianity, Hinduism, Buddhism, Islam and the remnants of classical Judaism; they have their myths and their rites—so to speak their "circumcision"—which gives each of them their distinction. There are the secular movements: Fascism and Communism, Secular Humanism, and Ethical Idealism. They try to avoid myths and rites; they represent, so to speak, uncircumcision. Nevertheless, they also claim ultimate truth and demand complete devotion. How shall Christianity face them? Shall Christianity tell them: Come to us, we are a better religion, our kind of circumcision or uncircumcision is higher than yours? Shall we praise Christianity, our way of life, the religious as well as the secular? Shall we make of the Christian message a success story, and tell them, like advertisers: try it with us, and you will see how important Christianity is for everybody? Some missionaries and some ministers and some Christian laymen use these methods. They show a total misunderstanding of Christianity. The apostle who was a missionary and a minister and a layman all at once says something different. He says: No particular religion matters, neither ours nor yours. But I want to tell you that something has happened that matters, something that judges you and me, your religion and my religion. A New Creation has occurred, a New Being has appeared; and we are all asked to participate in it. . . .

And now we ask again: What is this New Being? The New Being is not something that simply takes the place of the Old Being. But it is a renewal of the Old which has been corrupted, distorted, split and almost destroyed. But not wholly destroyed. Salvation does not destroy creation; but it transforms the Old Creation into a New one. Therefore we can speak of the New in terms of a *re*-newal: The threefold *"re,"* namely, *re*-conciliation, *re*-union, *re*-surrection.

In his letter, Paul combines New Creation with reconciliation. The message of reconciliation is: Be reconciled to God. Cease to be hostile to Him, for He is never hostile to you. The message of reconciliation is not that God needs to be reconciled. How could He be? Since He is the source and power of reconciliation, who could reconcile Him? Pagans and Jews and Christians—all of us have tried and are trying to reconcile Him by rites and sacraments, by prayers and services, by moral behavior and works of charity. But if we try this, if we try to give something to Him, to show good deeds which may appease Him, we fail. It is never enough; we never can satisfy Him because there is an infinite demand upon us. And since we cannot appease Him, we grow hostile toward Him. . . . This cannot be otherwise; for one is hostile, consciously or unconsciously, toward those by whom one feels rejected. Everybody is in this predicament, whether he calls that which rejects him "God," or "nature," or "destiny," or "social conditions." Everybody carries a hostility toward the existence into which he has been thrown, toward the hidden powers which determine his life and that of the universe, toward that which makes him guilty and that threatens him with destruction because he has become guilty. . . . There are two symptoms which we hardly can avoid noticing: The hostility against ourselves and the hostility against others. One speaks so often of pride and arrogance and self-certainty and complacency in people. But this is, in most cases, the superficial level of their being. Below this, in a deeper level, there is self-rejection, disgust, and even hatred of one's self. . . . And he who feels rejected by God and who rejects himself feels also rejected by the others. As he grows hostile toward destiny and hostile toward himself, he also grows hostile toward other men. . . . Be reconciled with God—that means, at the same time, be reconciled with the others! But it does *not* mean try to reconcile the others, as it does not mean to try to reconcile yourselves. Try to reconcile God. You will fail. This is the message: A new reality has appeared in which you *are* reconciled. To enter the New Being we do not need to show anything. We must only be open to be grasped by it, although we have nothing to show.

Being reconciled—that is the first mark of the New Reality. And being reunited is its second mark. Reconciliation makes reunion possible. The New Creation is the reality in which the separated is reunited. The New Being is manifest in the Christ because in Him the separation never overcame the unity between Him and God, between Him and mankind, between Him and Himself. This gives His picture in the Gospels its overwhelming and inexhaustible power. In Him we look at a human life that maintained the union in spite of everything that drove Him into separation. He represents and mediates the power of the New Being because He represents and mediates the power of an undisrupted union. Where the New Reality appears, one feels united with God, the ground and meaning of one's existence. One has what has been called the love of one's destiny, and what, today, we might call the courage to take upon ourselves our own anxiety. Then one has the astonishing experience of feeling reunited with one's self, not in pride and false self-satisfaction, but in a deep self-acceptance. One accepts one's self as something which is eternally important, eternally loved, eternally accepted. The disgust at one's self, the hatred of one's self has disappeared. There is a center, a direction, a meaning for life. All healing—bodily and mental—creates this reunion of one's self with one's self. Where there is real healing, *there* is the New Being, the New Creation. . . . And it creates reunion with the others. Nothing is more distinctive of the Old Being than the separation of man from man. Nothing is more passionately demanded than social healing, than the New Being within history and human relationships. . . .

And if the Church which is the assembly of God has an ultimate significance, this is its significance: That here the reunion of man to man is pronounced and confessed and realized, even if in fragments and weaknesses and distortions. The Church is the place where the reunion of man with man is an actual event, though the Church of God is permanently betrayed by the Christian churches. But, although betrayed and expelled, the New Creation saves and preserves that by which it is betrayed and expelled: churches, mankind and history.

The Church, like all its members, relapses from the New into the Old Being. Therefore, the third mark of the New Creation is re-surrection. . . . Resurrection is not an event that might happen in some remote future, but it is the power of the New Being to create life out of death, here and now, today and tomorrow. Where there is a New Being, *there* is resurrection, namely, the creation into eternity out of every moment of time. . . .

Reconciliation, reunion, resurrection—this is the New Creation, the New Being, the New state of things. Do we participate in it? The message of Christianity is not Christianity, but a New Reality. A New state of things has appeared, it still appears; it is hidden and visible, it is there and it is here. Accept it, enter into it, let it grasp you.*

Paul Tillich, 1886–1965. American theologian, philosopher.
The New Being.

The Way and "The Voice of the Beloved"

I am weary, often, to read and hear many things—
in Thee is all that I desire and long for.
Let all teachers hold their peace; let all
creatures be silent in Thy sight; speak unto me
Thou alone.

The Voice of the Beloved:
I am He who in one instant do lift up the humble
mind to comprehend more reasoning of eternal
Truth, than if one had studied ten years in the
schools . . .
The more a man is at one within himself and
becometh single in heart, so much the more and
higher things doth he without labor understand; for
that he receiveth the light of the understanding
from above . . .
If thou wilt have me come unto thee, and remain with
thee; purge out the old leaven, and make clean the
habitation of thy heart. I am the Lover of purity
and the Giver of all holiness. I seek a pure heart,
and there is the place of my rest . . .
If thou couldst but perfectly bring thyself to
nothing, and empty thyself of all created love, then

ought I with great grace to flow into thee . . .
Howsoever little any thing be, if it is inordinately
loved and regarded, it keepeth thee back from the
Highest, and corrupteth the soul . . .
My son forsake thyself and thou shalt find me.

O Thou Beloved:
Love eternal, my whole Good, Happiness which hath
no bounds, I desire to appropriate Thee with the
most vehement desire, and the most worthy
reverence.
I desire to reserve nothing unto myself.
O everlasting Light, surpassing all created
luminaries, flash forth Thy lightning from above,
piercing all the most inward parts of my heart.
Make clean, make glad, make bright and make alive
my spirit, with all the powers thereof, that I
may cleave unto Thee in ecstasies of joy.**

Thomas à Kempis, 1380–1471. German mystic.
The Imitation of Christ.

The Way as Actuation of Innate and Individual Wholeness

There is inherent in man a longing and tendency towards wholeness, and only when this longing is stilled is his negative state of tension wiped out and neutralized. This wholeness can only be achieved through knowledge of the missing part, that is when man has become fully conscious. That is what is meant, for instance, by the sentence in the Upanishads: "Brahma is the knowledge of Brahma."

Now this innate striving for wholeness is the decisive factor in any real understanding of the process whereby healing is brought about by consciousness. In every psychic system, there exists this desire for completeness which, making use of the life process, does its utmost to force [man] to realize his latent wholeness, whether we give the resultant sum total the name of "character" or "personality." Whenever in any given life this unity is not in process of being achieved the particular meaning and purpose of that life has gone astray. . . .

Therefore, in the end, consciousness, or better still, the process of becoming conscious, always implies becoming aware of one's real personality and of its predestined wholeness. It is as if there were a central image, an eidos, working behind all manifestations of life and determining them. The wholeness is achieved—in other words the entelechy has been fulfilled—in proportion as the central image, the eidos, determines every single act of the personality, and finds therein its full and undisturbed actualization.

There is an obvious difference between the purely biological and the psychological wholeness. With plants and animals—and to a relatively large extent also with primitive people and children—the actualization of the eidos is more or less achieved; they present an organic and unbroken wholeness. This explains their natural "beauty" and undisturbed rhythm. This beauty, however, is purely instinctive, "unconscious"; it might be described as belonging purely to the aesthetic sphere. With [civilized] man a completely new factor enters the situation which disturbs the instinctive wholeness: it is that of consciousness and with it discrimination and choice. An animal or a plant—and to a lesser degree a primitive or a child—is unconsciously whole. With consciousness this instinctive wholeness is at first lost. Man can actualize his *a priori* "human" wholeness only in and through continuously repeated acts of choice and decision.[13] The eidos of wholeness is present in him all the time, but it is not automatically and instinctively actualized as it is in the sphere of biological wholeness. As a matter of fact, the factor of conscious choice, of deliberate decision is the constituent element of human wholeness. The freedom of the individual might be defined as the preparedness to be formed by his own eidos, his inner image of wholeness which exists *a priori* in him. The more the individual becomes sensitive and receptive to his inner image, the more he becomes whole and "healed." The fact that language has one root for the words "whole," "holy" and to "heal" conceals a deep truth; he who is whole is also healed; to be healed is to be made whole. And it is just because this predestined, unique "wholeness," which is called personality, is the real meaning and purpose of each life, that consciousness of this wholeness produces healing. It is

[13]i.e., "Life itself, with all the experiences and duties which must be met, strives to make man fulfill his own individual task." [See p. 166 of the author's text and his chapter on "A Psychological Approach to Religion."—Ed.]

"holy" in so far as it represents a profound experience of a numinous character; the idea of wholeness is, in other words, an archetype[14] of deep significance. . . . Thus individuation implies a "coming to oneself." That is why the recognition of one's true self obliterates the cleavage and its accompanying fear. . . .

At the same time the integrated personality does not merely express the *individual* totality, for in the actualization of his own *a priori* wholeness the individual also discovers his relatedness to a super-individual centre. This centre is the self which is "paradoxically the quintessence of the individuum and at the same time of the collectivum."[15] In other words: the experience of wholeness coincides with the experience of a centre of the personality and a meaning of life which transcends the individual. This is expressed for instance in the words of Nicolaus of Cusa who makes God say to man: "Be thou thyself, and I shall be thine."*–**

Gerhard Adler, 1904–. English Jungian analyst.
Extracts from *Studies in Analytical Psychology.*

I said to my soul, be still, and let the dark come upon
    you
Which shall be the darkness of God . . .
I said to my soul, be still, and wait without hope
For hope would be hope for the wrong thing;
    wait without love
For love would be love of the wrong thing;
    there is yet faith
But the faith and the love and the hope are all in the
    waiting.
Wait without thought, for you are not ready for
    thought:
So the darkness shall be the light, and the stillness
    the dancing.

Whisper of running streams, and winter lightning.
The wild thyme unseen and the wild strawberry,
The laughter in the garden, echoed ecstasy

---

[14]Dynamic patterns or images making up the collective or suprapersonal unconscious (see fn. 27, p. 354).—Ed.

[15]Jung. *Paracelsica,* p. 167.

Not lost, but requiring, pointing to the agony
Of death and birth.

You say I am repeating
Something I have said before. I shall say it again.
Shall I say it again? In order to arrive there,
To arrive where you are, to get from where
you are not,
You must go by a way wherein there is no ecstasy.
In order to arrive at what you do not know
You must go by a way which is the
way of ignorance.
In order to possess what you do not possess
You must go by the way of dispossession.
In order to arrive at what you are not
You must go through the way in which you are not.
And what you do not know is the only thing you know
And what you own is what you do not own
And where you are is where you are not.*

* * * * * *

What we call the beginning is often the end
And to make an end is to make a beginning.
The end is where we start from . . .
Every phrase and every sentence is an end
and a beginning,
Every poem an epitaph. And any action
Is a step to the block, to the fire, down the sea's throat
Or to an illegible stone: and that is where we start.
We die with the dying:
See, they depart, and we go with them.
We are born with the dead:
See, they return, and bring us with them.
The moment of the rose and the moment of the
yew-tree
Are of equal duration . . .

We shall not cease from exploration
And the end of all our exploring
Will be to arrive where we started
And know the place for the first time.

Through the unknown, remembered gate
When the last of earth left to discover
Is that which was the beginning;
At the source of the longest river
The voice of the hidden waterfall
And the children in the apple-tree
Not known, because not looked for
But heard, half-heard, in the stillness
Between two waves of the sea.

Quick now, here, now, always—
A condition of complete simplicity
(Costing not less than everything)
And all shall be well and
All manner of thing shall be well
When the tongues of flame are in-folded
Into the crowned knot of fire
And the fire and the rose are one.*

T. S. Eliot, 1888–1965. English poet.
Extracts from "East Coker" IV
and "Little Gidding" V in *Four Quartets.*

CHAPTER II

The Implications of the Way

Which of you, desiring to build a tower, doth not first sit down and count the cost whether he have wherewith to complete it?

JESUS OF NAZARETH

You must strip yourself of all self-deception.

FRANCES G. WICKES

. . . and having found one pearl of great price, he went and sold all that he had, and bought it.

JESUS OF NAZARETH

Yes God! Yes God! Yes, yes and always yes."

NICOLAS DE CUSA

The selections in Chapter I presented paradoxical and general statements of the Way. Chapter II attempts to examine more specific steps in the religious growth process. Such steps rarely occur in the sequence described, but each step is somewhat essential to the progressive achievement of that inner change whereby a new Center is discovered and a greater wholeness permitted to function in an individual life.

These steps are designated as Choice, Purgation, Self-Knowledge and Self-Acceptance, Devotion to the Good, and Rebirth. What is implied? One chooses to try for wholeness rather than partialness. This involves submitting to a thoroughgoing revision of the personality, unconscious as well as conscious. It demands an integrity of purpose strong enough to endure the downfall of egocentric drives, and brave enough to build on the unfamiliar foundations of a newly discovered Inner Life which is so much more than "I want." Finally it implies a process of transformation which, because of its sweeping scope and its essential mystery, has often been described as a spiritual rebirth. The selections which follow give content to each of these implications.

Because some readers find an attitude of devotion difficult or meaningless, as they have had no recognizable experience (and thus no real conviction) of a supra-personal reality to which to direct their devotion, an Appendix "The Object of Devotion" has been included. In this Appendix are assembled ideas of God as expressed by philosophers, scientists, poets, psychologists, as well as by mystical writers of various periods. Because of the richness in approach which they represent, it is believed that most readers who explore the Appendix will find it rewarding. The editors consider it indigenous to Part One. Ed.

The Way Implies Choice

The choice is always ours. Then let me choose
The longest art, the hard Promethean way
Cherishingly to tend and feed and fan
That inward fire, whose small precarious flame,
Kindled or quenched creates
The noble or the ignoble men we are,
The worlds we live in and the very fates,
Our bright or muddy star.

Aldous Huxley, 1894–1963. English writer, literary critic.
The Cicadas

The creature has nothing else in its power but the free use of its will, and its free will hath no other power but that of concurring with, or resisting, the working of God in nature.

William Law, 1686–1761. English clergyman, mystic.
Serious Call to a Devout and Holy Life.

Until man appeared, evolution strove only, from an observer's point of view, to manufacture an organ, the brain, in a body capable of assuring its protection. All the ancestors of man were but irresponsible actors playing an imposed part in a play which they did not understand, or try to understand. Man continues to play his part but wants to comprehend the play. He becomes capable of perfecting himself, and he is even the only one capable of doing this. But in order to improve himself he must be free, since his contribution to evolution will depend on the use he makes of his liberty.

This transformation of man into an active, responsible individual is the new event which, more than any other, characterizes man. Of course the ancient mechanism of evolution, natural selection, will again enter into play. But, instead of depending as formerly on the slow action of biological laws and of chance, natural selection now depends on conscience, a manifestation of cerebral activity based on freedom which becomes, in each of us, the means put at our disposal to advance. According to the degree of evolution we have reached we will choose to progress or regress. Our choice will indicate precisely the state of perfection we have attained.

Lecomte du Noüy, 1883–1947. French biophysicist.
Human Destiny.

The distresses of choice are our chance to be blessed.

W. H. Auden, 1907–1973. English poet.
For the Time Being.

Wise Men

Not In but With our time Love's energy
Exhibits Love's immediate operation;
The choice to love is open till we die.

Shepherds

O Living Love, by your birth we are able
Not only, like the ox and ass of the stable,
  To love with our live wills, but love,
  Know we love.

Tutti

O Living Love replacing phantasy,
O Joy of life revealed in Love's creation;
Our mood of longing turns to indication:
Space is the Whom our loves are needed by,
Time is our choice of How to love and Why.

W. H. Auden, 1907–1973. English poet.
For the Time Being.—"A Christmas Oratorio."

All the length of our conscious life, God for Whom we were made, in Whom alone we can find what we want and understand what we mean, presents Himself to the apprehension of our soul, tempts our desire, pursues our will. To this pressure we must react, either with it or against it.

R. H. J. Steuart, S.J., 1874–1948. English priest.
The Inward Vision.

For the most part, of course, the presence and action of the great spiritual universe surrounding us is no more noticed by us than the pressure of air on our bodies, or the action of light. Our field of attention is not wide enough for that; our spiritual senses are not sufficiently alert. Most people work so hard developing their correspondence with the visible world, that their power of corresponding with the invisible is left in a rudimentary state.

The moment in which, in one way or another, we become aware of this creative action of God and are therefore able to respond or resist, is the moment in which our conscious spiritual life begins. In all the talk of human progress, it is strange how very seldom we hear anything about this, the most momentous step forward that a human being can make: for it is the step that takes us beyond self-interest.

There are many different ways in which the step can be taken. It may be, from the ordinary human point of view, almost imperceptible: because, though it really involves the very essence of man's being, his free and living will, it is not linked with a special or vivid experience. Bit by bit the inexorable pressure is applied, and bit by bit the soul responds; until a moment comes when it realizes that the landscape has been transformed, and is seen in a new proportion and lit by a new light. But sometimes the step is a distinct and vivid experience. Then we get the strange facts of conversion: when through some object or event—in the external world, another world and its overwhelming attraction and demand is realised. An old and limited state of consciousness is suddenly, even violently, broken up and another takes its place. It was the voice of a child saying "Take, read!" which at last made St. Augustine cross the frontier on which he had been lingering, and turned a brilliant and selfish young professor into one of the giants of the Christian Church; and a voice which seemed to him to come from the Crucifix, which literally made the young St. Francis, unsettled and unsatisfied, another man than he was before. It was while St. Ignatius sat by a stream and watched the running water, and while the strange old cobbler Jacob Boehme was looking at a pewter dish, that there was shown to each of them the mystery of the Nature of God. A spring is touched, a Reality always there discloses itself in its awe-inspiring majesty and intimate nearness, and becomes the ruling fact of existence; continually presenting its standards, and demanding a costly response. And so we get such an astonishing scene, when we reflect upon it, as that of the young Francis of Assisi, little more than a boy, asking all night long the one question which so many apparently mature persons have never asked at all: "My God and All, what are Thou and what am I?" and we realise with amazement what a human creature really is—a finite centre of consciousness, which is able to apprehend, and long for, Infinity.*

Evelyn Underhill, 1875–1944. English writer, mystic.
The Spiritual Life.

We think we must climb to a certain height of goodness before we can reach God. But He says not "At the end of the end of the way you may find me"; He says "I am the Way; I am the road under your feet, the road that begins just as low down as you happen to be." If we are in a hole the Way begins in the hole. The moment we set our face in the same direction as His, we are walking with God.

Helen Wodehouse, 1880–1964. English educator.
"Inner Light" I.

God impels nobody, for he will have no one saved by compulsion . . . God has given free will to men that they may choose for themselves, either the good or the bad. Christ said to his disciples, "Will ye go away?" as tho he would say, "You are under no compulsion," and, "God forces no one, for love cannot compel and God's service is, therefore, a thing of complete freedom."*

Hans Denck, 1495–1527. German mystic, spiritual reformer.
On the Law of God.

The world is tired of individualism (which economic-dominated minds call by its economic symptom, capitalism). Many men are so desperate that they will use violence to rid themselves of individualism, though it itself is the product of violence, and grows with violence. They are like men adrift and dying of thirst who in their madness drink seawater.

The compulsory economic communism is based on hate.

The psychological [communism] is based on love, on the steadily expanding power which grows by giving. Because consciousness and the psyche are more fundamental than the means of life, it will always be the emotion and motive, and not the supposed aim, that will govern and shape the actual achievement. If the psychology is right, then the right economics, the only economics bearable to a happy, just, social and charitic nature, will follow. If a man realises how he must and how he may lose his individuality, he will not thereafter cling to greed which can prevent his deliverance and ruin his happiness.

This, then, it would seem, is the future of religion, and one neither other-worldly nor distant. Men may enter on their happiness when they will, and they should not hesitate, for the old order is over anyhow. Man may be far more happy than any but the saints have so far been, or far more wretched than it is possible for a man to be and not to become a beast. Which he will choose to be no one can say. He may see the choice, make the effort and attain the new life. Or he may drift, persuade himself that things are well enough, and that they will last his time. But it is certain that here in our day the middle path ends. Nationalism and individualism are outraged by the integration of the world; they must cut these tendrils and rootlets that are binding the world together, or they will be obliterated. Physical science puts at their disposal forces that can really tear in pieces these connections and rupture every artery of the world's economic life. Everyone may destroy, and so none may escape.

Here therefore, and here alone, in the advance of religion there seems to lie to our hand the solution of the aeonic conflict of the individual, and with that solution, at the same stroke (for this is but its other side), the salvation of civilization. Here lies the reconciliation of the individual's intense passion to survive and the race's apparently disregardful continuance. Here is the door passing through which the individual returns to society, society becomes the race, the race is reunited with life, and life is one with the universe.*

Gerald Heard, 1889–1971.
English author, religious philosopher.
The Social Substance of Religion.

Every one who hears these words of mine and does them will be like a wise man who built his house upon the rock; and the rain fell, and the floods came, and the winds blew and beat upon that house, but it did not fall, because it had been founded on the rock. And every one who hears these words of mine and does not do them will be like a foolish man who built his house upon the sand; and the rain fell, and the floods came, and the winds blew and beat against that house, and it fell; and great was the fall of it.

Jesus of Nazareth.
New Testament (Matt. 7:24–27). Revised Standard Version.

The Way Implies Inner Purgation

If the doors of perception were cleansed, everything would appear to man as it is, infinite.

For man has closed himself up, till he sees all things thro' narrow chinks of his cavern.

William Blake, 1757–1827. English poet, artist, mystic.
The Marriage of Heaven and Hell.

Except for those rare spirits that are born without sin, there is a cavern of darkness to be traversed before that temple can be entered. The gate of the cavern is despair, and its floor is paved with the gravestones of abandoned hopes. There Self must die; there the eagerness, the greed of untamed desire must be slain, for only so can the soul be freed from the empire of Fate. But out of the cavern the Gate of Renunciation leads again to the daylight of wisdom, by whose radiance a new insight, a new joy, a new tenderness, shine forth to gladden the pilgrim's heart.

Bertrand Russell, 1872–1970.
English mathematician, philosopher.
Mysticism and Logic.

Abandon Hope All Ye That Enter Here

To die—for this into the world you came.

Yes, to abandon more than you ever conceived as possible:

All ideals, plans—even the very best and most unselfish —all hopes and desires,

All formulas of morality, all reputation for virtue or consistency or good sense; all cherished theories, doctrines, systems of knowledge.

Modes of life, habits, predilections, preferences, superiorities, weaknesses, indulgences,

Good health, wholeness of limb and brain, youth, manhood, age—nay life itself—in one word: To die—

For this into the world you came.

All to be abandoned, and when they have been finally abandoned,

Then to return to be used—and then only to be rightly used, to be free and open forever.

Edward Carpenter, 1844–1929. English author, poet.
Towards Democracy.

No man is free until he is free at the center. When he lets go there he is free indeed. When the self is renounced, then one stands utterly disillusioned, apart, asking for nothing. He anticipates the sorrows, the buffetings, the slights, the separations, the disappointments of life by their acceptance in one great renunciation. It is life's supreme strategic retreat. You can then say to life, "What can you do to me? I want nothing!" You can say to death, "What can you do to me? I have already died!" Then is a man truly free. In the bath of renunciation he has washed his soul clean from a thousand clamoring, conflicting desires. Asking for nothing, if anything comes to him, it is all sheer gain. Then life becomes one constant surprise.

Everything belongs to the man who wants nothing. Having nothing, he possesses all things in life, including life itself. Nothing will be denied the man who denies himself. Having chosen to be utterly solitary he now comes into possession of the most utterly social fact in the universe, the kingdom of God. He wants nothing of the world of man or of matter. He has God. That is enough. Now he is ready to come back into the world. He is washed clean of desires, now he can form new ones, from a new center and with a new motive. This detachment is necessary to a new attachment. The fullest and most complete life comes out of the most completely empty life.*

E. Stanley Jones, 1884–1973.
American, Christian missionary to India, author.

The recognition and careful observation of non-personal psychical factors entails and leads to a sacrifice of the ego —not in the form of an abolition, but in the form of a renunciation of its supremacy. It is no longer possible always to say: I want, I decide, I do, and so on, because it is evident that things happen to me, which are decided for me, and that factors other than the conscious "I" do or think in me. The ego is the vehicle for these other factors and it is responsible for them; but their roots are not in it but in the larger psyche. This is an attitude comparable to that of St. Paul when he says (Gal. ii 20): "I live; yet not I, but Christ liveth in me"; and it is certainly an attitude which can be called religious. It is, in a way, a kind of death of the ego and is often represented in dreams. This entails a deliberate renunciation of the hitherto dominating position of the ego, the conscious person as I know myself to be.*

Toni Wolff, 1888–1953. Swiss analytical psychologist.
Christianity Within.

Purgation of "Family Images"

Then he went home; and the crowd came together again, so that they could not even eat. And when his friends heard it, they went out to seize him; for they said, "He is beside himself."

Mark 3:19–21

And his mother and his brothers came; and standing outside they sent to him and called him. And a crowd was sitting about him; and, they said to him, "Your mother and your brothers are outside, asking for you." And he answered, "Who are my mother and my brothers?" And looking around on those who sat about him, he said, "Here are my mother and my brothers! Whoever does the will of God is my brother, and sister, and mother."

Mark 3:31–35

The first moves towards independence occur very early in life—as exemplified in the story of the twelve-year-old Jesus in the temple. And none of these moves is without pain and tragic guilt—as indicated in the anxiety of the parents of Jesus and the reproaches they made to Him. In the story above Jesus uses the family relations as symbols for a relation of a higher order, for the community of those who do the will of God. Something unconditional breaks into the conditional relations of the natural family and creates a community which is as intimate and as strong as the familv relations, and at the same time infinitely superior to it. The depth of this gap is emphasized in the attempt of His family to seize Him and to bring Him home because of His extraordinary behavior which makes them believe that He is out of His mind. And the gap is strongly expressed in His saying that He who loves father and mother more than Him cannot be His disciple, words even sharpened in Luke's version, where everyone is rejected by Him who does not "hate" father and mother and wife and children and brothers and sisters—and his own life.

All these words cut with divine power through the natural relation between the members of the family whenever these relations claim to be ultimates. They cut through the bondage of age-old traditions and conventions and their unconditional claims; they cut through the consecration of the family ties by sacramental or other laws which make them equal to the ties between those who belong to the new reality in the Christ. The family is no ultimate! The family relations are not unconditional relations. The consecration of the family is not a consecration for the final aim of man's existence. We can imagine the revolutionary character of such sayings in face of the religions and cultures of mankind. We can hardly measure their disturbing character in face of what has happened century after century within the so-called Christian nations—with the support of the Christian churches who could not stand the radical nature of the Christian message in this as in other respects. However, in spite of its radicalism, the Christian message does not request the dissolution of the family. It affirms the family and limits its significance.

We must risk tragic guilt in becoming free from father and mother and brothers and sisters. And we know today better than many generations before us what that means, how infinitely difficult it is and that nobody does it without carrying scars in his soul his whole life. For it is not only the real father or mother or brother or sister from whom we must become free in order to come into our own. It is something much more refined, the image of them, which from our earliest childhood has impregnated our souls. The real father, the real mother may let us go free, although this is by no means the rule in Christian families. But even if they have the wisdom to do it, their images can prevent us from doing what the will of God is in a concrete situation, namely, to do acts in which love, power and justice are united. Their image may prevent us from love by subjection to law. It may prevent us from having power by weakening our personal center. . . . But do not mistake me! Opposition and revolt are not yet freedom. They are unavoidable stages on the way to freedom. But they create another servitude if they are not overcome as much as the early dependence must be overcome. How can this happen? Certainly, in pathological cases, psychotherapy is needed, as Jesus Himself acted as a healer, bodily and mentally. But more is necessary, namely, the dependence on that which gives ultimate independence, the image of that which includes and transcends all father and mother images, the life of that which makes it possible to hate and to love every life, including our own. No human problem and certainly not the family problem can be solved on a finite level. This is true although we know that even the image of God can be distorted by the images of father and mother, so that its saving power is almost lost. This is the danger of all religion and a serious limit for our religious work. But it is not a limit for God, who again and again breaks through the images we have made of Him, and who has shown in Christ that He is not only father and mother to us, but also child, and that therefore in Him the inescapable conflicts of every family are overcome. The Father who is also child is more than a father as He is more than a child. Therefore, we can pray to the Father in heaven without transferring our hostility against the father image to Him. Because God has become child, it is possible for us to say the Our Father.*

Paul Tillich, 1886–1965.
American theologian, philosopher.
The New Being.

The pseudo-conscience which demands patterns, ways of life never individually examined and appraised, is the enemy of creativity. It says, "Thou shalt not," to living desires that stir within us. It demands, not obedience to the inner law of our being, but conformity to superimposed convention. A young woman, who had been taught to stifle the voice of desire, dreamed:

> "My father and I were buried in shoe boxes under the old apple tree. He lay comfortably curled in his box but mine was too small for me—I couldn't grow. It stifled me—I could not breathe. I felt myself move, push toward the light. Then I was out and the apple tree was in bloom. I might never have seen it."

The shoe box, receptacle for the shoe that one puts on one's feet before going forth into life, is now only a coffin. The father had accepted a life of small duties, of conventionally regulated thought and feeling. His daughter wanted to explore new ideas, to play the renegade from security. Should she be quiet in the place she had been put or break the confines and see the spring come to the apple tree?

She decided to follow the dream. The immediate reaction was as dramatic as the breaking of ice in a great river in spring. She felt an uprushing energy that swept away old restrictions with a ruthless disregard of their demands. She wanted only to be free. But what was this newly released demon who was flaunting her conscientiousness? Doubt swept over her; self-assertion was destructive. As the first turbulence subsided, she was aware of a new element that was alive in her, and knew she must trust it and let it live. Spring had come to her as well as to the apple tree. This experience of rebirth made it possible for her to accept a concept of creative living which her father had denied—to live more abundantly, sacrificing the lower value to the higher, substituting sacrifice to the god of livingness for mere self-sacrifice. Divine discontent had moved as a factor of creative energy.

This divine discontent is born of the spirit. It is the will toward freedom and life, not the discontent of the desirous ego that seeks its own aggrandizement, or the discontent of the child who clamors for small satisfactions. It is the discontent that will not let man rest until he has found the creative meaning of his own individual life. For true creativity is not concerned with the ego, but with the Self:

Frances G. Wickes, 1875–1970. American psychotherapist.
"The Creative Process."

"Beauty is Truth, Truth Beauty." The words to many are meaningless. And it is certain that by no poring over the words themselves can the vision which they express be attained. Nor, probably, if we turn them about, like a jewel of many facets, will they reflect a gleam.

We may turn them in many ways. We may say that the Real is Beautiful. The answer straightway is that the Real is full of ugliness and pain. And this is true: who will deny it? But the Beauty of the Real is a Beauty which resides as surely in pain and ugliness as in beauty itself. There is the sorrow which makes

Sorrow more beautiful than Beauty's self.

But that sorrow may still be called, by our human standards, beautiful. The Beauty of the Real is beyond this. It lies in the perfection of uniqueness which belongs to every thing, or thought, simply because it *is*.

But this is not Beauty. And indeed it is not what men commonly call Beauty, any more than the Love with which all high religion invests its Deity is what is commonly called Love among men, any more than the Perfection which, Spinoza said, belonged to every existence is what men commonly call perfection. None the less, the great sayings that "God is Love," and that "*Omnis existentia est perfectio,*" have their meaning for those who understand them. Keats uttered another saying worthy to stand with these simple and lucid finalities. "Beauty is Truth, Truth Beauty" belongs to the same order as they; nor can any one truly understand any one of these sayings without understanding the others.

. . . the only name for the faculty by which we can discern that element of Beauty which is present in every Fact, which we must discern in every Fact before it becomes Truth for us, is Love. . . . The relation between these things is simple and inextricable. When we love a Fact, it becomes Truth; when we attain that detachment from our passions whereby it becomes possible for us to love all Facts, then we have reached our Peace. If a Truth cannot be loved, it is not Truth, but only Fact. But the Fact does not change, in order that it may become Truth; it is we who change. All Fact is beautiful; it is we who have to regain our innocence to see its Beauty.

But this is inhuman, it may be said. And if it is indeed inhuman to be detached for a moment from all human passion, to see for a moment all things that happen as sheer happenings, to cease for a moment to feel what men call love and hate in the peace of a Love that is distinct from, and beyond them both, then it is inhuman. But this ultimate disinterestedness begins at home. It is achieved only by disinterestedness towards the pain and ugliness of one's own experience; and it is achieved chiefly by those to whom the pain of others has been as their own pain. This detachment is reached not through insensibility, but through sensibility grown intolerable.

None can usurp this height
But those to whom the miseries of the world
Are misery, and will not let them rest.

Whether or not it is easily intelligible, there is a meaning in "Beauty is Truth, Truth Beauty" . . . It is simple, but not easy; and it involves a great renunciation. . . . To attain the vision which Keats describes as the knowledge that "Beauty is Truth, Truth Beauty" we are required to put away all our human desires and beliefs and anxieties. Our joys and sorrows must become remote as though they happened to others than ourselves, or to ourselves in some other mode of existence from which we have awakened as from a dream. All the infinite, the all but total activities of man, conscious or unconscious, which are directed towards the maintenance and assertion of the instinctive will to live, must be put away. Cease they cannot, nor can we make them cease; but we must cease to be identified with them. They are the substrate of our vision; without them we cannot see as we desire to see. But when we have become an Eye, the Eye cannot belong to them, or they to it. It sees them with the same utter detachment with which it sees all things else. And this detachment is a real detaching. Than this no greater renunciation is possible.*–**

John Middleton Murry, 1889–1957. English author, critic.
Studies in Keats.

He that hath ears, let him hear.

The kingdom of heaven is like unto a treasure hidden in

the field; which a man found, and hid; and in his joy he goeth and selleth all that he hath, and buyeth that field.

Again, the kingdom of heaven is like unto a man that is a merchant seeking goodly pearls: and having found one pearl of great price, he went and sold all that he had, and bought it.

Jesus of Nazareth.
New Testament (Matt. 13:43–45).

Therefore if a heart is to be ready for him, it must be emptied out to nothingness, the condition of its maximum capacity. So, too, a disinterested heart, reduced to nothingness, is the optimum, the condition of maximum sensitivity.

Take an illustration from nature. If I wish to write on a white tablet, then no matter how fine the matter already written on it, it will confuse me and prevent me from writing down (my thoughts); so that, if I still wish to use the tablet, I must first erase all that is written on it, but it will never serve me as well for writing as when it is clean. Similarly, if God is to write his message about the highest matters on my heart, everything to be referred to as "this or that" must first come out, and I must be disinterested. God is free to do his will on his own level when my heart, being disinterested, is bent on neither this nor that.

Meister Johannes Eckhart, 1260–1327. German scholar, mystic.
Meister Eckhart. Trans. R. Blakney.

Compromise Untenable

After experience had taught me that the common occurrences of ordinary life are vain and futile, and I saw that all the objects of my desire and fear were in themselves nothing good nor bad, save in so far as the mind was affected by them; I at length determined to search out whether there were not something truly good and communicable to man, by which his spirit might be affected to the exclusion of all other things: yea, whether there were anything, through the discovery and acquisition of which I might enjoy continuous and perfect gladness forever. I say that I at length determined, because at first sight it seemed ill-advised to renounce things, in the possession of which I was assured, for the sake of what was yet uncertain. . . . I therefore turned over in my mind whether it might be possible to come at this new way, or at least to the certitude of its existence, without changing my usual way of life, (a compromise which I had often attempted before, but in vain). For the things that commonly happen in life and are esteemed among men as the highest good (as is witnessed by their works) can be reduced to these three, Riches, Fame, and Lust; and by these the mind is so distracted that it can scarcely think of any other good. With regard to Lust, the mind is as much absorbed thereby as if it had attained rest in some good: and this hinders it from thinking of anything else. But after fruition a great sadness follows, which, if it does not absorb the mind, will yet disturb and blunt it. . . . But love directed towards the eternal and infinite feeds the mind with pure joy, and is free from all sadness. Wherefore it is greatly to be desired, and to be sought after with our whole might . . . [and] although I could perceive this quite clearly in my mind, I could not at once lay aside all greed and lust and honour. . . . One thing I could see, and that was that so long as the mind was turned upon this new way, it was deflected, and seriously engaged therein; which was a great comfort to me; for I saw that those evils were not such as would not yield to remedies: and though at first these intervals were rare and lasted but a short while, yet afterwards the true good became more and more evident to me, and these intervals more frequent and of longer duration.*

Benedict Spinoza, 1632–1677. Dutch philosopher.
"De Intellectus Emendatione." Trans. Robert Bridges.

Renunciation of Immaturities

Every person must learn the art of renouncing many things in order to possess other things more securely and fully. This is a most important and difficult step. As children, we knew very little about the necessity of renunciation. The young mind simply has no experience in the postponement of satisfaction. Yet as we grow older we learn that every stage of human development calls upon us to weigh differing goods in the scales and to sacrifice some for the sake of others. . . .

The man [or woman] who wishes to achieve stature in the mature world will have to renounce many careers in order to fulfill one. The same truth exists in the realm of emotions. . . . Time is an irreversible arrow, and we can never return to the self that we sloughed off in childhood or adolescence. . . . Human existence means the closing of doors, many doors, before one great door can be opened—the door of mature love and of adult achievement.

No person can attain genuine self-respect until he achieves the knowledge of the consistent and the inconsistent. As an adult he must accept duties and responsibilities and cultivate his true fulfillment in the acre he has chosen—the acre of love and marriage, vocation, and avocation. He must be able not only to say, but to realize deeply within himself, that he is no longer an uninvolved free human atom. "Everything that I do," such a man must say, "is like the pebble thrown into a pool, making larger and larger ripples in the waters of other lives."

Renunciation is often painful, and we cling stubbornly to the romantic cloak-and-dagger characters of our fantasy life. But dangerous and vain is the attempt to relive in actuality the fantasies of childhood, or to attempt to breach those barriers between the possible and the impossible which maturing years have erected. . . .

It should be noted that there is a difference between renunciation and repression. A person who represses all his ambitions and wishes and denies any reality to them is on the road to misery. The person, on the other hand, who consciously renounces unrealizable and unworthy desires has straightened himself by daring to face his life as it is and making clear to himself why he has chosen that course of action. A man who can say to himself, "I know that there is still something of the adolescent within me, and yet I know that I can ruin my life and the lives of others if I should smash the mature pattern which I now possess; therefore, for the sake of abiding and permanent happiness, I willingly sacrifice the ephemeral temptation"—such a man has achieved the wisdom of renunciation without repression.

We shall become free of inner conflict and burden only when we have looked renunciation directly in the face and persuaded ourselves that it is essential for the fulfillment of our true and permanent happiness. Persons who have made such renunciation have learned to live not for the fleeting and perishable ecstasy of the moment, but for the eternal and abiding values which alone are the sources of self-respect and peace of mind.*

Joshua Loth Liebman, 1907–1948.
American rabbi, educator.
Peace of Mind.

Renunciation of the Spirit of the World

Every person, when he first applies himself to the exercise of the virtue of humility, must consider himself as a learner. He has not only as much to do, as he that has some new art or science to learn, but he has also a great deal to unlearn: He is to forget and lay aside his own Spirit, which has been a long while fixing and forming itself; he must forget, and depart from abundance of passions and opinions, which the fashion, and vogue, and spirit of the world have made natural to him. Because the vogue and fashion of the world, by which we have been carried away as in a torrent, before we could pass right judgments of the value of things, is, in many respects, contrary to humility.

To abound in wealth, to have fine houses and rich clothes, to be beautiful in our persons, to have title of dignity, to be above our fellow-creatures, to overcome our enemies with power, to subdue all that oppose us, to set out ourselves in as much splendor as we can, to live highly and magnificently, to eat, and drink, and delight ourselves in the most costly manner, these are the great, the honourable, the desirable things, to which the spirit of the world turns the eyes of all people. And many a man is afraid of standing still, and not engaging in the pursuit of these things, lest the same world should take him for a fool.

This is the mark of Christianity; you are to be dead, that is, dead to the spirit and temper of the world, and live a new life in the Spirit of Jesus Christ.

William Law, 1686–1761. English clergyman, mystic.
Serious Call to a Devout and Holy Life.

Forms of Self-love to be Renounced

In broadest outline we see the universe evolving life and life evolving to continually extended awareness. We see our individuality as a phase—perhaps a "hairpin bend" in the zig-zag spiral of ascent—and we see that our task in co-operating with the purpose of life and the universe is so to act and to think that we become increasingly aware of our extra-individuality—that is, the common life which unites us with our fellow creatures with all life and the universe . . .

The first aim is to keep the individual from losing his flexibility, sensitiveness, adaptability, power of growth. Against the constant tendency to settle down, stiffen, "to be subdued by what it works in," to accept as absolute the current assumptions and partial prejudices, the human spirit has to practise a compensatory expansion, a constant keeping in training, an athleticism . . . However, it is not denial, but a wider acceptance that is aimed at, an expansion which casts off, as atrophied, confining husks, its old practices and passions . . . So a rationed life is pursued in order that the individual may attain the maximum of growth with the minimum of effort—for few of us can grow as we would unless we give ourselves every available help.

Nearly everyone finds himself involved in a threefold entanglement of body, personality, and society . . . The mortificator would cut the knot . . . The knot cannot be cut, but must be untied, because, as individualism is a phase to be surmounted, there can, clearly, be no private salvation. The individual cannot forsake society or call life evil. He grows by developing each power until it transcends its limits and what, contracted, would have been a private vice becomes, expanded, a public virtue.

We must then examine in turn the three levels on which individuality is present, threatens to make itself permanent, but must and can be made transitional, leading to a larger, correlating consciousness.

(a) PHYSICAL: ADDICTION—The first level is the physical. Appetite may become an addiction, an end in itself. Then, as the original creative energy which informed it, volatilizes out of it, the pointless repetition becomes a habit. The pleasure grows less but the compulsion is irresistible, because the habit is so strongly confirmed . . . The power of interest in any other compensatory activity is gone and the individual becomes a slave to an ever-narrowing function. This can be avoided if appetite is kept as a means and so prevented from becoming a fixation . . . In the state of civilization where a larger cosmology was recognized, where consciousness was assumed to be more than the body, appetite could not be so dangerous. It is one of the unsuspected tragedies of a falsely intellectualized society (such as the mechanomorphic) that lust becomes the only aim and purpose . . . Its presence is the one sure guarantee of life—of death being still far away . . . The ecstasy of union through psychological means, through the fact that in its higher stages the individual consciousness blends with others, with all life, this ecstasy can, in a mechanomorphic age, only be obtained at the lower level.

Appetite, especially sexual appetite, needs then, direction. The hope that by leaving the reins on the horse's neck, by getting rid of all tabus and yielding freely to impulse, impulse would become eliminated is not true . . . The fact that our emotions are very flexible means that they easily become suited to any habit or lack of habit. . . . We know that sex begins by being diffused and reaches a focus, so in fully healthy living where the individual realizes his evolution and his present phasal condition, sex will expand again, after having passed through its specific focus. (Such seems to happen in successful parenthood where general tenderness takes the place of intense passion and cherishing is substituted for possessing.) . . .

The small insurance-cost which an ordered and rationed life entails is, after all, a slight exaction beside the bankrupting charges made by uncontrolled desire. It must be repeated, this is not to advocate the life of mortification or denial. The conventional ascetic is a very dangerous person. Better an addict who hates his failure, as nearly all do, than an arrogant who, as nearly all do, prides himself on his achievement. The aim of ordering appetite is not for ordering's sake—not for a sense of power or display—but as a means to a fuller life.

(b) SOCIAL: POSSESSIVENESS—Possessiveness, we have seen, already appears in sexual relationships. It extends, however, much more widely. Man has a necessary capacity for saving, but this passion, if he conceives of himself as nothing but an individual, and happens to be of a timid and cautious nature, will become morbid and dominant. This state is, however, easily cured, once the individual realizes the phasic nature of his individuality. Possessiveness itself is the characteristic symptom of individualism, and so the passion for security and over-saving have naturally marked the culmination and crisis of the mechanomorphic age, in which individuality was taken to be the final and absolute term.

There are, however, forms of possessiveness which are loftier and therefore more subtle and dangerous. . . . The individual argued out of his love of money-avarice, and forbidden it, may yet be uncured of the root passion. He will still suffer from a possessive wish to influence those particularly loved . . . He would coerce those over whom his love gives him power . . . "I must use authority to save them from my mistakes." It is the gentlest of violences and yet may do the authentic damage violence must always inflict. If, however, the individual realizes that he and his charge both have a vast time of development before them, he will no longer be tempted to take the short-cut. He will realize that everyone must freely accept for himself, and not to please another, the way of advance. . . . To attempt to influence consciously is either to arouse opposition—opposition all the more efficacious, the more it is unconscious—or to reduce the patient to a stage of psychological parasitism. Until all individualism is transcended and fused, unconscious influence alone is safe and pure . . .

From military influence and coercion, which "makes a desolation and calls it peace," to that possessive maternalism which will not let its child be "weaned" . . . it is clear that the better the end and motive, the more the mistaken means does such damage as to prevent the end being attained.

The man who is rationed has therefore few possessions, and these he would at any moment hand to any other who might use them better; they are simply the tools of his craft. Even in personal relationships he would guard against all possessiveness. . . . This is, need it be said, no scorn of life or coldness of heart, but the vivid and continual awareness that, until individuality is transcended, love and life have not in reality begun. Until each can recognize in each their common transcendent life, affection and sympathy are still no more than rudiments.

(c) PSYCHICAL: PRETENSION—The third danger is great because it inflames the judgment itself and has no natural limit or satiety. That danger is Pretension: pride, the claim to be honoured, respected, recognized, praised, deferred to, valued not for beauty or wealth but for character. It is all the more dangerous because it comes last and cannot indeed really envelop the man and net him in his individuality unless first he has rid himself, or been rid, of the two lower involvements—bodily addictions and ordinary possessiveness. He will not be able to dominate unless he is strong, and the man who is liable to be dominated by lust or love of goods is always liable to be beaten by the man who is superior to these lures. Most dictators are abstemious. Ambition, like morphia, takes away the more innocently animal lusts. The will for power is insatiable, for it can have no limit . . . Ambition, as the mythos says, is the individual determined to become god. Therefore it is deadly and all profound morality diagnoses it as the supreme sin. . . . Great wealth can be like a huge sledge hammer in one's hand—you try to touch gently with it, you cannot, it smashes at every touch. Great charm can be like the face of Moses—something which should be shrouded, for others will yield to its splendour, dazzled, and he who wields will soon wrest. It is true wisdom, confirmed by our present psychological knowledge, when Pantanjali rules as a preliminary step to advance: "You must yield up power[1] over anyone."

The fundamental principle whereby the growing spirit knows all those things which should be avoided is this: Whatsoever will keep the individual arrested in his individuality and incapable of growing into the enlarged life that lies ahead, that is deadly to life.*–**

Gerald Heard, 1889–1972.
English author, religious philosopher.
The Third Morality.[2]

Possessiveness and Attachment

Almost every form of religion has insisted that many possessions are a bar to spiritual progress, but while the Zen monk has certainly the minimum of material possessions, Zen interprets poverty as an attitude of mind rather than a physical condition. One of the most common ways of trying to fix life into rigid definitions is to qualify something, whether a person, a thing, or an idea, with the state-

[1]Power always corrupts; absolute power absolutely corrupts. All great men are bad."—Lord Acton

[2]This abridged selection was chosen from pp. 186–204 of the author's text. The reader will profit by a full reading of these pages.—Ed.

ment, "This belongs to me." But because life is this elusive and perpetually changing process, every time we think we have really taken possession of something, the truth is that we have completely lost it. All that we possess is our own idea about the thing desired, an idea which tends to remain fixed, which does not grow as the thing grows. Thus one of the most noticeable facts about those obsessed with greed for possessions, whether material goods or cherished ideas, is their desire that things shall remain as they are—not only that their possessions shall remain in their own hands, but also that the possessions themselves shall not change. There are theologians and philosophers who show the greatest concern if anyone questions their ideas about the universe, for they imagine that within those ideas they have at last enshrined ultimate truth, and that to lose those ideas would be to lose the truth. But because truth is alive it will not be bound by anything which shows no sign of life—namely a conception whose validity is held to depend partly on the fact that it is unchangeable. For once we imagine that we have grasped the truth of life, the truth has vanished, for truth cannot become anyone's property, the reason being that truth is life, and for one person to think that he possesses all life is a manifest absurdity. Just as no person can possess life, so no idea which a person can possess can define it; the idea of possession is illusory.

But Buddhism and Taoism go further than saying that nothing can ever be possessed; they declare that those who try to possess are in fact possessed, they are slaves to their own illusions about life. Spiritual freedom is just that capacity to be as spontaneous and unfettered as life itself, to be "as the wind that bloweth where it listeth and thou hearest the sound thereof but cannot tell whence it cometh nor whither it goeth." "Even so," said Jesus, "is everyone that is born of the Spirit." But non-attachment does not mean running away from things to some peaceful hermitage, for we can never escape from our own illusions about life; we carry them with us, and if we are afraid of them and wish to escape it means that we are doubly enslaved. For whether we are content with our illusions or frightened of them, we are equally possessed by them, and hence the non-attachment of Buddhism and Taoism means not running away from life but running with it, for freedom comes through complete acceptance of reality. Those who wish to keep their illusions do not move at all; those who fear them run backwards into greater illusions, while those who conquer them "Walk on."

Thus the poverty of the Zen disciple is the negative aspect of his spiritual freedom; he is poor in the sense that his mind is not encumbered with material and intellectual impedimenta—the significant Latin word for "baggage." This state of mind is the realization of the Mahayana doctrine of *sunyata,* of the emptiness of transitory things; nothing can be grasped for everything is emptiness. . . . For the Zen, life does not move in ruts; it is the freedom of the Spirit, unfettered by external circumstances and internal illusions. Its very nature is such that it cannot be described in words, and the nearest we can get to it is by analogy. It is like the wind moving across the face of the earth, never stopping at any particular place, never attaching itself to any particular object, always adapting itself to the rise and fall of the ground. If such analogies give the impression of a dreamy *laissez-faire,* it must be remembered that Zen is not always a gentle breeze, like decadent Taoism; more than often it is a fierce gale which sweeps everything ruthlessly before it, an icy blast which penetrates to the heart of everything and passes right through to the other side! The freedom and poverty of Zen is to leave everything and "Walk on," for this is what life itself does, and Zen is the religion of life.

Therefore the masters tell their disciples to forget all that they have ever learnt before coming to the practice of Zen, to forget even their knowledge of Buddhism. For the Buddha himself declared that his teaching was only a raft with which to cross a river; when the opposite bank has been reached it must be left behind, but so many of his followers mistook the raft for the opposite bank. Yet this negative aspect of Zen, this giving up, is only another way of expressing the positive fact that to give up everything is to gain all. "He that loseth his life shall find it."

Professor Suzuki points out that while it was the custom of some of the masters to express their poverty, others would refer rather to the complete sufficiency of things. Thus while Hsiang-yen says:

> My last year's poverty was not poverty enough;
> My poverty this year is poverty indeed.

In my poverty last year there was room for a gimlet's
point;
But this year even the gimlet has gone—

Mumon emphasizes the other side of the picture:

Hundreds of spring flowers, the autumnal moon,
A refreshing summer breeze, winter snow—
Free thy mind from idle thoughts,
And for thee how enjoyable every season is!

Here we find the acceptance and affirmation of the seasonal changes, and in the same way Zen accepts and affirms the birth, decay and death of men; there are no regrets for the past, and no fears for the future. Thus the Zen disciple gains all by accepting all, since ordinary possessiveness is loss—it is the denial of the right of people and things to live and change; hence the only loss in Zen is the loss of this denial.*–**

Alan W. Watts, 1915–1973.
American religious philosopher, lecturer, author.
The Spirit of Zen.

As he was starting again on his journey, a man came running up to him, and knelt at his feet and asked him,

"Good master, what must I do to make sure of eternal life?"

But Jesus said to him,

"Why do you call me good? No one is good but God himself. You know the commandments—'Do not murder, Do not commit adultery, Do not steal, Do not bear false witness, Do not defraud, Honor your father and mother.' "

But he said to him,

"Master, I have obeyed all these commandments ever since I was a child."

And Jesus looked at him and loved him, and he said to him,

"There is one thing that you lack. Go, sell all you have, and give the money to the poor, and then you will have riches in heaven; and come back and be a follower of mine."

But his face fell at Jesus' words, and he went away much cast down, for he had a great deal of property.

And Jesus looked around and said to his disciples,

"How hard it will be for those who have money to enter the Kingdom of God!"

But the disciples were amazed at what he said. And Jesus said to them again,

"My children, how hard it is to enter the Kingdom of God! It is easier for a camel to get through the eye of a needle than for a rich man to get into the Kingdom of God!"

Mark 10:17–25.
New Testament. Trans. E. J. Goodspeed.

Do not be troubled, God, though they say "mine"
of all things that permit it patiently.
They are like wind that lightly strokes the boughs
and say: MY TREE.

They hardly see
how all things glow that their hands seize upon,
so that they cannot touch
even the utmost fringe and not be singed.

They will say "mine" as one will sometimes call
the prince his friend in speech with villagers,
this prince being very great—and far away.
They call strange walls "mine," knowing not at all
who is master of the house indeed.
They still say "mine" and claim possession, though
each thing, as they approach, withdraws and closes;
a silly charlatan perhaps thus poses
as owner of the lightning and the sun.
And so they say: my life, my wife, my child,
my dog, well knowing all that they have styled
their own: life, wife, child, dog, remain
shapes alien and unknown,
that blindly groping they must stumble on.
This truth, be sure, only the great discern,
who long for eyes. The others WILL not learn
that in the beggary of their wandering
they cannot claim a bond with anything
but, driven from possessions they have prized,
not by their own belongings recognized,
they can OWN wives no more than they own flowers,
whose life is alien and apart from ours.

God, do not lose your equilibrium.
Even he who loves you and who knows your face
in darkness, when he trembles like a light
you breathe upon,—he cannot own you quite.
And if at night one holds you closely pressed.
locked in his prayer so you cannot stray,
you are the guest
who comes but, not to stay.

God, who can hold you? To yourself alone
belonging, by no owner's hand disturbed,
you are like unripened wine that unperturbed
grows ever sweeter and is all its own.

Rainer Maria Rilke, 1875–1926. German poet.
The Book of Hours.

Let Go. Return

This is the need, the deep necessity of every life:
To scatter wide seed in many fields,
But build one barn.

This is our blunder, to have built
Gilt shacks for every seed,
And followed our sowing on fast, anxious feet,
Desiring to grind the farmost grain.

Let go. Let go. Return
Heighten and straighten the barn's first beam.
Give shape and form. Discover the rat, the
splintered stair.
Throw out the dry, gray corn.

Then may it be said of you:
Behold, he had done one thing well,
And he knows whereof he speaks, and he means
what he has said,
And we may trust him.
This is sufficient for a life.

Josephine W. Johnson, 1910–. American novelist, poet.
Year's End.

"Real sacrifice" as a Deliberate Conscious Act

The act of making a sacrifice consists in the first place in giving something which belongs to me. Everything which belongs to me bears the stamp of "mineness," that is, it has a subtle identity with my ego. . . .[8]

In other words, out of the natural state of identity with what is "mine" there grows the ethical task of sacrificing oneself. . . . One ought to realize that when one gives or surrenders oneself there are corresponding claims attached, the more so the less one knows of them. The conscious realization of this alone guarantees that the giving is a real sacrifice. For if I know and admit that I am giving myself, foregoing myself, and do not want to be repaid for it, then I have sacrificed my claim, and thus a part of myself. Consequently, all absolute giving, a giving which is total from the start, is a self-sacrifice. Ordinary giving for which no return is received is felt as a loss; but a sacrifice is meant to be like a loss, so that one may be sure that the egoistic claim no longer exists. . . .

Yet, looked at in another way, this intentional loss is also a gain, for if you can give yourself it proves that you possess yourself. Nobody can give what he has not got. So anyone who can sacrifice himself and forego his claim must have had it; in other words, he must have been conscious of the claim. This presupposes an act of considerable self-knowledge, lacking which one remains permanently unconscious of such claims. . . .

The sacrifice proves that you possess yourself, for it does not mean just letting yourself be passively taken: it is a conscious and deliberate self-surrender, which proves that you have full control of yourself, that is, of your ego. The ego thus becomes the object of a moral act, for "I" am making a decision on behalf of an authority which is superordinate to my ego nature. I am, as it were, deciding against my ego and renouncing my claim. . . .

. . . in giving up my egoistic claim I shall challenge my ego personality to revolt. I can be sure that the power which suppresses this claim, and thus suppresses me, must

[8]The conscious willing factor of the personality structure—see fn. 4, p. 41. Also see Wolff, p. 83.—Ed.

be the self.[4] Hence it is the self that causes me to make the sacrifice; nay more, it compels me to make it. . . .

. . . We have seen that a sacrifice only takes place when we feel the self actually carrying it out on ourselves. We may also venture to surmise that in so far as the self stands to us in the relation of father to son, the self in some sort feels our sacrifice as a sacrifice of itself. From that sacrifice we gain ourselves—our "self"—for we only have what we give. But what does the self gain? We see it entering into manifestation, freeing itself from unconscious projection, and, as it grips us, entering into our lives and so passing from unconsciousness into consciousness, from potentiality into actuality. What it is in the diffuse unconscious state we do not know; we only know that in becoming ourself it has become man.*

Carl G. Jung, M.D., 1875–1961. Swiss psychiatrist.
Psychology and Religion: West and East.
Trans. R. F. C. Hull.

There is the fundamental and all-inclusive choice of a Way leading to Life. There is a sacrifice of both the support of collective opinion and the comfort of being unconscious. Having chosen to go this Way, man is from thenceforth engaged in a continual process of choosing, sacrificing, suffering, and healing. He becomes aware of more and greater pulls between opposites in the psyche and must learn to discriminate between them, choosing to go sometimes with one, sometimes with another, depending upon *where the Value needs him* (as opposed to where he egocentrically wants to go). Repeatedly he must sacrifice routes that seem direct and "good" for routes that are less direct, more encompassing, and more desirable in the long run.

Once egocentric patterns are seen with any clarity, there is a facing of the ways and means by which to break from them and not stay imprisoned in them. Once the unlived life is glimpsed, man must make choices for those ways in which he can express and integrate this life. These two together—breaking the ego defenses and freeing the unlived life—involve suffering because they usually force one to action against the predetermined and established forms of

[4]See fn. 3, p. 412 for Dr. Jung's discussion of the "self" which he states "might just as well be called the 'God in us.'"—Ed.

society in some way or other, as well as against one's own self-images. They also bring great joy of spirit and peace of mind.

Elizabeth B. Howes, contemporary Jungian analyst.
Sheila Moon, contemporary Jungian analyst, writer.
Man the Choicemaker.

It is tragic how few people ever "possess their souls" before they die. "Nothing is more rare in any man," says Emerson, "than an act of his own." It is quite true. Most people are other people. Their thoughts are some one else's opinions, their lives a mimicry, their passions a quotation.

When Christ says, "Forgive your enemies," it is not for the sake of the enemy, but for one's own sake that he says so, and because love is more beautiful than hate. In his own entreaty to the young man, "Sell all that thou hast, and give to the poor," it is not of the state of the poor that he is thinking, but of the soul of the young man, the soul that wealth was marring. . . .

But while Christ did not say to men, "Live for others," he pointed out that there was no difference at all between the lives of others and one's own life. By this means he gave to man an extended, a Titan personality. Since his coming the history of each separate individual is, or can be made, the history of the world.*–**

Oscar Wilde, 1856–1900. English playwright, author.
De Profundis.

The Way Implies Self-Knowledge and Self-Acceptance

One must be able to strip oneself of all self-deception, to see oneself naked to one's own eyes before one can come to terms with the elements of oneself and know who one really is.

Frances G. Wickes, 1875–1970.
American psychotherapist.
The Inner World of Man.

A man has many skins in himself, covering the depths of his heart. Man knows so many other things; he does not know himself. Why, thirty or forty skins or hides, just like an ox's or a bear's, so thick and hard, cover the soul. Go into your own ground and learn to know yourself.

Meister Johannes Eckhart, 1260–1327.
German scholar, mystic.
Meister Eckhart. Trans. R. Blakney.

To get at the core of God at his greatest, one must first get into the core of himself at his least, for no one can know God who has not first known himself. Go to the depths of the soul, the secret place of the Most High, to the roots, to the heights; for all that God can do is focused there.

Meister Johannes Eckhart, 1260-1327.
German scholar, mystic.
Meister Eckhart. Trans. R. Blakney.

We should mark and know of a very truth that all manner of virtue and goodness, and even that Eternal Good, which is God Himself, can never make a man virtuous, good or happy so long as it is outside the soul, that is, so long as the man is holding converse with outward things through his senses and reason, and doth not withdraw into himself and learn to understand his own life, who and what he is.

Anonymous (one of the "Friends of God").
Fourteenth century.
Theologia Germanica.

If the desire to be honest is greater than the desire to be "good" or "bad," then the terrific power of one's vices will become clear. And behind the vice the old forgotten fear will come up (the fear of being excluded from life) and behind the fear the pain (the pain of not being loved) and behind this pain of loneliness the deepest and most profound and most hidden of all human desires: the desire to love and to give oneself in love and to be part of the living stream we call brotherhood. And the moment love is discovered behind hatred all hatred disappears.

Fritz Kunkel, M.D., 1889–1956. American psychiatrist.
In Search of Maturity.

THE NATURE OF SELF[5]

---

[5]The Way rests on the basic assumption of a "false" and a "true" element within the structure of the personality. This distinction is expressed variously by different authors, i.e. "The

The Seeming-Self and the Real Self

All feelings about one's value and worth and about what one can or cannot do are embodied in the Ego. So distorted and inaccurate are they that the Ego is always a false image of the Self—yet to the individual it seems to be what he really is and he acts accordingly.

In seeking to understand the effect of this Seeming-Self upon the life of the individual, it is helpful to think of the Ego as something in the nature of a psychological shell encasing the Self which may be thought of as the heart at the centre of personality. No figure or comparison can ever be relied upon to depict fully the reality we are now discussing. At the moment the figure of the shell encasing the "heart" serves us well in understanding the psychological situation.

This shell, with all its mistaken feelings and inaccurate ideas, does indeed wall up the Self. The more firmly these errors are fixed—the more inflexible one's ideas and feelings—the thicker and more rigid this wall is. That means that the Ego limitations placed upon one's productivity are greater and more inflexible, and the Self is more and more restricted in its expressions. Life is less rich and meaningful and creative than it might be otherwise, yet the individual often has no idea of how vast are the unrealized potentialities of his being.

Every human being is unconsciously shut up within a system of mistaken ideas and feelings which thwart the fullest expression of the powers of the Self. They add to the necessary limitations of the natural laws of his being which he must take into account.

The individual is limited, also, by the defects of the culture of his time. Its biases, prejudices, unscientific assumptions, historic errors, mistaken beliefs all bind him with fetters that seem to be unbreakable and often are never discarded. Such is our human fate that however good may be the intentions of our educators, in the broad sense, we suffer from the mistakes they unconsciously reflect in their dealings with us. Being human, all such persons express in

---

Seeming-Self" and the "Real Self"; "The Conventional Self" and the "Self of an Individual Vocation"; the "old" man and the "new" man; the "outer" self and the "inner" self, etc. See fn. 4, p. 41.—Ed.

their behaviour the mistakes of their own Ego and unconsciously influence us accordingly.

Under that influence we accept their own errors for ourselves, or develop other mistaken ideas to counterbalance them. We enact these errors and mistakes into laws which we now unconsciously accept and submit to as the natural laws of our being. Thus we come back to the basic psychological truth that the Ego serves as a shell, limiting the expression of the capacities of the Self.

Now it follows that one basic task of man is the removal of this shell. A lifelong problem is the discovery of the errors built into one's Ego, for only by discovering them does one come to crack his shell and remove its limitations even piecemeal. This discovery grows only out of the realization that one's system of living does not work.

It is possible for one to learn his mistaken ways from the reasonably calm contemplation of his life in the light of kindly observations by a friend or helpful suggestions in a book. But we must distinguish between an intellectual insight into the broad fact that the Ego is only our second, not our real, nature—and the actual breakdown of the shell. In only a very few instances is insight alone sufficient. In the end, it seems that nothing short of the severest kind of pressure is enough to shatter the shell.

This drastic experience we call the major crisis. All egocentricity leads toward it. Moreover, it should be welcomed; for through its suffering, as will be seen, we may move into that joy and peace which comes from releasing the Self within from the limitations of its shell into the creative, productive, courageous, loving expressions of which it is capable. That is indeed the abundant life.*—**

Fritz Kunkel, M.D., 1889–1956, American psychiatrist,
and Roy E. Dickerson, 1886–. American author.
How Character Develops.

The False Self and the True Self

Both Hinayana and Mahayana Buddhism have a common basis in the elementary principles of the Buddha's doctrine. Briefly, this doctrine is that man suffers because of his craving to possess and keep forever things which are essentially impermanent. Chief among these things is his own person, for this is his means of isolating himself from the rest of life, his castle into which he can retreat and from which he can assert himself against external forces. He believes that this fortified and isolated position is his best means of obtaining happiness; it enables him to fight against change, to strive to keep pleasing things for himself, to shut out suffering and to shape circumstances as he wills. In short it is his means of resisting life. The Buddha taught that all things, including this castle, are essentially impermanent and that as soon as man tries to possess them they slip away; this frustration of the desire to possess is the immediate cause of suffering. But he went further than this, for he showed that the fundamental cause is the delusion that man *can* isolate himself from life. A false isolation is achieved by identifying himself with his castle, the person, but because this castle is impermanent it has no abiding reality, it is empty of any "self-nature" (*atta*) and is no more the Self than any other changing object. What, then, is the Self? The Buddha remained silent when asked this question, but he taught that man will find out only when he no longer identifies himself with his person, when he no longer resists the external world from within its fortification, in fact, when he makes an end of his hostility and his plundering expeditions against life. In contrast to this pholosophy of isolation the Buddha proclaimed the unity of all living things and charged his followers to replace this hostility by divine compassion (*karuna*).

The Mahayana considers that a true self is found when the false one is renounced. When man neither identifies himself with his person nor uses it as a means for resisting life, he finds that the Self is more than his own being; it includes the whole universe.

Alan W. Watts, 1915–1973.
American religious philosopher, lecturer, author.
The Spirit of Zen.

The "Outward" and "Inner" Man

The Scriptures say of human beings that there is an outward man and, along with him, an inner man.

To the outward man belong those things that depend on the soul but are connected with the flesh and blended with it, and the cooperative functions of the several members such as the eye, the ear, the tongue, the hand, and so on.

The Scriptures speak of all this as the old man, the earthy man, the outward person, the enemy, the servant.

Within us all is the other person, the inner man, whom the Scriptures call the new man, the heavenly man, the young person, a friend, the aristocrat.

Relative to the aristocracy of the inner, spiritual man the the commonalty of the outward, physical person, the heathen philosophers, Tully and Seneca, maintain that no rational soul is without God. The seed of God is in us. Given an intelligent farmer and a diligent fieldhand, it will thrive and grow up to God whose seed it is and, accordingly, its fruit will be God-nature. Pear seeds grow into pear trees; nut seeds into nut trees, and God-seed into God.

Meister Johannes Eckhart, 1260–1327. German scholar, mystic.
Meister Eckhart. Trans. R. Blakney.

Ego Investigation

We should ask ourselves what type of egocentricity may be ours. In the main, the Ego conforms more or less to one single pattern, and it is ordinarily possible for a person through self-observation to recognize which role he is acting, even though it is true that appearances are often deceptive. It seems almost as if the Ego were a living being seeking to deceive us by wearing a mask so lifelike that it is almost impossible to distinguish it from the reality it covers.

The best way to conduct this Ego investigation is to ask oneself what goal we would like to attain, if we could choose.[6] It is important to imagine this choice as made quite alone or together with some completely understanding comrade, not in the presence of moralizing friends or relatives. We must be prepared to recognize a choice which may seem somewhat embarrassing to us because it would not be commended and might even be condemned. Frankly, perhaps even jokingly, we should imagine ourselves in the situation in which we should really like to be,

[6]Sometimes it is useful to try to recall one's earliest recollections in order to find out what kind of fear or wish may have been developed. Our experience has shown that the choice of our early recollections is influenced by our Ego and therefore our idea about our earliest recollections may reflect our egocentricity and help us discover our type.

laying aside all idealism. Otherwise, our moral or philosophical or religious convictions would be likely to keep us from being quite honest with ourselves. This choice is bound to reflect the mistakes in our Ego. We seek that understanding because we are misled and deceived by these mistakes.

We must have something akin to Paul's reaction.[7] We feel like saying, "It is I and yet not I. This choice seems to represent what I am, yet it is not. If I were freed from the influence of my egoistic thinking, I would choose differently. I would be no longer egocentric but objective. I would see clearly. My Self would be free from its shell, and my choices would be sound and wholesome. Until that freedom comes, I, like all others, am the victim of the human process by which the Ego is developed, and I am misled as they are." That is the inevitable fate of every human being. All others have had the same experience. If we could really know their egocentricity, we should find in them mistakes and errors which are on the same level as any of ours even though of quite a different type. There is no necessity of judging ourselves harshly if we find that we are seeking that which should not be sought. Our responsibility in character development is to face what we find unflinchingly and when we have become aware of mistakes to correct them as soon as we can.

Suppose now that, pursuing your inquiry in this spirit and for this purpose, you discover you feel you want to be secure, peaceful, unpretentious, left alone in calmness with sufficient supply of food. Are you acting objectively as a follower of Rousseau and a priest of pure nature? Or would it be more honest to admit that you are thinking of yourself in a rather well-formed Gaby Ego pattern?

If your goal, your highest value, is security with indulgence, and the protection of a good, reliable person: if you are looking all the time to see whether this godlike person —a priest or employer or husband or wife—may find you (without thinking too much of trying to find him or her yourself), are you then a loyal and modest servant of the good? Or wouldn't you acknowledge that you are reacting according to the passive and dependent Clinging-Vine pattern.

[7]Romans 7:15–17.

If you dream of laurels, fame, glory, and riches in order to be admired, or of splendid achievements in arts or sciences, probably you are playing the role of an egocentric Star. You may object that good achievements are objectively necessary for cultural progress and that your ideal is to serve the whole race and not just your Ego. Well, that may be. If so, you would not be offended if you invent something greatly beneficial to mankind and another person becomes famous because of it. Could you even imagine this without rebellion? And if you could, you must somewhat distrust your reaction and be ready to recognize some egocentric remnants in your We-feeling attitude. Even the martyr to injustice may be acting a Star role.

Finally, if power is what you want and you think you want it for the service of humanity, don't trust your thinking too much. It is better to test it carefully. Imagine, for example, that you do everything necessary to form and build up a new and needed organization, but someone else, who has done nothing, is made president and exercises many privileges, great authority, and extensive influence. Would you be satisfied? St. Francis built a monastery and then lived in it as a simple monk, one of the others being the abbot. He seems clearly not to have had a Nero type Ego. And you? The more you really want the power for the power's sake only—and that means for your own sake—the less you would feel you could tolerate such injustice! And the more you are playing the part of a Nero.

The next step is to consider the abyss. For all of us there is something that seems to be an abyss into which we must not fall, an experience or situation so dreadful that we can scarcely bear to imagine it for ourselves. This abyss is always closely connected with our Ego. It is the depth of life which is the very extreme opposite of the heights of experience which our Ego leads us to seek. Therefore, to know one's abyss is to know much about one's Ego type.

What would be the most unbearable, most horrible situation in which you could imagine yourself? What seems to you worse than death? Is it more the loss of esteem and recognition (*e.g.*, the preacher who is laughed at), the loss of power (*e.g.*, the officer whose commands are not obeyed), the loss of security and protection (*e.g.*, the spoiled rich woman who loses all her money) or the loss of seclusion and privacy (*e.g.*, the official who retired early but who is called back to service again)?

We should work out this part of our investigation as carefully as possible, preferring always to think of the concrete situation—the scene, the immediate experience—and not of the abstract term or name for our reactions and apparent qualities. Only at last, having collected many memories and made many "experiments by imagination," can we come to see what intermixture of types is involved in our Ego.*–**

Fritz Kunkel, M.D., 1889–1956, American psychiatrist, and Roy E. Dickerson, 1886–, American author. *How Character Develops.*

So long as one has not attained perfection, one can know one's self but imperfectly. The same self-love which causes our faults is very subtle in hiding them both from ourselves and from others. Self-love cannot endure to see itself; it would die of shame and vexation! If by chance it gets a glimpse, it at once places itself in some artificial light, so as to soften the full hideousness and find some comfort. And so there will always be some remains of self-delusion clinging to us while we still cling to self and its imperfections. Before we can see ourselves truly, self-love must be rooted up, and the love of God alone move us; and then the same light which showed us our faults would cure them. Till then we only know ourselves by halves, because we are only half God's, and hold a great deal more to ourselves than we imagine or choose to see. When the truth has taken full possession of us, we shall see clearly, and then we shall behold ourselves without partiality or flattery, as we see our neighbors. Meanwhile God spares our weakness, by only showing us our own deformity by degrees, and as He gives strength to bear the sight. He only shows us to ourselves, so to say, by bits; here one and there another, as He undertakes our correction.

François Fénelon, 1651–1715. French Archbishop of Cambray. *Spiritual Letters of Archbishop Fénelon.* Trans. H. L. Lear.

Difficulties and the Role of Pressure

The point at which the egocentric person is most readily touched is his egocentric welfare; therefore, the original impulse toward self-education often must be formulated as an appeal to our egocentricity, wherein a strange paradox becomes apparent. We must face the alternative either of suffering the consequences of our egocentricity even to the extent of experiencing a major crisis or of taking this next step in the direction of religious and social progress. The paradox is that even from the egocentric viewpoint it seems to be advisable to decrease our egocentricity for the sake of decreasing the suffering from it.

This paradox is the very kernel of our theory of the crisis. Even egoism itself recommends that we become less egoistic. Here we meet the first principle in the art of self-education as the We-Psychology is to display it. Its name is: Pressure.

The task of character development is the destruction of our own egocentric shell in order to set free and develop the We-feeling productivity which was shut up within the shell. That would be well-nigh an impossible task without the help of some power coming from without. At first the shell is realized in the form of the Ego. When I say I, I usually mean my Ego. The imprisoned Self is felt—if at all—as an It, a kind of unknown, almost foreign force of which one is ordinarily afraid. Thus the task is that I, saying I, should not identify myself—as formerly—with the Ego, but now with the Self. My viewpoint should shift from the Ego centre, the Seeming-self, to the true centre, the real Self.[8]

If this were possible by mere will-power the shell and the egocentricity would not be what they are—the old fortifications against anguish and fear. Suppose that I have learned that I have to be the "good," that is, the obedient, child. In playing my egocentric role, I am impelled to look for approval and to avoid everything which may displease my companions, but when I lay it aside I display the courage and We-feeling qualities of my Self by opposing injustice and objecting to my companions when they are wrong.

Insofar as I act my egocentric role, I feel afraid that my reactions might, in a certain case, be the kind inspired by We-feeling and courage. I fear such reactions because they

[8]In the later stages of development, when "I" has grown to mean the Self, the Ego is—not always but sometimes—realized as the It, *i.e.*, the bad old habit, the moral weakness we repudiate, or even something like "the fiend" or temptation.

seem to be dangerous to what seems to be my best interests seen from the viewpoint of the Ego or the Seeming-Self. Thus, the greedy Star fears his kindly impulses because they tend to separate him from his money, which seems so essential to his stardom, and the Nero fears his We-feeling impulses because they are seemingly tendencies to that weakness which would make others less fearful of him and therefore less submissive. Therefore we unconsciously oppose the destruction of these walls—these egocentric fortifications—even though we are consciously trying to demolish them and to laugh at them as being obsolete, useless, and childish.

We cannot pull ourselves out of the swamp by our own hair as the famous knight in the fairy tale did. Therefore, we cannot succeed here unless an outer force—the pressure—comes to our assistance. Mere idealism, or moral endeavour, or, in most cases, even insight would not be sufficient. . . .

Pressure, it must be said, is inevitable. Egocentric living involves acting on mistaken ideas, pursuing false goals, being swayed by unsound emotions, and all this leads certainly to difficulty and distress. Life cannot be lived on untrue premises or filled with deluded behaviour without creating pressure sooner or later even though it be felt only in the haunting fears or vicious nightmares of one's dreams.

It follows, then, that one ought not to rebel against pressure. Like bodily pain, this psychic discomfort is unpleasant and should be relieved as soon as possible by dealing wisely with its cause. But like pain, it is a beneficent thing, because it warns of danger. It points out an unwholesome condition which might otherwise go unnoticed far longer than it should. One of the first lessons in self-education is that one should welcome the discomfort of pressure because of the opportunities for growth which it is capable of revealing. One ought not to be sorry for himself but rather glad that some source of difficulty in one's life may be disclosed by the pressure.

In discussing pressure we see that it is difficult to know when real pressure, as opposed to mere imaginative suffering, is at work and to what sources it can be traced. It is hard to distinguish between the two so that we know when we have to deal with nothing more than neurotic, imaginative suffering.

Here a certain amount of objective research is a necessary part of the self-education that develops character. Unconscious connections must be discovered and cleared up; faults, weak spots, fears, or aims of which we were not hitherto aware must be explored. We must look at them with the curiosity of the scientist, not with shame or moral devaluation or horror, as would be the case with the moralist.

The moralistic standpoint strengthens the egocentric resistance against self-knowledge, as we never see what our mistakes are, if we wish to be "stainless." The most serious errors in the Ego will not be realized as such because they are an essential part of this Seeming-Self. The only way to escape self-deception and to unmask ourselves successfully is to suspend all moral and ethical judgment until the investigation has been ended. We must add at once a psychological observation very important in our day. Many persons live in what we call "reversed valuation." The mistakes of their Ego are such that they would not have inferiority feelings even if recklessness or sensuality or wantonness were discovered in the depth of their unconscious life. On the contrary, they would be pleased. In these cases the egocentric goal (+100) is something such as being the Don Juan who conquers the greatest number of girls or the "good fellow" who drinks the most wine or the shrewd trader who "gets ahead of" every person with whom he deals. Those who pursue such goals would feel devalued if this research would prove them more "moral" than they want to be.

From this viewpoint of their Ego, they cannot value loyalty, kindness, righteousness, love, and religion. They are "forbidden" and repressed or suppressed and seem intolerable when viewed from the viewpoint of the Seeming-Self. Therefore, even in these cases it is necessary, if a person would discover his mistakes, for him to suspend at first all valuation of a situation as moral or immoral.

This unconscious defence of our Ego—the Seeming-Self may be very helpful in our efforts to investigate our own lives. It may supply us with an important clue as to our own weaknesses. The more we feel offended by what we interpret as a reproach, the more it is probable that the criticism hits the nail on the head, even if we do not at the time find anything in our conscious life to support the reproach.

Strong negative emotions like anger, irritation, and indignation usually but not always indicate that our weak spot has been touched consciously or unconsciously. In order to discover our true inner situation, it is necessary to overcome our own egocentric inner resistance which often takes the form of negative moods. We should, therefore, learn to understand and handle them.*

Fritz Kunkel, M.D., 1889–1956, American psychiatrist, and Roy E. Dickerson, 1886–, American author. *How Character Develops.*

Meeting One's Own "Shadow"

The man who looks into the mirror of the waters does, indeed, see his own face first of all. Whoever goes to himself risks a confrontation with himself. The mirror does not flatter, it faithfully shows whatever looks into it; namely, the face we never show to the world because we cover it with the persona, the mask of the actor. But the mirror lies behind the mask and shows the true face.

This confrontation is the first test of courage on the inner way, a test sufficient to frighten off most people, for the meeting with ourselves belongs to the more unpleasant things that may be avoided as long as we possess living symbol-figures in which all that is inner and unknown is projected.

The meeting with oneself is the meeting with one's own shadow. To mix a metaphor, the shadow is a tight pass, a narrow door, whose painful constriction is spared to no one who climbs down into the deep wellspring. But one must learn to know oneself in order to know who one is. For what comes after the door is, surprisingly enough, a boundless expanse full of unprecedented uncertainty, with apparently no inside and no outside, no above and no below, no here and no there, no mine and no thine, no good and no bad. It is the world of water, where everything living floats in suspension; where the kingdom of the sympathetic system, of the soul of everything living, begins; where I am inseparably this and that, and this and that are I; where I experience the other person in myself, and the other, as myself, experiences me.

No, the unconscious is anything but a capsulated, personal system; it is the wide world, and objectivity as open as the world. I am the object, even the subject of the object, in a complete reversal of my ordinary consciousness, where I am always a subject that has an object. There I find myself in the closest entanglement with the world, so much a part of it that I forget all too easily who I really am. "Lost in oneself" is a good phrase to describe this state. But this self is the world, if only a consciousness could see it. This is why we must know who we are.*

Carl G. Jung, M.D., 1875–1961. Swiss psychiatrist.
The Integration of the Personality. Trans. S. Dell.

The "projection" of which Dr. Jung writes in the preceding selection is a common device whereby one unconsciously places his own unpleasant shadow[9] qualities on the outside—usually on other persons—resulting in intense negative reactions toward them. Since it is with the shadow, also, that man's unused and undeveloped potentials lie, he tends to project them as well, trying thus to escape his own development. Exaggerated adulation or hostility toward others usually yields clues to positive and negative shadow projection of this kind.

Obviously, then, an important factor in self-knowledge is the becoming aware of such projective maneuvers. It is necessary, furthermore, to find ways progressively to reclaim and integrate those lost parts of oneself in order to become a "whole" person. But the facing of the repressed contents and neglected potentials within the personality, and the conscious co-operation leading toward their integration, is likely to be a long and often a painful process, since it involves the loss of illusions, and the breakup of old securities. A man needs a steady stance and a developed faith to undergird the progressive "meeting with his own shadow." –Ed.

In the end, the individual is brought face to face with the necessity for "accepting" his own evil. To begin with, this

[9] "The 'shadow' is that part of the psyche which could and should become conscious, yet of which we are unaware." It contains bright undeveloped potentials as well as dark, unpleasant repressed elements—painful memories, etc. See *Knowing Woman* by Irene Claremont de Castillejo (Putnam and Sons 1973).

statement may appear unintelligible; it is certainly true that its full significance can by no means be realised at the first glance. The act of the acceptance of evil should not be minimised or disguised by any attempt at relativisation which may try to reassure us by pretending that this evil which has to be accepted is not so bad, after all; and the situation is not made any easier by the fact that evil no longer appears in the form of a collectively recognised phenomenon.

"My" evil may not be an evil at all in my neighbour's eyes, and vice versa; it is precisely this that constitutes the moral difficulty of the situation. Group valuation and group responsibility cease at the point where no approval by the generally accepted standard can take away the ego's insight that it has acted in an evil manner, and where, on the other hand, no condemnation by the collective has either the power or the right any more to replace the ego's own orientation.

The differentiation of "my" evil from the general evil is an essential item of self-knowledge from which no-one who undertakes the journey of individuation is allowed to escape. But as the process of individuation unfolds, the ego's former drive towards perfection simultaneously disintegrates. The inflationary exaltation of the ego has to be sacrificed, and it becomes necessary for the ego to enter into some kind of gentleman's agreement with the shadow—a development which is diametrically opposed to the old ethic's ideal of absolutism and perfection.

This process of coming to terms with the shadow leads in fact to an apparent moral levelling-down of the personality. The recognition and acceptance of the shadow presupposes more than a mere willingness to look at one's dark brother—and then to return him to a state of suppression where he languishes like a prisoner in a gaol. It involves granting him freedom and a share in one's life. But the process of allowing the shadow to take part in one's life is only possible on a "deeper" moral level. The ego is obliged to step down from its pedestal and realize the state of individual, constitutional and historical imperfection which is its appointed fate.

The acceptance of one's own imperfection is an exceedingly difficult task. Each one of us, irrespective of his psychological type and sex, has an inferior function and a shadow; that is why we all find the assimilation of this side of the personality equally difficult.

Erich Neumann, 1905–1960. Psychologist and writer.
Depth Psychology and a New Ethic.

I recently came across an almost intuitive expression of the shadow, from a Japanese Buddhist who had probably read no western psychology whatsoever.

He refers first to a poem by his grandfather carved on the back of the family tombstone:

"How frightened I am
To behold my shadow
Lying large amid the frost
Of the wintry night."

Then he comments: "In observing for the first time the frightening distortion of our own shadow, we can realize how warped our character and personality must appear to others—how warped indeed they really are."

The writer was General Hidiki Tojo. It was written while he awaited execution as a war criminal. He came through to a serene and illuminated faith[10] in the Grace of Buddha before the end.

Terisina Havens, contemporary American teacher of religion.
Excerpt from a letter.

Facing the Darkness

There has come to me an insight into the meaning of Darkness. The reason one must face his darkness, and enter into that darkness is not that he may return purified to face God. One must go into the darkness because that is where God is. The darkness is not sin, not evil. Those are by-ways, side paths by which one can escape. The darkness is pure terror, and the last terror of all is to know as one turns downward that there is no God. Then the darkness is upon you, and there is God Himself, for God is the greatest destroyer of gods.

---

[10]The moving story of his awakening is told by Shunsho Hanayama, a devout Buddhist chaplain, in his book *The Way of Deliverance,* p. 223 (Scribner, 1950). The quotations in the above selection are taken from this book.—Ed.

It seems as though we must each make himself a god of his own, one not too big to carry. For some, the good will be God, or Nature, or the Creative Idea, or the Indulgent Father. One must stay with Him and in His universe, or go down into the darkness alone. It is as though one had to take a hammer and smash his god to bits, only to find that there on the instant stood God, God Himself, filling the universe and personally near.

The meaning of the Crucifixion must be like this. One can imagine the disciples talking among themselves: "How could God have let him be killed? He was so good, so kind. He was surely doing God's work if ever a man did. What kind of a God is it that lets His own followers, His best follower die so?" Until at last, they had to deny their God, the God who would not waste a good man's life—and in that instant they found the God who sent them all over the world, the God about whom no more can be said than that He Is.

God is. That is so real, that to talk of His love, or of serving Him is saying less, not more. He is, and He is with us, and there is no need of promises.

Alfred Romer, 1907–. American professor of physics.

. . . We must assume our existence as broadly as we in any way can; everything, even the unheard-of, must be possible in it. That is at bottom the only courage that is demanded of us: to have courage for the most extraordinary, the most singular and the most inexplicable that we may encounter. That mankind has in this sense been cowardly has done life endless harm; all those things that are so closely akin to us, have by daily parrying been so driven out of life that the senses with which we could have grasped them are crippled. To say nothing of God. But fear of the inexplicable has not alone impoverished the existence of the individual; the relationship between one person and another has also been cramped by it, as though it had been lifted out of the river bed of endless possibilities and set down in a fallow spot on shore to which nothing happens. For it is not laziness alone that is responsible for human relationships repeating themselves from case to case, indescribably monotonous and unrenewed; it is shyness before any sort of new, unforeseeable experience with which one does not think oneself able to cope. But only he who is ready for everything, who excludes nothing, not even the most enigmatical, will live the relation to another as something alive and will himself wholly expend his own being. For if we think of this existence of the individual as a larger or smaller room, it appears evident that most people learn to know only a corner of their room, a window bay, a strip on which they walk up and down. Thus they have a certain security. And yet that dangerous insecurity is so much more human which drives the prisoners in Poe's stories to feel out the shapes of their fearful dungeons and not be strangers to the unspeakable terror of their abode. We, however, are not prisoners. No traps or snares are set about us, and there is nothing which should intimidate or worry us. We are set down in life as in the element to which we best correspond, and over and above this we have through thousands of years of adjustment become so like this life, that when we hold still we are, through a happy mimicry, scarcely to be distinguished from all that is around us. We have no reason to mistrust our world, for it is not against us. Has it terrors, they are our terrors; has it abysses, those abysses belong to us; are dangers at hand, we must try to love them. And if we only arrange our life according to that principle which counsels us that we must always hold to what is difficult, then that which now still seems to us the most hostile, will become what we most trust and find most faithful. How should we be able to forget about those ancient myths that are at the beginning of all peoples, the myths about dragons that at the last moment turn into princesses; perhaps all the dragons of our lives are princesses who are only waiting to see us once beautiful and brave. Perhaps everything terrible is in its deepest being something helpless that wants help from us.

Rainer Maria Rilke, 1875–1926. German poet.
Letters to a Young Poet. Trans. M. D. Herter Norton.

I bore up against everything with some stubbornness of will and much rebellion of nature, till I had absolutely nothing left in the world but one thing. I had lost my name, my position, my happiness, my freedom, my wealth. I was a prisoner and a pauper. But I still had my children left. Suddenly they were taken away from me by the law. It was a blow so appalling that I did not know what to do, so I flung myself on my knees, and bowed my head, and wept, and said, "The body of a child is as the body of the Lord: I am not worthy of either." That moment seemed to save me. I saw then that the only thing for me was to accept everything. Since then—curious as it will no doubt sound—I have been happier. It was of course my soul in its ultimate essence that I had reached. In many ways I had been its enemy, but I found it waiting for me as a friend.

Now I find hidden, somewhere away in my nature, something that tells me that nothing in the whole world is meaningless, and suffering least of all. That something hidden away in my nature, like a treasure in a field, is Humility.

It is the last thing left in me, and the best: the ultimate discovery at which I have arrived, the starting-point for a fresh development. It has come to me right out of myself, so I know that it has come at the proper time. It could not have come before, nor later. Had any one told me of it, I would have rejected it. As I found it, I want to keep it. I must do so. It is the one thing that has in it the elements of life, of a new life, a Vita Nuova for me. Of all things it is the strangest; one cannot give it away and another may not give it to one. One cannot acquire it, except by surrendering everything that one has. It is only when one has lost all things, that one knows that one possesses it.

The important thing, the thing that lies before me, the thing that I have to do, if the brief remainder of my days is not to be maimed, marred, and incomplete, is to absorb into my nature all that has been done to me, to make it part of me, to accept it without complaint, fear or reluctance. . . .

When first I was put into prison some people advised me to try and forget who I was. It was ruinous advice. It is only by realising what I am that I have found comfort of any kind. . . . Now I am advised by others to try on my release to forget that I have ever been in a prison at all. I know that would be equally final. It would mean that I would always be haunted by an intolerable sense of disgrace and that those things that are meant for me as much as for anybody else—the beauty of the sun and moon, the pageant of the seasons, the music of daybreak and the silence of great nights, the rain falling through the leaves, or the dew creeping over the grass and making it silver—would all be tainted for me, and lose their healing power, and their power of communicating joy. To regret one's own experience is to arrest one's own development. To deny one's own experience is to put a lie into the lips of one's own life. It is no less than a denial of the soul.*

Oscar Wilde, 1856–1900. English author.
De Profundis.

Santos: New Mexico

Return to the most human, nothing less
Will nourish the torn spirit, the bewildered heart,
The angry mind: and from the ultimate duress,
Pierced with the breadth of anguish, speak for love.

Return, return to the deep sources, nothing less
Will teach the stiff hands a new way to serve,
To carve into our lives the forms of tenderness
And still that ancient necessary pain preserve.

O we have moved too far from these, all we who look
Upon the wooden painted figure, stiff and quaint,
Reading it curiously like a legend in a book—
But it is Man upon the cross. It is the living saint.

To those who breathed their faith into the wood
It was no image, but the very living source,
The saviour of their own humanity by blood
That flows terribly like a river in its course.

They did not fear the strangeness, nor while gazing
Keep from this death their very precious life.
They looked until their hands and hearts were blazing
And the reality of pain pierced like a knife.

We must go down into the dungeons of the heart,
To the dark places where modern mind imprisons
All that is not defined and thought apart.
We must let out the terrible creative visions.

Return to the most human, nothing less

Will teach the angry spirit, the bewildered heart,
The torn mind, to accept the whole of its duress,
And pierced with anguish, at last act for love.

May Sarton, 1912–. American author, poet.
The Lion and the Rose.

Progress in self-knowledge leads inevitably to progress in humility and to self-acceptance—an acceptance which admits not only the "false" self which needs "losing," but which includes the "real" self, which is to be "preserved." —Ed.

Meekness in itself is nought else, but a true knowing and feeling of a man's self as he is . . . And therefore swink and sweat in all that thou canst and mayest, for to get thee a true knowing and feeling of thyself as thou art; and then I trow that soon after that thou shalt have a true knowing and a feeling of God as He is. Not as He is in Himself, for that may no man do . . . but as it is possible, and as He vouchsafeth to be known and felt of a meek soul living in this deadly body.

And think not because I set two causes of meekness, one perfect and another imperfect, that I will therefore that thou leavest the travail about imperfect meekness, and set thee wholly to get the perfect. Nay, surely; I trow thou shouldest never bring it so about. I think to tell thee how that a privy love pressed in cleanness of spirit upon this dark cloud of unknowing betwixt thee and thy God, truly and perfectly containeth in it the perfect virtue of meekness without any special or clear beholding of any thing under God. And because I would that thou knewest which were perfect meekness, and settest it as a token before the love of thine heart, and didst it for thee and for me. And because I would by this knowing make thee more meek.

[For] ofttimes it befalleth that lacking of knowing is cause of much pride as me thinketh. For peradventure [if] thou knewest not which were perfect meekness, thou shouldest ween when thou hast a little knowing and a feeling of this that I call imperfect meekness, that thou hadst almost gotten perfect meekness: and so shouldest thou deceive thyself, and ween that thou wert full meek when thou wert all belapped in foul stinking pride. And therefore try for to travail about perfect meekness; for the condition of it is such, that whoso hath it, and the whiles he hath it, he shall not sin, nor yet much after.*–**.

Unknown English mystic, fourteenth century.
The Cloud of Unknowing. Ed. Evelyn Underhill.

SELF-ACCEPTANCE

The biological will is to biological self-perpetuation; the metabiological will is to the perpetuation of significant variations. But these wills are not, save in rare conditions of ultimate crisis, discrepant. Self-perpetuation is the condition of the perpetuation of significant variations.

The position is this. The first necessity is metabiological unity; only when emotion and intellect have achieved their own synthesis is the true metabiological will operative. Instead of a will to this or that posited and ideal end, there is a will to pure self-emergence. We learn to wait upon the unknown which we are; we are dedicated to whatever of creative newness may emerge through us. In that condition, is given the possibility of complete self-acceptance; and that is the whole duty of men.

Than complete self-acceptance man can go no further. By taking upon himself the final responsibility, he has reached the point where he has none. What values he is destined to perpetuate, those will be perpetuated in and through him; what values he is destined to let die, those will die in and through him. He can no more; nor is it conceivable that he should desire more. Whether he has been a significant variation, the organic process will ultimately and irrevocably decide.

To those who ask: "What shall I do?" we have finally one simple answer: "Accept yourself." To those who ask: "But when I have accepted myself, what then?" we answer: "By your question you show that you have read without comprehension." To those who demur: "But you say nothing of man's duties—the world problems—peace or war—social reform—morality," we reply: "No, we say nothing of these things." His attitude to these things each man must let his accepted self determine. We have our own attitude to these things, but it is not required to be formulated or defended here. What values a man will perpetuate, what values he can perpetuate, is for himself to decide. We claim no more than perhaps to help him to a condition where these questions decide themselves with a different and higher authority than any imposed decisions of the unintegrated self could ever possess.

John Middleton Murry, 1889–1957. English author, critic.
God.

I Charge You

When men shall face their destiny like stones
with powerful indifference;
When men shall have the strength to say "Yes"
to the deepest hell
And walk unmoved across depths most desperate
and most absolute;

When they shall assume the burdens of darkness
and pass joyfully through all stench
Because in them abides the deathless fragrance
of their own soul;

When they shall forget their own little self,
their little purity and little comfort
And grow tragically into the great serenity,
quintessence of all storms;

When they shall wipe out the horrors of past days,
by facing evil as the elder brother of good,
Accepting the dead with the strength of living
and the understanding which is the core of love;

When they shall look beyond to Him
who tore from gods the fire of Self
And blessed us all with its curse,
bearing in their hearts His cross and His glory;

Then shall there be peace and beauty in the lands of men.

Dane Rudhyar, 1895–.
American poet, artist, philosopher.
White Thunder.

Recently I received a letter from a former patient which describes the necessary transformation in simple but trenchant words. She writes: "Out of evil, much good has come to me. By keeping quiet, repressing nothing, remaining attentive, and by accepting reality—taking things as they are, and not as I wanted them to be—by doing all this, unusual knowledge has come to me, and unusual powers as well, such as I could never have imagined before. I always thought that when we accepted things they overpowered us in some way or other. This turns out not to be true at all, and it is only by accepting them that one can assume an attitude towards them.[11] So now I intend to play the game of life, being receptive to whatever comes to me, good and bad, sun and shadow forever alternating, and, in this way, also accepting my own nature with its positive and negative sides. Thus everything becomes more alive to me. What a fool I was! How I tried to force everything to go according to the way I thought it ought to!"

Only on the basis of such an attitude, which renounces none of the Christian values won in the course of Christian development, but which, on the contrary, tries with Christian charity and forbearance to accept even the humblest things in one's own nature, will a higher level of consciousness and culture become possible. This attitude is religious in the truest sense, and therefore therapeutic, for all religions are therapies for the sorrows and disorders of the soul. The development of the Western intellect and will has given us an almost fiendish capacity for aping such an attitude, with apparent success, despite the protests of the unconscious. But it is only a matter of time before the counterposition asserts itself all the more harshly. Aping an attitude always produces an unstable situation that can be overthrown by the unconscious at any time. A safe foundation is found only when the instinctive premises of the unconscious win the same respect as the views of the conscious mind. No one should blind himself to the fact that this necessity of giving due consideration to the unconscious runs violently counter to our Western, and in particular the Protestant, cult of consciousness. Yet, though the new always seems to be the enemy of the old, anyone with

[11]And thus become freer of the compulsive power ("participation mystique") that arises from over identification with them. —Ed.

a more than superficial desire to understand cannot fail to discover that without the most serious application of the Christian values we have acquired, the new integration can never take place.

Carl G. Jung, M.D., 1875–1961. Swiss psychiatrist.
Alchemical Studies. Trans. R. F. C. Hull.

EMERGENCE OF THE REAL SELF

True self-revelation has always as its counter-part a growth in knowledge of God. For it is only in the light of God that we see ourselves for what we are. Hence self-abnegation in its full import is not a merely negative thing. According as the soul ceases to be *"self-regarding"* in its activities, it becomes *"God-regarding."* As the soul is being emptied of what is material, transient and perishable, it is being filled with what is spiritual, enduring and incorruptible.

Edward Leen, 1885–1944. Irish Catholic cleric, educator.
Progress Through Mental Prayer.

I am aware of something in myself whose shine is my reason. I see clearly that something is there, but what it is I cannot understand. But it seems to me that, if I could grasp it, I should know all truth.

Anonymous.

Though God is everywhere present, yet He is only present to thee in the deepest and most central part of thy soul. The natural senses cannot possess God or unite thee to him; nay, thy inward faculties of understanding, will and memory can only reach after God, but cannot be the place of his habitation in thee. But there is a root or depth of thee from whence all these faculties come forth, as lines from a centre, or as branches from the body of the tree. This depth is called the centre, the fund or bottom of the soul. This depth is the unity, the eternity—I had almost said the infinity—of thy soul; for it is so infinite that nothing can satisfy it or give it rest but the infinity of God.

William Law, 1686–1761. English clergyman, mystic.
Serious Call to a Devout and Holy Life.

Do you know that you are God's temple and that God's

Spirit makes its home in you? If anyone destroys the temple of God, God will destroy him. For the temple of God is sacred, and that is what you are.

Saint Paul, first century Christian Apostle.
New Testament (I Cor. 3:16–17). Trans. E. J. Goodspeed.

The Way Implies Devotion to the Good[12]

Being true to oneself is the law of God, trying to be true to oneself is the law of man.

There is only one way for a man to be true to himself. If he does not know what is good, a man cannot be true to himself. . . . He who learns to be his true self is one who finds out what is good and holds fast to it.

Tsesze, Chinese philosopher, grandson of Confucius.
The Golden Mean of Tsesze.
Trans. Ku Hungming and Lin Yutang.

Cleanse your own heart, cast out from your mind pain, fear, envy, ill-will, avarice, cowardice, passion uncontrolled. These things you cannot cast out unless you look to God alone; on him alone set your thoughts, and consecrate yourself to his commands. If you wish for anything else, with groaning and sorrow you will follow what is stronger than you, ever seeking peace outside you, and never able to be at peace; for you seek it where it is not, and refuse to seek it where it is.

Epictetus, born about 60 A.D. Greek philosopher.
Discourses and Manual of Epictetus. Trans. R. E. Matheson.

I have often said that a person who wishes to begin a good life should be like a man who draws a circle. Let him get the center in the right place and keep it so and the circumference will be good. In other words, let a man first learn to fix his heart on God and then his good deeds will have virtue; but if a man's heart is unsteady, even the great things he does will be of small advantage.

Meister Johannes Eckhart, 1260–1327.
German scholar, mystic.
Meister Eckhart. Trans. R. Blakney.

---

[12]See Appendix, "The Object of Devotion," p. 439.—Ed.

Let us settle ourselves, and work and wedge our feet downward through the mud and slush of opinion, and prejudice, and tradition, and delusion and appearance, that alluvion which covers the globe, through Paris and London, through New York and Boston and Concord, through church and state, through poetry and philosophy and religion till we come to a hard bottom and rocks in place, which we can call reality, and say, This is, and no mistake; and then begin, having a *point d'appui,* below freshet and frost and fire, a place where you might found a wall or a state, or set a lamppost safely, or perhaps a gauge, not a Nilometer, but a Realometer, that future ages might know how deep a freshet of shams and appearances had gathered from time to time.

Henry David Thoreau, 1817–1862. American philosopher.
Walden.

Devotion and the Role of Ideals

We must have some passionate devotion to give us the necessary drive of life. If that passionate devotion is given to established and accepted ideals, we cannot seek and find the new possibilities that arise with changing conditions. Where, then, shall we find an object of passionate devotion? Such an object is that order of value which enters into our present state of existence, but which also includes the highest possibilities of value however unknown and undefined by us as yet. Without such a devotion, we maintain, maturity is not attained, the art of living is not mastered, and the way is blocked that leads to the good life in our present age of science, machinery, and industry when all things are changing so rapidly.

There are two ways in which we can deal with the socially accepted ideals, these achieved structures of value and known possibilities. We can live with them as though they were final, as though they were the supreme good, as though there were nothing on beyond them to seek and explore, or we can use them not as final goods, not as our home and resting place, but as merely torches and trails, leading on. In other words, there are two ways of life according to what we make supreme. We may give our highest allegiance to the socially accepted ideals, the known possibilities, the goods achieved, while the unknown possibilities are for us more nebulosity and dreamland. Or, on the other hand, we may give our supreme loyalty to this realm of meanings yet to be achieved, these possible structures of value not yet defined and mastered, while the known possibilities and socially accepted ideals are for us mere tools and instruments to be used in this higher devotion. This is the contrast between religion forever on the defensive and in peril and religion invincible.*

The Invincibility of Devotion to the Good

Why does dedication to the supreme and unknown good engender a striving so invincible? For three reasons. First, because the object of devotion which then inspires the striving is invaluable, being the best there is in all reality actual and possible, and hence worth everything that may be endured or given. Second, because it is not irrevocably identified with any known object or undertaking, these all being more or less tentative and exploratory; hence failure or disaster to any of these does not blot out from life the star of value which leads on. Third, under the dominance of such a devotion all experience becomes a seeking of this highest value, an adoration of it and a reaching after it. Hence all experience becomes a way of experiencing the best there is in all reality. Even failure of any specific enterprise, even pain and all evil, since these along with pleasure and successful fulfillments make up the medium of experience in which we seek for and reach after the supreme good, are ways of experiencing this object of our supreme devotion.

Henry Nelson Wieman, 1884–1973.
American philosopher, theologian, educator.
Issues of Life.

Hold fast to God and he will add every good thing. Seek God and you shall find him and all good with him. To the man who cleaves to God, God cleaves and adds virtue. Thus, what you have sought before, now seeks you; what once you pursued, now pursues you; what once you fled, now flees you. Everything comes to him who truly comes to God, bringing all divinity with it, while all that is strange and alien flies away.

Meister Johannes Eckhart, 1260–1327.
German scholar, mystic.
Meister Eckhart. Trans. R. Blakney.

We have to believe that in the final good designed by Him not a cell of Being will be found missing or unfulfilled. Nor is this a selfish view to take of the travail of the world in which we find ourselves as if we were to regard the whole purpose of it as converging on our own private and exclusive good. For my final good does not in any way obstruct or interfere with the good of any other individual; and my good is in the end no other than the good of God Himself. I am not lost in God in the sense that my individuality ceases to be my own. It is just that in its perfection my happiness is no other than the happiness of God, though all the more truly my own. I do not cease to be myself because I have surrendered myself wholly to him; there will be no surrender, no possession, no completion, if there be no I.

R. H. J. Steuart, S.J., 1874–1948. English priest.
The Inward Vision.

Partial allegiance to a perfect god is almost the last thing in futility and dreariness. Nothing but thoroughness can save us here. Half carrying, half dragging the yoke of fellowship will chafe and gall. Casual, shallow, trivial, reserved obedience will not answer. You can go the whole length with him and live, live royally, live exultingly and victoriously, but if you only partially enthrone him, or if you crown him with mental reservations, you will not get far.

William Fraser McDowell, 1858–1937.
American Methodist bishop.
This Mind.

Doing the Will of God

"It is not everyone who says to me 'Lord! Lord!' who will get into the Kingdom of Heaven, but only those who do the will of my Father."

Jesus of Nazareth.
New Testament (Matt. 7:21). Trans. E. J. Goodspeed.

The whole gist of the matter lies in the will, and this is what our Dear Lord meant by saying, "The Kingdom of God is within you." It is not a question of how much we know, how clever we are, nor even how good; it all depends upon the heart's love. External actions are the results of love, the fruit it bears; but the source, the root, is in the deep of the heart.

François Fénelon, 1651–1715.
French Archbishop of Cambray.

And he is truly very learned, that doeth the will of God, and forsaketh his own will.

Thomas a Kempis, 1380–1471. German mystic.
The Imitation of Christ.

Science seems to me to teach in the highest and strongest manner the great truth which is embodied in the Christian conception of entire surrender to the will of God. Sit down before fact as a little child, be prepared to give up every preconceived notion, follow humbly wherever and to whatever abysses nature leads, or you shall learn nothing. I have only begun to learn content and peace of mind since I have resolved at all risks to do this.

Thomas Huxley, 1825–1895. English biologist.
Life and Letters of Thomas Huxley.

Look now forwards and let the backwards be. And see what thou lackest and not what thou hast; for that is the readiest getting and keeping of meekness. All thy life now must all ways stand in desire, if thou shalt advance in degree of perfection. This desire must all ways be wrought in thy will, by the hand of Almighty God and thy consent. But one thing I tell thee: he is a jealous lover and suffereth no fellowship, and he liketh not to work in thy will unless he be only with thee by himself. He asketh no help but only thyself. He wills thou do but look upon him and let him alone. And keep thou the windows and the door from flies and enemies assailing. And if thou be willing to do this, thou needest but meekly to set upon him with prayer, and soon will he help thee. Set on then: let me see how thou bearest thee. He is full ready, and doth but abide thee.

Unknown English mystic, fourteenth century.
The Cloud of Unknowing. Ed. Dom Justin McCann.

Loving God

Then an expert in the Law got up to test him and said, "Master, what must I do to make sure of eternal life?"

Jesus said to him,

"What does the Law say? How does it read?"

He answered,

" 'You must love the Lord your God with your whole heart, your whole soul, your whole strength, and your whole mind,' and 'your neighbor as you do yourself.' "

Jesus said to him,

"You are right. Do that, and you will live."

Luke 10:25–28.
New Testament. Trans. E. J. Goodspeed.

To love God with all our hearts and all our souls and all our minds means that every cleavage in human existence is overcome.

Reinhold Niebuhr, 1892–1973.
American theologian, educator.
Interpretation of Christian Ethics.

Some people want to see God with their eyes as they see a cow and to love him as they love their cow—they love their cow for the milk and cheese and profit it makes them. This is how it is with people who love God for the sake of outward wealth or inward comfort. They do not rightly love God when they love him for their own advantage. Indeed, I tell you the truth, any object you have on your mind, however good, will be a barrier between you and the inmost truth.

Meister Johannes Eckhart, 1260–1327.
German scholar, mystic.
Meister Eckhart. Trans. R. Blakney.

You will ask me questions how a man can give himself to that which he has no feeling of, especially when it relates to an Object which he does not see, nor never had acquaintance with? Sir, every day of your life you love things you do not see. Do you see for instance the wisdom of your friend? Do you see his sincerity, his disinterestedness, his virtue? You cannot see those objects with the eyes of the body, yet you prize and value them, and love them in that degree that you prefer them in your friend to riches, and outward beauty, and to everything that strikes the eye. Love then the wisdom and supreme goodness of God, as you love the wisdom and imperfect goodness of your friend. And if you cannot presently have a sensible feeling of love, you at least may have a love of preference in your will and desire, which is the essential point. . . .

[And] when you come to be sensibly touched, the scales will fall from your eyes; and by the penetrating eyes of love you will discern that which your other eyes will never see.*

François Fénelon, 1651–1715.
French Archbishop of Cambray.
Spiritual Letters of Archbishop Fénelon. Trans. H. L. Lear.

Because we are born of the flesh, it must needs be that our desire, or love, begins from the flesh; and if it is directed by right order, advancing by its several degrees under guidance of grace, it will at last be consummated by spirit: for "that was not first which is spiritual, but that which is natural; afterwards that which is spiritual." And first we must bear "the image of the earthly," afterwards "the image of the heavenly."

First, then, man loves himself for his own sake; he is flesh, forsooth, and can have no taste for aught beyond himself. And when he sees that he cannot subsist of himself, he begins by faith to seek God as necessary to him, and to love him. Thus he loves God in the second degree, but for his own sake, not for Himself. But when by occasion of his own necessity, he has begun to worship and approach him, by meditation, reading, prayer, obedience; by a certain familiarity of this kind, little by little and gradually, God becomes known and consequently grows sweet; and thus, having tasted how sweet is the Lord, he passes on to the third degree, so that he loves God, not now for his own sake, but for Himself.

Assuredly the abiding is long in this degree; and I know not if the fourth is perfectly attained by any man in this life, so that, that is, a man love himself only for the sake of God. Let those, if any, who have experienced, tell us; to me, I confess it seems impossible. But it will be beyond question when the good and faithful servant is brought into the joy of his Lord, and inebriated with the plenty of the house of God. For in a certain wondrous fashion oblivious of himself, and as it were utterly abandoning himself, he will wholly pass on into God, and henceforth, joined to the Lord, will be one in spirit with him.*

Saint Bernard, 1091–1153. French Abbot of Clairvaux.
On the Love of God. Trans. E. G. Gardner.

It is when a man begins to know the ambition of his life not simply as the choice of his own will but as the wise assignment of God's love; and to know his relations to his brethren not simply as the result of his own impulsive affections but as the seeking of his soul for these souls because they all belong to the great Father-soul; it is then that life for that man begins to lift itself all over and to grow towards completion upward through all its length and breadth.*

Phillips Brooks, 1835–1893. American clergyman.
Sermons of Phillips Brooks.

I have but one word to say to you concerning love for your neighbor, namely, that nothing save humility can mould you to it; nothing but the consciousness of your own weakness can make you indulgent and pitiful to that of others. You will answer, "I quite understand that humility should produce forbearance towards others, but how am I first to acquire humility?" Two things combined will bring that about; you must never separate them. The first is contemplation of the deep gulf whence God's All-powerful Hand has drawn you out, and over which He ever holds you, so to say, suspended. The second is the Presence of that All-penetrating God. It is only in beholding and loving God that we can learn forgetfulness of self, measure duly the nothingness of that which has dazzled us, and accustom ourselves thankfully to "decrease" beneath that Great Majesty Which absorbs all things. Love God, and you will be humble; love God, and you will throw off the love of self; love God, and you will love all that He gives you to love for love of Him.

François Fénelon, 1651–1715.
French Archbishop of Cambray.
Spiritual Letters of Archbishop Fénelon. Trans. H. L. Lear.

When I was brought down from my prison to the Court of Bankruptcy, between two policemen, ——— waited in the long dreary corridor that, before the whole crowd, whom an action so sweet and simple hushed into silence, he might gravely raise his hat to me, as, handcuffed and with bowed head, I passed him by. Men have gone to heaven for smaller things than that. It was in this spirit, and with this mode of love, that the saints knelt down to wash the feet of the poor, or stooped to kiss the leper on the cheek. I have never said one single word to him about what he did. I do not know to the present moment whether he is aware that I was even conscious of his action. It is not a thing for which one can render formal thanks in formal words. I keep it there as a secret debt that I am glad to think I can never possibly repay. When wisdom has been profitless to me, philosophy barren, and the proverbs and phrases of those who have sought to give me consolation as dust and ashes in my mouth, the memory of that little, lovely, silent act of love has unsealed for me all the wells of pity; brought me out of the bitterness of lonely exile into harmony with the wounded, broken, and great heart of the world.*

Oscar Wilde, 1856–1900. English author.
De Profundis.

This was the commandment. "Thou shalt love thy neighbour as thyself," but when the commandment is rightly understood, it also says the converse. "Thou shalt love thyself in the right way." If anyone, therefore, will not learn from Christianity to love himself in the right way, then neither can he love his neighbour; he may perhaps, as we say, "for life and death"—cling to one or several other human beings, but this is by no means loving one's neighbour. To love one's self in the right way and to love one's neighbour are absolutely analogous concepts, are at bottom one and the same. When the "as thyself" of the commandment has taken from you the selfishness which Christianity, sad to say, must presuppose as existing in every human being, then you have rightly learned to love yourself. Hence the law is: "You shall love yourself as you love your neighbour when you love him as yourself." Whoever has some knowledge of men will certainly admit that as he has often wished to be able to influence men to give up their self-love, so he has also often wished that it were possible to teach them to love themselves. When the busy man wastes his time and energy on vain and unimportant projects, is this not because he has not rightly learned to love himself? When the frivolous man abandons himself, almost as a mere nothing, to the folly of the moment, is not this because he does not rightly understand how to love himself?

When the melancholy man wishes to be done with life, aye, with himself, is this not because he will not learn strictly and earnestly to love himself? When a man, because the world or another man faithlessly betrayed him, yields himself up to despair, how was he to blame (for we are not here speaking of his innocent suffering), except for not having loved himself in the right way? When a man in self-torment thinks to do God a service by torturing himself, what is his sin except this, of not willing to love himself in the right way? Ah, and when a man presumptuously lays his hand up on himself, does not his sin precisely consist in not loving himself in the way in which a man ought to love himself? Oh, there is so much said in the world about treachery and faithlessness, and, God help us! this is unfortunately only too true, but let us still never forget that the most dangerous traitor of all is the one every man has in his own breast. This treachery, whether it consists in a man's selfishly loving himself, or in the fact that he selfishly does not wish to love himself in the right way, this treachery is certainly a mystery because there is no outcry about it, as is usual in cases of treachery and faithlessness. But is it not therefore all the more important that we should repeatedly be reminded about the Christian teaching: that a man should love his neighbour as himself, that is, as he ought to love himself?

Sören Kierkegaard, 1813–1855. Danish philosopher.
Works of Love. Trans. David F. Swenson.

FOLLOWING THE INNER LIGHT

If one listens to the faintest but constant suggestions of his genius, which are certainly true, he sees not to what extremes, or even insanity, it may lead him; and yet that way, as he grows more resolute and faithful, his road lies. The faintest assured objection which one healthy man feels will at length prevail over the arguments and customs of mankind. No man ever followed his genius till it misled him. Though the result were bodily weakness, yet perhaps no one can say that the consequences were to be regretted, for these were a life in conformity to higher principles. If the day and the night are such that you greet them with joy, and life emits a fragrance like flowers and sweet-scented herbs, is more elastic, more starry, more immortal—that is your success. All nature is your congratulation, and you have cause momentarily to bless yourself. The greatest gains and values are farthest from being appreciated. We easily come to doubt if they exist. We soon forget them. They are the highest reality. Perhaps the facts most astounding and most real are never communicated by man to man. The true harvest of my daily life is somewhat as intangible and indescribable as the tints of morning or evening.

Henry David Thoreau, 1817–1862. American philosopher.
Walden.

It is always a difficult thing to express, in intellectual terms, subtle feelings that are nevertheless infinitely important for the individual's life and well-being. It is, in a sense, the feeling that we have been "replaced," but without the connotation of having been "deposed." It is as if the guidance of life had passed over to an invisible centre.

This remarkable experience seems to me a consequence of the detachment of consciousness, thanks to which the subjective "I live" becomes the objective "It lives me." This state is felt to be higher than the previous one; it is really like a sort of release from the compulsion and impossible responsibility that are the inevitable results of *participation mystique.* This feeling of liberation fills Paul completely; the consciousness of being a child of God delivers one from the bondage of the blood. It is also a feeling of reconciliation with all that happens, for which reason, according to the *Hui Ming Ching,*[13] the gaze of one "who has attained fulfillment" turns back to the beauty of nature.

In the Pauline Christ symbol the supreme religious experiences of West and East confront one another: Christ the sorrow-laden hero, and the Golden Flower that blooms in the purple hall of the city of jade. What a contrast, what an unfathomable difference, what an abyss of history! A problem fit for the crowning work of a future psychologist!*

Carl G. Jung, M.D., 1875–1961. Swiss psychiatrist.
Alchemical Studies. Trans. R. F. C. Hull.

---

[13]*The Book of Changes*—Ancient Chinese Scripture.

Dwelling in the Light, there is no occasion at all for stumbling, for all things are discovered with the Light. Thou that lovest it herewith is Thy Teacher. When thou art walking abroad it is present with thee in thy bosom. Thou needest not to say, lo, here, or lo, there; and as thou liest in thy bed it is present to teach thee and judge thy wandering mind which wanders abroad and thy high thoughts and imaginations and makes them subject. For following thy thoughts thou art quickly lost. By dwelling in this Light it will discover to thee the body of sin and thy corruptions and fallen estate where thou art. In that Light which shows thee all this, stand; neither to the right nor to the left.

George Fox, 1624–1691.
English, founder of the Society of Friends.

Your eye is the lamp of your body. When your eye is sound, your whole body is light, but when it is unsound, your body is dark. So take care! Your very light may be darkness! If, therefore, your whole body is light with no darkness in it at all, it will all be as light as a lamp makes things for you by its light.

Jesus of Nazareth.
New Testament (Luke 11:34–36). Trans. E. J. Goodspeed.

The Way Implies a Rebirth

For thousands of years, rites of initiation have been teaching rebirth from the spirit; yet, strangely enough, man forgets again and again the meaning of divine procreation. Though this may be poor testimony to the strength of the spirit, the penalty for misunderstanding is neurotic decay, embitterment, atrophy, and sterility. It is easy enough to drive the spirit out of the door, but when we have done so the meal has lost its savour—the salt of the earth. Fortunately, we have proof that the spirit always renews its strength in the fact that the essential teaching of the initiations is handed on from generation to generation. Ever and again there are human beings who understand what it means that God is their father. The equal balance of the flesh and the spirit is not lost to the world.

Carl G. Jung, M.D., 1875–1961. Swiss psychiatrist.
Freud and Psychoanalysis. Trans. R. F. C. Hull.

This dying to self by dying into life results, as Keats had discovered, in the birth of a new self. For the mind through which man acquires his sense of personal identity, is not luxuriously relaxed. The intensity of effort involved is vividly revealed in the lines in which Keats described his agonzied approach to the altar steps. But this effort implies something other than the negative concentration of self-restraint which Mr. Babbitt preaches. It is a positive crucifixion of self, whereby the mind ceases to be conscious of its own petty rights and scruples, and knows in itself the Mind of life labouring in the imperfect matter of humanity towards a perfect realization of being.

For every moment of pure consciousness is a kind of death. The self dies as a separate entity. It lives as a perfect unity. By giving itself to the death that is in life, it receives the life that is in death, and receives it, not with clouded faculties or in some swoon of sense, but with a heightened awareness of reality. The self is so disinterested that nothing is alien to it; it is so conscious of its own and so of life's creative purpose that nothing is meaningless to it.*

Hugh I'Anson Fausset, 1895–1965. English critic, poet.
Proving of Psyche.

Here it is necessary to distinguish two paths through the crisis to a new start. We call the first one the human or earthly path. It ends in a certain sense of fellowship in a We that consists of humans—an earthly or human We. The second one may be characterized as the religious path. Its outlet is—at least in our time—Christianity with its sense of the manifestation of God in the We.

In the first case, the person has renounced all the former aims and values of his Ego. In anticipation this process seemed to be death itself, yet now, having passed through it, he realizes that he is alive in spite of the terrible breakdown. Now he sees that the world is quite different from what he formerly believed it to be. He seems to look upon life with new eyes, seeing connections, facts, values, goals, ways, possibilities he never saw before. A serious offense, which yesterday seemed to be unbearable, is now a mere trifle. Like old clothes, worn out and worthless, his egocentric prejudices, notions, and ideas have been discarded for something better. Formerly it was supposed that without these egocentric values life would be empty, meaningless, nothing at all—that when these old egocentric ideas had been dropped nothing would be left, that the rest of life would be emptiness. But now the person discovers how mistaken he was. For a new world opens up before him with a whole new life, richer and more colorful and more differentiated than anything he knew before.

This appearance in his life of the new values, new feelings and new aims, which completes the new insight into the actual realities of life, is the very essence of the crisis, and perhaps the essence of human life itself. As has been said before, it is inexplicable, and we must limit ourselves to describing it as carefully as possible. In the case of the human or earthly path through crisis, we come to feel that this "miracle of rebirth" seems to be a natural element in human life. In the case of the religious path, we feel behind the sunrise of the new life a higher Living Power who brings it about.

Fritz Kunkel, M.D., 1889–1956. American psychiatrist,
and Roy E. Dickerson, 1886–, American author.
How Character Develops.

Among the Pharisees there was a man named Nicodemus, a leader among the Jews. This man went to Jesus one night, and said to him,

"Master, we know that you are a teacher who has come from God, for no one can show the signs that you do, unless God is with him."

Jesus answered him,

"I tell you, no one can see the Kingdom of God unless he is born over again from above!"

Nicodemus said to him,

"How can a man be born when he is old? Can he enter his mother's womb over again and be born?"

Jesus answered,

"I tell you, if a man does not owe his birth to water and spirit, he cannot get into the Kingdom of God. Whatever owes its birth to the physical is physical, and whatever owes its birth to the Spirit is spiritual. Do not wonder at my telling you that you must be born over again from above. The wind blows wherever it chooses, and you hear the sound of it, but you do not know where it comes from or where it goes. That is the way with everyone who owes his birth to the Spirit."

John 3:1–8
New Testament. Trans. E. J. Goodspeed.

Nicodemus asked, expecting to end the discussion which had grown too transcendental: Can a man enter again his mother's womb and be reborn? That undoubtedly is the question with which civilization is faced today: Can there be rebirth, or must the attempt of metamorphosis always mean death?

It is on that peculiar and vital point that we have today through science a most significant addition to our knowledge. Today we know that this way of rebirth is the way whereby all great critical advances have been made by Life. All profoundly new development, all development after the stage of complete functional power has been attained, must be and can only be by a profound sloughing and, more, by a recasting of the elder form and a completely fresh growth build up from basic materials. This is the great principle called now in science Foetalization, since its supreme biological importance has been discovered, but known for long to the "artists of thought" as metamorphosis or rebirth.

Naturally, faced by this demand of Life, with this dilemma to take in more reality and to fulfill more courageously the psychological demands of his nature, man shrinks from the only way forward—to keep on opening his mind, his heart, and his apprehensions. He feels that he is being torn asunder and dissolved. Birth is as terrible an agony as death. That it shall be birth and not death depends on the creature's vitality. One thing is certain, that the old narrower life is over. For a short time we shall see the violences of this profound conflict, by those who suffer from them, thrown out into the outer world of action. We shall see the outer violences of class wars, experts' wars, nations' wars and age-group wars—all projections of inner conflict striving to avoid the crisis that must be fought out in itself. But in the end the force within us, which we are now attempting to get rid of by our violent actions in the world without, will turn in upon ourselves. For we are not answering its demand that we should change ourselves by these our violent efforts to overset the world. We cannot say whether we shall learn in time where lies the true centre of our distress and so realize how it may be cured, and cease before we have done fatal damage by striking blindly about us as lunatics strike with mad fury at the phantasms projected by their diseased minds. What our present knowledge does tell us is either we shall shortly emerge into a new world in which value and reality can be seen reconciled, or we shall die, leaving a lesson and an empty field for those next chosen by Life to attempt this crisis of creation. We can see the deep rend under us today so clearly because today it is risen to the surface and is sweeping us to the brink.*

Gerald Heard, 1889–1971.
English author, religious philosopher.
These Hurrying Years.

I had learned, it seemed, that a spiritual progress was possible to man, by which out of the discordant elements of his being—the desire of the Heart and the knowledge of the Mind—a harmony was created. This harmony was a new kind of being, and it had been called by Jesus and Eckhart and Keats, the Soul. This Soul was at once a new condition of the total human being and a faculty of knowledge. It was aware of the universe as a harmony, and of itself as a part of that harmony; and this awareness was a joyful awareness. This was the ground of the mystical faith that the Soul was consubstantial with God. God, in this mystical sense, was the inseparable counterpart of the Soul; and the Soul, in the process and very moment of becoming aware of its own self-existence, became also aware of the existence of an omnipresent God of which itself was, as it were, a focus of self-knowledge.

This strange and simple process was the "rebirth" which Jesus had taught, and which was the central mystery of all high religion. It could occur in complete independence of any particular religion; it was the outcome of an internecine conflict between the desire of the Heart and the knowledge of the Mind.

This conflict between Heart and Mind, between feeling and knowledge, was obviously independent of religion, in any ordinary sense of the word. It was simply incidental to humanity. Man, being man, was bound to endure this conflict. If he did not endure it, he was less than man, in the sense that he was turning away from something which it was his duty as a man to look upon.

Some drugged themselves with a religion which assured them that the desires of the Heart would be realized, and that death was only the doorway to life; some sought forgetfulness in busy plans for the amelioration of human circumstance; some sought to live in the moment. But there were always a few on whom these opiates failed to work. By some queer destiny the conflict was forced upon them. Heart and Mind in them insisted each upon its rights, and the claims could not be reconciled. There was a deadlock in the centre of their being, and they passed steadily into a condition of isolation, inanition, abandonment and despair. Their inward division was complete.

Then came, out of that extreme and absolute division, a sudden unity. A new kind of consciousness was created in them. Mind and Heart, which had been irreconcilable enemies, became united in the Soul, which loved what it knew. The inward division, which had divided the human being also from the universe of his knowledge, was healed; in a single happening, man became one in himself and one with all that was without him. He knew that he was called upon to play his part in the harmony revealed to him.

This was the great secret of religion; but only because it was the great secret of life. Men who learned and obeyed it, became different. They were a new kind of men.*

John Middleton Murry, 1889–1957. English author, critic.
God.

CHAPTER III

Progression on the Way

People who are far from God think they are very near to him, when they begin to take a few steps to approach him. The most polite and most enlightened people have the same stupidity about this as a peasant who thinks he is really at court, because he has seen the king.

FRANCOIS FENELON

*There are too many who are content to learn words by heart, and to put words in the place of experience. No one can really understand these things unless he has experienced them himself.**

CARL G. JUNG

*He that hath ears, let him hear.**

JESUS OF NAZARETH

"O Lord, this is not the work of one day, nor children's sport; nay, in this short work[1] is included all the perfection of religious persons." In this statement Thomas à Kempis voices an appropriate warning to all who enter upon the religious Way, for it is not a quick, nor an easy undertaking. The rebirth that occurs is a continuous process. It challenges to a persistent and concentrated effort, such as is required in learning to apprehend and enter into the nature of reality in any new area. In the spiritual realm the demands are greater than in all others, for the goal is the apprehension of the nature of the real self ("Within, yet beyond the person") and the organization of personality around that Central Reality.

The warning of this fifteenth-century religious refers to a grave misunderstanding regarding the Way, one that has led to countless discouragements and failures, *i.e.*, the com-

[1] "Let go all, and thou shalt find all."

monly held belief that the change of conscious attitude which the Way involves will bring an immediate and lasting transformation of personality. For many there may be a tremendously clarifying initial experience, but for relatively few of whom there is record, is there the cataclysmic conversion of a Paul or an Augustine. For most people the transformation is a long and slow process because of those obstacles of personality and social structure which so effectively block the needed reorientation.

So much emphasis has been placed on *beginning* the religious Way, and so little emphasis has been put on *following* it, that a startling ignorance concerning the very fact of progression prevails. Doubtless some of the disrepute into which religion falls can be traced to this unrealism. Its effect is twofold.

It leads to the disillusionment of many aspirants, who, following the first enthusiastic flush of devotion, gradually find themselves faced with the same conflicts, tensions, and fears as before. What seems disturbing to them is that these appear in intensified form. They conclude, therefore, that they are growing worse instead of better and so frequently fall by the wayside. They are the ones who may be heard to exclaim, "I have tried religion, and it doesn't work." Thus many lose faith and discontinue their efforts, at least until their inner longing leads them to a different approach to the Way, whereupon they are benefited by another clarifying experience. This stop-and-go method is wasteful and largely unnecessary, for we learn from the first rank religious as well as psycho-therapeutic helpers, that progress in self-knowledge leads inevitably to the uncovering of heretofore hidden egocentric motives—to a greater awareness of a faulty condition that has existed for a long time. This is a sign of progress, and not of failure. (See pp. 104, 125, 155–158.)

The other situation stemming from this unrealism is even more disturbing, because victims are seldom aware of their plight. They are those who start out with good promise, but not realizing the range of progress which may be possible for them, nor the training that will facilitate progress toward the further goals, gradually settle down into a mediocrity that is complacent, and sterile. They may be, indeed, many of them are, loyal church members. They believe themselves to be leading the "good life" whereas they have barely stepped over the threshold, for they have not yet come to grips with their deepest inner nature. They have made little progress in eradicating the "false" elements within the self and therefore the "real" elements remain still to be discovered. Thus they continue to project upon society their unknown and unresolved conflicts, and fail to project what could emerge through them—some measure of the creative, loving power of God.

When mediocrity of achievement thus becomes the rule, it comes also to be accepted as the only possible, practical goal. It is easy to see how the religious Way, viewed with such distortion, ceases to hold out the answer to man's longing for fulfillment, and falls into disrepute.

We may wonder why advice concerning progression has not been made more available. The reasons are too involved to discuss here. However, there is no present excuse for lack of information in this area, for in addition to the enlightened instruction of early religious directors which has long been available, and too frequently neglected, there is a comparatively new body of information provided by psychology which throws light on the unconscious factors involved in any change of character. Also there has come an increased influx of translations made from the wealth of ancient Hindu and Buddhist sources concerning the means whereby man can learn to apprehend Reality. The Westerner can profit from some of the methods which these religions have developed, even though many of them are not suitable to the Western temperament.

The information and advices which follow have been garnered from these three areas of insight, as well as from contemporary religious teachers.

Limitation of space obviously prevents a thorough consideration of all that is known concerning progression on the Way. The reader will profit by further study concerning them. (See Recommended Reading.) It should be said that the factors governing the rate and range are complex and individually determined. Biological heritage, mental and emotional endowment, temperament, as well as environmental factors enter in. Recent psychological studies on both physical and temperamental types are proving helpful in spiritual training.[3]

---

[3]*Psychological Types* by Carl G. Jung, and *Varieties of Temperament* by William H. Sheldon. Also see p. 325.—Ed.

We may often need to remind ourselves that every step along the way brings immeasurable benefits. It is up to us therefore to use every sound means for accelerating our progress on the Way—knowing, however, that the final range of achievement depends not on our own efforts—but on the grace of God.—Ed.

Stages of Progression

A tree that it takes both arms to encircle grew from a tiny rootlet. A many storied pagoda is built by placing one brick upon another brick. A journey of three thousand miles is begun by a single step.

Lao-tzu, sixth century B.C. *Chinese philosopher*
Lao-tzu's Tao and Wu-Wei.
Trans. Bhikshu Wai-dau and D. Goddard.

Our safety does not lie in the present perfection of our knowledge of the will of God, but in our sincerity in obeying the light we have, and in seeking for more.

Edward Worsdell, 1853–1908. English teacher.
The Gospel of Divine Help.

In the great mystics we see the highest and widest development of that consciousness to which the human race has yet attained. We see its growth exhibited to us on a grand scale perceptible of all men. . . . The germ of that same transcendent life, the spring of the amazing energy which enables the great mystic to rise to freedom and dominate his world, is latent in all of us; an integral part of our humanity. Where the mystic has a genius for the Absolute, we have each a little buried talent, some greater, some less; and the growth of this talent, this spark of the soul, once we permit its emergence, will conform in little, and according to its measure, to those laws of organic growth, those inexorable conditions of transcendence which we found to govern the Mystic Way.

Every person, then, who awakens to consciousness of a Reality which transcends the normal world of sense is put upon a road which follows at low levels the path which the mystic treads at high levels. . . .

I do not care whether the consciousness be that of artist

or musician, striving to catch and fix some aspect of the heavenly light or music, and denying all other aspects of the world in order to devote themselves to this: or of the humble servant of Science, purging his intellect that he may look upon her secrets with innocence of eye: whether the higher reality be perceived in the terms of religion, beauty, suffering; of human love, of goodness, or of truth. However widely these forms of transcendence may seem to differ, the mystic experience is the key to them all. . . . Each brings the self who receives its revelation in good faith, does not check it by self-regarding limitations, to a humble acceptance of the universal law of knowledge: the law that "we behold that which we are," and hence that "only the Real can know Reality." Awakening, Discipline, Enlightenment, Self-surrender, and Union, are the essential phases of life's response to this fundamental fact: the conditions of our attainment of Being. . . .*

Evelyn Underhill, 1875–1944. English writer, mystic.
Mysticism.

No one can be enlightened unless he first be cleansed or purified and stripped. So also can no one be united with God unless he be first enlightened. Thus there are three stages: first, the purification (or purgation); secondly, the enlightening; thirdly, the union.

Anonymous (one of the "Friends of God").
Fourteenth century.
Theologia Germanica. Trans. Susanna Winkworth.

There is need for sharper differentiation in religious literature between what appear to be two different goals in the religious process. While the difference may stem partly from a confusion in terms—arising from attempts to describe authentic, "numinous" experiences for which language has no adequate parallel—it also seems to point to a basic disagreement which we feel should be carefully examined.[a]

One goal is expressed in classic mystic writings as "union with God," *when it is interpreted as identification,* leading to a loss of individual uniqueness—to a kind of anonymity

[a]Rufus Jones' books contribute greatly toward such an examination. See Recommended Reading list.

—the goal of the training which the nun in *The Nun's Story* found impossible to fulfill. This same goal can be recognized in the Neoplatonic mystics as well as in Hindu mysticism and in the Buddhist concept of Nirvana, whenever it is interpreted to mean the obliteration[4] of all individual attributes, resulting in a complete "participation mystic." For some, indeed, this total naughting of the self, whether in favor of an "Abstract Infinite" or of a "Divine Order of the Church," may be the Way (psychologically right, and even necessary). The editors, however, would point the reader to selections in this anthology which stress the goal as one of *relationship,* rather than identification—individuation, rather than anonymity—a "union with God" in which the personality is fulfilled and consciousness extended, rather than negated (see Jung, pp. 61–65; Wolff, p. 83; Leibman, p. 90; Heard, p. 92; Steuart, p. 132; Jacobi pp. 158–159, etc.).

Father Steuart writes: "I am not lost in God in the sense that my individuality ceases to be my own . . . I do not cease to be myself because I have surrendered myself wholly to Him." Dr. Jacobi further differentiates this for us when she refers to the experience of being identified with or "lost" in God as the *Mana phase of the Way*—where one becomes "united with God in spiritual childhood"—and warns that this stage is to be moved *through* and not lodged *in.* The editors find substantiation for this desirable and necessary "moving on" from the Mana stage in the writings of many religious teachers[5] and the soundness of it substantiated by the findings of depth psychology,[6] particularly of analytical psychology.

Martin Buber, speaking from the best in modern Jewish

---

[4]Research in recent years reveals that the *true* Nirvana experience results in a transformed and extended consciousness rather than in a loss of ego structure.

[5]Jacob Boehme, Hans Denck, Thomas Traherne, François Fénelon, Martin Luther, Rufus Jones, Paul Tillich, Martin Buber and others.

[6]Freud's negative attitude toward religion may have stemmed partly from the regressive dangers he saw in the goal of identification, such as the danger in the loss of ego function. These dangers may also account for the resistance many lay persons have toward the more extreme forms of mysticism.

mysticism, superbly enunciates the goal of the religious way in terms of relationship. He describes the meeting of man with God, the Eternal Thou, as a dialogic one, out of which "man becomes most truly a person." He writes: "In the act of true dialogic (I-Thou) relation man becomes a *self*. And the fuller its sharing in the reality of the dialogue the more real the self becomes."[1]

And it is especially striking that in the teachings of Jesus all statements of method—such as "losing life," "selling all," "doing the Will"—are completed by statements of a goal related to individual identity—to "saving" or "preserving" life. To miss this point is, we feel, to miss one of the sources of uniqueness in the life and teaching of Jesus. It is to miss some of the significance of the second great commandment: "And thou shalt love thy neighbor as thyself." For to love, one has to *"be."* Without unique identity one can love neither God, nor neighbor, nor self.

In any discussion of stages of the religious Way, whether phrased in mystical terminology, as in Underhill, Baker, and others; or by Martin Buber (who writes of direction, actuality, meaning, duality, and unity); or expressed psychologically as in Kunkel, and Jacobi (pp. 108–110), or by Jung (who designates the stages as catharsis, elucidation, education and transformation)—one needs to keep in mind that all categories, when applied to any living process are only attempts to communicate and interpret phases of experience which should never be expected to follow one another consecutively as on a straight line. The process is more likely to be experienced as a spiral development—where many of the same problems are confronted over and over but on a different level and with a deeper meaning. Or, it can be expressed as an unfoldment—such as a flower unfolding—according to its own inner design. There are, to be sure, changes in the quality and level of experience that can be noted throughout the whole religious journey. But one needs to avoid the temptation of becoming preoccupied with trying to figure out *where one is*. Rather, the attention should be focused on fulfilling the conditions of the Way and on honoring and nurturing whatever is revealed at each step—instead of on any particular result to be expected at any particular time.

---

[1]*Eclipse of God*, p. 125 (Harper, 1952).

A discussion of stages can be helpful if one will appropriate what belongs to him, while bearing in mind that, as Dr. Jung says, "every period of life has its own psychological truth." It can contribute in letting one know that there is always "something beyond" in the maturing, transforming process. It can often throw interpretive light on the variety of experiences, whether "valley" or "mountaintop," which may be encountered along the Way.—Ed.

"STAGES" AS RELATED TO THE EVOLUTIONARY PATH

We must start without delay on the painful, steep, humiliating path of undoing our busy, deliberately deluded selves. So only will the Kingdom come, where it must come fully and where we alone can decide whether it shall come—in ourselves. "The Kingdom of God is within you," yes, but only if we are prepared to let that powerful germ of eternal life grow. . . . Unless we, this person with his tightly bound triple self-love—love of his physical appetites and comforts, of his possessions of his place, rank, and recognition—unless that hard and hardening nut is buried and rots and is eaten away by the new life's germ, there is no hope. Indeed we may say that the whole secret of the spiritual life is just this painful struggle to come awake, to become really conscious. And, conversely, the whole process and technique of evil is to do just the reverse to us: to lull us to sleep, to distract us from what is creeping up within us; to tell us that we are busy workers for the Kingdom when we are absent-mindedly spreading death, not life.

That, then, is the first step, known by the grim technical term, purgation. I must start with myself, and stay with myself until some intention appears in my actions, some consistency between what I say and do. I must not escape into denunciation, coercion, or even superior concern for anyone else. I shall do so if I can; that is the invariable trick of the ego. . . . Then, after complete abandonment of serving two masters—my view of myself as a master-builder gaining recognition by my active goodness, and of God—then comes the next step, illumination. I am still far below being capable of a creative act. That is God's prerogative. But I am permitted at last to see things as they are. Fear and hurry and anxiety leave me. Why? Because, though still extremely ignorant, I know one thing at last. I know that God exists. There is utter Reality, complete creative power holding the entire creation in its grasp. The whole of time and space is no more than an incident, a minute episode in the immeasurable order, power, and glory of complete Being. Once I have seen, really seen, that, once I am illuminated, then I have fully attained one step in approaching God's Kingdom and in letting it approach; I no longer am standing in the way. I cease to be a reason for people not believing in God. The Light shines through those who have so let themselves be opened. Thank God we have all of us known one or two of them. And there may be more of them than we notice, for they are the reverse of showy. They may be very active, but when we think of them it is not of the activity of which we think. It is of some still, firm quality, some essence deeper than deeds, that we see in them. They see Reality, are always looking at it; there is in them a quality of entire Being.

Is there anything beyond that stage? That is indeed much. . . . The first stage is that of servantship, when we learn not to disobey. The second stage is one of friendship, when we learn why we have had to obey, and to abstain from much that seemed harmless and even, in its way, right. Then comes the third stage, that of creative action, the station and work of sons. They are not merely privileged onlookers, they are co-workers. This is the well-known (but seldom climbed) ladder of the mystics. Is it not also, here in front of us today, unmistakably, an evolutionary path? Is not this the way to the Kingdom and is not the attainment of that final station itself the Kingdom? To some people this may seem something of an anticlimax. Is the dream of the Kingdom to end simply with the ivory-tower ideal of a large crop of saints? If we think that goal anything less than the highest, that can be because we have never met any of that highest rank—as well may be. They are themselves rare and those who would understand them must in themselves have already something of the nature they would appreciate. If we are quite blind, however intense the sun, we shall still see only darkness. Theirs is of the essential nature of their Father, a quality, an intensity of Being, which is, unless they screen it from us, disquieting, uncanny. Real creativeness is far more terrible than what we call destruction.

Can we ourselves hope to climb this tremendous way to the Kingdom? Certainly: there will be no Kingdom unless and until we do so climb to that station. For only those who have attained may safely be given the powers, the spiritual powers whereby, and only whereby, God's Kingdom may come on earth. How can we learn to climb to such immense heights? We have seen the first steps. The very first is to know that I as I am, am an obstacle to the Kingdom. I must start, before anything else, by clearing myself out of the way. I must learn, right down to my reflexes, to say and mean and know, "Let my name perish, so Thy Kingdom come."*–**

Gerald Heard, 1889–1971.
English author, religious philosopher.
The Creed of Christ.

STAGES FROM THE VIEWPOINT OF DEPTH PSYCHOLOGY

The more we can observe the details of the process the more we discover the well-known features of the "Great Turn," or the "Great Way," as it has been described by spiritual leaders all through the history of religion. Seen from the viewpoint of depth-psychology the essential stages of the journey are three.

The first stage is regression and reintegration. It corresponds to the "purgation" of medieval mysticism. The Ego or the idol, the rigid structure of the former life, collapses, together with all its valuations, prejudices, resentments, desires and fears. The "censorship," the screen between consciousness and the unconscious, breaks down. Old images, forgotten emotions, repressed functions, come to life again; primitive obsessions and projections, visions and nightmares endanger the equilibrium of the good citizen. Without adequate inner or outer help, religious and psychological, he will be in an evil predicament.

This is the situation which the psalmists have described with amazing exactitude: "The sorrows of death compassed me, and the floods of ungodly men made me afraid. The sorrows of hell compassed me about: the snares of death prevented me" (Psalm 18:4,5). And again: "Many bulls have compassed me; strong bulls of Bashan have beset me round" (Psalm 22:12). The outer and the inner evil fuse; death or insanity seems to be certain; all the negativity of the universe seems to be arrayed against us. There is only one way out: the religious way: "Yea, though I walk through the valley of the shadow of death, I will fear no evil: for thou art with me" (Psalm 23:4).

The power of the images,[8] terrifying as it may be, is borrowed power. It appears to be genuine and invincible only as long as we do not know the real center. The appeal to the center,[9] therefore, is the only thing left for the person who is "beset by the bulls" of the collective unconscious.[10] Even the atheist, if anything disagreeable takes him by surprise, reacts with a superficial turn to the center. He says "O God!" or "For goodness sake!" If the believer can do the same thing in a more serious way, even though in the moment of fear or pain his concept of God may be vague or childish, it will help him more than anything else.

The turning towards the center is the second stage of the journey. But the center itself, the aspect of God which can be experienced in such a situation, is quite different from what most people expect it to be. Either we project some learned or emotional ideas into the universe; or, knowing we must have no image of God, we use an empty frame, three feet square, and according to our creed we think God will fit the frame. Yet he does not. His appearance, if he appears at all, crushes our beautiful frame. We are frightened and offended and decree that the power which destroyed our convictions must be the devil.

The nearer we come to the center, the more we leave the images behind, the more are our fears turned into anxiety. And anxiety, if we face it, is turned into awe. What seemed to be the power of darkness now manifests itself as the power of light. After the great and strong wind comes the earthquake, then the fire, and then the still small voice (I Kings 19:11–13).

The terrible and destructive aspect of the godhead—the "tremendum" in theological language—originates as a subjective human experience, though an unavoidable one if our religious convictions and our rigid theology are smashed by the Grace of God. We live in a jail which we

[8]Symbols in dreams and fantasy.

[9]The "Real Self"—"God within."

[10]That deep, inborn layer of the unconscious which is not individual but universal in content.—Ed.

call our castle; a foreign soldier breaks through the doors, come to free us by blasting the walls of our castle—and we fight him with the last might of our broken Ego, calling him scoundrel, knave and devil, until we are exhausted, overwhelmed and disarmed. Then looking at the victor with disinterested objectivity we recognize him: St. Michael smilingly sheathes his sword.

The power which brought about the fight was grace. The "evil" which caused our anxiety was, in the last analysis, grace. And even the real scoundrels, our competitors in egocentricity who betrayed us and wounded us so unjustly, even they, as we discover now, were already working unknowingly and unwillingly in the service of the superhuman strategy of grace. This fact is no excuse for their evil-doing; but it shows the transcendent power and wisdom of the coming Kingdom of Heaven. And above all it shows that the Kingdom is there already and is working in spite of and even through the errors and felonies of its prospective citizens.

Here begins the third stage of the journey, identical with the "illumination" of the old mystics. It is not only an intellectual insight but is at the same time an emotional experience of utmost reality and a volitional change which overthrows the whole system of our values, goals and means. It gives us a new viewpoint, or rather a double viewpoint, which enables us to see people at the same time as rascals and as children of God. Evil reveals its creative implications, and what we deemed to be good now shows its fiendish danger as the devil's bait. Deeper insight, more power, increasing responsibility, and above all a higher kind of love, more detached and more comprehensive—these are the characteristics of the new life, as far as we are able to describe them in a language of our empirical, and that means humanly limited, psychology.

The "unconscious of the past," we may say, was conditioned by our images and their historical forms. The "unconscious of the future" is conditioned by the center itself. It is creative power, using the images, now cleansed and timeless, according to its creative plans, which are our own unconscious goals. The crisis then is the transition from an eccentric less conscious and less powerful life—pivoting around the Ego-image or an idolized image—to a well-centered, more conscious and more powerful life—pivoting around the real Self. This Self proves to be the center both of the individual and of the group, and therefore transforms the individual into a servant of the group—that is love; and proves to be also our relation to God, and therefore transforms individuals and groups into servants of God—that is faith. The crisis, if it is complete, means conversion.[11]*–**

Fritz Kunkel, M.D., 1889–1956. American psychiatrist.
In Search of Maturity.

The first stage [in the process of "individuation"[12]] leads to the experience of the *shadow*, which symbolizes our "other aspect," or "dark brother," who belongs inseparably to our totality. The meeting with the shadow often coincides with the making conscious of the functional type to which one belongs.[13] The shadow is an archetypal figure that often appears even today personified in many forms in the conceptions of primitives. It forms a part of the individual, a kind of split-off part of his being which is nevertheless joined with him just "like a shadow." Confronting one's shadow means becoming unsparingly critically conscious of one's own nature. The shadow stands, so to speak, on the threshold of the way to the unconscious. Only when we have learned to distinguish ourselves from it, having accepted its reality as a part of our being and remaining always aware of this fact, can the encounter with the other psychic pairs of opposites succeed. Then, and then only, commences that objective attitude towards one's own personality without which there is no progress along the way to totality.

The second stage of the individuation process is characterized by the meeting with the figure of the "soul-image," named by Jung the *anima* in the man, the *animus* in the woman.

The soul-image is a more or less firmly constituted functional complex, and the inability to distinguish one's self from it leads to such phenomena as those of the moody man, dominated by feminine drives, ruled by his emotions, or of the rationalizing, animus-obsessed woman who al-

[11]What the mystics called "union" is a later event.

[12]See 61–65 Jung's description of this process.—Ed.

[13]The four functions are: feeling, sensation, thinking, intuition. 325.—Ed.

ways knows better and reacts in a masculine way, not instinctively. One has then the impression that another, a strange person has "taken possession" of the individual.

The variety of forms in which the soul-image can appear is nearly inexhaustible. It is seldom unambiguous, almost always a complexly opalescent phenomenon, equipped with all properties of the most contradictory nature in so far as these are typically feminine or masculine respectively.

"The first bearer of the soul-image is probably always the mother; later it is those women who excite the man's fancy, whether in a positive or negative sense." The release from the mother is one of the most important and most delicate problems in the realization of personality. The primitives possess for this purpose a whole series of ceremonies, initiations to manhood, rites of rebirth, *etc.*, in which the initiant receives such instructions as shall enable him to dispense with the guardianship of the mother. The European, however, must gain "acquaintanceship" with his feminine or masculine psychological component through the process of making conscious this component in his own psyche. That the figure of the soul-image, the contrasexual in one's own psyche, especially with the Occidental is so deeply repressed in the unconscious and accordingly plays a decisive and often troublesome role is in great part the fault of our patriarchically oriented culture. The repression of feminine traits and inclinations in a man leads naturally to an accumulation of these needs in the unconscious. Thus it can often be his own worst weakness that the man marries, which explains many a "queer marriage," and it happens no differently to the woman.

The animus is mostly represented by a multiplicity of figures, by "something like an assemblage of fathers and other authorities who pronounce *ex cathedra* incontestable, 'sensible' judgments." Often these are, in the first place, uncritically accepted opinions, prejudices, principles, which mislead the woman to wrangling and argumentation. But just as the anima is not merely symbol of the dangers of the drives waiting their chance for seduction in the dark of the unconscious, but at the same time signifies man's light and inspiring guide, leading him onwards, not downwards, so is the animus not only the "devil of opinions," the renegade from all logic, but "also a productive, creative being, albeit not in the form of masculine productiveness but as fructifying word, as *"logos spermatikos."* As the man gives birth to his work out of his inner "femininity," as a rounded whole, and the anima thereby becomes his inspiring muse, so the inner "masculine" of the woman often brings forth creative germs able to fertilize the feminine in the man. Thus the two sexes complement each other here as well in a fortunate interplay, not only on the physical level but also in that mysterious stream pregnant with images that flows through and unites the depths of their souls.

We generally choose our partners so that they stand for the unknown, unconscious part of our psyche. When this part has been made conscious, one no longer shoves off his own faults onto the feminine or masculine partner, *i.e.*, the projection is resolved. Thus a quantity of psychic energy, which up to then lay bound in the projection, is taken back and can be placed at the disposal of one's own ego. In this way too one comes "to one's self"—not in the way of self-complacency indeed, as in narcissism, but in the way of self-recognition. If one has seen through and made conscious the contrasexual in his own psyche, then one has himself and his emotions and affects in hand. That means above all real independence, although at the same time—isolation, that isolation of the "inwardly free" whom no love relation or partnership can hold in chains, for whom the other sex has lost its mystery because they have learned to know its fundamental traits in the depths of their own psyche. Such a man, too, will scarcely be able to "fall in love" any more, for he can no more lose himself in another; but he will be capable of so much the deeper "love" in the sense of consciously giving himself to the other. For his isolation does not estrange him from the world; it only gives him a proper distance from it. It makes possible to him a devotion to fellow-men still more unrestricted because no longer dangerous to his individuality. True, it requires in most cases half a lifetime until this step is reached. Probably no one attains it without a struggle. A full measure of experience—indeed of disappointment—likewise belongs thereto. The encounter with the soul-image is therefore not a task of youth but of maturity. Probably on this account it becomes only in the course of later life a necessity to dispose of this problem.

As the making conscious of the shadow makes possible the knowledge of our other, dark aspect, so does the making conscious of the soul-image enable us to gain knowledge of the contrasexual in our own psyche. When this image is recognized and revealed, then it ceases to work from out of the unconscious and allows us finally to differentiate this contrasexual component and to incorporate it into our conscious orientation, through which an extraordinary enrichment of the contents belonging to our consciousness and therewith a broadening of our personality is attained.

A further portion of the way is now made free. When all the difficulties of the confrontation with the soul-image are overcome, then new archetypes arise that compel the individual to a new reckoning and a new definition of his position. The whole process is, as far as we can see, directed towards a goal.

The personification of the spiritual principle can be distinguished as the next milestone of inner development. Its counterpart in the individuation process of the woman is the *Magna Mater,* the great earth-mother, which represents the cold and objective truth of nature. The moment has arrived for analysing and exploring no longer the contrasexual part of the psyche, as in the case of the anima and the animus, but that part of it which constitutes, so to speak, our very essence—for going back to the primordial image after which it has been formed. It is necessary to make conscious the whole range of possibilities one carries within one's self, from the crudest "primordial being" up to the highest, most differentiated and most nearly perfect symbol. To this end both figures, the "Old Wise Man" as well as the "Magna Mater," may appear in an infinite variety of shapes. Jung calls these archetypal figures of the unconscious "Mana personalities." To possess mana means to have effective power over others, but also to run the danger of becoming presumptuous and vainglorious thereby. The making conscious of those contents which constitute the archetype of the mana personality signifies therefore "for the man the second and true liberation from the father, for the woman that from the mother, and therewith the first perception of their own unique individuality." Only when the individual has come thus far can he, may he in the true sense of the word "become united with God in a spiritual childhood." The basically double nature of the psyche is recognized. Yet the forces activated in the individual by these insights only stand really at his disposal when he has learned to distinguish himself from them in humility.

Now we are no longer far from the goal. The archetypal image that leads out of this polarity to the union of both partial systems—consciousness and the unconscious—through a common mid-point is named: the *self*. It marks the last station on the way of individuation, which Jung calls self-realization. Only when this mid-point is found and integrated can one speak of a "whole" man. Only then, namely, has he solved the problem of his relation to the two realities to which we are subject, the inner and the outer, which constitutes an extraordinarily difficult, both ethical and epistemological task.

The birth of the Self signifies for the conscious personality not only a displacement of the previous psychological centre, but also as consequence thereof a completely altered view of and attitude towards life, a "transformation" in the fullest sense of the word.*–**

Jolande Jacobi, 1890–1973. Swiss analytical psychologist.
The Psychology of Jung. Trans. K. W. Bash.

Progression Presented Allegorically

"Picture men in an underground cave-dwelling, with a long entrance reaching up towards the light along the whole width of the cave; in this they lie from their childhood, their legs and necks in chains, so that they stay where they are and look only in front of them, as the chain prevents them turning their heads round. Some way off, and higher up, a fire is burning behind them, and between the fire and the prisoners is a road on higher ground. Imagine a wall built along this road, like the screens which showmen have in front of the audience, over which they show the puppets."

"I have it," he said.

"Then picture also men carrying along this wall all kinds of articles which overtop it, statues of men and other creatures in stone and wood and other materials; naturally some of the carriers are speaking, others are silent."

"A strange image and strange prisoners," he said.

"They are like ourselves," I answered. "For in the first place, do you think that such men would have seen anything of themselves or of each other except the shadows thrown by the fire on the wall of the cave opposite to them?"

"How could they," he said, "if all their life they had been forced to keep their heads motionless?"

"What would they have seen of the things carried along the wall? Would it not be the same?"

"Surely."

"Then if they were able to talk with one another, do you not think that they would suppose what they saw to be the real things?"

"Necessarily."

"Let us suppose one of them was released, and forced suddenly to stand up and turn his head, and walk and look towards the light. What do you think he would say if he were told by some one that before he had been seeing mere foolish phantoms. And, further, if each of the several figures passing by were pointed out to him, and he were asked to say what each was, do you not think that he would be perplexed, and would imagine that the things he had seen before were truer than those now pointed out to him?"

"Yes, much truer," he said.

"Then if he were forced to look at the light itself, would not his eyes ache, and would he not try to escape and turn back to things which he could look at, and think that they were really more distinct than the things shown him?"

"Yes," he said.

"But," I said, "if some one were to drag him out up the steep and rugged ascent, and did not let go till he had been dragged up to the light of the sun, would not his forced journey be one of pain and annoyance; and when he came to the light would not his eyes be so full of the glare that he would not be able to see a single one of the objects we now call true?"

"Certainly, not all at once," he said.

"Yes, I fancy that he would need time before he could see things in the world above. At first he would most easily see shadows, then the reflections in water of men and everything else, and, finally, the things themselves. Last of all, I fancy he would be able to look at the sun and observe its nature, not its appearances in water or on alien material, but the very sun itself in its own place?"

"Inevitably," he said.

"And that done, he would then come to infer concerning it that it is the sun which produces the seasons and years, and controls everything in the sphere of the visible, and is in a manner the author of all those things which he and his fellow-prisoners used to see?"

"It is clear that this will be his next conclusion," he said.

"Well, then, if he is reminded of his original abode and its wisdom, and those who were then his fellow-prisoners, do you not think that he will pity them and count himself happy in the change?"

"Certainly."

"Would he not rather suffer anything rather than be so the victim of seeming and live in their way?"

"Yes," he said, "I certainly think that he would endure anything rather than that."

"Then consider this point," I said. "If this man were to descend again and take his seat in his old place, would not his eyes be full of darkness because he had just come out of the sunlight?"

"Most certainly," he said.

"And suppose that he had again to take part with the prisoners there in the old contest of distinguishing between the shadows, while his sight was confused and before his eyes had got steady (and it might take them quite a considerable time to get used to the darkness), would not men laugh at him, and say that having gone up above he had come back with his sight ruined, so that it was not worth while even to try to go up? And do you not think that they would kill him who tried to release them and bear them up, if they could lay hands on him, and slay him?"

"Certainly," he said.

"Now this simile, my dear Gloucon, must be applied in all its parts to what we said before. In the world of knowledge the Form of the good is perceived last and with difficulty, but when it is seen it must be inferred that it is the cause of all that is right and beautiful in all things, producing in the visible world light and the lord of light, and being itself lord in the intelligible world and the giver of trust and reason and this Form of the good must be seen by whosoever would act wisely in public or in private."

"I agree with you," he said, "so far as I am capable."

"A sensible man would remember that the eyes may be confused in two ways, and for two reasons—by a change from light to darkness, or from darkness to light. He will consider that the same may happen with the soul, and when he sees a soul in trouble and unable to perceive, he will not laugh without thinking; rather he will examine whether it has come from a brighter light and is dim because it is not accustomed to the darkness, or whether it is on its way from ignorance to greater brightness and is dazzled with the greater brilliance; and so he will count the first happy in its condition and its life, but the second he will pity."

"Then," I said, "if these things be true, education is not what certain of its professors declare it to be. They say, if you remember, that they put knowledge in the soul where no knowledge has been, as men putting sight into blind eyes."

"Yes, they do," he said.

"But our present argument," I said, "shows that there resides in each man's soul this faculty and the instrument wherewith he learns, and that it is just as if the eye could not turn from darkness to light unless the whole body turned with it; so this faculty and instrument must be wheeled round together with the whole soul away from that which is becoming, until it is able to look upon and to endure being and the brightest blaze of being; and that we declare to be the good. Do we not?"

"Yes."

"Education then," I said, "will be an art of doing this, an art of conversion, and will consider in what manner the soul will be turned round most easily and effectively. Its aim will not be to implant vision in the instrument of sight. It will regard it as already possessing that, but as being turned in a wrong direction, and not looking where it ought, and it will try to set this right."*

Plato, 427?–347 B.C. Greek philosopher,
disciple of Socrates and teacher of Aristotle.
The Republic. Trans. A. D. Lindsay.

Obstacles to Progression[14]

Something hath puddled his clear spirit. . . . And in such cases, men's natures wrangle with inferior things, though great ones are their object.*

William Shakespeare, 1564–1616.
Othello.

Contradictions within Modern Culture

Making use of anthropological findings we must recognize that some of our conceptions about human nature are rather naïve, for example, the idea that competitiveness, sibling rivalry, kinship between affection and sexuality are trends inherent in human nature. Our conception of normality is arrived at by the approval of certain standards of behavior and feeling within a certain group which imposes these standards upon its members. But the standards vary with culture, period, class and sex.

Modern culture is economically based on the principle of individual competition. The isolated individual has to fight with other individuals of the same group, has to surpass them and, frequently, thrust them aside. The advantage of the one is frequently the disadvantage of the other. The psychic result of this situation is a diffuse hostile tension between individuals. Everyone is the real or potential competitor of everyone else. This situation is clearly apparent among members of the same occupational group, regardless of strivings to be fair or of attempts to camouflage by polite considerateness. It must be emphasized, however, that competitiveness, and the potential hostility that accompanies it, pervades all human relationships. It pervades the relationships between men and men, between women and women, and whether the point of competition be popularity, competence, attractiveness or any social value it greatly impairs the possibilities of reliable friendship. It also, as already indicated, disturbs the relations between men and women, not only in the choice of the partner but in the entire struggle with him for superiority. It pervades school

[14] Also see Chap. II under "Self-Knowledge" and Chap. VI under "Psychotherapy."—Ed.

life. And perhaps most important of all, it pervades the family situation, so that as a rule the child is inoculated with this germ from the very beginning. The rivalry between father and son, mother and daughter, one child and another, is not a general human phenomenon but is the response to culturally conditional stimuli.

The potential hostile tension between individuals results in a constant generation of fear—fear of the potential hostility of others, reinforced by a fear of retaliation for hostilities on one's own. Another important source of fear in the normal individual is the prospect of failure. The fear of failure is a realistic one because, in general, the chances of failing are much greater than those of succeeding, and because failures in a competitive society entail a realistic frustration of needs. They mean not only economic insecurity but also loss of prestige and all kinds of emotional frustrations.

All these factors together result psychologically in the individual feeling that he is isolated. Even when he has many contacts with others, even when he is happily married, he is emotionally isolated. Emotional isolation is hard for anyone to endure; it becomes a calamity, however, if it coincides with apprehensions and uncertainties about one's self.

It is this situation which provokes, in the normal individual of our time, an intensified need for affection as a remedy. Obtaining affection makes him feel less isolated, less threatened by hostility and less uncertain of himself. Because it corresponds to a vital need, love is overvalued in our culture. It becomes a phantom—like success—carrying with it the illusion—although in our culture it is most often a screen for satisfying wishes that have nothing to do with it—but it is made an illusion by our expecting much more of it than it can possibly fulfill. And the ideological emphasis that we place on love serves to cover up the factors which create our exaggerated need for it. Hence the individual—and I still mean the normal individual—is in the dilemma of needing a great deal of affection but finding difficulty in obtaining it.

The situation thus far represents a fertile ground for the development of neuroses. The same cultural factors that affect the normal person . . . affect the neurotic to a higher degree and in him the same results are merely intensified.

When we remember that in every neurosis there are contradictory tendencies which the neurotic is unable to reconcile, the question arises as to whether there are not likewise certain definite contradictions in our culture, which underlie the typical neurotic conflicts. It would be the task of the sociologist to study and describe these cultural contradictions. It must suffice for me to indicate briefly and schematically some of the main contradictory tendencies.

The first contradiction[15] to be mentioned is that between competition and success on the one hand, and brotherly love and humility on the other.

The second contradiction is that between the stimulation of our needs and our factual frustrations in satisfying them. The psychic consequence for the individual is a constant discrepancy between his desires and their fulfillment.

Another contradiction exists between the alleged freedom of the individual and all his factual limitations. The individual is told by society that he is free, independent, can decide his life according to his own free will. In actual fact, for the majority of people all these possibilities are limited. The result for the individual is a wavering between a feeling of boundless power in determining his own fate and a feeling of entire helplessness. While the normal person is able to cope with the difficulties—in the neurotic all the conflicts are intensified to a degree that makes a satisfactory solution impossible.

It seems that the person who is likely to become neurotic is one who has experienced the culturally determined difficulties in an accentuated form, mostly through the medium of childhood experiences, and who has consequently been unable to solve them, or has solved them only at great cost to his personality. We might call him a stepchild of our culture.*

Karen Horney, M.D., 1885–1952. American psychoanalyst.
The Neurotic Personality of Our Time.

THE ONE-SIDEDNESS OF MAN'S DEVELOPMENT

I think the answer [to the present dilemma] is to be found in our general one-sided attitude, in our exaggerated materialism and gross overvaluation of the physical world and of man's achievements in the physical world. It is so

[15]See the author's text for a fuller discussion of these contradictions, pp. 281, 290.—Ed.

because this one-sidedness is a product of long and steady growth. In itself it is not so very reprehensible. It is, after all, the time-honoured way whereby man makes his living and increases his holding in the black forest and among the blind forces of nature about him. The trouble only starts when the process is pushed too far, for then a law of diminishing returns sets in and threatens the integrity of man's spirit. Other aspects of man which have been overlooked and neglected because of this favouritism towards one part of himself tend to rise in angry rebellion against him. He is forced then, if he is not to be torn asunder, to reverse a process to which he owes much and to suspend a most valuable evolutionary trend. This is something which few individuals and no nation yet seem to have accomplished without the *help* of disaster. Oh, the phenomenon is not new! The favoured aspect varies from age to age, but the machinery for this kind of excess breeding more excess and then begetting its own vengeful redress, is as old as life itself. It is a constantly recurring theme in the Greek tragedies. Chinese thinking is deeply influenced by it and expresses the belief that everything in life sooner or later goes over into its opposite. "At midnight noon is born," the Chinese proverb says. Thus the legends and mythology of the world are all full of a submerged warning to man against the danger of indefinitely exceeding a part of himself at the expense of totality in personality.

There, for instance, we have the key to the significance of the one-eyed giants who stride so strangely through Greek and Roman mythology. I suspect that their gruesome presence there does not mean that a race of one-eyed colossi once walked the earth with seven-leagued strides and brushed the thunder clouds out of their hair. Only on the most elementary and literal levels can they be taken to represent a man grown into monstrous physique with only one eye in the middle of his forehead. But in the aboriginal language of the spirit, in the underlying thought processes of man . . . the giant is the image of a man who has grossly exceeded himself in a part of himself. Only one eye is planted in the cretin head to indicate that he has not the two-way vision that the complete spirit needs but only this one-way look into a world of outward-bound senses. So also the two eyes of contemporary man when they focus as *one* on the outer physical world give him only one-way sight and admit of only one-way traffic. European man is fast forgetting to balance the fixed outward stare with a questioning inward glance, and therein lies our great and growing danger. In the manner immemorial of the spirit this aspect of fundamental meaning is first made accessible to the mind by dramatic personification. The giant and his one eye are projected like an image in a cinema onto the darkened screen of our minds to draw attention to this constantly recurring danger which besets man on his odyssey back from honourable battle in the physical world towards the fulfillment he has earned on the island-self he left behind him when he was young. The poet Blake, too, illustrates and confirms this in a manner closer to our own time. Blake had a uniquely inspired intuition of inner reality. Not only is his poetry full of unconscious truth but also his many canvases are charged with magnetic personifications of the neglected titans and unused energies in modern man's averted nature. In "The Marriage of Heaven and Hell" he showed an acute awareness of one of the abiding problems of culture in a world "of dark satanic mills," a problem which is inextricably entangled with the situation we are discussing today. He was one of the first to spot the "one-eyed giant" of our time poking his head up above the clear horizon of what was considered to be the beginning of an era of permanent enlightenment and reason. His intuitive awareness of the presence of this danger was so accurate and acute . . . that he actually wrote of the "one-eyed vision of science." . . . The age of one-eyed giants is never over. If they disappear temporarily from one aspect of our being they quickly reappear in another. They are always within us and about us. . . . Though our cave is furnished with up-to-date comfort and equipped with all modern conveniences, though it is air-conditioned and bright with electric light, it is an archaic prison of a vital part of ourselves nonetheless. . . . Thus we are sealed off, as Odysseus and his crew were in the cave, from the sun, the moon, the stars. The unmanned ship grates its urgent keel on the yellow foreshore, its sails flap idly in the wind that would carry us home from some warring beachhead in the world without to wholeness with the half we left behind on an island self when young.*

Laurens Van der Post, 1906–. British author.
The Dark Eye in Africa.

The neglect of the inner or subjective aspect of life has led, particularly for woman, to a certain falsification of her living values. For example, in the conventional judgment of the past a woman had one prime adaptation to make, the adaptation of wife and mother. If she married well she succeeded, if she failed to marry she was all too likely to be considered a failure. . . . If any difficulty arose in her relation to her husband her tendency was, and still often is, to seek for an external remedy. . . . The subjective side of the problem was [and still is] in most cases discounted and allowed to vent itself only in moods or bad temper, or in some neurotic disturbance.

. . . In more recent times a woman faced with home problems of this character, perhaps a badly maladjusted child, would learn something of modern psychology and child training and try by applying what she had learned, objectively, to accomplish by an external technique what would really follow naturally if she did but know how to apply her own feminine feelings and reactions to the situation. But in so far as her own subjective life is disregarded, this natural effect of her being is nullified and she is left with no resource but a mechanical technique, at best a poor substitute for a living reality.

Today, the success or failure of a woman's life is not judged to anything like the same extent on the exclusive criterion of marriage. Her adaptation to life may now be made in various ways, each of which offers some opportunity for solving the problems of work, of social relations, and of her emotional needs. If, however, in order to gain discipline and development on all sides of her personality she seeks to make an adjustment to life which is not one-sided but is as many faceted as her own nature, her task is a most complex one. For while the stirrings within, which require a field of activity in the outer objective world, are accepted by herself and others as legitimate, other longings, which also have their origin deep within her being and which seek for a spiritual and subjective fulfillment, are not so generally acknowledged. . . .

So pressing have these subjective problems become, however, in many instances, that the psychological factor which the older physical scientist eliminated is now being eagerly sought out and analyzed. . . . For every human being has not only impulses and instincts which need a life lived collectively in the social group for their satisfaction but other instincts and impulses also which urge him to find himself as a unique individual. Each one has a nature which seeks for love and relationship, and also there is imbedded in everyone the necessity to strive for impersonal truth. These opposing tendencies are expressions of the duality of human nature which is both objective and subjective. In all human beings such an opposition is at work and leads inevitably to conflict. In the Western world of today this conflict is most severe and bears hardest upon women because Western civilization lays especial emphasis on the value of the outer, and this fits in more nearly with man's nature than with woman's. The feminine spirit is more subjective, more concerned with feelings and relationships than with the laws and principles of the outer world. And so it happens that the conflict between outer and inner is usually more devastating for women than for men.

There is another reason why this problem is a particularly urgent one for women today. This is related to the recent development of the masculine side of woman's nature which has been so marked a feature of recent years.[16] This masculine development is definitely related to her life in the world of affairs; in the majority of cases it is even sought as a prerequisite for earning a living in the world, practicing a profession, or following a trade. The change of character, which has accompanied this evolution, does not stop at the professional part of a woman's life but affects her whole personality and has caused profound changes in her relation to herself and to others. . . .

. . . These changes have produced for woman an unavoidable inner conflict between the urge to express herself through work, as a man does, and the inner necessity to live in accordance with her own ancient feminine nature.[17] This conflict seems to condition the whole experience of life for all those modern women who are at all aware of themselves as conscious individuals. For them a one-sided life is not sufficient; the conflict between the opposing ten-

[16]For a fuller discussion of this subject see M. E. Harding, *The Way of All Women* (Longmans, Green, 1933).—Ed.

[17]*Ibid.* Also see the full text of *Woman's Mysteries;* and see *Human Relationships* by Eleanor Bertine, M.D. (Refer to Recommended Reading list.)—Ed.

dencies of masculine and feminine within them has to be faced. They cannot resume the feminine values in the old instinctive and unconscious way. Through acquiring a new degree of consciousness they have cut themselves off from the easy road of nature. If they are to get in touch with their lost feminine side it must be by the hard road of a conscious adaptation.*

M. Esther Harding, M.D., 1888–1971. American psychiatrist. *Woman's Mysteries.*

Protestant Christianity has, almost from its inception, been overweighted on the rational side, leading inevitably to an impoverishment of the feeling and irrational aspects. Although the Reformation brought with it precious and needed correctives which contributed to man's phenomenal thrust toward consciousness—with the consequent release of his inventive genius and the assumption of greater individual responsibility—its enthronement of Logos (the Word) and the subsequent devaluation of Eros (feeling) helped create an imbalance which is only beginning to be recognized, since it still remains so largely unconscious.

The "Sermon" and the "Bible" were elevated to primary positions in religious services while Ritual, Symbol and the Mysteries, even of Grace itself, became suspect. Yet it is through the symbol[18]—the language of the unconscious—that the deeper levels of man's being have always expressed themselves. Stripped of this means of communication, man becomes cut off from a reservoir of meaning which seems to be available to him in no other way.

Also the masculine emphasis on perfection has tended to exclude the more feminine aspect of "wholeness" or "completeness" as a part of the religious goal and to that extent has distorted the religious process. This one-sidedness has had a profound influence on our whole culture as can be seen in our educational institutions with their tendency toward a scientific, success-ridden orientation, as well as in our religious institutions and practices.

It is startling to most people to realize that the Christian concept of the Holy Trinity is wholly masculine, at least as usually recognized in contemporary Protestantism. The

---

[18]Symbols represent realities whose meaning is still partially, if not wholly, beyond conscious or rational comprehension (see p. 248–250).—Ed.

Catholic Church, to be sure, has long allowed for the feminine element and has expressed it through an emphasis on the Virgin Mary[19] ("Mother of God"), so recently and significantly honored by the Church through the newly established dogma of the Assumption of the Blessed Virgin. But Protestant awareness of the roots of this imbalance has been slow in emerging. As it does appear, and there are signs that it is beginning to do so, it can doubtless be expected to assume an entirely different kind of configuration and probably on a much more conscious and thus integrative level.

The impact of this patriarchal orientation has been felt as well in political life—both national and international. It may be one of the underlying causes of the difficulty in the "Meeting of East and West," each representing to the other, as it does, the unknown—and thus usually to be feared—"other side." The Eastern glorification of the feminine, contemplative, subjective aspect contrasts sharply with the Western activist, materialistic, objective approach to life. We are being forced to recognize the effects of this disparity in our culture since it engenders attitudes that ignore the twofold approach to reality inherent in the very nature of the personality structure. It thus exacts a fearful toll as is witnessed increasingly in the consulting rooms of both ministers and psychotherapists.

It is encouraging to note that the difficulties arising from this one-sidedness are already leading to a fresh appraisal of the situation at its root base, i.e., a re-examination of the nature of both feminine and masculine principles such as function as integral parts of man's nature. The discovery is being made anew that each of us is essentially whole—both masculine and feminine—Yin and Yang (earth and sky)—Eros and Logos; and that an individual or a society when geared to only one aspect is bound to become distorted and incomplete in both development and effect. The West, and we believe the East as well, is beginning to recognize in this connection that sex equality is a reality and not a myth; and, further and most important, that it must be given a

[19]What was known as the Cult of Mary originated in the tenth century and flourished up to the thirteenth century. The Reformation represented a reaction against the matriarchal emphasis of that early period.

chance to function in actuality as such. Western civilization needs to acknowledge the value of the feminine side and learn to perceive the validity of the maxim expressed by Lao-tzu so long ago, "He who, being a man, remains a woman, will become a universal channel." This truth seen in its larger context and in converse form represents the "totality" toward which all life and all civilizations strive.

Dr. M. Esther Harding points up the crucial need of our modern situation when she writes in *Woman's Mysteries:* "Unless an understanding of the principle of woman can be apprehended anew no further step can be taken either in psychological development of woman herself, nor in the nature of the relationship which is possible between men and women. Indeed we can go a step further than that, for men also need a relation to the feminine principle, not only that they may better understand women, but also because their contact with the inner or spiritual world is governed not by masculine but by feminine laws as Jung has pointed out in his writings.[20] So that a new relation to this woman principle is urgently needed today to counteract the one-sidedness of the prevailing masculine mode of Western civilization."

The Effect of Mechanization—a Woman's Viewpoint

. . . The world today does not understand, in either man or woman, the need to be alone. How inexplicable it seems. Anything else will be accepted as a better excuse. If one sets aside time for a business appointment, a trip to the hairdresser, a social engagement, or a shopping expedition, that time is accepted as inviolable. But if one says: I cannot come because that is my hour to be alone, one is considered rude, egotistical or strange. What a commentary on our civilization, when being alone is considered suspect. . . .

Women [especially] need solitude in order to find again the true essence of themselves: that firm strand which will be the indispensable center of a whole web of human relationships. . . . [Yet], solitude alone is not the answer; it is only a step toward it, a mechanical aid. . . . The problem is more how to still the soul in the midst of its activities. In

[20]See *Two Essays on Analytical Psychology* (Princeton Univ. Press 1953).—Ed.

fact, the problem is how to feed the soul. For it is the spirit of woman that is going dry, not the mechanics that are wanting. Mechanically, woman has gained in the past generation. . . . [But] with our garnered free time, we are more apt to drain our creative springs than to refill them. With our pitchers, we attempt sometimes to water a field, not a garden. We throw ourselves indiscriminately into committees and causes. Not knowing how to feed the spirit, we try to muffle its demands in distractions. . . .

In other times, women had in their lives more forces which centered them whether or not they realized it. . . . Their very seclusion in the home gave them time alone. Many of their duties were conducive to a quiet contemplative drawing together of the self. They had more creative tasks to perform. Nothing feeds the center so much as creative work, even humble kinds like cooking and sewing. Baking bread, weaving cloth, putting up preserves, teaching and singing to children, must have been far more nourishing than being the family chauffeur or shopping at supermarkets, or doing housework with mechanical aids. . . . In housework, as in the rest of life, the curtain of mechanization has come down between the mind and the hand. . . .

[Yet] the answer is not in going back, in putting woman in the home and giving her the broom and the needle again. A number of mechanical aids save us time and energy. But neither is the answer . . . in the feverish pursuit of centrifugal activities which only lead in the end to fragmentation. Woman's life today is tending more and more toward the state William James describes so well in the German word, "Zerrissenheit—torn-to-pieces-hood." She cannot live perpetually in "Zerrissenheit." She will be shattered into a thousand pieces. On the contrary, she must consciously encourage those pursuits which oppose the centrifugal forces of today. . . . It need not be an enormous project or a great work. But it should be something of one's own. Arranging a bowl of flowers in the morning can give a sense of quiet in a crowded day—like writing a poem, or saying a prayer. What matters is that one be for a time inwardly attentive. . . .

To the possession of the self the way is inward, says Plotinus. The cell of self-knowledge is the stall in which the pilgrim must be reborn, says St. Catherine of Siena. Voices from the past. In fact, these are pursuits and virtues of the past. But done in another way today because done consciously, aware, with eyes open. Not done as before, as part of the pattern of the time. Not done because everyone else is doing them; almost no one is doing them. Revolutionary, in fact, because almost every trend and pressure, every voice from the outside is against this new way of inward living.

Woman must be the pioneer in this turning inward for strength. In a sense she has always been the pioneer. Less able, until the last generation, to escape into outward activities, the very limitations of her life forced her to look inward. And from looking inward she gained an inner strength which man in his outward active life did not as often find. But in our recent efforts to emancipate ourselves, to prove ourselves the equal of man, we have, naturally enough perhaps, been drawn into competing with him in his outward activities, to the neglect of our own inner springs. . . . Why have we been seduced into abandoning this timeless inner strength of woman for the temporal outer strength of man? This outer strength of man is essential to the pattern, but even here the reign of purely outer strength and purely outward solutions seems to be waning today. Men, too, are being forced to look inward—to find inner solutions as well as outer ones. Perhaps this change marks a new stage of maturity for modern extrovert, activist, materialistic Western man. Can it be that he is beginning to realize that the kingdom of heaven is within?*

Anne Morrow Lindbergh, 1906–. American poet, writer.
Gift from the Sea.

Society Based on Organized Lovelessness

Our present economic, social and international arrangements are based, in large measure, upon organized lovelessness. We begin by lacking charity towards Nature, so that instead of trying to cooperate with Tao or the Logos on the inanimate and subhuman levels, we try to dominate and exploit, we waste the earth's mineral resources, ruin its soil, ravage its forests, pour filth into its rivers and poisonous fumes into its air. From lovelessness in relation to Nature we advance to lovelessness in relation to art—a lovelessness so extreme that we have effectively killed all the fundamental or useful arts and set up various kinds of mass production by machines in their place. And of course this lovelessness in regard to art is at the same time a lovelessness in regard to the human beings who have to perform the fool-proof and grace-proof tasks imposed by our mechanical art-surrogates and by the interminable paper work connected with mass production and mass distribution. With mass-production and mass-distribution go mass-financing, and the three have conspired to expropriate ever-increasing numbers of small owners of land and productive equipment, thus reducing the sum of freedom among the majority and increasing the power of a minority to exercise a coercive control over the lives of their fellows. This coercively controlling minority is composed of private capitalists or governmental bureaucrats or of both classes of bosses acting in collaboration—and, of course, the coercive and therefore essentially loveless nature of the control remains the same, whether the bosses call themselves "company directors" or "civil servants." The only difference between these two kinds of oligarchical rulers is that the first derive more of their power from wealth than from position within a conventionally respected hierarchy, while the second derive more power from position than from wealth. Upon this fairly uniform groundwork of loveless relationships are imposed others which vary widely from one society to another, according to local conditions and local habits of thought and feeling. Here are a few examples: contempt and exploitation of coloured minorities living among white majorities, or of coloured majorities governed by minorities of white imperialists; hatred of Jews, Catholics, Free Masons, or of any other minority whose language, habits, appearance or religion happens to differ from those of the local majority. And the crowning superstructure of uncharity is the organized lovelessness of the relations between state and sovereign state—a lovelessness that expresses itself in the axiomatic assumption that it is right and natural for national organizations to behave like thieves and murderers, armed to the teeth and ready, at the first favourable opportunity, to steal and kill.

So long as the organized lovelessness of war and preparation for war remains, there can be no mitigation, on any large, nation-wide or world-wide scale, of the organized lovelessness of our economic and political relationships. War and preparation for war are standing temptations to make the present bad, God-eclipsing arrangements of society progressively worse as technology becomes progressively more efficient.*

Aldous Huxley, 1894–1963. English writer, literary critic.
The Perennial Philosophy.

The Habitual Cast of Thought

Novices in the spiritual life know of sin only as a positive violation of God's Law, and are unaware that there is an habitual cast of thought that is more dangerous than an actual evil act. They come imbued with the spirit of the world and fashioned to the habits, formed by the years of living according to that spirit. Life has been for them a tissue of those ideas, judgments, sentiments, principles, hopes, fears, desires, regrets and dreams which envelop the souls of men, corrupt their vision and little by little hide from them heaven and the eternity for which they are destined. To those entering on the spiritual life, things spiritual have appealed but vaguely, whilst all that can be seen, weighed, touched and handled, alone have had value in their eyes. . . . The beginning of the interior life is therefore much occupied with intellectual activity. It is devoted to the consideration of what we are, of what God is.*

Edward Leen, 1885–1944. Irish Catholic cleric, educator.
Progress Through Mental Prayer.

How many people swell with pride and vanity, for such things as they would not know how to value at all, but that they are admired in the world? Would a man take ten years more drudgery in business to add two horses more to his coach, but that he knows that the world most of all admires a coach and six? How fearful are many people of having their houses poorly furnished, or themselves meanly clothed, for this only reason, lest the world should make no account of them, and place them amongst low and mean people?

How often would a man have yielded to the haughtiness and ill-nature of others, and shewn a submissive temper, but that he dares not pass for such a poor-spirited man in the opinion of the world? Many a man would often drop a resentment, and forgive an affront, but that he is afraid if he should, the world would not forgive him.

How many would practice Christian temperance and sobriety in its utmost perfection, were it not for the censure which the world passes upon such a life? Thus do the impressions which we have received from living in the world, enslave our minds, that we dare not attempt to be eminent in the fight of God, for fear of being little in the eyes of the world. But as great as the power of the world is, it is all built upon a blind obedience, and we need only open our eyes, to get quit of its power.

And therefore, I hope, you will not think it a hard saying, that in order to be humble, you must withdraw your obedience from that vulgar spirit, which gives law to Fops and Coquets, and form your judgments according to the wisdom of Philosophy, and the piety of Religion. Who would be afraid of making such a change as this?

William Law, 1686–1761. English clergyman, mystic.
Serious Call to a Devout and Holy Life.

The Lack of Psychical Culture

It may easily happen that a Christian who believes in all the sacred figures is still undeveloped and unchanged in his inmost soul because he has "all God outside" and does not experience Him in the soul. His deciding motives, his ruling interests and impulses, do not spring from the sphere of Christianity, but from the unconscious and undeveloped psyche, which is as pagan and archaic as ever. Not the individual alone but the sum total of individual lives in a people proves the truth of this contention. The great events of our world as planned and executed by man do not breathe the spirit of Christianity, but rather of unadorned paganism. These things originate in a psychic condition that has remained archaic and has not been even remotely touched by Christianity. . . . Christian civilization has proved hollow to a terrifying degree: it is all veneer, but the inner man has remained untouched and therefore unchanged. His soul is out of key with his external beliefs; in his soul the Christian has not kept pace with external developments. Yes, everything is to be found outside—in image and in word, in Church and Bible—but never inside. Inside reign the archaic gods, supreme as of old; that is to say the inner correspondence with the outer God-image is undeveloped for lack of psychological culture and has therefore got stuck in heathenism. Christian education has done all that is humanly possible, but it has not been enough. Too few people have experienced the divine image as the innermost possession of their own souls. Christ only meets them from without, never from within the soul; that is why dark paganism still reigns there, a paganism which, now in a form so blatant that it can no longer be denied and now in all too threadbare disguise, is swamping the world of so-called Christian culture. . . .

. . . It has yet to be understood that the *mysterium magnum* is not only an actuality but is first and foremost rooted in the human psyche. The man who does not know this from his own experience may be a most learned theologian, but he has no idea of religion and still less of education.*

Carl G. Jung, M.D., 1875–1961. Swiss psychiatrist.
Psychology and Alchemy. Trans. R. F. C. Hull.

It is important that all of us become wise enough to recognize where we go astray in our attitudes toward ourselves and how we become enslaved to false notions of what we are and what we ought to be. Some of us think we are loving ourselves when we are really strangling or suffocating ourselves with morbid self-concern. We maintain a cruel contempt for our own capabilities and virtues or become unconscious victims of a paralyzing egocentricity. When we free ourselves from that false self-love which is narcissism, that destructive self-hatred which is masochism, we become for the first time integrated enough to become friendly with ourselves and with others. We are on the road to proper self-love. Such self-love implies many things, but above everything else it is rooted in self-respect. And no man or woman can have self-respect unless he has learned the art of renunciation and the equally vital art of self-acceptance.*

Joshua Loth Liebman, 1907–1948. American rabbi, educator.
Peace of Mind.

The Obstacles in the Personal Unconscious

The true self-sacrifice is the one that sacrifices the hidden thing in the self which would work harm to ourselves and to others. It is an effort to become more and more conscious of all the forces in the unconscious, of the unworthy personal motives that work underground, as well as the inherited forces, so that our lives shall become more and more full of understanding and of really conscious choice. In this way we do "descend into hell," the depth of the unconscious where lie all those things that would destroy our conscious attitude and which we most fear to face and acknowledge. From such a descent can come a new life if the new understanding is accepted by the individual.

This new life carries on the vital thing which has been born from the old. It often appears in dreams as a child, thus adopting the symbol of the religious concept and giving it form in the rebirth of the individual. Jung, in his dream analysis, calls this the "*puer aeternus,*" the ever-living child. In dreams this child often takes on characteristics which symbolize the special need of the individual, and which give a clue to the new adaptation needed in order to further his integration.

Our greatest task is to have the courage to face the thing that rises in us, whether it take the form of doubt which must be thought out, or the knowledge of the unacceptable thing in ourselves with which we must reckon. In this way only can be found the acceptance of greater consciousness.*

Frances G. Wickes, 1875–1970, American psychotherapist.
The Inner World of Childhood.

Reservations

If you really look into the state of things between God and your soul, you will find that there are certain limits beyond which you refuse to go in offering yourself to Him. People often hover around such reservations, making believe not to see them, for fear of self-reproach, guarding them as the apple of the eye. If you were to break down one of these reservations, you would be touched to the quick and inexhaustible in your reasons for self-justification, a very sure proof of the life of evil. The more you shrink from giving up any such reserved point, the more certain it is that it needs to be given up. If you were not fast bound by it, you would not make so many efforts to convince yourself that you are free.

It is but too true that these and the like frailties hinder God's work in us. We move continually in a vicious circle round self, only thinking of God in connection with ourselves, and making no progress in self-renunciation, lowering of pride or attaining simplicity. Why is it that the vessel does not make way? Is the wind wanting? Nowise; The Spirit of Grace breathes on it, but the vessel is bound by invisible anchors in the depths of the sea. The fault is not God's; it is wholly ours. If we will search thoroughly, we shall soon see the hidden bonds which detain us. That point in which we least mistrust ourselves is precisely that which needs most distrust.

François Fénelon, 1651–1715.
French Archbishop of Cambray.
Spiritual Letters of Archbishop Fénelon. Trans. H. L. Lear.

The Unconscious "Guiding Image" as a Major Obstacle

The purpose of every objective function is service to the world. The purpose of every egocentric function is service to the ego. That is why the egocentric, whether he knows it or not, always acts according to self-evaluation. He has an ego-ideal which he strives to attain, a guiding image by which he measures his worth or worthlessness. He judges everything that happens on the basis of whether it brings him nearer this guiding image or not. The nearer he fancies himself, the happier he is; his unhappiness grows with increase in distance.

This guiding image can be variously formed. It may be, "I want to be as rich as Rothschild," or "as famous as Goethe," or "as poor as Francis," or "suffer as much as Christ on the Cross." The ego-ideal is always distinguished by the fact that its possessor tries to make the material world serve him, while the objective human being places himself (*i.e.,* his ego) at the service of the world.

The number of forms in which egocentricity may appear is infinite. A good portion of an understanding of human nature is necessary to ferret it out of all its disguises and hiding places. It is generally easier to discover egocentricity in others than in ourself, for its discovery in others raises our own ego. Everything is easy for us which serves to elevate our secret picture of ourself.

The more egocentric we are, the more distinctly effective in us are the two extreme levels of the ladder of self-valuation. The wretcheder we feel, the higher lies the level of happiness to which we make claim. The less money we have, the greater the sum which we dream we shall inherit or win in a lottery. The nearer we feel to our ideal, the deeper the level of which we are afraid. The more important a man believes himself, the more irritated he is when he does not receive the customary greeting from a mere mortal.

Characteristic of egocentricity is always the inexorableness of its demands. The ego acts like a monarch who tolerates no contradiction.

Egocentricity without self-deception is not possible. Even he who says, like Richard III, "I am determined to prove a villain," fools not only the world by hiding his weakness in violence; he fools also himself. He conceals from himself the fact that he hates only because he has not the courage to love, and that he says no to the joys of the world because he does not want to say yes to his own suffering. Every egocentric human being deceives himself. Complete insight and egocentricity cannot exist side by side, which is why insight is lessened by egocentricity. It is also why it is possible to discover a little self-deceit in everyone (for everyone is a little egocentric). The more egocentric a person is, however, the more cunningly does he arrange his self-deceit, and the slyer the subterfuges he uses to protect himself against an unmasking. He feels, without admitting it, that his egocentricity would go to pieces in the face of the truth.*

Fritz Kunkel, M.D., 1889—1956. American psychiatrist.
Let's Be Normal.

Hiding from Truth

This is the happy life which all desire, to joy in the truth all men desire. Why then joy they not in it? Why are they not happy? Because they are more strongly taken up with other things which have more power to make them miserable, than that which they so faintly remember to make them happy. For there is yet a little light in men; let them walk, let them walk, that the darkness overtake them not.

But why doth "truth generate hatred," and the man of thine, preaching the truth, become an enemy to them—whereas a happy life is loved, which is nothing else but joying in the truth? They love truth when she enlightens, they hate her when she reproves. For since they would not be deceived, and would deceive, they love her, when she discovers herself unto them, and hate her, when she discovers them. Whence she shall so repay them, that they who would not be made manifest by her, she both against their will makes manifest, and her self becometh not manifest unto them. Thus, thus, yea thus doth the mind of man, thus blind and sick, foul and ill-favoured, wish to be hidden, but that aught should be hidden from it, it wills not. But the contrary is requited it, that itself should not be hidden from the Truth; but the Truth is hid from it. Yet even thus miserable, it has rather joy in truths than in falsehoods. Happy then will man be, when, no distraction interposing, he shall joy in that only Truth, by Whom all things are true.

All consult Thee on what they will, though they hear not always what they will. He is Thy best servant, who looks not so much to hear that from Thee, which himself willeth; as rather to will that, which from Thee he heareth.*–**

Saint Augustine, 354–430. Latin church father.
Confessions. Trans. E. B. Pusey.

Failure in Understanding the Two-sidedness of Personality

I discovered that there is all the difference in the world between knowing something intellectually and knowing it as a "lived" experience. . . . I found that there were different ways of perceiving and that the different ways provided me with different facts. There was a narrow focus which meant seeing life as if from blinkers and with the centre of awareness in my head; and there was a wide focus which meant knowing with the whole of my body a way of looking which quite altered my perception of whatever I saw. . . .

It seemed to me that my difficulties could most conveniently be considered in terms of a failure to understand that every human personality is two-sided, that every man or woman is potentially both male and female. . . . I had unknowingly assumed that the only desirable way to live was a male way—the way of objective understanding and achievement. . . . As soon as I tried to question my experience I began to discover impulses towards a different attitude, impulses which eventually led me to find out the meaning of my own femininity. . . .

Most of the people I knew [both men and women] had made a cult of the male intellect, that is, of objective reasoning as against subjective intuition. I had apparently been submissive towards this fashion, and had for years struggled to talk an intellectual language which for me was barren, struggled to force the feelings of my relation to the universe into terms that would not fit. For I had not understood that a feminine attitude to the universe was just as legitimate, intellectually and biologically, as a masculine one. . . . I found that although the feminine attitude needs the male intellect if it is to understand itself, most of those I knew who possessed competent intellects were not sufficiently both-sided themselves to have any notion of the meaning of subjective intuition whether in a man or a woman. . . .

My early discovery about how delight came when I stopped trying, may have been a first achievement in the understanding of real femininity. I had realized that these good moments occurred when I was able to wipe out my own identity and let the thing I was looking at take possession of me. . . But I had not before understood that the obsession with purposes which had seemed to keep me from such surrender might be in part the attempt to express an inevitably present maleness. . . . I finally learned that my main purpose was to have no purpose, to learn how to give up effort. . . . But why had I been so slow in discovering that by relinquishing I could produce riches . . . ?

What was the source of this fear of surrender in terms of the bisexuality of the human psyche? Was it that to my blind thinking, with its inability to see more than one thing at once, the satisfaction of the female meant the wiping out of the male for ever? To satisfy the feminine to the full without the loss of one's individuality, perhaps this was an idea beyond the powers of blind thinking to grasp. And in its terror of losing the male in the female it had in fact lost both. For I never could be actively myself, throw myself into work or play with complete absorption. I was always on guard lest this urge to femininity should catch me out. So real male achievement in action was inhibited by anxiety and expressed itself in that continual effort after purposes which made femaleness impossible. . . .

My discovery of a natural rhythm of awareness was perhaps the discovery that reflective thinking requires a subtle balance of male and female activity. . . . For the irrational fears had prompted me to contract, to spread round myself a protective ring of tenseness, a sort of "shamming dead," a living in the head high out of reach of the vital interchange of experience, prevented from spreading my perceptive feelers and becoming utterly still and receptive by this panic chatter of pseudo-male purposes. . . .

It seemed, then, that my failure to reflect, my inability to know what I liked or what I wanted, or to draw any conclusions from the welter of my experience, was due to letting my musings remain in the form of an unconscious monologue. . . . I had certainly understood nothing of my own inner life until I had learnt to make that male act of separation and detachment by which I stood aside and looked at my experience. And it seemed that my reluctance to do this was, superficially, the fear of what I might find there, but actually, the fear of a blind urge of femininity.*–**

Joanna Field, contemporary English analyst and author.
Extracts from *A Life of One's Own.*[21]

Impatience and the Lack of Humility

Why should we be in such desperate haste to succeed, and in such desperate enterprises? If a man does not keep pace with his companions, perhaps it is because he hears a different drummer. Let him step to the music which he hears, however measured or far away. It is not important that he should mature as soon as an apple tree or an oak. Shall he turn his spring into summer? If the condition of things which we were made for is not yet, what were any reality which we can substitute? We will not be shipwrecked on a vain reality. Shall we with pains erect a heaven of blue glass over ourselves, though when it is done we shall be sure to gaze still at the true ethereal heaven far above, as if the former were not?

---

[21]This book, first published in 1934, gives a fascinating account of the author's attempt to come to self-knowledge on her own, long before she became an analyst.—Ed.

Do not seek so anxiously to be developed, to subject yourself to many influences to be played on; it is all dissipation. Humility like darkness reveals the heavenly lights. The shadows of poverty and meanness gather around us, "and lo! creation widens to our view." You are then confined to the most significant and vital experiences; you are compelled to deal with the material which yields the most sugar and the most starch. It is life near the bone where it is sweetest.

We are acquainted with a mere pellicle of the globe on which we live. Most have not delved six feet beneath the surface, nor leaped as many above it. We know not where we are. Besides, we are sound asleep nearly half our time. Yet we esteem ourselves wise, and have an established order on the surface. Truly, we are deep thinkers, we are ambitious spirits! As I stand over the insect crawling amid the pine needles on the forest floor, and endeavoring to conceal itself from my sight, and ask myself why it will cherish those humble thoughts and hide its head from me who might, perhaps, be its benefactor, I am reminded of the greater Benefactor and Intelligence that stands over me, the human insect.*–**

Henry David Thoreau, 1817–1862. American philosopher.
Walden.

Role of Suffering and Crisis[23]

We suffer, yet do not allow the mission of suffering to be accomplished in us. I pray the Lord that we may none of us fall into that torpid state in which our crosses do us no good.

François Fénelon, 1651–1715.
French Archbishop of Cambray.
Spiritual Letters of Archbishop Fénelon. Trans. H. L. Lear.

He who dreams must be awakened, and the deeper the man is who slumbers, or the deeper he slumbers, the more important it is that he be awakened, and the more powerfully must he be awakened. In case there is nothing that awakens the youth, this dream-life is continued in manhood. The man doubtless thinks that he is dreaming no more, and in a sense he is not; perhaps he scorns and de-

[23]See difficulties and the Role of Pressure,"

spises the dreams of youth, but precisely this shows that his life is a failure. In a sense he is awake, yet he is not in an eternal sense and in the deepest sense awake. And so his life is something far less significant than that of the youth, and it is his life rather which deserves to be despised; for he has become an unfruitful tree, or like a tree which has died, whereas the life of youth verily is not to be despised. The dream-life of childhood and youth is the time of blossoming. But in the case of a tree which is to bear fruit, the time of blossoming is a time of immaturity. It may indeed seem like retrogression when the tree which once stood naked and then burst into bloom, now casts off its blossoms; but it also may be progress. Fair is the time of blossoms, and fair is the blossoming hope in the child and in the youth; and yet it is immaturity.

Then comes affliction to awaken the dreamer, affliction which like a storm tears off the blossoms, affliction which nevertheless does not bereave of hope, but recruits hope.

Affliction is able to drown out every earthly voice, that is precisely what it has to do, but the voice of eternity within a man it cannot drown. Or conversely: it is the voice of eternity within which demands to be heard, and to make a hearing for itself it makes use of the loud voice of affliction. Then when by the aid of affliction all irrelevant voices are brought to silence, it can be heard, this voice within.

O thou sufferer, whosoever thou art, if only thou wilt listen! People generally think that it is the world, the environment, external relationships, which stand in one's way, in the way of one's good fortune and peace and joy. And at bottom it is always man himself that stands in his own way, man himself, who is too closely attached to the world, to the environment, to circumstances, to external relationships, so that he is not able to come to himself, come to rest, to have hope, he is constantly too much turned outward, instead of being turned inward, hence everything he says is true only as an illusion of the senses.

For Affliction Recruits Hope. It does not bestow hope, but it recruits it. It is man himself who acquires it, this hope of eternity which is deposited in him, hidden in his inner man; but affliction recruits it. For affliction prevents him mercilessly from obtaining any other help or relief whatsoever; affliction compels him mercilessly to let go of everything else; affliction schools him mercilessly, schools him thoroughly, that he may learn to grasp the eternal and to hold on to the eternal. Affliction does not help directly, it is not affliction that acquires or purchases hope and makes a present of it to a man; it helps repellently, and can do no otherwise, because hope is in man himself. Affliction preaches awakening. Affliction is no congratulatory caller who comes bearing hope in his hand as a present. Affliction is the villain who cruelly says to the sufferer, "I shall recruit hope for thee all right." But as it always is in life, that he who has to play the villain is never appreciated, that nobody takes the time to put himself in the villain's place and to recognize how admirably he plays his part and conforms to his role, how admirably, without letting himself be moved by any sighs or tears or ingratiating prayers—so it is also with affliction, it always has to hear itself spoken ill of. But just as little as it troubles the physician that the sick man in his pain scolds and clamours, or even kicks at him, just so little is affliction put out at this; God be praised, it is not put out—it recruits hope. Just as Christianity, precisely by all that unappreciation and persecution and injustice which the truth must suffer, proves that righteousness must exist (oh, marvellous inference!), so there is in the extremity of affliction, when it passes hardest, this inference, this ergo: Ergo there is an eternity to set one's hope upon.

Imagine hidden in a simpler exterior a secret receptacle wherein the most precious treasure is deposited—there is a spring which has to be pressed, but the spring is hidden, and the pressure must have a certain strength, so that an accidental pressure would not be sufficient—so likewise is the hope of eternity hidden in man's inmost parts, and affliction is the pressure. When it presses the hidden spring, and strongly enough, then the contents appear in all their glory.

Sören Kierkegaard, 1813–1855. Danish philosopher.
Christian Discourses. Trans. Walter Lowrie.

It must be remembered that even though the Ego is the individual's inaccurate conception of himself, it seems to him to be what he is.

It follows that all the thinking and striving of the egocentric person is basically concerned with avoiding all damage to his cherished Ego—his Seeming-self. He constantly fights against the breakdown of his Ego because its collapse seems to him to mean the destruction of his very Self, but even by these defensive efforts he inevitably brings about that breakdown which he dreads most. This is the result of the so-called vicious circle.

In his consciousness the egocentric person may feel that he is rather secure and successful, but unconsciously he feels that some critical moment for his Ego is close at hand. Being increasingly cut off by his egocentricity from the We—the source of real life—he suffers from a lack of inner psychic vitality and becomes less and less creative. This makes him insecure and anxious first in his unconscious and then more and more in his conscious mind.

Seemingly inexplicable inferiority feelings, irritability, sensitiveness and other signs of increasing "nervousness" always stand out more distinctly. The more the individual comes to feel that egocentric goals probably will not be attained, the more he seems to attach value to them, and now he strives for them more than ever. The unconscious anxiety whispers to him more distinctly in the form of bad dreams, melancholic or troubled moods or even as physical disturbances. At last they speak out loud, and mercilessly say that, in spite of all endeavour and apparent success, he has really failed. Life is passing. Perhaps much has already gone, but he has not yet really lived.

But now these symptoms which seemed to be bad and inimical, namely, this anxiety or guilt, prove themselves to be helpful and friendly, for they intrude themselves in order to bring healing by awakening this living yet unalive person. They are the voice of this life which is not lived, and their force is the power of life itself. They are the messengers of the We which represents this power of life, even within the egocentric mind.

Fritz Kunkel, M.D., 1889–1956, American psychiatrist,
and Roy E. Dickerson, 1886—. American author.
How Character Develops.

Affliction is a treasure, and scarce any man hath enough of it. No man hath affliction enough that is not matured, and ripened by it, and made fit for God by that affliction.

John Donne, 1573–1631. English poet, divine.
Devotions upon Emergent Occasions.

At first one passes some time in suffering from things

which seem to come from other persons, or from circumstances outside oneself. Gradually one finds a great part (or all) one's troubles are in oneself!

When we come to know that our whole environment and everything that happens is God's hand upon us, and that we are in touch with Him at every moment, because every detail of life is a means arranged to lead us to Himself; then we find that our great trouble is self. Only the very top of our soul is quite united to God; and all the rest is horribly unquiet, and makes us miserable. This is an unavoidable process of "purification," or Purgatory!

We used to think we were good—now we know we are not. We suffer from this, and, as we realise our imperfections more and more, we seem to be going backwards. Only we have got to be resigned to seeing these imperfections. We must not make light of them, in the sense of not hating them; but it is quite good to laugh at them [and] say, "You see, O Lord, how silly I am—this is all you can expect!"; or "I am delighted to see how imperfect I am—reveal more to me of my wretchedness."

We also say, of course: "You see what I am, without Your grace." Only don't think God is not giving you a great deal of grace. It is an enormous grace to be left to be conscious of our own want of recollection and want of energy.

Hence this second state consists in a continual perception that we are wanting. Consequently the earlier stage was much more comfortable; but, on looking back, we see it was a half-truth, or a tenth-truth!

The first stage: "I feel I habitually am doing and suffering God's Will in everything."

The second stage: "But I see this is only half-hearted and not thorough."

The third stage: "Habitually I perceive that I am never really doing God's Will, except most miserably and imperfectly; and I am, therefore, habitually miserable about it."

Consequently we begin to realise that we can only get union with God by very unpleasant suffering, and not by very enjoyable feelings! I gather from your letter that you are making real progress. All progress in virtue is progress in humility—knowledge of our own wretchedness.

Only try to enjoy knowing it! Thank God for showing it to you, and long to see it more and more.

(Only of course don't dwell upon it. All this introspection is unavoidable, but the shorter it is, the better.)

Fervour consists in dissatisfaction with ourselves—provided we also have confidence in God. He never takes us by the way we should expect. So do not worry, but accept all your imperfections—when past or present—as inevitable, and use them as steps up. But future ones are neither to be wished for, nor to be worried about.*–**

Dôm John Chapman, O.S.B., 1865–1933.
English biblical and patristic scholar.
Spiritual Letters of Dôm John Chapman.

Even if we have to face the utmost negative possibility, death, or what may be really worse than death, chronic sickness, imprisonment, accidental injuries, we must understand that life includes these possibilities and that an apparently harmless decision may bring about such a terrible thing. Should we shun therefore, every decision? Would it be better to close our eyes to all the perils of life and to enjoy the present moment as long as it is possible?

The too superficial person, as well as the too scrupulous one, is not able to face real life. All escape from crisis leads into more serious crises, and the only way out is to learn how to endure life as it is, including all its terrible dangers as well as its wonderful gifts. . . .

It is human to go through negative experiences, disappointments and frustrations. It is one of the ways leading us to maturity. Indeed, it is the opportunity to become We-feeling, objective, creative. . . .

We should find in our own past one or two small experiences which give us the assurance, at least in subsequent analysis, that the abyss, the dark situation which we fear more than death, can be faced daringly and confidently—and that it proves then to be the door leading us to objectivity and creativeness. Fear of failure, frustration, defeat and at last even fear of death has to be faced, explored, lived through, in vivid imagination. Gradually all the "perils of the soul," all catastrophes of life, lose their terrifying aspects, though certain very serious results from them may still remain. They become parts of human life, and we learn to think of them without anxiety. Fear of death disappears and religious confidence develops the more, the more we discover the deepest values of life, understanding that human life tends to lead us into maturity of character, We-feeling units of individuals and the creative development of personality.

The more we realize that this is true, the less we are afraid of making mistakes and the more we are able to make creative decisions. Then our courage and confidence increase through favourable experiences. Our readiness to take risk and responsibility grows. Life becomes fuller, richer, more successful and our confidence increases. The deeper meaning of human life, the meta-physical goals of history and culture become almost perceptible, though it may not be possible to formulate any statement about them. A new kind of security and confidence is felt—a confidence that does not need guarantees, that is based simply on our growing inner experience. This is in accordance with the experience of many religious personalities. Out of this experience may one day arise the highest value of our life—real, living, efficient faith.*

Fritz Kunkel, M.D., 1889–1956, American psychiatrist, and Roy E. Dickerson, 1886–, American author. *How Character Develops.*

I should like this to be accepted as my confession. There is no limit to human suffering. When one thinks: "Now I have touched the bottom of the sea—now I can go no deeper," one goes deeper. And so it is for ever. I thought last year in Italy, any shadow more would be death. But this year has been so much more terrible that I think with affection of the Casetta! Suffering is boundless, it is eternity. One pang is eternal torment. Physical suffering is—child's play. To have one's breast crushed by a great stone—one could laugh!

I do not want to die without leaving a record of my belief that suffering can be overcome. For I do believe it. What must one do? There is no question of what is called "passing beyond it." This is false.

One must submit. Do not resist. Take it. Be overwhelmed. Accept it fully. Make it part of life.

Everything in life that we really accept undergoes a change. So suffering must become Love. This is the mystery. This is what I must do. I must pass from personal love to greater love. I must give to the whole of life what I gave to one. The present agony will pass—if it doesn't kill.

It won't last. Now I am like a man who has had his heart torn out—but—bear it—bear it! As in the physical world, so in the spiritual world, pain does not last forever. It is only so terribly acute now. It is as though a ghastly accident had happened. If I can cease reliving all the shock and horror of it, cease going over it, I will get stronger.

Here, for a strange reason, rises the figure of Doctor Sorapure. He was a good man. He helped me not only to bear pain, but he suggested that perhaps bodily ill-health is necessary, is a repairing process, and he was always telling me to consider how man plays but a part in the history of the world. My simple kindly doctor was pure of heart as Tchekhov was pure of heart. But for these ills one is one's own doctor. If "suffering" is not a repairing process, I will make it so. I will learn the lesson it teaches. These are not idle words. These are not the consolations of the sick.

Life is a mystery. The fearful pain will fade. I must turn to work. I must put my agony into something, change it. "Sorrow shall be changed into joy."

It is to lose onself more utterly, to love more deeply, to feel oneself part of life—not separate.

Oh Life! accept me—make me worthy—teach me.*

Katherine Mansfield, 1890–1923. English writer, critic.
Journal of Katherine Mansfield.

God's Crosses Safer Than Self-chosen Crosses

The crosses which we make for ourselves by over-anxiety as to the future are not Heaven-sent crosses. We tempt God by our false wisdom, seeking to forestall His arrangements, and struggling to supplement His Providence by our own provisions. The fruit of our wisdom is always bitter. God suffers it to be so that we may be discomfited when we forsake His Fatherly guidance. The future is not ours: we may never have a future; or, if it comes, it may be wholly different to all we foresaw. Let us shut our eyes to that which God hides from us in the hidden depths of His Wisdom. Let us worship without seeing; let us be silent and lie still.

The crosses actually laid upon us always bring their own special grace and consequent comfort with them; we see the Hand of God when It is laid upon us. But the crosses wrought by anxious foreboding are altogether beyond

God's dispensations; we meet them without the special grace adapted to the need—nay, rather in a faithless spirit, which precludes grace. And so everything seems hard and unendurable; all seems dark, helpless, and the soul which indulged in inquisitively tasting forbidden fruit finds nought save hopeless rebellion and death within. All this comes of not trusting to God, and prying into His hidden ways. "Sufficient unto the day is the evil thereof," our Lord has said, and the evil of each day becomes good if we leave it to God. Let us throw self aside, and then God's Will, unfolding hour by hour, will content us as to all He does in or around us. The contradictions of men, their inconstancy, their very injustice, will be seen to be the results of God's Wisdom, Justice, and unfailing Goodness; we shall see nought save that Infinitely Good God hidden behind the weakness of blind, sinful men. Let us be glad when our Heavenly Father tries us with sundry inward or outward temptations; when He surrounds us with external contrarieties and internal sorrow, let us rejoice, for thus our faith is tried as gold in the fire. What! shall we be disheartened while God's Hand is hastening His work? We are perpetually calling on Him to do it, and so soon as He begins we are troubled, our cowardice and impatience hinder Him. I said that in the trials of life we learn the hollowness and falseness of all that is not God—hollowness, because there is nothing real where the One Sole Good is not; and falseness, because the world promises, kindles hopes, but gives nought save vanity and sorrow of heart—above all, in high places. Unreality must be unreal everywhere, but in high places it is all the worse because it is more decorated; it excites desire, kindles hope, and can never fill the heart. That which is itself empty cannot fill another. All that is not God will be found to be vanity and falsehood, and consequently we find them in ourselves. What is so vain as our own heart? With what delusions do we not deceive ourselves? Happy he who is thoroughly undeceived, but our heart is as vain and false as the outer world; we must not despise that without despising ourselves. We are even worse than the world, because we have received greater things from God.*

François Fénelon, 1651–1715.
French Archbishop of Cambray.
Spiritual Letters of Archbishop Fénelon. Trans. H. L. Lear.

Meeting of Temptation and Failure

Defeat must necessarily split attention and create unhappiness, unless in some way it is possible, in the pursuit of definite ends, to combine an unlimited attachment with an unlimited detachment.

William Ernest Hocking, 1873–1966. American philosopher.
The Meaning of God in Human Experience.

Victorious living does not mean freedom from temptation. Nor does it mean freedom from mistakes. We are personalities in the making, limited and grappling with things too high for us. Obviously, we, at very best, will make many mistakes. But these mistakes need not be sins. Our actions are the result of our intentions and our intelligence. Our intentions may be very good, but because the intelligence is limited the action may turn out to be a mistake—a mistake, but not necessarily a sin. For sin comes out of a wrong intention. Therefore the action carries a sense of incompleteness and frustration, but not of guilt. Victorious living does not mean perfect living in the sense of living without flaw, but it does mean adequate living, and that can be consistent with many mistakes.

Nor does it mean maturity. It does mean a cleansing away of things that keep from growth, but it is not full growth. In addition to many mistakes in our lives, there will be many immaturities. Purity is not maturity. This gospel of ours is called the Way. Our feet are on that Way, but only on that Way; we have not arrived at the goal.

Nor does it mean that we may not occasionally lapse into a wrong act, which may be called a sin. At that point we may have lost a skirmish, but it doesn't mean we may not still win the battle. We may even lose a battle and still win the war. One of the differences between a sheep and a swine is that when a sheep falls into a mudhole it bleats to get out, while the swine loves it and wallows in it. In saying that an occasional lapse is consistent with victorious living I am possibly opening the door to provide for such lapses. This is dangerous and weakening. There must be no such provision in the mind. There must be an absoluteness about the whole thing. But nevertheless victorious living can be consistent with occasional failure.

E. Stanley Jones, 1884–1973.
American, Christian missionary to India, author.
Victorious Living.

My son, if thou come to serve the Lord,
Prepare thy soul for temptation.
Set thy heart aright, and constantly endure,
And make not haste in time of trouble.
Cleave unto him, and depart not away,
That thou mayest be increased at thy last end.
Whatsoever is brought upon thee take cheerfully,
And be patient when thou art changed to a low estate.
For gold is tried in the fire,
And acceptable men in the furnace of adversity.
Believe in him, and he will help thee;
Order thy way aright, and trust in him.

Ecclesiasticus 2:1–6. About the second century B.C.
Apocrypha.

Most men have a dual interpretation of themselves—two pictures of their two selves in separate rooms. In one room are hung all the portraits of their virtues, done in bright, splashing, glorious colors, but with no shadows and no balance. In the other room hangs the canvas of self-condemnation.

Instead of keeping these two pictures isolated from one another, we must look at them together and gradually blend them into one. In our exalted moods we are afraid to admit guilt, hatred, and shame as elements of our personality; and in our depressed moods we are afraid to credit ourselves with the goodness and the achievement which really are ours.

We must begin now to draw a new portrait and accept and know ourselves for what we are. We are relative, and not absolute, creatures; everything we do is tinged with imperfection. So often people foolishly try to become rivals of God and make demands of themselves which only God could make of Himself—rigid demands of absolute perfection. . . .

A splendid freedom awaits us when we realize that we need not feel like moral lepers or emotional pariahs because we have some aggressive, hostile thoughts and feelings toward ourselves and others. When we acknowledge these feelings we no longer have to pretend to be that which we are not. We discover that rigid pride is actually the supreme foe of inner victory, while flexible humility, the kind of humility that appears when we do not demand the impossible or the angelic of ourselves, is the great ally of psychic peace.

We should learn to rejoice in the truth that we human beings consist of a variety of moods, impulses, traits, and emotions. . . .

If we become pluralistic in thinking about ourselves, we shall learn to take the depressed mood or the cruel mood or the uncooperative mood for what it is, one of many, fleeting, not permanent. As pluralists we take ourselves for worse as well as for better, cease demanding a brittle perfection which can lead only to inner despair. There are facets of failure in every person's makeup and there are elements of success. Both must be accepted while we try to emphasize the latter through self-knowledge.*

Joshua Loth Liebman, 1907–1948.
American rabbi, educator.
Peace of Mind.

March 21, 1690.

As light increases, we see ourselves to be worse than we thought. We are amazed at our former blindness as we see issuing forth from the depths of our heart a whole swarm of shameful feelings, like filthy reptiles crawling from a hidden cave. We never could have believed that we had harboured such things, and we stand aghast as we watch them gradually appear. But we must neither be amazed nor disheartened. We are not worse than we were; on the contrary, we are better. But while our faults diminish, the light by which we see them waxes brighter, and we are filled with horror. Bear in mind, for your comfort, that we only perceive our malady when the cure begins. So long as there is no sign of cure, we are unconscious of the depth of our disease; we are in a state of blind presumption and hardness; the prey of self-delusion. While we go with the stream, we are unconscious of its rapid course; but when we begin to stem it ever so little, it makes itself felt.

François Fénelon, 1651–1715
French Archbishop of Cambray.
Spiritual Letters of Archbishop Fénelon. Trans. H. L. Lear.

That the greatest pains or pleasures of this world were not to be compared with what he had experienced of both kinds of a spiritual state: so that he was careful for nothing and feared nothing, desiring only one thing of God, viz., that he might not offend Him.

That when he had failed in his duty, he simply confessed his fault, saying to God, I shall never do otherwise, if Thou leavest me to myself; 'tis Thou must hinder my falling, and mend what is amiss. That after this, he gave himself no farther uneasiness about it.

That we ought to act with God in the greatest simplicity, speaking to Him frankly and plainly, and imploring His assistance in our affairs, just as they happen. That God never failed to grant it, as he had often experienced.

That we should not wonder if, in the beginning, we often failed in our endeavours; but that, at last, we should gain a habit, which would naturally produce its acts in us, without our care, and to our exceeding great delight.

That the whole substance of religion was faith, hope, and love; by the practice of which we became united to the will of God; that all beside is indifferent, and to be used only as a means, that we may arrive at our end, and be swallowed up therein, by faith and love.

That all things are possible to him who believes, that they are less difficult to him who hopes, that they are easier to him who loves, and still more easy to him who perseveres in the practice of these three virtues.*

Brother Lawrence (Nicholas Herman), 1611–1691.
French Carmelite friar.
The Practice of the Presence of God. Trans. unknown.

For I am sure that neither death, nor life, nor angels, nor principalities, nor things present, nor things to come, nor powers, nor height, nor depth, nor anything else in all creation, will be able to separate us from the love of God in Christ Jesus our Lord.

Saint Paul, first century Christian Apostle.
New Testament (Rom. 8:38–39).

PART TWO

The Techniques

It is one thing from the woody top of a mountain to see the land of peace, and not to find the way thither; and another to keep on the way that leads thither.

SAINT AUGUSTINE

If we are to have vision, we must learn to participate in the object of the vision. The apprenticeship is hard.

ANTOINE DE SAINT-EXUPERY

"Behold, I stand at the door and knock . . ."

REVELATIONS

CONTENTS

Part Two

INTRODUCTION

Part One enunciated the conditions of the Way taken by men and women in all ages who have in varying degrees become free and creative in spirit. Therein was seen that heightened awareness is, in most cases, achieved slowly, and that it generally seems to lead through several stages. Throughout the whole process, but especially during its early stages, the seeker finds himself in need of every available help. His progress depends upon many factors, among them being the depth and kind of his original experience of commitment to Reality—to wholeness[1] of being; the degree of rigidity in his unconscious egocentric purposes, and the effectiveness of the techniques he develops for the maintenance and growth of the new attitude. This section is concerned with such techniques.

Techniques are necessary and difficult. But if one will face the extent of revision and reorientation needed of all functions and processes of the conscious and unconscious personality (will, emotions, intellect, imagination), one will see the necessity for advice and help from those who seem to have achieved the deepest religious and psychological insight. These point to ways by which man is brought into contact with an inner creative richness which otherwise tends to be lost—ways by which he relates to the inner and outer aspects of a supreme Reality.

Such teachers seem to agree that some disciplines are essential. In order to be effective they must be able to transform the egocentric set of man's own psyche which tends to choke out his new resolve, in releasing the undeveloped and repressed areas of his psyche, and in establishing new behavior patterns consistent with the new direction. Special

[1] "Wholeness," as contrasted to exclusively "ego-centered."

disciplines are as necessary here as in any other kind of proficiency one may desire to attain.

One method used throughout the centuries is prayer and meditation. Many still shy away from the practice of prayer due to inadequate early experiences or to prescribed prayers which to them are meaningless. The choice of subject matter for meditation should always be determined by what is most real and meaningful to each individual. Whether it be on the life and teachings of Jesus, or other historical figures in whom God appears manifest to a high degree, or on certain stirring philosophical hypotheses, or on the intimations of God received through dreams, art, nature, science, evolution or history; whether one meditates upon the dynamic of the Real Self (advanced by several psychotherapeutic systems as well as by early Hindu, Buddhist, and Christian mystics), or upon some other significant approach, one will be provided with enormously inspiring subject matter.

The next technique discussed in this section is that of psychotherapy. It is striking to note how many of the insights and practices of this science were known and used by great teachers of the past. Interesting evidence of such forerunning knowledge is seen in ancient Buddhist, Hindu and early Christian training systems.

The scientific classification of what was already known, and the extensive development of that knowledge through experimental processes presents us with a useful body of psychological data regarding the structure and functioning of personality. It not only throws light on self-knowledge and therefore on those obstacles to growth which stem from the unconscious, but frequently is successful in probing to and effecting a removal of the roots of those obstacles—thus helping in the release of the transforming, integrative factors.

Besides the light which psychotherapy throws on the understanding of the process of progression, and besides the valuable suggestions for general self-education which it has originated, it has developed its own particular technique by which it seems to understand the unconscious through the aid of dream analysis. This method is direct as contrasted to the indirect method of prayer. One of the dangers in the direct method is the tendency to become overly absorbed in the revelations of the unconscious and thus to sidetrack the primary goal which is the release of the living reality. Another danger is that the egocentric demands frequently are only modified instead of being steadily reduced and eliminated. This is partly due to the partial view of man's world which is accepted by so many psychologists[2]—one in which the human mind and body, the human external and internal environments, are considered the whole of the real world. Both of these dangers, however, can be avoided through the wise choice of professional help. Fortunately there are therapists of profound insight who are qualified to assist one by this method. The material included on psychotherapy is necessarily inadequate. No trustworthy introduction to this important field can be gained without careful study of several well chosen books in the field. (See Recommended Reading list.)

Concerning the third suggestion for further progression, little introduction is needed. It is obvious that for strength of purpose to carry on through the perplexities and discouragements met along the Way the value of intimate fellowship is immeasurable. Many small, seriously-intented groups can be discovered though it may require patience to seek them out. Success in any venture of fellowship may be difficult, but in an intimate fellowship of this kind there are particular dangers which may arise from the tendency of the members to idealize one another, while at the same time disregarding those individual differences in temperament and experience which vary the rate of progress as well as determine the particular emphasis which the progress will take in each. In spite of the hazards, however, there are few experiences as rich as that of such fellowship.

Finally, there is what we call the technique of Action. (Chap. VIII) Unless there is action up to the height of insight there will be no increase in insight. It is the habit of saying 'yes' to Life and to what life is saying, both outwardly and inwardly.

But how successfully in most of us does the loud clamor of egocentric interests prevent the hearing of what "life" is saying! It is to recover this hearing faculty that spiritual

---

[2]The Analytical Psychology of Jung and the We-psychology of Kunkel are exceptions.

training is recommended. A contemporary religious[4] puts it something like this: The spiritual life resembles a fertile egg whose embryo is surrounded by the exact sustenance needed for its development. It grows by feeding on its environment, achieving the strength needed finally to peck through the shell. So, likewise, "the spark of the soul" within each human being is surrounded by the exact food necessary for its development. This food consists of the essence of all the circumstances, the difficulties, the opportunities, the relationships—personal and universal—in which each person at every moment of time is environed. But man tends to resist, even to fight against this given sustenance. He fails to recognize it as the perfect nutriment for his spiritual and psychological development. It is to awaken this recognition of what "life" is offering in the way of food that the techniques described herein are important.

[4]Howard Thurman, former Dean of the Chapel of Boston University.

CHAPTER IV

Prayer and Meditation

The practice of reflective meditation, which consists in holding certain ideas in the mind long enough to enable them to form emotional connections, tends to break up the crust of habit and to create a new will.

WALTER MARSHALL HORTON

Worship in all its aegrees is an education in charity, a purgation of egoism.

EVELYN UNDERHILL

Prayer is the most perfect and most divine action that a rational soul is capable of. It is of all other actions and duties the most indispensably necessary.

F. AUGUSTINE BAKER

General Definitions of Prayer[1]

Prayer is disciplined opening of the self to God. My social, verbal, officious, work-a-day self has something closed and set about it. It is a mass of predispositions, preconceptions, inhibitions, settled beliefs and expectations. There is a convenient fixity about it. It assures me of my identity, it provides me with the least laborious responses to the stresses of my environment, it gives me a stable base from and on which to grow. But that fixity must never be suffered to become final. This would be death. Prayer is the persistent effort to guard against that death—the effort toward effortlessness, receptivity. So long as the tenseness of

[1]These definitions do not particularize the different kinds of prayer. For that see under "Kinds and Degrees of Prayer," pp. 223–241.

the daily struggle remains, one battles the old problems with the old resources and the old insights. If one could only suspend that conscious fight, one might be able to meet the same reality that is to be subdued with a larger, more complete, more relaxed self: one might harness to the fight not only the thin upper surface of one's resolutions but a more massive undercurrent of habit and emotion. This is just what can be achieved by the difficult art of prayer, and its discipline of silence.

For there is strength in you greater than any strength of your own, the Will that stirs within you when your own will is at rest.*

Gregory Vlastos, 1909–. Canadian professor of philosophy.
The Religious Way.

Prayer is the act by which man opens himself to the total values for wholeness that exist in each situational moment of his life. It is an affirmation (reaffirmation) of a fundamental dedication to each moment's emergent highest Value. It assumes the Other, the eternal Thou as a given. It assumes the presence of a mystery, and of the possibility of grace (the unbidden abundance of God). In the words of the first commandment, prayer is the act of loving God with as much of the all (of heart, soul, strength, mind) as can possibly be brought into consciousness. In contrast to various forms of meditation, prayer is a relationship between the *I*, the situation in which the *I* is functioning, and the Meaning transcending both the *I* and the situation but manifesting itself within both. It is a continual yes-saying to the fact that there is a direction more encompassing than mine, a Purpose larger than mine, for which I can work. It is also a willingness to be open to alternatives to opposite ways of action or response. When prayer makes this openness possible, it is a marvelous preventer of egocentricity. And this decision to say 'yes' to whatever alternative seems to belong to Purpose, must be taken in advance before any of the specifics of moments are or can be known.

Elizabeth B. Howes, Jungian analyst and writer.
Sheila Moon, Jungian analyst and writer.
Man the Choicemaker.

---

*The use of a single asterisk indicates that the selection has been abridged; two asterisks indicate that it has been slightly rearranged.—Ed.

By worship I mean a reflective activity of the "total mind" by means of which the Self relates itself to its Total Environment in so far, that is, as the Self can become aware of and responsive to its Total or Effective Environment. In my view it is true to say that we can worship Nature or Humanity or Art, or God. I believe that all of these are the same activity, but that they differ in quality. They differ in the sense that Whitehead means when he speaks of "high-grade" and "low-grade" experiences. The chief difference between these "grades" of worship can be measured by the differences in the objects of worship and in the effects produced by higher or lower-grade worship upon the organization of the personality of the worshipper and upon his experience. Worship requires, firstly, stillness in the "ego"; secondly, openness to or awareness of the object of worship; and, thirdly, the establishment of mutual relations between the worshipper and the object of worship. In essence, worship is the whole process of valuation. In Christian worship, God in Christ is the Divine Object.

Howard E. Collier, M.D., 1890–1970. English physician.
The Place of Worship in Modern Medicine.

Moral and religious reality cannot be perceived without transformation of self, without submission of the individual to its exigencies. One condition has to be met; the decision must be taken in advance not only in words but in reality to say "yes" to the light. And this attitude is called prayer. In fact it is prayer even before we realize that we should call it so. One should therefore say that the only search for God is through prayer—but what prayer? Not the formulas of ritual, not the multiplication of words . . . "I am nothing; I know nothing, save the fact that I am here, full of need and misery, full of ignorance, doubt and fear. But, I am finding my direction; I turn inward toward an ideal of higher, purer spirituality; I will the good, even the good unknown to me; I aspire and trust; I crave; I open myself; I abandon myself to the God whose inspiration I feel at work in the depths of myself; I will the light; I call upon it; I am confident that it will answer me and I accept in advance everything that it will exact from me." Moreover this prayer must not only be dreamed about it, it must be prayed in every fact, explicitly. It is not sufficient to approve of it as a theoretical principle, to admit its necessity in an abstract movement of pure mind; at one precise moment of time, withdrawing in one's self and seizing hold of that self to its uttermost depths, one must make it give birth to the act in its reality. Only with the fulfillment of this condition will one's search be fully sincere, and not a vain lie and a mere sham. If one felt I know not what obscure aversion for this act, that would be the best proof that the fact of experience does add something to simple reflection on it. And this aversion we would then have to conquer, for it would mark in us a secret refusal of the ethical demand.*

Edouard LeRoy, 1870–1954. French philosopher.
Le Problème de Dieu. Extract trans. Dora Wilson.

There is no fear of the charge of autosuggestion in prayer that so haunted the last generation. It is freely admitted from the outset that large elements of prayer are and should be of that character. All that is meant by this word "autosuggestion," or self-suggestion, is that the suggestion is selected and presented by the person to himself. We have come to recognize that all we know has been suggested to us either by our external or internal environment in the form of what is called hetero-suggestion.

In entering prayer we have a perfect right to choose from this random mass of heterosuggestions some that we regard as more significant than others, and to dwell upon them. Autosuggestion is no more than this act of dwelling upon selected aspects of experience. By the mere act of dwelling upon them we do not necessarily prove them to be true. Nor did we intend to. That matter of truth is both a prior and a subsequent matter of tests and interpretations to which either auto- or heterosuggestions must be submitted. These selected aspects of experience with which we may enter prayer are, however, only a threshold of past experience that we cross in order to engage with what is there. And they are subject to revision and to addition as the prayer brings its bearer to new levels of insight.

Douglas V. Steere, 1901–.
American author, professor of philosophy.
Prayer and Worship.

Worship, or prayer, is the especial sphere of the will in religion. It is an act of approach to God; and while this act involves a lifting of thought to God, it is more than an act of thought—it intends to institute some communication or transaction with God wherein will answers will.

Within the motive of worship there is to be discerned, I believe, a weariness of the old, the habitual, the established —a hunger for what is radically new and untried. This is, in part, the significance of that deliberate undoing of all bonds and attachments, all received knowledges and properties, which is part of the preparation for the mystical experience in all ages. If it were possible for the soul to become aware of all its attachments and habits, how could it be better disposed for originality? The scientific discipline of the mind is of the same effect in its own sphere; to disaffect oneself as far as may be of prepossessions; to recognize and allow for the biases of the person, the body, and the age. It is not improbable, then, that worship may include this value of preparing the soul for the reception of novelty with its primary value of uniting the worshipper with his God.

Worship is indeed a reasonable act, even when instinctive and momentary: it is informed of God; it uses and contains all available knowledge of the being whom it addresses. But in worship the universality of thought is overcome; and God is appropriated uniquely to the individual self. Worship brings the experience of God to pass in self-consciousness with a searching valency not obligatory upon the pure thinker: in some way it *enacts* the presence of God, sets God into the will to work there. In the nature of the case, the aspect of deity which reason discovers is an unconditional, inevitable, universal presence: from such a presence there can be no escape—and so no drawing near —save by the movements of deliberate attention. But the drawing-near of worship is more than a movement of attention.

Worship may be regarded as an attempt to detach oneself from everything else in uniting with God. It seeks God first as an object, that Other of all worldly objects; and it seeks to join itself to that absolute Other. The mystic proceeds by negation; this and that, he says, are not God; it is not these that I seek. The effort of worship measures the soul's power of detachment. And my power of detachment measures the whole of my freedom, the whole of my possibility of happiness, the whole of my possible originality, the whole depth and reach of my morality and of my human contribution!

What the mystic reaches is, in terms of his world-conceptions, a zero; not indeed the Whole of reality, but Substance, the heart of God. It is just such a zero as one encounters when he seeks his own soul behind the shifting content of his experience, or when he seeks the soul of another, in distinction from that other's various external expressions. This zero is not a place to stay in; but it may be pre-eminently a place to return to, and *to depart from*. In worship one touches the bottom of that bottomless pit of Self and perceives at hand the real Origin of things; gaining not the whole of any knowledge, but the beginning and measure of all knowledge.

May not worship be described as the will to become, for a moment and within one's own measure, what existence is; or more simply, as the act of recalling oneself to *being?* It might be described as a spontaneous impulse for spiritual self-preservation; for self-placing, for the ultimate judgment of life, and for the perpetual renewal of the worth of life. And in thus returning to the sources of being we may still more dimly discern, it may be, a self-preservation of farther scope, such as immortality may hang on; a glint of ontological bearing of unlimited importance. . . .

The worth of God's presence to the genuine mystic is a sufficient and absolute good; and he often expresses himself as if the ecstasy of his moment were its own justification. But every immediate value must be sanctioned by its bearings in the system of all values, must have a meaning which can give account of itself in the form of knowledges such as we have suggested. Worship must not be an intoxication which alienates the soul from the duller interests of experience; and hence, as mysticism has learned its own meaning, it has realized that subjective delight recommends nothing, and that the supremacy of the moment of its experience must be judged by the staying powers of its insight.*

William Ernest Hocking, 1873–1966. American philosopher.
The Meaning of God in Human Experience.

Prayer is not asking for things—not even for the best things; it is going where they are. The word, with its inevitable sense and stain of supplication, is therefore best abandoned. It is meditation and contemplation; it is opening another aperture of the mind, using another focus, that is the real recreative process.

Gerald Heard, 1889–1972.
English author, religious philosopher.
The Third Morality.

Let any true man go into silence; strip himself of all pretense, and selfishness, and sensuality, and sluggishness of soul; lift off thought after thought, passion after passion, till he reaches the inmost depth of all; remember how short a time and he was not at all; how short a time again, and he will not be here; open his window and look upon the night, how still its breath, how solemn its march, how deep its perspective, how ancient its forms of light; and think how little he knows except the perpetuity of God, and the mysteriousness of life:—and it will be strange if he does not feel the Eternal Presence as close upon his soul as the breeze upon his brow; if he does not say, "O Lord, art thou ever near as this, and have I not known thee?"—if the true proportions and the genuine spirit of life do not open on his heart with infinite clearness and show him the littleness of his temptations and the grandeur of his trust. He is ashamed to have found weariness in toil so light, and tears where there was no trial to the brave. He discovers with astonishment how small the dust that has blinded him, and from the height of a quiet and holy love looks down with incredulous sorrow on the jealousies and fears and irritations that have vexed his life. A mighty wind of resolution sets in strong upon him and freshens the whole atmosphere of his soul, sweeping down before it the light flakes of difficulty, till they vanish like snow upon the sea. He is imprisoned no more in a small compartment of time, but belongs to an eternity which is now and here. The isolation of his separate spirit passes away; and with the countless multitude of souls akin to God, he is but as a wave of his unbounded deep. He is at one with Heaven, and hath found the secret place of the Almighty.

James Martineau, 1805–1900. English religious director.
Endeavors After the Christian Life.

Value and Function of Prayer[2]

For World Salvation

The world can be saved—by one thing only and that is worship. For to worship is to quicken the conscience by the holiness of God, to feed the mind with the truth of God, to purge the imagination by the beauty of God, to open the heart to the love of God, to devote the will to the purpose of God.

William Temple, 1881–1944. Archbishop of Canterbury.
The Hope of a New World.

For Unity

"People cannot be loyal to what they have not experienced." If so, meditation would seem to be almost necessary to most religious people who wish to remain sincere and consistent. Meditation gives opportunity to ponder over the subtler realities which are not easily or hastily perceived but which are nevertheless constantly operative and controlling life. Meditation provides opportunity for weighing values. Insofar as will is choice or perceiving a pattern, it is aided by meditation. Meditation also provides opportunity for us to examine our assumptions about human nature, about the spirit, about our relations to one another and to God. Often these assumptions lie at the base of our choice and our action. Meditation is of special value for those who desire peace.

During the greater part of man's history, fight or flight were his only two ways of getting physical security. Owing to the great increase of integration and awareness and sensitiveness of modern society as a result of modern transport and communications, our physical security now depends much more on intangible relationships, on trust, on moral and psychological imponderables than it is used to. The psychological equivalent of physical security is inner unity, the integration of spiritual and moral unity between men. Men's chief insecurity now is caused by separateness or di-

[2]Also see "Confessional Meditation," pp. 318–322, Ed.

visiveness. Therefore unity means security. The search for inner unity is thus the psychological equivalent of physical fight or flight. When once attained, that inner unity must of course be translated into corresponding consistent action. The search for spiritual unity is one important means of attaining spiritual, moral, psychological, and even physical security. Hence the importance of meditation.*

Richard Gregg, 1882–1966.
American author, professor of philosophy.
Inward Light.

Revelation of Self-Love

Prayer, if properly carried out, will have as its effect the gradual revelation to the soul of the disease of self-love which so intimately penetrates the very fibres of its being as to pass unobserved by the person that does not lead an interior life. In prayer the soul gradually draws into the radiant purity and truth of the soul of Jesus. It becomes bathed through and through with that radiance; and in this splendour all in it that is of self and not of God stands clearly revealed to that soul's gaze.

Prayer reveals the presence of this self-love and secures the aid of God in its extermination.*

Edward Leen, 1885–. Irish Catholic cleric, educator.
Progress Through Mental Prayer.

To Combine Thought and Devotion

Of all things that militate against the spiritual life, none is more disastrous and far-reaching in its effect than the divorce of thought from devotion. The divine precept which bids us love God with all our mind seems to many to have but little connection with thought.

Where the understanding is exercised upon the things of God, there the will begins to energise toward the Divine and love bursts into flame. Meditation begets a deep yearning; apprehension and adhesion march together. We understand with the heart; we love with the mind.

Emily Herman, 1876–1923. English writer.
The Touch of God.

Making Faith Real

If our Faith is to be made vivid, it must be by meditation. We are told that "Faith cometh by hearing." But we have to do more than hear it, merely. Meditation is meant to make our Faith real to us, so that we shall realise in our lives what we know and believe.

Dom John Chapman, O.S.B., 1865–1933.
English biblical and patristic scholar.
Spiritual Letters of Dom John Chapman.

Adjustment to Cosmic Reality

This solitary response to reality is the deepest religious experience one can have. It is turning from the periphery of life to the core of existence. In this solitary moment it is as if one entered into the scheme of things. He penetrates the outer glare and comes into a sombre retreat where perspective is steady and clear. But the solitary view does more than intensify the subjective focus; it illumines the objective reference. It deafens one's ears to folk noises and fills them with the sound of vastness. It stirs one from the mood of living to a sense of life in its immensities. Solitariness makes one world-conscious. And in becoming world-conscious he becomes God-conscious.

I have known solitary moments such as these to bring me a peculiarly intimate understanding of the movement of life. It was as if I were momentarily lifted from the scene of details to a lone plateau where a broader vista was possible. The universe as an entity seemed to be moving through space-time, an earnest, living organism of huge dimensions, pulsating with innumerable life-activities, yet, like a massive liner at sea, plowing its own course through waves of time, whither, there was no knowing. There is a feeling of eternity or timelessness that comes over one in such a glimpse of the total course of things that seems to give dignity and worth to the temporal passage of events.

Contemplating this vast, on-going process of life in this intimate way makes one vividly aware of the great community of cosmic activities which sustain and promote life. The cosmos becomes a community, near and neighborly. It is, indeed, a vivid awareness of God.

In this solitary hour, the worshiper, looking beyond himself, is moved to prayer. The awareness of reality quickens him. He feels the surge drawing him, the creature, toward the source of being. Prayer of this sort is not just meditation; it is tropism of a human sort. It is a profound organic movement that impels man to reach toward reality and to lay hold of the "gift of life" that issues from that profound reciprocity.

A clear awareness of self in relation to reality silhouettes the worshiper against the cosmic background. Thus solitariness confronts him with what he is. It strips him of his social shroud and reveals him in creature form. It gives voice to his silenced thoughts and unmasks his impurities that threatened his health of soul. This religious solitude may also inspirit the worshiper with what he might be. It may arouse in him the feel of his authentic self.

In this solitary hour of awareness, the religious man's response is not always an easy adjustment. Exposure before reality carries no guarantee of blessing. He may find "God the enemy." And the revealment may leave him tentatively damned. Faced with "what is permanent in the nature of things," many men and women *are* wretched creatures, sorely out of adjustment with what fulfills life. If there is no original sin in the sense of a predestined bent toward maladjustment, there certainly is a vicious inclination away from the better self, easily acquired and difficult to overcome.

The prayer of penitence is an essential step in the process of adjustment, for it brings the wrong-doer boldly, however humbly, into the presence of the reality he has shunned. Wrong-doing persists as long as the offender continues to shun reality.

Like men of all ages, modern man is threatened with dissolution or with failure to fulfill his life-process. The religious man, aware of this possible death or defeat of spirit, reaches out continually toward goals that inspire and toward realities that sustain and fulfill. His prayer, then, is made redemptive through his adjustment to realities that may bear or break his being. He recovers himself and the course toward fulfillment through penitence, aspiration, and devotion.*

Bernard Eugene Meland, 1899–.
American philosopher, professor of religion.
Modern Man's Worship.

As Method for Achieving Integral Thought

Evolution did not cease with the evolution of man. On the contrary henceforward it became vastly accelerated. Instead of having to be carried on through change of physique it can now be advanced through change of tools, tools which are extensions of limbs created by an extension of consciousness, a more intense form of consciousness than that which was formerly homogeneous with the physique. This, however, necessitates a separation in the individual consciousness, one level still running the body while a new range experiments with the external world. Henceforward therefore progress must be a balance and each aspect of consciousness—the inward- and the outward-looking—must keep pace in their advance and intensification of focus. Finally a direct consciousness emerges and man discards evolution through tools, as he, when he became man, disregarded the first aenoic evolution through the developement of new bodily organs.

Man then is seen as a creature who is achieving pure consciousness and, in the end, achieving it as a purely voluntary act.

It is in this frame of reference that we can set and see the life of prayer, prayer as a pure act of the will, seeking an integral understanding of and union with the Whole, the One. We can see prayer as not only the continuation of evolution in consciousness by consciousness but the essential method whereby today man achieves integral thought when analytical thought is threatening to unbalance him. For analytical thought is the only thought which the ego-consciousness can command (though sometimes the higher, integral thought breaks up and through the threshold of the ego) and analytical thought is a form which can only give rise to means and powers. Integral thought which springs from the deep mind alone can give rise to meaning, value, sanctions and truly creative integration.

Gerald Heard, 1889–1971.
English author, religious philosopher.
A Preface to Prayer.

Handling Periods of Inflation and Deflation

Once he has gone some distance on the inward journey, a man will know that there is one thing above all he needs to do. On every occasion that presents itself, from facing death in the dark to waiting for the bus, from being caught in a sterile patch to being carried away by panic fear, he . . . should consciously, deliberately, with all his strength, centre.

How best to do this each must find in his own way. To anyone who knows what it is for a Quaker Meeting to "centre down," then it is to do like that, to hold a meeting of one. To anyone who has said to himself in a life-or-death emergency, "I must pull myself together and face this," it is such a pulling together. For the man of responsibility it is, as it were, to follow that responsibility down to its ultimate roots in the depths of his physical and moral being. It is the deep convulsive breath with which, in an agony of fear, we seek and find ourselves. And the injunction that goes with this is, pray; especially that form of prayer which consists in a wordless, imageless, lifting of the soul—the "naked intent directed unto God" as *The Cloud of Unknowing* puts it. For it is by this means that the "different spiritual dimension" becomes manifest, interpenetrating and transcending the space-time cause-effect world in which our bodies exist.

Especially is it necessary to centre and to pray in the "Infirm glory of the positive hour." In disaster one naturally has recourse to these means. In success it is otherwise: and success, notoriously, can be far more dangerous than disaster. And not in a time of outward success only but also, and particularly, of inward success, is it necessary to "give the glory to God." Whenever we feel we have come through to something vital . . . seen for the first time what we have been getting wrong, traced down what it was that has been separating us from those we love, that is the time to centre and pray. For it is then that inflation threatens; and the unclean spirit gathers his seven companions for the counter-attack.

Above all is it vital to centre and pray whenever, as from time to time will happen, the whole pattern of life breaks up: sometimes the outer life, sometimes the inner life, sometimes both at once. Then a man is in mortal peril: and the further he has gone in the experiment, the greater the danger. In such straits it is well to remember that individuation[8] necessarily consists of such periods of flux: that for the wider integration to be made, some measure of disintegration is essential. But intellectual considerations at such a time mean relatively little. What is needed is that the integrative and consolidating process shall come into operation no less swiftly and no less powerfully than the disintegrative. And for this, centre and pray, descendite ut ascendatis, is the effective means.*

P. W. Martin, 1893–. English social scientist.
Experiment in Depth.

For Spiritual Effectiveness

If we ask of the saints how they achieved spiritual effectiveness, they are only able to reply that, in so far as they did it themselves, they did it by love and prayer. A love that is very humble and homely; a prayer that is full of adoration and of confidence. Love and prayer, on their lips, are not mere nice words; they are the names of tremendous powers, able to transform in a literal sense human personality and make it more and more that which it is meant to be—the agent of the Holy Spirit in the world. Plainly then, it is essential to give time or to get time somehow for self-training in this love and this prayer, in order to develop these powers. It is true that in their essence they are "given," but the gift is only fully made our own by a patient and generous effort of the soul. Spiritual achievement costs much, though never as much as it is worth. It means at the very least the painful development and persevering, steady exercise of a faculty that most of us have allowed to get slack. It means an inward if not an outward asceticism; a virtual if not an actual mysticism. . . .

Evelyn Underhill, 1875–1944. English writer, mystic.
Concerning the Inner Life.

Handling of Personal and Social Life

Meditation is essential. Imports must balance exports. Everyone should first learn by himself what he would prac-

[8]See p. 61–63.—Ed.

tise in public. Through insight acquired in solitude he must study to recognize the underlying pattern and coherencies so that when he comes out into the contemporary confusion he may still detect and discriminate the fundamental design and meaning, though it be blurred by the surface disturbances. Only those who have first taught themselves by listening to clear unambiguous enunciation to recognize a language new to their ear, can hope to pick up from the clipped and elided vernacular the meaning of casual speech. To less practised ears it sounds no more than a confusion of indistinguishable noises incapable of any specific meaning. The individuals whom any other individual sees are not in themselves immediately appealing, still less inspiring. They seem pointless, futile, boring. They, as he, are engrossed in their own cares and careers. Even if he tries to treat them as creatures with immense capacities within them, he sees they are not that now. On the contrary, they are blind to what they might be, and unless he can take the initiative with a generous and assured conviction, which is positively creative, it is they who convince him of his individualism and separateness, not he who convinces them of their general eternal life and common union.

He cannot, then, begin by feeling a creative, non-personal generosity, which they deny and he rather desires than possesses. The first step, therefore, is practice—practice in throwing the mind open by meditation to its larger being, practice in throwing off the individuality where there is space—in the silence where the pressing claims and strident assertions of others' individualism are not challenging him and rousing his own reaction to protect himself against such incursions, encroachments, and collisions.

The slowness of self-change, against which so many rebel and because of which even greater numbers abandon this essential process, becomes more endurable when we realize two things. The first is that, considering the results to be produced, change, if it to be effective, could not be faster. To change oneself—that seems a small preliminary thing. In fact it is nothing of the sort. It is the most radical of alterations. To change oneself is not merely to alter one's relations to all fellowmen, to alter the whole of self and social nexus. That is much. We are, even the most independent, unsuspectedly integrated with our society. We cannot move without affecting all those around us: they have made and make us largely what we are. Self-change must always be social change: that is why moral courage is rarer than physical courage; the determination to alter the social will needs more energy than the determination to sacrifice the self to that will.

To change oneself is to have to do that, but it is also to do far more. It is to alter one's outlook literally—to attend to what has been overlooked, to see through what has riveted attention. It is to see another world. Once that other world is seen, once the new faculty has grown, then a new way of action is natural and inevitable. Seeing, realization of the further range of reality, that is the step that really counts. The task is an immense one, for by remaking the self, we remake, and can only remake the world.*

Anonymous.

Anatomical and Functional Modifications

Certain spiritual activities may cause anatomical as well as functional modifications of the tissues and the organs. These organic phenomena are observed in various circumstances, among them being the state of prayer. Prayer should be understood, not as a mere mechanical recitation of formulas, but as a mystical elevation, an absorption of consciousness in the contemplation of a principle both permeating and transcending our world. Such a psychological state is not intellectual. It is incomprehensible to philosophers and scientists, and inaccessible to them. But the simple seem to feel God as easily as the heat of the sun or the kindness of a friend. The prayer which is followed by organic effect is of a special nature. First, it is entirely disinterested. Man offers himself to God. He stands before Him like the canvas before the painter or the marble before the sculptor. At the same time, he asks for His grace, exposes his needs and those of his brothers in suffering. Generally, the patient who is cured is not praying for himself. But for another. Such a type of prayer demands complete renunciation—that is, a higher form of asceticism. The modest, the ignorant, and the poor are more capable of this self-denial than the rich and the intellectual. When it possesses such characteristics, prayer may set in motion a strange phenomenon, the miracle.

In all countries, at all times, people have believed in the existence of miracles, in the more or less rapid healing of the sick at places of pilgrimage, at certain sanctuaries. But after the great impetus of science during the nineteenth century, such belief completely disappeared. It was generally admitted not only that miracles did not exist, but that they could not exist. As the laws of thermodynamics make perpetual motion impossible, physiological laws oppose miracles. Such is still the attitude of most physiologists and physicians. However, in view of the facts observed during the last fifty years this attitude cannot be sustained. The most important cases of miraculous healing have been recorded . . . The process of healing changes little from one individual to another. Often, an acute pain. Then a sudden sensation of being cured. In a few seconds, a few minutes, at the most a few hours, wounds are cicatrized, pathological symptoms disappear, appetite returns. Sometimes functional disorders vanish before the anatomical lesions are repaired. The skeletal deformations of Pott's disease, the cancerous glands, may still persist two or three days after the healing of the main lesions. The miracle is chiefly characterized by an extreme acceleration of the processes of organic repair. There is no doubt that the rate of cicatrization of the anatomical defects is much greater than the normal one. The only condition indispensable to the occurrence of the phenomenon is prayer. But there is no need for the patient himself to pray, or even to have any religious faith. It is sufficient that some one around him be in a state of prayer. Such facts are of profound significance. They show the reality of certain relations, of still unknown nature, between psychological and organic processes. They prove the objective importance of the spiritual activities, which hygienists, physicians, educators, and sociologists have almost always neglected to study. They open to man a new world.*

Alexis Carrel, 1873–1944. French surgeon, biologist.
Man the Unknown

Kinds and Degrees of Prayer

Although the material on kinds and degrees of prayer will be of special interest to the student of mysticism, it will also yield valuable insights to any one sincerely interested in spiritual progress.

As we have seen, the impotence of many religious people is partly due to the widespread ignorance concerning the range of progress, the unconscious factors involved therein, and the degrees of prayer through which those who achieve the higher ranges in freedom of the spirit seem to pass. Most of us are content with "a little wave of feeling" in our practice of prayer. We have failed to realize that the remodelling of the unconscious attitude requires persistence and time, that it bears little relation to desultory "feeling."

Brother Lawrence who underwent twelve years of training before he achieved an habitual sense of the presence of God, spoke eloquently of the blindness of mankind regarding the range of spiritual progress. From the book *The Practice of the Presence of God* we find concerning him:

"He [Brother Lawrence] complains much of our blindness and exclaims often that we are to be pitied, who content ourselves with so little. God's treasure, he says, is like an infinite ocean; yet a little wave of feeling, passing with the moment, contents us. Blind as we are, we hinder God, and stop the current of His graces. But when He finds a soul permeated with a living faith, He pours into it His graces and His favours plenteously; into the soul they flow like a torrent, which, after being forcibly stopped against its ordinary course, when it has found a passage, spreads with impetuosity its pent-up flood.

"Yes, often we stop this torrent, by the little value we set upon it. But let us stop it no longer; let us enter into ourselves and break down the barrier which holds it back. Let us make the most of the day of grace, let us redeem the time that is lost."

Mystic terminology abounds in this material on degrees of prayer and may prove difficult and even disturbing for some readers. For whomever this is the case it is suggested that he read only as much as will give a general idea of the several degrees—that he pass over the detailed description of the higher degrees until some later time when his experience may make them more understandable.

Perhaps the future will see a more fully developed religious psychology which will have penetrated far enough into an understanding of the processes of prayer to develop a terminology more understandable to the lay reader. Fritz

Kunkel took a long step in this direction. Carl G. Jung has made major contributions to the psychological value and function of kinds of prayer, meditation, and religious symbols in the "individuation" process. Important work in this direction is also being accomplished by The Guild of Pastoral Psychology in England; and by some newer groups, such as The Guild for Psychological Studies in California, the Academy of Religion and Psychology of New York and others. Of course ideational knowledge about prayer and meditation will always be limited because it is necessary to go beyond intellect to immediate experience where the nonverbal, spontaneous insight is operative and where so much depends on the "Grace of God." All tested aids to inner catharsis which help clear the way for contact with the Transforming Center, whether of religious or phychotherapeutic origin, are of tremendous importance. Many emphases of psychotherapy surely are providing requisite supplements to the usual prayer procedures.—Ed.

DEGREES OF PRAYER

A careful study and analysis of the various states or degrees of prayer as given by spiritual writers enable us, avoiding subtle and, for practical purposes, unnecessary distinctions, to define three main steps by which the soul progresses toward a more perfect prayer.

1. Mental or Discursive Prayer.[4]
2. Affective Prayer, or the Prayer of Simplicity.
3. Active or Acquired Contemplation.

The essential note of progress in prayer is simplification. Beginning with mental prayer, in which there is a large use of the understanding, having as its end the motivating of the will, the soul, more or less unconsciously and by virtue of its fidelity, passes to a prayer in which the understanding moves the will much more rapidly—one thought, and that more and more single and simple, actuating to the acts of prayer. This, in turn, leads to a state in which recollection is almost constant, and the soul's prayer is but a more deliberate and direct centering of itself upon God at special times. Whereas, in mental prayer careful and deliberate attention had, as it were, to be forced upon Divine realities,

[4]See also "Confessional Meditation," p. 318–322.—Ed.

and the will moved to act by definite and prolonged reasoning, in the prayer of simplicity, acts follow thought without any appreciable interval, until in acquired contemplation the multiplicity of acts give way to a single direction of the soul toward God in which acts of prayer, as hitherto practised, are merged in an intuitive sight in which the soul no longer meditates upon God, nor addresses Him in varied acts, but simply, adoringly, and lovingly contemplates Him as its Supreme Good.

Those who will apply themselves faithfully to the practice of the interior life, who set their prayer in its rightful place and are prudently zealous in the matter of mortification, especially of self-will, ought to arrive in a comparatively short time at affective prayer.

I have already emphasized the fact that all souls are called to perfection, and this implies a more or less steady progress in the life of prayer, which, without any forcing, tends to seek that acquired contemplation which is the highest state possible to the soul's efforts aided by Divine grace. "Contemplation," says St. Thomas, "is for man the end of human life."

"It is the very aim of the teaching of Fr. Baker and his school that extraordinary prayer, contemplation, should be an ordinary state for Christian souls," said Bishop Hedley; also the Abbot of Pershore, "In point of fact, some of the best mystics and contemplatives are to be found in the world."

That this truth is so little recognised is largely due not only to the prevailing ignorance about any prayer except vocal prayer, intercessions and the like, but also because any mention of the higher states usually connotes to the mind such extraordinary phenomena as visions, locutions, raptures, ecstasy, which are comparatively rare and are not to be sought for or expected by any soul.

Further, many are held back by the thought that any advance would be only a mark of presumption in one so imperfect and full of failure. They are obsessed by the common error which seeks a self-made goodness as a condition for receiving the gifts of God, and give all their attention to efforts of their own when they should be simply abandoning themselves to the guidance of the Holy Spirit.

Another difficulty often arising in the minds of those who find themselves giving much more time to affective acts of the will, to the reiteration of a few acts or even one act of adoration, etc., than to actual meditation, or who remain motionless before God contemplating the Divine Majesty and Beauty, is the fear that they are "doing nothing." There is, of course, a danger of the soul drifting into a mere dreamy reverie in which nothing is done, and this must be checked at once by a return to considerations, acts[5] or resolutions, but when the eye of faith is riveted on God, the memory, imagination and will possessed by and drawn to Him, there is nothing to fear, for this is a state of prayer commended by all the Saints.

Père Surin says that there are three signs by which we may know that this kind of prayer is good and should be adhered to. First, that during the prayer the soul is in peace without any sense of weariness or ennui; second, that it goes forth from prayer with a great resolution to persevere in good; third, that during the day it sees clearly how to conduct itself and has much strength in the practice of virtue.*

Bede Frost, 1877–. English priest, Church of England.
The Art of Mental Prayer.

The education of the self in the successive degrees of orison has been compared by St. Theresa, in a celebrated passage in her life, to four ways of watering the garden of the soul so that it may bring forth its flowers and fruits. The first and most primitive of these ways is meditation.[5] This, she says, is like drawing water by hand from a deep well: the slowest and most laborious of all means of irrigation. Next to this is the orison of quiet,[6] which is a little better and easier: for here soul seems to receive some help, *i.e.*, with the stilling of the senses the subliminal faculties are brought into play. The well has now been fitted with a windlass—that little Moorish water-wheel possessed by every Castilian farm. Hence we get more water for the energy we expend—more sense of reality in exchange for our abstraction from the unreal. Also "the water is higher, and

[5]This first degree of Prayer is termed variously by different writers as Meditation, Recollection, Discursive Prayer, Mental Prayer, etc.—Ed.

[6]Prayer of Simplicity.—Ed.

accordingly the labour is much less than it was when the water had to be drawn out of the depths of the well. I mean that the water is nearer to it, for grace now reveals itself more distinctly to the soul." In the third stage, or orison of union, we leave all voluntary activities of the mind—the gardener no longer depends on his own exertions, contact between subject and object is established, there is no more stress and strain. It is as if a little river now ran through our garden and watered it. We have but to direct the stream. In the fourth and highest stage, God Himself waters our garden with rain from heaven "drop by drop." The attitude of the self is now that of perfect receptivity, "passive contemplation," loving trust. Individual activity is sunk in the "great life of the All."

Evelyn Underhill, 1875–1944. English writer, mystic.
Mysticism.

Detailed Description of Each Stage

Recollection ("Discursive Prayer")

All the scattered interests of the self have here to be collected; there must be a deliberate and unnatural act of attention, a deliberate expelling of all discordant images from the consciousness—a hard and ungrateful task.

The unfortunate word *Recollection,* which the hasty reader is apt to connect with remembrance, is the traditional term by which mystical writers define just such a voluntary concentration, such a gathering in of the attention of the self to its "most hidden cell." That self is as yet unacquainted with the strange plane of silence which so soon becomes familiar to those who attempt even the lowest activities of the contemplative life. It stands here between the two planes of its being; the Eye of Time is still awake. It knows that it wants to enter the inner world, but it must find some device to help it over the threshold—rather, in the language of psychology, to shift that threshold and permit its subliminal intuition of the Absolute to emerge.

This device is as a rule the practice of meditation, in which the state of Recollection usually begins: that is to say, the deliberate consideration of and dwelling upon some one aspect of Reality—an aspect most usually chosen from amongst the religious beliefs of the self. Thus Hindu mystics will brood upon a sacred word, whilst Christian contemplatives set before their minds one of the names or attributes of God, a fragment of Scripture, an incident of the life of Christ; and allow—indeed encourage—this consideration, and the ideas and feelings which flow from it, to occupy the whole mental field. This powerful suggestion, kept before the consciousness by an act of will, overpowers the stream of small suggestions which the outer world pours incessantly upon the mind. The self, concentrated upon this image or idea, dwelling on it more than thinking about it—as one may gaze upon a picture that one loves—sinks into itself, and becomes in the language of asceticism "recollected" or gathered together.

To one in whom this state is established, consciousness seems like a blank field, save for the "one point" in its centre, the subject of the meditation. Towards this focus the introversive self seems to press inwards from every side; still faintly conscious of the buzz of the external world outside its ramparts, but refusing to respond to its appeals. Presently the subject of meditation begins to take on a new significance; to glow with life and light. The contemplative suddenly feels that he knows it. . . . More, through it, hints are coming to him of mightier, nameless things. . . .

In these meditative and recollective states, the self still feels very clearly the edge of its own personality; its separateness from the Somewhat Other, the divine reality set over against the soul. It is aware of that reality: the subject of its meditation becomes a symbol through which it receives a distinct message from the transcendental world. There is yet no conscious fusion with a greater Life; no resting in the divine atmosphere, as in the "Quiet"; no involuntary and ecstatic lifting up of the soul to direct apprehension of truth, as in contemplation. . . .

This description makes it clear that "recollection" is a form of spiritual gymnastics; less valuable for itself than for the training which it gives, the powers which it develops.*

Evelyn Underhill, 1875–1944. English writer, mystic. *Mysticism.*

Prayer of Quiet

More important is the next great stage of orison; that curious and extremely definite mental state which mystics call the Prayer of Quiet or Simplicity, or sometimes the Interior Silence. This represents the result for consciousness of a further degree of that inward retreat which Recollection began.

Out of the deep, slow brooding and pondering on some mystery, some incomprehensible link between himself and the Real, or the deliberate practice of loving attention to God, the contemplative—perhaps by way of a series of moods and acts which his analytic powers may cause him "nicely to distinguish"—glides, almost insensibly, onto a plane of perception for which human speech has few equivalents. . . . Here the self passes beyond the stage at which its perceptions are capable of being dealt with by thought. It can no longer "take notes": can only surrender itself to the stream of an inflowing life, and to the direction of a larger will. Discursive thought would only interfere with this process; as it interferes with the vital processes of the body if it once gets them under its control.

With this surrender to something bigger, as with the surrender of conversion, comes an immense relief of strain. The giving up of I-hood, the process of self-stripping, which we have seen to be the essence of the purification of the self, finds its parallel in this phase of the contemplative experience.

To one who is entering this state, so startling, very often, is the deprivation of all his accustomed mental furniture, that the negative aspect of the condition dominates consciousness; and he can but describe it as a nothingness, a pure passivity, an emptiness, a "naked" orison. He is conscious that all, even in this utter emptiness, is well. Presently, however, he becomes aware that *Something* fills this emptiness. Ceasing to attend to the messages from without, he begins to notice That which has always been within. His whole being is thrown open to its influence: it permeates his consciousness.

There are, then, two aspects of the Orison of Quiet: the aspect of deprivation, of emptiness which begins it, and the aspect of acquisition, of something found, in which it is complete. In its description, all mystics will be found to lean to one side or the other, to the affirmative or negative element which it contains. The austere mysticism of Eckhart and his followers, their temperamental sympathy with the Neoplatonic language of Dionysius the Areopagite, caused them to describe it—and also very often the higher state of contemplation to which it leads—as above all things an emptiness, a divine dark, an ecstatic deprivation. They will not profane its deep satisfactions by the inadequate terms proper to earthly peace and joy. To St. Theresa, and mystics of her type, on the other hand, even a little and inadequate image of its joy seems better than none. To them it is a sweet calm, a gentle silence, in which the lover apprehends the presence of the Beloved: a God-given state, over which the self has little control.

The emptying of the field of consciousness, its cleansing of all images—even of those symbols of Reality which are the objects of meditation—is the necessary condition under which alone this encounter can take place.

"Quiet" of all forms of mystical activity has been the most abused, the least understood. Its theory, seized upon, divorced from its context, and developed to excess, produced the foolish and dangerous exaggerations of Quietism. The accusation of Quietism has been hurled at mystics whose only fault was a looseness of language which laid them open to misapprehension. Others, however, have certainly contrived, by a perversion and isolation of the teachings of great contemplatives on this point, to justify the deliberate production of a half-hypnotic state of passivity. With this meaningless state of "absorption in nothing at all" they were content; claiming that in it they were in touch with the divine life, and therefore exempt from the usual duties and limitations of human existence.

There can be no doubt that for selves of a certain psychical constitution, such a "false idleness" is only too easy of attainment. They can by wilful self-suggestion deliberately produce this emptiness . . . To do this from self-regarding motives, or to do it to excess . . . is a mystical vice. It leads to the absurdities of "holy indifference" and ends in the stultification of mental and moral life. The true mystic never tries deliberately to enter the orison of quiet. Where it exists in a healthy form, it appears spontaneously, as a phase in normal development; not as a self-induced condition, a psychic trick.[8]

The true condition of quiet, according to the great mystics, is at once active and passive . . . The departmental intellect is silenced, but the totality of character is flung open to the influence of the Real. Personality is not lost: only its hard edge is gone. A "rest most busy," says Hilton.

But though the psychological state which contemplatives call the prayer of quiet is a common condition of mystical attainment, it is not by itself mystical at all. It is a state of preparation: a way of opening the door. That which comes in when the door is opened will be that which we truly and passionately desire.*–**

Evelyn Underhill, 1875–1944. English writer, mystic.
Mysticism.

Contemplation

We must consider under the general name of contemplation those developed states of introversion in which the mystic attains somewhat: the results and rewards of the discipline of Recollection and Quiet. If this course of spiritual athletics has done its work, he has now brought to the surface, trained and made efficient for life, a form of consciousness—a medium of communication with reality—which remains undeveloped in ordinary men. In Contemplation, the self transcends alike the stages of symbol and of silence; and "energizes enthusiastically" on those high levels which are dark to the intellect but radiant to the heart. We must expect this contemplative activity to show itself in many different ways and take many different names, since its character will be largely governed by individual temperament. It appears under the forms which ascetic writers call "ordinary" and "extraordinary," "infused" or "passive" Contemplation; and as that "orison of union" which we have already discussed.

First, then, as to Contemplation proper: what is it? It is supreme manifestation of that indivisible "power of know-

[8]Much of the teaching of modern "mystical" cults is thus crudely quietistic. It insists on the necessity of "going into the silence," and even, with a strange temerity, gives preparatory lessons in subconscious meditation: a proceeding which might well provoke the laughter of the saints.

ing" which lies at the root of all our artistic and spiritual satisfaction. . . . It is an act, not of the Reason, but of the whole personality working under the stimulus of mystic love. Hence, its results feed every aspect of that personality: minister to its instinct for the Good, the Beautiful, and the True. Psychologically it is an induced state, in which the field of consciousness is greatly contracted: the whole of the self, its conative powers, being sharply focused, concentrated upon one thing. We pour ourselves out or, as it sometimes seems to us, *in* towards this overpowering interest: seem to ourselves to reach it and be merged with it. Whatever the thing may be, in this act it is given to us and we *know* it, as we cannot know it by the ordinary devices of thought.

The turning of our attention from that crisp and definite world of multiplicity, that cinematograph-show, with which intelligence is accustomed and able to deal, has loosed new powers of perception which we never knew that we possessed. Instead of sharply perceiving the fragment, we apprehend, yet how we know not, the solemn presence of the whole. Deeper levels of personality are opened up, and go gladly to the encounter of the universe. That universe, or some Reality hid between it and ourselves, responds to "the true lovely will of our heart." Our ingoing concentration is balanced by a great outgoing sense of expansion, of new worlds made ours, as we receive the inflow of its life. So complete is the self's absorption that it is for the time unconscious of any acts of mind or will; in technical language, its "faculties are suspended." This is the "ligature" frequently mentioned by teachers of contemplative prayer, and often regarded as an essential character of mystical states.

The object of the mystic's contemplation is always some aspect of the Infinite Life: of "God, the one Reality." Hence, that enhancement of vitality which artists or other unself-conscious observers may receive from their communion with scattered manifestations of Goodness, Truth, and Beauty, is in him infinitely increased . . . In the contemplative act, his whole personality, directed by love and will, transcends the sense-world, casts off its fetters, and rises to freedom . . . There it apprehends the supra-sensible by immediate contact, and knows itself to be in the presence of the "Supplier of true Life." Such Contemplation—such positive attainment of the Absolute—is the *whole act* of which the visions of poets, the intuition of philosophers, give us hints.

It is a brief act. The greatest of the contemplatives have been unable to sustain the brilliance of this awful vision for more than a little while . . . "My mind," says St. Augustine, in his account of his first purely contemplative glimpse of the One Reality . . . "with the flash of one hurried glance, attained to the vision of *That Which Is* . . . but I could not sustain my gaze: my weakness was dashed back, and I was relegated to my ordinary experience, bearing with me only a loving memory, and as it were the fragrance of those desirable meats on the which as yet I was not able to feed." This fragrance, as St. Augustine calls it, remains forever with those who have thus been initiated. They can never tell us in exact and human language *what* it was that they attained . . . though by their oblique utterances, they give us the assurance that the Object of their discovery is one with the object of our quest . . .

Contemplation is not, like meditation, one simple state, governed by one set of psychic conditions. It is a general name for a large group of states, partly governed—like all other forms of mystical activity—by the temperament of the subject, and accompanied by feeling-states which vary from the extreme of quietude or "peace in life naughted" to the rapturous and active love in which "thought into song is turned." Some kinds of Contemplation are inextricably entwined with the phenomena of "intellectual vision" and "inward voices." In others we find what seems to be a development of the "Quiet": a state which the subject describes as a blank absorption, a darkness, or "contemplation in caligine."*–**

Evelyn Underhill, 1875–1944. English writer, mystic.
Mysticism.[9]

Indications of Progress

What are the normal signs which mark the transition from one stage to another? Actually, two movements have to be considered: first, the passage from the ordinary men-

---

[9]See *Mysticism* pp. 298–379 for a full and illuminating description of the degrees of prayer. The selections included here necessarily present them in an abridged form.—Ed.

tal prayer of beginners to affective prayer, and second, that from affective prayer to ordinary, acquired contemplation. In the first case there is a gradual but increasing ability to pass more rapidly from considerations and the use of the imagination to acts of prayer. The soul finds in a single thought, or even in the act of placing herself in the presence of God, a desire and a facility to pour herself out in affective acts of prayer—catches fire, as it were, at once, without the labour of reflection hitherto necessary. It is not so much that meditation becomes more difficult as that it becomes less necessary . . . The test which determines the need and the time of making this advance in the prayer-life is the attraction the soul feels toward a more actual prayer, as contrasted with the exercise of the mind, etc., which leads to prayer . . .

The signs which mark the transition between affective prayer and ordinary or acquired contemplation are three in number: (1) An inability to make reflections or to exercise the imagination upon Divine truths, coupled with an aridity resulting from the endeavour to make such acts wherein previously light and consolation were present. So long as meditation is fruitful, it should be persevered in; nor must it be supposed that the entry upon contemplation precludes any return to formal meditation, for until the new state has become habitual, "sometimes one, sometimes the other," occurs in this time of proficiency in such a way that very often the soul finds itself in this loving or peaceful attendance upon God, with all its facilities in repose, and very often also will find it necessary, for that end, to have recourse to meditation. (2) Secondly, the will is more firmly rooted in God. It sees more clearly that thoughts about God and the means by which He is apprehended and approached are not God; that they are to be used, not rested in or enjoyed in themselves. (3) The third sign, "which is the most certain of the three," consists in the fact that the soul finds itself at peace in this prayer, undisturbed by any scruples that it is doing nothing, or that it is losing ground.

It is important to note that all three signs must be present before the soul may safely give up the practice of ordinary mental prayer . . . But the third sign sets its seal upon the others, providing the soul with an assurance that, despite the subtlety and delicacy of this new state, it has begun to find the fruit sought in the labour of mental prayer. It is the end—itself unending, for there can be no end in the sense of a full stop to the soul's growth in the loving knowledge of God.*–**

Bede Frost, 1877–. English priest, Church of England.
The Art of Mental Prayer.

One person who has mastered life is better than a thousand persons who have mastered only the contents of books, but no one can get anything out of life without God. If I were looking for a master of learning, I should go to Paris to the colleges where the higher studies are pursued, but if I wanted to know about the perfection of life, they could not tell me there.

Where, then, should I go? To (someone who has) a nature that is pure and free and nowhere else: there I should find the answer for which I so anxiously inquire.

Meister Johannes Eckhart, 1260–1327.
German scholar, mystic.

The young Tobias, when commanded to go to Rages, said: "I have no knowledge of the way." "Go then," replied his father, "and seek out some man to guide thee." "I say the same to you, my Philothea. Do you wish in good earnest to set out on the way to devotion? Seek out some good man to guide and conduct you; it is the admonition of admonitions." "Although you may search," says the devout Avila, "you will never find out the will of God so assuredly, as by the way of this humble obedience, so much recommended and practised by all the devout men of old."

Saint Francis de Sales, 1567–1622. French Bishop of Geneva.
Introduction to the Devout Life. Trans. Allan Ross.

The real purpose of direction, he (Dom Chapman) insisted, was to keep the soul humble, and prevent it from trusting to its unaided judgment, or putting too much confidence in its own lights. He was fully alive to the dangers to which an imprudent Director could expose his penitents, realising how disastrous it was if—as sometimes happened—direction should degenerate into an orgy of self-analysis or over-introspection. A good Director, he held, must be a nurse, no more. He should confine himself to the task of teaching his penitent how to walk alone and unaided. That done, he should be ready to retire into the background;

only emerging on rare occasions when unusual circumstances or some particular crisis called for his assistance. Directors of this kind would be no danger to simplicity or humility, while an over-dogmatic or too eager Director, giving unsuitable or unnecessary advice with relish and impressiveness, would harm both his penitent and himself.

The spiritual life is nourished—to speak of natural means only—chiefly by prayer and by reading. With regard to books, he insisted on two definite principles; first, that one should read only what appealed to one, and secondly, that different books were necessary at different times in the soul's progress.

Dom John Chapman, O.S.B., 1865–1933.
English biblical and patristic scholar.
Spiritual Letters of Dom John Chapman.

Role of the Spiritual Director

The director of souls in the spiritual life must have a very clear, definite and convinced knowledge (1) of the scope and limitations of his office; (2) the end which is to be sought; (3) the means to be used; (4) the manner of applying those means to various classes of souls. [See author's text for long discussion of 4th point.]

(1) The office of a director is a subordinate, dependent one. His sole work is to wait upon God, to seek to discern the Divine will for each soul, to co-operate with the Divine leading by aiding the soul to see, understand and follow it. "It is necessary that the confessor should be an interior man, a man of prayer, a man well versed in spiritual things, as much by his own experience as by study and reading; that he should have no purely natural designs, either of vanity or self-interest, but that he should only consider the glory of God and the good of souls; that he should never act according to the leadings of his own spirit, but that he should judge of the things of God by the spirit of God" (Grou, Manual for Interior Souls, p. 128).

The director, then, must have a high regard and deep reverence for souls, and for the designs of God for each soul. Directors too often fall into the temptation of forcing souls according to their own predilections, of domineering and dictating, assuming a personal authority which is quite unjustifiable. "Their aim should be, then, not to guide souls by a way of their own suitable to themselves, but to ascertain, if they can, the way by which God Himself is guiding them. If they cannot ascertain it, let them leave these souls alone and not disquiet them" (St. John of the Cross, *The Living Flame*, Stanza iii). Mgr. Gay, whom Mgr. d'Hulst called "the master of spiritual direction in the nineteenth century," writes to a penitent who desired to follow his direction with the exact obedience of a servant to a master: "I shall not employ, at least habitually, in spite of your desire, the imperative formulas of which you speak. It seems to you that so you would find peace. Yes, but a natural peace which is not what I wish. Such commands would relieve you of the burdens of life, but it is good that you should feel the weight of them. I would help you, not substitute myself for you. Strong natures have need of obedience; weak ones, such as yours, have a gentleness which inclines to idleness. It is necessary to give to each according to their needs. I do not want you to be a slave—the word is your own—a word excessive and reprehensible. I wish you to be a son, and a son reasonable, enlightened by the counsels of his father . . . but walking as a man, not as a child." (Lettres, iv. 10)

It necessarily follows that a soul cannot be directed until it is known, and that what is principally to be known is the particular will of God for it. "In the direction of a soul it is necessary to begin, and this is all-important, with an understanding of its interior state. If you know well the state of a soul, the operation of God and the action of grace within it, you have gained a very clear knowledge of the designs of God for it. But that is not all; the obstacles which grace finds there must also be seen, the action of the soul and its character, the vices and faults which exist. Further, to cause a soul to advance it must be brought back to the principle of sanctity within it, to Divine grace. I regard it as essential in direction that one shall allow grace to act with a great freedom, seek to distinguish false attraits from the true, and prevent souls from wandering from, or going beyond, the limits of such attraits."

(2) The end to be sought. This is nothing less than the end for which man was created, to seek, find, know, praise, reverence and serve God.

Now this emphatically does not mean that we set before our eyes a certain ideal of sanctity and endeavour to force all souls into the paths by which that ideal was attained, for, although the end is one, it has to be reached in the particular way desired by our Lord. . . . The whole setting of a soul has to be considered, and what needs far more insistence upon than it commonly gets is the truth that the sanctification of a soul depends upon its fulfilling the duties of its state as perfectly as possible with the aid of grace.

(3) The means to be used. . . . Too much direction is moral rather than spiritual, more concerned with sin than with God, with self-examination and self-improvement rather than with the search for God. "It is a great grace from God to practise self-examination, but too much is as bad as too little, as they say, believe me, by God's help, we shall advance more by contemplating His divinity than by keeping our eyes fixed on ourselves" (St. Teresa, *Interior Castle*, M.I., chap. ii 9).

A director should always adopt a certain attitude of reserve toward those whom he directs. Frequent intercourse is undesirable; long visits, conversations and profuse correspondence to be avoided; the relation between director and directed should always be *in Christo.*

Far from attaching souls to himself, the director must do all that lies in his power to enable them to walk in entire dependence upon the guidance and in the power of the Holy Spirit. People will ask, for instance, what particular mortification they should undertake, and it is often better to answer by pointing out that, the end of all mortification being the bringing of our will into union with the Divine Will, they can probably think of something which they have not yet done, and which they need to do, to effect this more completely.

In order that a soul should not only begin well, but also advance in the way of perfection, there are certain essential points which directors should keep in mind. The first is the need of establishing the soul in a true peace. To this end not only is a general confession advisable, but also a full and frank account of one's life, circumstances, difficulties, graces received, etc. A soul cannot be directed, as I have said, unless it is known, and many go on making routine confessions for years without ever knowing themselves or making themselves known in such a way that any adequate direction can be given. There is always an unknown region in which, consciously or unconsciously lie the roots of sins confessed again and again, and this suffices to prevent that peace without which no progress can be made.

Second, the director's work being to further the will of God in souls, he must make them see the personal nature of religion, personal love, devotion, and service for God in Jesus Christ; not a mere tame acquiescence in a moral code, but a burning enthusiasm for a Master. For—strange as it may sound the Christian religion is this, the joyous, heroic, magnificent thing the Saints have seen and lived; not the dull, cold, safe, respectable and comfortable travesty to which the English eighteenth and nineteenth centuries reduced it.

The director should never tend to rigorism. The Saints, ever hard upon themselves, were ever tender towards others.

Père Ginhac, S.J., says, "Severe directors teach virtue rather than perfection. To acquire virtue, fear is useful, but to progress toward perfection, love is necessary. Fear makes servants; love, the children of God." (Cagnac, *Lettres Spirituelles en France,* 11. 262.)

The common desire, too, to immerse themselves in active works should be closely watched, for their chief concern at first must be with their own souls, their most necessary practices, prayer and mortification. If some active work seems to be desirable, it should be of as hard and as hidden a nature as possible. There are already too many unspiritual amateurs doing "parochial work"; priests will be well advised to see that any work done for God and for souls can only be done by humble, obedient, loving, practising Christians, and to spend some of the time in producing such, being content to wait, seeing many things left undone, until he has trained souls who are in some degree capable of being the instruments of Divine grace. Third, to establish a true peace in souls and to nourish their good desires means that their prayer-life must be the director's first and continuous concern. Unless such are taught to pray, they are taught nothing. To inspire a soul with the true idea of prayer, to get it interested in its prayer, is the greatest thing we can do for it. The director, then, must inquire as to the knowledge of the end, value and practice of prayer possessed, the kind of prayer made, the particular difficulties encountered, the attraits and special devotions to which the soul is led, and. where necessary, he must choose for and direct the soul in such methods of prayer as seem most suitable.

Now nothing of this can be done unless the director is himself convinced of the necessity and value of prayer, and this will be in proportion to his own practice and experience of prayer. Study of the science of prayer is most necessary, as necessary as it is wanting, but no degree of study alone will give that sense of conviction which is needed in order to be convincing. "Without prayer, our work will be sterile, our words dry, our direction altogether unfruitful. . . . All the faults which arise in the direction of souls come from the fact that directors do not apply themselves to the holy exercise of prayer (M. Olier, *Spresit 'D'un Directeur,* Art. i.).*–**

Bede Frost, 1877–. English priest, Church of England.
The Art of Mental Prayer.

Important Aids to Prayer and Meditation

The Practice of Mortification[10]

Mortification or deliberate dying to self is inculcated with an uncompromising firmness in the canonical writings of Christianity, Hinduism, Buddhism and most of the other major and minor religions of the world, and by every theocentric saint and spiritual reformer who has ever lived out and expounded the principles of the Perennial Philosophy. But this "self-naughting" is never (at least by anyone who knows what he is talking about) regarded as an end in itself. It possesses merely an instrumental value, as the indispensable means to something else.

That mortification is the best which results in the elimination of self-will, self-interest, self-centered thinking, wishing and imagining. Extreme physical austerities are not likely to achieve this kind of mortification. But the acceptance of what happens to us (apart, of course, from our own sins) in the course of daily living *is* likely to achieve this kind of mortification. If specific exercises in self-denial are undertaken, they should be inconspicuous, non-compet-

[10]The full discussion of mortification in Chap. VI of *The Perennial Philosophy* will richly reward the careful reader. —Ed.

itive and un-injurious to health. Thus, in the matter of diet, most people will find it sufficiently mortifying to refrain from eating all the things which the experts in nutrition condemn as unwholesome. And where social relations are concerned, self-denial should take the form, not of showy acts of would-be humility, but of control of the tongue and the moods—in refraining from saying anything uncharitable or merely frivolous (which means, in practice, refraining from about fifty per cent of ordinary conversation), and in behaving calmly and with quiet cheerfulness when external circumstances or the state of our bodies predisposes us to anxiety, gloom or an excessive elation.

Perhaps the most difficult of all mortifications is to achieve a "holy indifference" to the temporal success or failure of the cause to which one has devoted one's best energies. If it triumphs, well and good; and if it meets defeat, that also is well and good, if only in ways that, to a limited and time-bound mind, are here and now entirely incomprehensible.

Sufficient not only unto the day, but also unto the place, is the evil thereof. Agitation over happenings which we are powerless to modify, either because they have not yet occurred, or else are occurring at an inaccessible distance from us, achieves nothing beyond the inoculation of here and now with the remote or anticipated evil that is the object of our distress. Listening four or five times a day to newscasters and commentators, reading the morning papers and all the weeklies and monthlies—nowadays, this is described as "taking an intelligent interest in politics." St. John of the Cross would have called it indulgence in idle curiosity and the cultivation of disquietude for disquietude's sake.

In the practice of mortification as in most other fields, advance is along a knife-edge. On one side lurks the Scylla of egocentric austerity, on the other the Charybdis of an uncaring quietism. The holy indifference inculcated by the exponents of the Perennial Philosophy is neither stoicism nor mere passivity. It is rather an active resignation. Self-will is renounced, not that there may be a total holiday from willing, but that the divine will may use the mortified mind and body as its instrument for good.*–**

Aldous Huxley, 1894–1963. English writer, literary critic.
The Perennial Philosophy.

The Practice of Daily Reading

If we look into the daily regimen of the men and women who seem to us to be growing in the religious life, we shall seldom find them neglecting to read nor failing to acknowledge that what they have read has profoundly influenced what they have done.

Not all lawyers emulate Sir Thomas More. Yet I happen to know two of the ablest legal minds in Philadelphia who are the most eager readers of devotional works and who find this nurture an imperative in keeping inwardly fresh and sensitive. These men are hungry. They are conscious of need and they are not too proud to ask for help. Close friends of mine ask one another, "What do you feed on?" "Where are you finding light?" "Who has pointed you most directly to what is real?" They want bread, not a diet of *hors d'oeuvres*. They want to be directed, not diverted. They are becoming less interested in reading about religion and religious controversy than in reading works that have sprung out of the religious response to life and hence that minister to it in themselves. In short, they are in search of books that will strengthen, increase, and intensify devotion. And devotion, we recall, means the "promptitude, fervor, affection, and agility" in our response to the burning ray of love that attends us. Here there is a longing for voices that speak of discovery, of its way, and of its object.

"People do not read this *sacred* literature today: they are too 'emancipated.' They will read Dostoevsky with avidity —chiefly because he lived a large part of his time in Hell, with the topography of which they are themselves perfectly familiar. But they forget that Dostoevsky himself was a passionate student of the New Testament. They are sensationalists; they want strong, rich meat, and find the dry bread of true spiritual teaching unassimilable. Yet I am bold to suggest that they will discover in the end that they cannot afford to dispense with it. . . . It is not going too far to suggest that every individual who pursues his search for spiritual illumination with sufficient persistence finally finds himself obliged to leave secular literature behind him. He must sit at the feet of those who, even if they are less sympathetic figures, owe their authority to the fact that they are standing on more elevated ground. He must study scripture."[11]

How many times one has laid the *Bible* aside in favor of what seemed more real and compelling or more attractive and readable witnesses to the religious life, only to be driven back to it again by the great hunger to let the measured dignity and beauty of its language stir in him an emotion like that which comes in listening to classical music or in seeing a finely proportioned building.

Revealing writing shares its treasures progressively and only at a price. It exacts a willingness on the reader's part to let go his tense, tightly-clenched efforts at inner security, and a willingness to let the angel freely trouble the waters of his life to his healing. But for one who is in growth, and is seeking to yield, the *Bible* becomes an indispensable companion because it does reveal the way and because it seems to point beyond to infinitely more of the same source of light which he has already experienced.

The cloud of witnesses and teachers, however, did not end at the close of the first century. And those who seek for nurture in the religious life are acutely conscious of the fact that revelation is continuous. It has never stopped. In the eighteen intervening centuries a whole row of rich classics has appeared. They will not all speak to the needs of each person who reads them. We often find real companions who are to be cultivated by long intimacy, only at the end of a considerable search, a search that we must make for ourselves . . .

"Sacred Literature," to use Lawrence Hyde's term, does not, however, exhaust the materials that may be used in devotional reading. Well-chosen biography is another source of reading that quickens devotion.

In reading devotional literature, the limitations of time and the wisdom of those who have used it most profitably agree in urging the wise use of the veto. We cannot read all. We must select. Find a few spiritual "*staples*" and feed on them until you know them. Be proud to be ignorant of vast areas of the "religious book" field. Nowhere does novelty count so little as in devotional reading. Few young people today and too few of those in my generation have

[11]Lawrence Hyde, *Prospects of Humanism,* pp. 161–163 (Scribner, 1931).

ever carefully read the same book through five times or even three. A real devotional book is one that you can live with year after year and that never stales or never fails to speak to some needs in your life.*–**

Douglas V. Steere, 1901–.
American author, professor of philosophy.
Prayer and Worship.

PSYCHO-PHYSICAL AIDS

"We only believe those thoughts which have been conceived not in the brain but in the whole body."[12] This is a significant insight. For it is well known that the Western approach to life (owing so much to the Greeks) is intellectual, cerebral, syllogistic. In the realm of prayer, for instance, spiritual writers have ingeniously analyzed man's memory, understanding, and will: but they have had little to say about his breathing, his abdomen, his eyes, and his hands. The East, on the other hand, still remembers that man can adore God with his whole body, and has developed methods of concentration that go back to prehistoric days. And from all this, the West can learn much. For surely, as Yeats so truly remarks, the notional assent given to the conclusion of a syllogism often has little real motive power in a man's life and may be lightly cast aside in moments of emotional crisis; but the conviction conceived in the whole body is less easily lost.

William Johnston, S.J., contemporary professor and writer.
The Stillpoint.

What the body does during prayer and meditation is almost as important as what the mind and spirit do. It therefore behooves anyone who wants to go beyond the rudiments of prayer to pay intelligent attention to the immutable laws of God concerning his marvelous body instrument.

Relaxation— . . . we are in reality thinking an impossibility when we talk about relaxing the average un-coordinated mind-body organism during prayer, until we have tackled the root-problem of coordination during all one's

[12]W. B. Yeats, *Certain Noble Plays of Japan.*

hours, whether one be lying, sitting, standing or walking. [However,] in lieu of solving the major problem of body-mind coordination, here are a few suggestions which have proved their usefulness.

The place to begin to relax is in the neck, which is not only the bridge between the body and the head but is also the key which locks or unlocks most of the body's tensions. The trouble is that most beginners who try to relax try too hard. The best way is not to try at all, but simply to sit quietly and wait, mentally stepping aside and *allowing* the neck to relax itself in its own skillful way. Other parts of the body may be treated in the same way: hands, feet, shoulders, chin, eyes, throat, abdomen. But after one has learned the simple trick of letting go with the neck, the rest of the body should automatically lose much of its tightness.

Even after the neck is relaxed, the eyes may need special consideration. For most eyes have from childhood built up a habit of strain which it sometimes takes patience to overcome. One may need to stop a moment and remind the eyes to let go. Or one may cover the closed eyes with the crossed hands in that ancient attitude of prayer, which has to its advantage not only the value of association but also a physiological result from the warmth of the hands.

Breathing—Slow, rhythmic breathing is a great means to body-mind relaxation and has always been considered one of the chief steps in acquiring that serenity and poise which must precede and accompany fruitful meditation. . . . To re-learn rightly the natural skill of breathing may take serious instruction and practice. Nevertheless, there is much that anyone who really desires it can do for himself.

The first thing to remember is to begin slowly. Think about breathing for only very short periods at first, then gradually increase the time. The second thing to remember is that nobody has to strain to take in air. Our world of atmospheric pressure gives us freely each breath of air in good measure, providing only that we expand and contract the thoracic air-box and receive the breath that is poured into it. Much harm can be done by forgetting to be receivers only and trying to be grabbers.

Another point to remember is that the air as it comes in should go as far back in the body as possible. One can test himself by laying a hand on the chest and watching to see whether it moves as he breathes. If it does, inhibit this rising and falling of the chest-wall and think of the air as going down the *back* of the body-cavity. Of course, it actually fills the whole lung-space, but this device of thinking it down—and up—the inside of the backbone helps to involve the back-muscles, without the danger of unnatural effort and strain. Contrary to most people's habits, these back muscles should move rhythmically out and in with each inhalation and expulsion of breath.

In this way one may sit or lie quietly and breathe slowly in and out, perhaps counting at first in order to establish rhythm, letting the rhythmic swing of the diaphragm accomplish those many physical and mental results which must be accomplished before serenity and detachment can be expected. Such rhythmic breathing, once established during a conscious period of preparation for meditation, is put into the unconscious by a standing-order to maintain this kind of rightness during the meditation period—and after. The hint is soon taken, providing: that we don't strain or try to take in too much air, that at first the reminders are short enough and frequent enough, and that they are in line with the wonderfully co-ordinated mechanism with which we were originally endowed.

Posture— . . . the position of the body during prayer is important. It should be a relaxed and balanced position. Of course the traditional Christian position for prayer is down on the knees. This posture [includes] the body [in with] the spirit's adoration and humility. It is, however, a difficult position to maintain for many moments at a time and is therefore not usually best for those who believe that time and a sense of leisureliness are needed for prayer.

The other great traditional position is that used by many Eastern and some Western meditators—sometimes called the meditation position—in which one sits cross-legged on the floor, arms crossed or a hand on each thigh. This position is difficult for Western muscles, accustomed only to sitting on chairs, but if one begins with a five minute period and gradually increases the time, it soon becomes comfortable—perhaps even more conducive to wholeness and recollection than any other position. . . . [It] stretches the spine naturally, frees the circulation and the breathing and helps the body to be "whole."

All these matters of breathing, posture and physical relaxation may seem entirely too physiological to be important to anyone whose chief concern is with his spirit. They may, however, make the difference between a blocked channel and one that is open for the waters of God to flow through. In a matter of such supreme import no detail is unworthy of our serious attention and action.*–**

Helen Molyneaux Salisbury, 1883–1958.
American poet, teacher of Body-Mind Co-Ordination.
Written for this anthology.

The Element of Time

We have to make access to our subconscious and we know that it is difficult for us individualized, materialized Westerners. We must then approach that threshold when the diurnal tide favours, when the body-mind is passing from its rest on the sleep-facet to its rest on its waking-facet. It is no use attempting to cross a bar when the tide is out. Evening and morning are therefore probably the best times. When the mind is recovering from sleep it has now been established that it takes a full hour to close one aperture and open fully the other. Dreams, most people know, last often for an hour or two in the memory and then like hoar-frost are gone. When the mind is approaching sleep, it again passes across the threshold. Hypnotic and all subconscious suggestion-therapy has shown that there is a belt of accessibility to the deeper mind, or, perhaps a better, more exact simile, a stage of compromise when the two apertures of apprehension (that of the conscious and that of the subconscious mind) partly overlap. Then exchange can take place and the consciousness which has insight can inform the normal consciousness which, because it looks out exclusively on the world of physical action, has possession of material means.

For an hour after sleep, while dreams can still be recalled and an hour before, when the mind is preparing for sleep, intercommunication is possible. It is wise to reserve a considerable portion of these periods for spiritual exercises.*

Anonymous.

The Place of the Symbol

We cannot know our inner world directly—in the same way as we can know our heart beat or our pulse. The actions and reactions of our inward archetypes are known by way of symbols. We "know" through images that stand for something other than, and greater than, themselves. True symbols always have vistas of mystery standing behind them. If they do not, they are signs—as a traffic signal is a sign rather than a symbol.

By our symbols we shall be known. They carry and express our uniqueness and our ordinariness. They impart to life its bright or dark imaginativeness. The artist cannot live without symbols, and sometimes knows it. The child lives unconsciously and spontaneously through them . . . Most adults live without being aware that they are constantly surrounded by symbols and therefore their existences are lusterless and often meaningless. If the earth could speak it might say "How can I tell man I am here to serve him and be served by him? I will tell him through buds and blossoms in spring, through full fruit at harvest, through winter silences." And if the unconscious world of man could speak it might say, "How can I tell him I too am here to serve and be served? I will tell him through symbols woven into dreams, myths, religious rituals, art, the play of children, and into all persons or situations or things which move him with joy, grief, fear, anger, despair, love." As soon as we look into the mirror of the waters we are face to face with the multiplicity of our being—best to worst—by way of symbols. And if the "all" is to be used toward a wholeness of living and loving, religiously meaningful life needs to be based on symbolic life made conscious.

Elizabeth Boyden Howes, contemporary Jungian analyst.
Sheila Moon, contemporary Jungian analyst and poet.
Man the Choicemaker.

Our epoch is scientifically and technically minded. We want first of all to understand and to know and we believe in reason. And so we try to do the same in understanding religious ideas. But religious ideas are always and everywhere symbolic truths. They can never be understood in a rational way alone. They are, as symbols, both rational and irrational; they are paradoxical. They unite psychical facts of the conscious and unconscious mind. Though they appeal to our reason and knowledge, they have contents which we cannot yet know because they are only in the making. Religion is in its essence symbolic and every religious symbol, when it originated, was an experience surpassing conscious knowledge. When a religion becomes established, symbols are worked into dogmas. The Roman Catholic Church understands even the dogma to be a symbolic truth. "The dogma unites knowing and not knowing, something which is intelligible and something which is unintelligible, a clarity and at the same time a mystery."[13]

One of the most valuable achievements of Professor Jung is to have reopened the way to symbolic thinking. By this he has led us to understand religious ideas of every race and time. He also helps the modern individual either to understand his own religion in a deeper and more vital way or to find and to experience symbols which come to him from the depths of the unconscious, from that creative psyche which has always been the mother of all the things and ideas which move humanity. The symbols which are born in someone with the help of psychology are individual, but are at the same time universal, because they derive from that layer in man which is common to all. Thus the individual is enriched by an inner creative life which is full of meaning, and at the same time he is connected with mankind in a more vital way than merely rational and conscious efforts could achieve. He may not adhere to a given church or creed, but the Christian spirit which should unite all mankind cannot be denied to him.*

Toni Wolff, 1888–1953. Swiss analytical psychologist.
Christianity Within.

---

[13]*Die Gnosides Christentums* (Salzburg, 1939).

CHAPTER V

Prayer and Meditation

(Continued)

If worship is the highest activity of man's spirit we shall expect to find it difficult. But we shall also expect to find that there are avenues leading to worship for all sorts and conditions of men.

AUTHOR UNKNOWN

Such practise of inward orientation is no more counsel for monks retired in cloisters. This practise is the heart of religion.

THOMAS R. KELLY

Procedures and Patterns for Meditation

The procedures and patterns included here are suggestions only—stimuli to original meditation plans. If classified, they would fall mainly under discursive meditation. Continued practice should move one toward the more simplified forms wherein one touches the mystery and wonder of something More, both within and beyond oneself.

Since one of the purposes of meditation is to convince the conscious as well as influence the unconscious mind concerning the existence of a supra-personal reality and develop an openness toward it, the choice of material should be guided by one's own background and experience—by what speaks to one. It may take initiative and patience to discover an approach that is meaningful, that will aid in recalling to one's mind and heart what is of the highest Value.

There is a variety of terminology used in this chapter, some of which may be a hindrance to certain readers. However, as one's inner experience deepens, such differences will become less and less important. Running through the meditations can be noted a number of inner movements or steps. In general they are: "facing up" to one's condition and the condition of society—seeing the "shadow" side of each and their interrelatedness and need; recalling the power, love and transforming creativity of God—realizing it as present *now;* surrendering oneself to God for guidance: and resolving to make whatever changes in attitudes and habit patterns are revealed as necessary in following the Way.

The two elements in the Life-giving process are included in the above steps—the emptying and the filling—the purgative and the illuminating. It is obviously important that there is a balance of these two in one's meditative practice.

Two classic methods are included in this material which emphasize the life and "mysteries" of "our Lord." If they do not appeal to the reader he need only move on to the more modern approaches. It is well, however, not to overlook the significant evidence that such classic writings offer concerning the effectiveness of meditation on the life and teachings of Jesus (and, indeed, on those others in whom the spirit of God has been regnant). The visualizing of incidents in the life of Christ has long been one of the most inspiring and transforming for vast numbers of people. The records of Jesus' life are open to all. A fresh study of them can yield richly in subject matter[1] for meditation, as well as for a general heightening of vision and purpose—something of which one is in constant need.

The important step is to *start* one's inner work—to persist each day in taking time to "center down." One can begin developing the ability to become quiet and to become aware of the deep Values through such a simple exercise as focusing one's attention on a flower or other meaningful symbol, or on a short phrase around which to bind one's attention. One simply opens oneself and allows the symbol

[1]See the new paperback edition of the psychological interpretation of the Gospel of Matthew by Fritz Kunkel entitled *Creation Continues* (Word Publisher 1973), and *The Kingdom Within* (Lippincott) by John Sanford. Both are remarkable studies, using both psychological and religious insights in their approach. Another book on Jesus of the three gospels by Elizabeth Boyden Howes is now in process.

to speak. Thus does an artist "perceive"—by becoming quietly absorbed in what he wishes to observe. This practice quiets the ego and relaxes the mind so that one is more ready to move into a consideration of deeper realities.

One often finds it necessary to actually "steal" the time from other "important" activities in order to practice the necessary, recentering disciplines. But what could be more important or rewarding than to work toward allowing one's life to be transformed. Meditation is one of the methods which encourages such transformation.—Ed.

CLASSIC METHODS OF TRAINING

There are six Classic Schools of mystic training represented in the Catholic tradition. They are: The Ignatian, The Carmelite, The Salesian, The Liguorian, The Franciscan and The Oratorian. While each has its unique emphasis they agree fundamentally on method. Brief advices and procedures for the beginner from only two are represented here.

The Salesian Method

But perhaps you do not know, Philothea, how to make mental prayer; for it is a thing which unhappily few persons in this age of ours know how to practice. For this reason, I will give you a simple and brief method to that end, until such time as, by reading some of the good books which have been composed on this subject, and above all by practice you may be more fully instructed.

The Preparation. I note first the preparation, which consists in two points, the first of which is to place yourself in the presence of God, and the second to invoke his assistance —principal ways of placing yourself in the presence of God.

1. The first consists in a lively and attentive apprehension of the omnipresence of God, which means that God is in everything and everywhere, and that there is not any place or thing in this world where he is not most assuredly present; so that, just as the birds, wherever they fly, always encounter the air, so, wherever we go, or wherever we are, we find God present. Everyone knows this truth, but everyone is not attentive to grasp it—before prayer we must always

stir up our souls to an attentive thought and consideration of this presence of God.

The second is to think that not only is God in the place where you are, but that he is in a very special manner in your heart and in the depth of your spirit.

The third way consists in making use of the imagination alone, representing to ourselves the Saviour in his sacred humanity, as though he were near to us.

2. The invocation is made in this manner: your soul, having realized that she is in the presence of God, prostrates herself with profound reverence, acknowledging her unworthiness.

3. After these two ordinary points of the meditation, there is a third which is not common to all sorts of meditations; it is that which is called by some the composition of place. This is no other thing than to represent to the imagination the scene of the mystery upon which the meditation is made, as though it were actually taking place in our presence.

By means of this imaginary scene we confine our spirit within the mystery upon which we intend to meditate, so that it may not range hither and thither. Yet some will tell you that, in the representation of these mysteries, it is better to make use of the simple thought of faith, and of a simple apprehension entirely mental and spiritual, or else to consider that the things are done within your own spirit; but that is too subtle for a commencement, and until such time as God may raise you higher, I counsel you, Philothea, to remain in the low valley which I have shown you.

The Considerations. After the action of the imagination, follows the action of the understanding, which we call meditation, which is no other thing than one or many considerations made in order to stir up our affections towards God and divine things: and herein meditation differs from study and from other thoughts and considerations which are not made to acquire virtue or the love of God, but for other ends and intentions, as, for example, to become learned, to write, or to argue. Having then confined your spirit, as I have said, within the enclosure of the subject upon which you intend to meditate, you will begin to make considerations on it; if you find sufficient relish, light and fruit in one of these considerations, stay there without passing on to another, proceed quite gently and simply in this matter, without undue haste.

The Affections and Resolutions. Meditation produces good movements in the will or affective part of our soul, such as the love of God and of our neighbour, imitation of the life of our Lord, compassion, admiration, joy, confidence in the goodness and mercy of God, confusion for our bad lives in the past; and in these affections our spirit should expand and extend itself as much as possible.

You must not dwell upon these general affections to such an extent that you omit to convert them into special and particular resolutions for your correction and amendment. For example, the first word that our Lord spoke on the cross will doubtless stir up in your soul a good affection of imitation—namely, the desire to pardon your enemies and to love them. But I say now that this is of little value, if you do not add to it a special resolution to this effect: Well then! I will not hereafter be offended by such or such annoying words, nor by such or such an affront which may be put upon me by this person or by that: on the contrary, I will say and do such or such a thing to gain him.

Of the Conclusion and Spiritual Nosegay. Finally, the meditation must be closed by three acts which should be made with as much humility as possible. The first is the act of thanksgiving. The second is the act of oblation. The third is the act of petition, by which we demand of God and implore him to communicate to us the graces and virtues of his Son, and to bless our affections and resolutions, so that we may be able faithfully to put them into practice.

To all this I have added that one should gather a little nosegay of devotion. My meaning is as follows: Those who have been walking in a beautiful garden do not leave it willingly without taking away with them four or five flowers, in order to inhale their perfume and carry them about during the day: even so, we should choose one or two or three points in which we have found most relish, and which are specially proper to our advancement, in order to remember them throughout the day.*

Saint Francis de Sales, 1567–1622.
French Archbishop of Geneva.
Introduction to the Devout Life. Trans. Allan Ross.

The Franciscan Method

M. Bremond describes the method of Père Joseph du Tremblay as "one of the most stimulating, most attractive and simplest that I know of."

The method consists of three parts:

I. The Preparation, in which are four acts:

(1) Of making a right intention.

(2) Of profound humiliation.

(3) Of recalling to mind the subject chosen.

(4) Of withdrawal from distractions.

II. The Meditation. The application of the memory, imagination and intellect to the subject in four acts, by which we seek a knowledge:

(1) Of God, the prototype of the particular perfection manifested in the mystery we are considering.

(2) Of oneself.

(3) Of what our Lord does or suffers in this mystery.

(4) Of the end for which He works or suffers.

In an hour's prayer, about twenty minutes are to be spent on this part.

III. Affections of the Will:

(1) Of Oblation.

(2) Of Petition.

(3) Of Imitation.

(4) Of Union.

It will be seen that this method, whilst reminiscent of the Ignatian plan, is infused with the Franciscan spirit, and, intended primarily, as it was, for Capuchin novices, is designed to lead them to the higher degrees of prayer. The first act of the meditation emphasises the preeminence of God Whose perfections and ways should ever be the first object of our worship and our prayer.*

Bede Frost, 1877–. English priest, Church of England.
The Art of Mental Prayer.

CONTEMPORARY PROCEDURES

Five Steps Outlined

In worship we are reshaping ourselves in such manner

that we as personalities with all our behavior can serve as connecting links between disconnected parts and thus enable the integrating process of the world to fulfill itself. We are pressed into place and so through us the circuit is closed and the wider and richer integration which God achieves is brought to pass. In worship we are thus finding the way to join ourselves with God in his work of integration.

The first step in the act of worship is to relax and to become aware of that upon which we are dependent, that which sustains us in every breath, that which shapes the cells of our bodies and the impulses of our hearts according as we adjust to it in this way or that.

It is not a state in which one is thinking about anything in particular. One is simply relaxed, waiting and endeavoring to be filled with the consciousness of that encompassing and sustaining and integrating reality which, if he is psychologically capable of using the word God, he calls God.

The second step in worship is to call to mind the vast and unimaginable possibilities for good which are inherent in this integrating process called God. These possibilities are actualized in us and in others and in all the world round about us in so far as we and others find and establish the required adjustment between ourselves and this cosmic process which is God.

No matter how we may doubt the possibilities of personal improvement and social transformation and reconstruction of physical conditions, there is that noblest kind of personality, that highest degree of health, that clearness of mind and largeness of purpose, that measure of equality of opportunity, of cooperation and mutual understanding and deep organic community of heart and mind between all men, which may be attained by the best possible adaptation of means to ends. It is this possibility which we now bring to mind. By bringing it to mind we do not mean that one pictures what it shall be or forms any definite idea of it at all. What this best state of affairs may be we do not know and cannot know. What these highest possibilities may be we do not need to know in order to hold them in mind in the sense here indicated. We only need to know that there are such possibilities, however undefined and unexplored. In this second act of worship we become acutely aware of the fact of such possibilities and of the fact that they can be actualized through the working of the encompassing Reality and our better adjustment to it.

The third step is to face the chief problem with which we are struggling. If we are living earnestly we are always struggling with a problem which taxes our powers. We shall frequently have the sense of being baffled because we do not see the way to its solution. But most of the time, unless we take opportunity for the kind of worship we are here describing, we shall not face the problem in its entirety and get it in its true perspective. We are too busy dealing with some pressing detail to face it in all its fullness. But in this third stage of worship, after we have become aware of God (called by another name if we must) and of the total maximum of possibility for good which inheres in God and our relations to him, we face our problem. We survey it as comprehensively and acutely as possible to find what most needs to be done.

Every practical problem is solved by attaining some integration of parts through which the life-sustaining energies of the universe can flow. But the most important and vital thing which every individual must do if this end is to be attained in any particular case is to develop in himself the right mental attitude and consequent behavior.

The fourth step is self-analysis[2] to find what change must be made in our own mental attitudes and personal habits. No problem was ever solved, no desired result ever attained, by worship or in any other way, which did not require some personal readjustment on the part of the person through whom it was attained. Worship has practical value and is a way of doing things only because it enables us (1) to discover what personal readjustment is required of us and (2) to establish that readjustment in ourselves.

The fifth step in worship is to formulate in words as clearly and comprehensively as possible the readjustment of personality and behavior which I have discovered is required of me if I am to close the circuit between certain

[2]We will make more effective progress in self-analysis if we will avail ourselves of the Self-education methods of depth psychology. They can help us penetrate into the unconscious where are to be found the egocentric images and motives that so frequently block the readjustments which our worship reveals are necessary. See pp. 110–119 and Chap. VI.—Ed.

disconnected factors in the world round me. This verbal statement of the needed readjustment is very important. It should be accurate, comprehensive, concise. Above all it must be affirmative; not negative. For in worship we are not primarily trying to break a connection but to establish a connection.

Suppose we discover, as a consequence of our worshipful self-analysis, that we have been too egoistic, too much concerned about our own prestige, too envious of others and too anxious about holding a place of recognized superiority over those we consider our inferiors. One might, then, put the needed readjustment of personality in some such words as these: "I enter into deep, organic community of heart and mind with . . ." and then mention the people who are concerned, if posible. Or he might say: "I am simple, lowly, sensitive and sympathetic toward . . ." and here again mention explicitly certain individuals, groups or classes.

This statement of the required readjustment should be repeated many times in the spirit of worship which has been engendered by the preceding stages. The repetition is necessary in order to establish the readjustment and get it rooted deeply and firmly as a subconscious attitude of the personality which will give the needed character to all thoughts, feelings, words and overt behavior of the individual in any situation that may arise without the need of giving conscious thought to it. In fact anything which requires the guidance of conscious thought is never so skillful and effective as that which is so deep-rooted in the character of the individual that it is done spontaneously without conscious thought.

Through this repetition of words you are simply establishing as an enduring habitual attitude of the total personality that adjustment to God which you have attained through worship.*–**

Henry Nelson Wieman, 1884–.
American philosopher, theologian, educator.
Methods of Private Religious Living.

Meditation to Aid the Ego's[3] Struggle

There are many ways to observe one's own ego and to

[3]See p. 27 — of this anthology.

bring into consciousness its struggle for growth. One very simple but effective way is to meditate on such questions as: How many opportunities were there today where I had to make a decision? Was I really the chooser? How many times was my ego driving me? How many times, inwardly or outwardly, was I pushed around instead of my allowing the "Creative I" to make the choice? When was I taken over by autonomous behavior instead of acting from my Self?

When was I present today? Was I ever present in any sense? Did I see any of the people that I talked to today? Did I see the sunset, the flowers? Did I see my animal? Meditating on such simple questions as these can be a genuine aid in the knowing and being able to use the true ego. "A sacrifice proves you possess yourself, for it does not mean just letting yourself be passively taken; it is a conscious and deliberate self-sacrifice which proves you have full control of yourself, that is, of your ego . . . the ego must make itself self conscious of its claim and the Self[5] must cause the ego to renounce it." What a supreme challenge it is for the ego, conscious of its claims, to be ready to sacrifice itself for the deeper aspect of the Self!*–**

Meditate on the deep implication of this "sacrifice."

Affirm the giving over of yourself to the guidance of this inner aspect of God (the Self).

Elizabeth Boyden Howes, contemporary Jungian analyst.
Adapted from *Intersection.*

Meditation Based on Several Religious Strains

When I arrive at my office early in the morning, undisturbed by telephone or traffic, I sit quietly giving my attention first to my dreams of the night before. I analyze them, or at least ponder what the dream is saying to me. This is the *psycho-analytic* aspect of my meditation.

Then I devote ten or fifteen minutes to an "opening"

---

[4]Growth away from egocentric attitudes and toward creative and objective ones.

[5]The "imprint of God" in the psyche.

process. I clear my mind as nearly as possible of every content, meditating on nothingness. This, as I experience it, takes me into the deeper levels of being. The haste, the pressures and deadlines that haunt us all in the workaday world drop away; the "machinery" is temporarily halted. The jealousies, resentments and all the mess of backbiting to which human consciousness is heir also tend to evaporate. This experience of being brings with it relief, pleasure, and a very mild ecstasy.

At times my experience of being moves to a deeper dimension and consciousness. I then experience what I can only call Being with a capital *B*. The experience of Being brings a greater ecstasy, a pervasive calmness and sense of beatitude. Anxiety about death, for example, also vanishes: I feel myself part of eternity, part of the Being which was eons of years before I was born and will be eons of years after I die. This is an expression, it seems to me, of "The peace of God which passeth understanding."

This phase of meditation I learned from friends who have spent years in India. Though it has elements of Zen Buddhism, I shall call it the *Hindu* contribution to my meditation.

Third, there is generally some kind of message, some guidance that appears. It comes more readily if I do not stridently *demand* it; if I listen to my "deeper" self, sooner or later it will speak to me. The message which forms itself out of the darkness—when one does come—often takes me by surprise. This is generally a sign of its authenticity. This third phase owes a good deal to my *Protestant-Christian* background. It would be surprising if I could cut off my cultural body, nor do I want to. And the Protestant-Christian influence is also present in the images which come to me in my state of receptivity. Sometimes it is the vague form of a heroic-sized man, sometimes a woman, sometimes a moving cauldron of indistinguishable figures, but usually it is the unformed matter permeated with a profound feeling of peace.

Sometimes I meditate on the word and experience of "abyss," and sometimes on the "holy void," both concepts I got from Paulus.[6] I try to keep open in the sense of not getting into any rut, and vary the technique from time to time . . .

[6]Paul Tillich.

This meditation gives me a sense of integration. It aids the process of centering my self. After it, I am more confident of my stance. Whereas before I may have felt like the man who jumped on his horse and galloped off in all directions, I now find these different tendencies coming together into a pattern. As when one travels away from mountains, the foothills decrease in size and the sheer mountains loom higher.*

Rollo May, 1909–. American psychoanalyst.
Paulus.

Loose-Rope Meditation

Loose-rope meditation is a way to follow a particular symbol (from a dream, a phrase, a ritual, etc.). The symbol[1] is "fastened" to the peg of intentions. Once it is securely fastened to its peg by the resolve to remain aware of the I-Thou relationship, one can risk letting it go as one would let an animal go that was fastened to a stake by a long tether. The symbol can then wander off, in a combination of free association and amplification. For example, I may be haunted by a tune. I sit down with it, resolved to learn what it wants of me. I try to remember what it is, and I try to hum it through and cannot, which angers me. Then I recall how my aunt always used to hum off-key while she washed dishes. I go into an imaginary scene of telling my aunt how this bothers me—which I never could actually have done. So I begin to build strength where heretofore I had been weak. At this point I realize where I have gone. I recall my original intention and return to the tune. Four or five such wanderings may be necessary before I realize the deepest symbolic meaning of the tune—each one conjures up a rush of different and meaningful images. I have gained more with each wandering and return.

With this method, of course, there is the continual danger that the inner censor will keep us from seeing what we need to see. This censor can be dealt with by always remembering it may be there, and by making the yes-saying

[1]See definition in footnote, p. 173; also see pp. 248–250.

to the "Cry"[8] and the wholeness, stronger than the censor's no-saying.*–**

Elizabeth Boyden Howes,
contemporary American Jungian analyst.
Sheila Moon,
contemporary American Jungian analyst and writer.
Man the Choicemaker.

A Meditation on Being Open

Since there are as many ways of meditating as there are people, what follows is anything but a pattern to be imposed on anyone. It is simply one person's way found to be (at least for the present) rewarding.

First: *Adoration.* Giving the depth of one's being to that whose depth has no end, as Teilhard de Chardin says. Or as Evelyn Underhill would have it, offering up a glad sense of creatureliness. To me it is more like greeting a Presence which I am learning to look at with love and awe—without too much self consciousness. Another way of putting it is this: Sitting erect with the soles of the feet flat on the floor, I say inwardly on the intake of breath: "I breathe your blue sky deeply in (exhale) to blow it gladly back again. (inhale) I breathe Christ's strength and cheer gratefully in . . . to share it joyously wherever I go. I breathe the resurrection power in . . . to vibrate in me through and through." This brief workout is to remind the real me that I am letting the transcendent Spirit become immanent, a vital force operating in and through my here and now.

Second: *Riddance.* The hands are stretched out as if emptying onto the compost all those noisome products of egocentricity of which I am presently aware; the arrogance of being right, of being an authority; the self importance that grabs more than my share of power and attention; the worry lest somebody rip it off me; the resentment and the resulting guilt feelings that prevent my living wholeheartedly in the present moment.

Third: *The gesture of eager expectancy!* Having at least partially emptied my mind of a few of the stale and possibly poisonous irrelevancies that have been accumulating, and realizing that I have a little more room now for

---

[8]See p. 11.

what is most important and real, I close my eyes and cup my hands the way a child does when he is about to receive special gifts. New eyes—enabling me to see as if for the first time those I have been taking for granted? Freshly sensitized ears to catch from the tone of voice what people trying to communicate with me are really saying? Stepped up power of empathy enabling me to imagine myself in the skin of those from whom I am alienated? A quickened conscience that will prompt me to implement social concern intelligently, responsibly? A guided will to someone thinking of suicide or other ways of giving up—in trust that telepathy if not some other micro-wave will carry strength to that other's deep will?

But all this is preliminary to the *quieting*—not just of the restless tongue and the chattering mind, but quieting of the always importunate self will.

Fourth: *Relinquishment*. Therefore, and last of all, turning off the effort to have the right attitude (whatever that is), I relinquish myself and those on my heart into more competent hands than my own. For a few minutes I simply give myself over to God—let God have a chance to change my habits, my sense of direction and my way of thinking. Distractions no longer matter. I step aside and allow God, deep down, to do the work.

Allan A. Hunter, 1893–. Minister, author.
Written for this anthology.

Meditation Based on Three Levels of Personality

Meditation is to help me to "live under the aspect of Eternity" by cleansing my consciousness from the mistaken sense of Life as included within time and of Self in separateness.

I am convinced that the realization and enjoyment of Life involves the loss of life in the egocentric conception of it. The more completely self-will can draw into consciousness all the implications of personality of which it is the center, and the more completely it can relinquish self and them, the more nearly empty and open is consciousness for the flooding of a realization of the Unity that transcends personality.

As I breathe deeply and quietly, therefore, I inhale to

the thought "I" with a widening inclusiveness of that self-concept, and exhale to the thought "am," yielding the self to the boundlessness of true existence.

I draw into the individuation of my "I" my vegetative level—all the unconscious functioning that makes for assimilation and nourishing. I realize that in "my" chemistry I am akin to earth and water; I recognize my kinship with flowers and grass and trees, with brooks and lakes and rivers, and I feel their rhythms flow through me with peace and power, as I yield my sense of them-in-separateness to the Unity which is their underlying reality.

I draw into my widening sense of self my circulation-level, the blood, with all that implies of emotion and passion and creative power. I feel my kinship with animals and man, man of all races and colors, man with his untamed impulses and instincts; all that surges through the darkness of the unconscious I recognize as part of my inheritance. I acknowledge it and accept responsibility for it and outbreathe it into the "allness" where it can function creatively and unrestrictedly.

I recognize my respiratory level as the one that links the conscious and unconscious in personality, and I use it, in quiet breathing, to reconcile the two. Breath is like the wind that "bloweth where it listeth," we "know not whence it cometh or whither it goeth." It symbolizes the spirit which broodeth over the face of the dark mysterious waters. I feel the kinship of my quiet breath with the breath of Life which God breathed into man's nostrils. God's breath fans me and winnows me, and hastens the relinquishing of what I hold pent within my sense of separateness.

"I" am *standing* at my mental level as I draw level after level of personality into my thought. The mental is the role in which I conceive my "I." It must kneel in contrition for the arrogance of its denial of the more basic levels, and for its proud assurance of my personality's greatest mistake: its sense of itself as an isolated identity. I link myself lovingly with other lonely consciousnesses, feeling my oneness with them and outbreathing them with mine, yielding our ignorance to the all-knowing, our impotence and futility to the all-powerful, our little partialness to the great Whole.

My self-will and self-consciousness expand thus, through the widening sense of kinship, outward toward the limits of separateness; but it is still only "kinship" not "Unity" that self-consciousness can conceive. With all the completeness possible I now empty myself of myself and wait—dark and empty, and silent—waiting if peradventure I may be filled, irradiated, orchestrated by *that* which in *its* Infinity and Eternity transcends personality.*

Ruth Raymond, 1878–1969. American, art educator.
Written for this anthology.

Morning and Evening Prayer

Immediately you awake set your first thought on God. Keep your mind on him for a few seconds. Do not think of him subjectively, as to your relation to him, your failures, your sins, or your needs, but rather objectively. Let your whole self become conscious of him. This need only take a moment or two once the habit has been formed, but it is of inestimable importance. It sets the tone for the whole day. Even if one is awakened by the peremptory shout of a raucous voice, or the nerve-shattering rattle of an alarm clock, the real Presence can be apprehended almost instantaneously. If unpleasant memories press in upon you so that you cannot fasten your mind on him, do not worry about it. Laugh at yourself and think, "What a good thing God does not look at me as I look at myself! He sees something thoroughly lovable in me." He sees the inherent ability, the hidden beauty, the unused power of spirit in each of us. Do not get out of bed, therefore, until you have set your thought on God. Then remind yourself that he is waiting to illumine your spirit each morning as you awake.

Consider yourself not ready to start the day, ill equipped, unprepared to mix with your fellows, until you have spent at least fifteen minutes in prayer. Count it as much a social necessity as washing.

The cultivation of the spirit should be considered with at least as much intelligence as the cultivation of corn. If the field is of good soil and well plowed, if good seed is sown in it, if each day it gets a normal amount of sunshine and rain, if the four winds of heaven blow upon it, good corn inevitably appears. So it is with ourselves. If our mind is prepared and disciplined, if the teaching of Christ is sown in it, if each day it is set toward God and without anxiety and fuss laid open to his influence, good character inevitably appears. "Is it likely," asks Henry Drummond, "that the growth of corn should be regulated by law and the growth of character by mere caprice?"

The day will not be the jewel, the poem, the joy it might be unless one can come to the pitch when one can say the prayer: "Behold me, O Lord, in thy hands ready for all; spin me backward or spin me forward, for I desire nothing other than the doing of thy will!"

There are many who depend on their morning prayer for strength to tackle the difficulties ahead of them. Yet they would soon cease to think of these difficulties ahead if they habitually linked themselves to God with their waking thought. Our puniness turns into strength as we think of him, so that even the fact of our being well or ill depends to a large extent on how many seconds out of the twenty-four hours we have God in our minds.

Self-consciousness—that bane of youth—disappears, as we practice praying. During this hour we become more conscious of God than of our fellows and learn that that achievement is worth more than anything else in life. During the morning prayer-time new aspirations form themselves in one's mind. If we want to play our part in this cosmic process, we have to hold ourselves in readiness to do anything at any time and in any circumstances. "I would fain be to the Eternal Goodness what his own right hand is to a man."

Never get into bed with a burdened or a heavy mind; whether it be a vague oppression or a definite fear, shame or remorse, anger or hate; get rid of it before you lie down to sleep—at least start to deal with it, whatever it is. Our unconscious mind is active during our slumber. Settle down restfully to let your mind get clear and your spirit unclogged. It would be better to sit up half the night, wrestling in spirit until you have won your way to peace and wholeness rather than embark upon hours of unconsciousness with an unfaced conflict, an unacknowledged fear, or an unforgiven friend in your mind. It is a folly ever to shirk the issue of a single, worrying, doubting thought. Face each one before you get into bed, face them in the presence of your Father who knows all your muddled feelings and understands your tempestuous passions.

Silent in God's presence, you can relax yourself completely. The restfulness of being alone at last, facing reality, may even make you laugh aloud for joy as you open your mind in perfect confidence and summon the whole bustling medley of burdensome thoughts before Him. Let them come, waiting quietly for each, without a shadow of dread. See how they show up in the deep calm of God's presence. "That anger I felt this morning, it was like murder, it did real harm to the person it was vented upon, others are reacting to it still. God forgive me. It is not remission of penalty I am asking for when I say 'forgive.' " It is a longing to be made whole again, a passionate desire to save my victim from the consequences of my anger, a willingness to do anything to make amends. Anger is a force and I have let it loose upon the world; it may have wrecked the happiness of several people today.

As one waits quietly, other thoughts of fear or anxiety come to the forefront and are faced in the same way. Most of them disappear, vanish incontinently in the presence of God. One is at peace now. Then, as drowsiness increases, the words of committal can be used. "Father, into thy hands I commit my spirit."*–**

Muriel Lester, 1883–1970. English author, social worker.
Ways of Praying.

Meditation on Freedom

Give freedom to the ones who dwell close to your heart, not by separating yourself from them, trying to draw apart, for that often holds them in closer bonds. Give freedom in every thought, give love, overflowing love—with no restriction in your mind, no question of any kind. As you fully let go, each one will swing into his own accepted place.

Nothing relinquished is lost; everything finds its true balance, its equilibrium, in God. Leave each soul loose and free in your mind to swing into universal Life—a creative being in God, alone, at one with God.

Be not held by false illusions of your worth. Pride and self-condemnation walk side by side. Rid yourself of all condemnation, and give freedom to the ones you felt called upon to please.

Rejoice over the falling leaves of self—you will be light and free indeed when all sense of ownership is gone forever.

Realize that each soul is related to you. When you recognize that everyone is part of you, you will find that you cannot withdraw from another. Open your soul to the sun; you know how to loosen every knot, release every cord, and leave everyone free.

No one comes to you by chance. Give of your bread to all who would approach—then give them space, quietude, love.

Love gives; love never withdraws. Love warms and frees the will of man, so he may receive his own inheritance and make his own decisions.*

Elise Morgan, 1876–1954. American writer, mystic.
Your Own Path.

Thou who art over us,
Thou who art one of us,
Thou who *art*—
Also within us,
May all see Thee—in me also . . .

Dag Hammarskjöld, 1905–1961.
Secretary General of United Nations.
Markings.

Meditation on Forgiveness

. . . the task for me is to bring what I find in myself and in my relationships to the eternal Thou, where I can experience forgiving. . . . To say, "I forgive you" has in it always the danger of inflation. I am not the forgiver. I must try to participate in that which is making forgiveness possible. . . . I need to have an "altar," some place where I can feel the Presence, and to that "altar," whether in a church, in my house or in a personal symbol, I can bring whatever I have done to another, or what another has done to me, and there I can feel accepted, forgiven or forgiving, despite what I have done or what has been done to me. . . . What has been done—by me or another must be faced—not that the results will be eradicated, but that they may be altered and energy pent up in them released. All of it must be accepted, worked with lovingly and thus eventually transformed. And it can be transformed if it is brought to an "altar"—wherever that may be for me.*–**

Anonymous.

Meditation Pattern

Recall One's Need: When it is difficult to "center down" it is helpful to recall one's need—one's failures, lack of love, inner wars. Although negative realization is not a place to *stay*, it can rekindle one's zeal for inner work. It should not end with oneself but expand to include the relation between personal problems and those of your family, community, nation and the world. See the latter as partly due to projections of your own distorted, unfree self. Therefore for yourself and for others you are moved to a genuine desire for meditation as a means of transformation.

Recall Value: Affirm your faith in the power of God, its availability, its transforming efficiency; in the activity of God—His/Her initiative toward all human beings.

Concentrate on *God without*—throughout the universe. This consideration will vary according to what God means to each person. For some it may mean "the supreme and unknown Value," for others the Father, the Creator. Or it may mean the evolutionary thrust or "Cry" that is pushing all creation toward fulfillment. Let the transcendency of God be recalled with great vividness, remembering always that one's present limited vision can be extended only by the willingness to let it go. See it superseded, even nullified by what may appear more comprehensive and real.

Concentrate on *God Within*—the Real self as opposed to the false self. Repeat these three statements over and over. Let them expand in meaning.

> God is Existence (Transforming Power Creativity - Being).
>
> God is Knowledge (Meaning Wisdom).
>
> God is Bliss (Joy - Redeeming Love - beyond good or bad, success or failure, pleasure or pain).

Then say to yourself: "I am not existence; God is Existence." "I am not wisdom, God is Wisdom." "I am not bliss; God is Bliss."

Somehow this realization of the presence of an inner Source begins to relieve you of any exaggerated feeling of responsibility. Give over the need to control. Let it shift from the ego to the "Center." Open yourself to the Presence. Let it Be. Let yourself be in it. Heed what comes out of it.

Anonymous.[9]

Meditation on "Grace"

Graces are the free gifts of help bestowed by God upon each one of us, in order that we may be assisted to achieve our final end and purpose, namely, unitive knowledge of divine reality. Such helps are very seldom so extraordinary that we are immediately aware of their true nature as God-sends. In the overwhelming majority of cases they are *so* inconspicuously woven into the texture of common life that we do not know that they are graces, unless and until we respond to them as we ought, and so receive the material, moral or spiritual benefits which they were meant to bring us. If we do not respond to these ordinary graces as we ought, we shall receive no benefit and remain unaware of their nature or even of their very existence. Grace is always sufficient, provided we are ready to co-operate with it. If we fail to do our share, but rather choose to rely on self-will and self-direction, we shall not only get no help from the graces bestowed upon us; we shall actually make it impossible for further graces to be given. When used with an obstinate consistency, self-will creates a private universe walled off impenetrably from the light of spiritual reality; and within these private universes the self-willed go their way, unhelped and unillumined, from accident to random accident, or from calculated evil to calculated evil. It is of such that St. Francis de Sales is speaking when he says, "God did not deprive thee of the operation of his love, but thou didst deprive His love of thy co-operation. God would never have rejected thee, if thou hadst not rejected Him."

To be clearly and constantly aware of the divine guidance is given only to those who are already far advanced in the life of the spirit. In its earlier stages we have to work, not by the direct perception of God's successive graces, but by faith in their existence. We have to accept as a working hypothesis that the events of our lives are not merely for-

[9]Both Christian and Hindu teachers recommend that one think of God as within, as in the heart. This meditation, indeed, was inspired by a Vedanta teacher.

tuitous, but deliberate tests of intelligence and character, specially devised occasions (if properly used) for spiritual advance. Acting upon this working hypothesis, we shall treat no occurrence as intrinsically unimportant. We shall never make a response that is inconsiderate, or a mere automatic expression of our self-will, but always give ourselves time, before acting or speaking, to consider what course of behaviour would seem to be most in accord with the will of God, most charitable, most conducive to the achievement of our final end. When such becomes our habitual response to events, we shall discover, from the nature of their effects, that some at least of those occurrences were divine graces in the disguise sometimes of trivialities, sometimes of inconveniences or even of pains and trials. But if we fail to act upon the working hypothesis that grace exists, grace will in effect be non-existent so far as we are concerned. We shall prove by a life of accident at the best, or, at the worst, of downright evil, that God does not help human beings, unless they first permit themselves to be helped.

Aldous Huxley, 1894–1963.
English writer, literary critic.

To Will One Thing

Father in Heaven! What is a man without Thee! What is all that he knows, vast accumulation though it be, but a chipped fragment if he does not know Thee! What is all his striving, could it ever encompass a world, but a half-finished work if he does not know Thee: Thee the One, who art one thing and who art all! So may Thou give to the intellect, wisdom to comprehend that one thing; to the heart, sincerity to receive this understanding; to the will, purity that wills only one thing. In prosperity may Thou grant perseverance to will one thing; amid distractions, collectedness to will one thing; in suffering, patience to will one thing. Oh, Thou that givest both the beginning and the completion, may Thou early, at the dawn of day, give to the young man the resolution to will one thing. As the day wanes, may Thou give the old man a renewed remembrance of his first resolution, that the first may be like the last, the last like the first, in possession of a life that has willed only one thing. Alas, but this has indeed not come to pass. Something has come in between. The separation of sin lies in between. Each day, and day after day something is being placed in between: delay, blockage, interruption, delusion, corruption. So in this time of repentance may Thou give the courage once again to will one thing. True, it is an interruption of our ordinary tasks; we do lay down our work as though it were a day of rest, when the penitent (and it is only in a time of repentance that the heavy-laden worker may be quiet in the confession of sin) is alone before Thee in self-accusation. This is indeed an interruption. But it is an interruption that searches back into its very beginnings that it might bind up anew that which sin has separated, that in its grief it may atone for lost time, that in its anxiety it might bring to completion that which lies before it. Oh, Thou that givest both the beginning and the completion, give Thou victory in the day of need so that what neither a man's burning wish nor his determined resolution may attain to, may be granted unto him in the sorrowing of repentance: to will only one thing.

Sören Kierkegaard, 1813–1855. Danish philosopher.
The Prayers of Kierkegaard.

Yes God! Yes God! Yes, yes and always yes.

Nicolas de Cusa, 1401–1464. German mystic.

Prayer for Growing Old

Eternal God, I thank you that I am growing old. It is a privilege many have been denied. Awareness of this mercy gives fresh wonder to every day. . . . I thank you for the joys I now can grasp because age has pried my fingers loose from trivial things—for simpler life; for swallows skimming over sunlit meadows; for unhurried moments to nourish faith on thoughts of your past mercies; for sacred instants when all things that once seemed disjointed fall into place and the sad things of earth are swallowed up in holy joy.

Heavenly Father, grant us awareness of the beauties of life's autumn, a time of fulfillment and harvest. May age be seen as part of your design for the world and for us, so that the years may rest less like a burden and more like a benediction. Spare us from the self-pity that shrivels the soul. Though our wrinkles multiply and bodies tire, may there be no withering of our spirit. May every day witness some rebirth of beauty, some eager exploration of a new, unspoiled hour . . . If appetite for food should fade, may our eyes still savor tenderness in others, consume the dawn, feast on starlight . . . Like Job, may we see that the order of the planets is more significant than our sores. Though our money may be limited, let us be spendthrifts with love . . . And grant us daily some moments living on tiptoes, lured by the eternal city just beyond the hills of time.

Author unknown.

THE LAKE OF BEAUTY

Let your mind be quiet, realising the beauty of the world, and the immense, the boundless treasures that it holds in store.
All that you have within you, all that your heart desires, all that your Nature so specially fits you for—that or the counterpart of it waits embedded in the great Whole, for you. It will surely come to you.
Yet equally surely not one moment before its appointed time will it come. All your crying and fever and reaching out of hands will make no difference.
Therefore do not begin that game at all.
Do not recklessly spill the waters of your mind in this direction and in that, lest you become like a spring lost and dissipated in the desert.
But draw them together into a little compass, and hold them still, so still;
And let them become clear, so clear—so limpid, so mirror-like;
At last the mountains and sky shall glass themselves in peaceful beauty,
And the antelope shall descend to drink, and to gaze at his reflected image, and the lion to quench his thirst,
And Love himself shall come and bend over, and catch his own likeness in you.

Edward Carpenter, 1844–1929. English author, poet.
Towards Democracy.

As I walk, as I walk
The universe is walking with me
Beautifully—it walks before me
Beautifully—it walks behind me
Beautifully—it walks below me
Beautifully—it walks above me
Beautifully—on every side
As I walk—I walk with Beauty.**

From the *Navajo Indian Rain Ceremony.*
Trans. unknown.

My feet are restored to me.
My legs are restored to me.
My body is restored to me.
My mind is restored to me.
The dust of my feet is restored to me.
My spittle is restored to me.
The hair of my head is restored to me.
The world around me is restored in beauty.
All things [around] me are restored in beauty. . . .
My voice is restored in beauty.
It is finished in beauty.
It is finished in beauty.
It is finished in beauty.
It is finished in beauty.*–**

From a Navajo Prayer.[10]

The Use of the Holy Sentence

Some modern teachers believe in the use of the holy sentence. At times the aspirant will find that his mind lingers naturally over one word or sentence, and that his consciousness seems to be permeated with its meaning, to the exclusion of other thoughts. As he meditates, the actual words seem to fade, and he finds himself plunged straight into their meaning, apprehending truth directly, in a new mode.

Holy sentences, like symbols, get past the conscious into the subconscious mind; like symbols, they are full of pious

[10]Taken from a prayer of a Navajo medicine man for the exorcising of evil spirits. Adapted with permission from the translation in *The Pollen Path* by Margaret Schevill Link, pp. 185–189 (Stanford University Press, 1956).—Ed.

associations, powerful, evocative. Round it, as time goes on, clusters the mystic's religious experience. The Hindu's initiation formula, the Christian's text, can express the particular aspect of divine truth with which he has most affinity and on which he may most profitably meditate.

Aelfrida Tillyard, 1882–. English lecturer, writer.
Spiritual Exercises and Their Results.

SUGGESTED "SENTENCES" FOR MEDITATION

"And ye shall seek me, and find me, when ye shall search for me with all your heart."

Jeremiah

". . . lo, the Kingdom of God is within you."

Jesus of Nazareth

"The first sip from the beaker of knowledge separates man from God, but at the bottom of the beaker God waits for those who seek him."

Author unknown.

". . . and having found one pearl of great price, he went and sold all that he had and bought it."

Jesus of Nazareth

"No man is free until he is free at the center. When he lets go there he is free indeed."

E. Stanley Jones

"To be free, to be able to stand up and leave *everything* behind—without looking back. To say *Yes*—"

Dag Hammarskjöld

"One must be able to strip oneself of self-deception."*

Frances G. Wickes

"For as long as the root of wickedness is hidden—it is strong, but when it is recognized it is dissolved."

The Gospel of Phillip

"He who harbors an evil inclination has a great advantage, for he can serve God with it."

Martin Buber

"Lead me from the unreal to the real! Lead me from darkness to light!"

Upanishads

"What is meant by light? To gaze with undimmed eyes on all darkness."

Nikos Kazantzakis

"I saw that there was an ocean of darkness and death, but [also] an infinite ocean of light and love, which flowed over the ocean of darkness; and in that also I saw the infinite love of God."

George Fox

"True self-revelation has always as its counterpart a growth in the knowledge of God."

Edward Leen

"Do you know that you are God's temple and God's spirit makes its home in you? If anyone destroys the temple God will destroy him. For the temple of God is sacred and that is what you are."

Saint Paul

"Surely this place is Holy Ground."

Moses

"Blessed is the man whose strength is in thee; in whose heart are thy ways.
Who going through the vale of misery useth it for a well; and the pools are filled with water."

Psalm 84:5–6

"They that wait on the Lord shall renew their strength,
They shall mount on wings, like eagles,
They shall run and not be weary,
They shall walk and not faint."

Isaiah 40:31

"If ever, my God, it should happen through ignorance and passion that I persist in desires contrary to thine, may I be disappointed and punished, not by thy justice, but by thy pity and great mercy."

Pere de Caussade

"If I speak with the tongues of men and of angels but have not love I am become a sounding brass or a clanging cymbal."

Saint Paul

"Why should we not love our enemies? Our enemy is our greatest friend. Those who speak ill of me, exposing my weakness, do me the greatest good."

Vinobe Bhave

"And whenever you stand up to pray, if you have a grievance against anyone, forgive him."

Jesus of Nazareth

"Every event is a creative opportunity, every contact is an insight, a revelation."

Anonymous

Flash Mantras

"In this moment I am free to be me."

If it took You two billion years to bring me here; help me to *be all* here—as You are.

I accept Your forgiveness—to let it flow toward all my enemies.

"I will look for You in people's eyes and hope that they will feel Your love in mine."

Allan Hunter and his friends.

Meditation on Facing One's Psychic Abyss

One of the most helpful forms of meditation is that in which the individual seeks to face his own particular psychic abyss, his minus 100, the thing that seems worse than death to him since it represents the elimination of his false self. He should try to feel and imagine himself as being actually in this worst-of-all situations. He should seek to visualize what the objective reaction, as contrasted to the egocentric fear-driven reaction, would be. He should remind himself that minus 100 situations are after all very human and general and that even in these "worst" situations there have been men and women who have responded in the creative, courageous, serene way and that the same kind of inner courage and wisdom is available to him. He should remind himself that it is available if he will but learn to face and understand his own inner fear, thus lessening its hold on him; and if he will affirm the transforming power of the Spirit within. It is to the progressive realization of this inner Spirit—this Real-self—that he must commit himself.[11]

Anonymous.

Meditations on Death[12]

How closely numinous symbols come together! Jesus dying on the lowly cross, on which criminals were punished, is all of us transfigured by death and redeemed in time. He died at the age of thirty-two in the prime of life. Those around him found in themselves a transformation of being as a result of his agony. In that last communion, those to be transformed ate of "his flesh and blood," that is, they took on new life as a result of his death. Isn't each one of us, particularly those of us who honestly feel we have been "chosen"—what I call the unlucky-lucky ones—participants in this eternal process of death and transformation? By our deaths are others nourished and given added life and meaning?

Who am I to say in this great mystery in which all human beings are enshrouded that this is not the purpose of God calling me in the middle of life, harsh as it seems, unfair as it sometimes appears. I do not know about the children, but the discovery of real and genuine relationship may help the others, my family and some of my close friends, to undergo partial transformations themselves and be nourished by my facing of my destiny. If the kingdom of heaven is within, then is not this truth closely related to it, an intimate part of it?

---

[11]This meditation is based on one of Fritz Kunkel's helpful ideas for recognizing and dealing with unconscious egocentric images. See *Let's Be Normal*. Also see p. 111 of this anthology regarding "the abyss."

[12]These meditations were taken from the author's Journal during the last year before his death in 1956. He was forty-six years old.

* * * * *

Whence come these feelings that everything is not really to be trusted, that all is illusion? My faith, my beliefs, my imagination, my soul, the whole construction of my life that gives it meaning? That actually there is nothing, nothing at all. I participate here in the common problem of twentieth century man, but there is a more personal source for this basic distrust of life, and from what part of my difficult childhood experience does this spring? All of these things require separate meditations for no other purpose than that I should discover the truth about myself, and the truth shall set me free. To my mechanistic friends all this examination will seem morbid, but there is a vast difference between introspection and introversion; if life is to have meaning it must have personal meaning. Existence on the shallow surface of things can be an escape from reality, and reality is deep within our natures. By experience in depth we become whole, and wholeness for each of us is the only solution, in our fragmented century. . . . If we are whole within, life can partake of this wholeness which we bring to it.

* * * * *

Right now I feel that every hour is precious, the moments like strings of pearls. Before this I had long hours of despair, and I am trying to rescue myself from the pull back into oblivion, and to find where life is. I must try to monopolize these hours as if I were a sole owner of a diamond trust. . . .

Since this latest illness, although I have had some comfort from sporadic reading, I have had a revulsion against books. Books are my business. But now I find more pleasure in looking out the window at the garden, or in the expression on the faces of the children. One burst into the room in a spin of delight, one grabbed at my pen shouting, "I want to kiss you." One arrived after dinner to play an hour of poker with me. One bounced in the air because he just received a prize in a speech contest. The dog in furry delight sneaked into the bedroom to lick my big toe, and finally my wife touched my hand as she said, "Good night," to give me strength and courage, for she is the one who can really take it and keep her head above water. Such rich delights are of a different kind from what I am used to.

I lie and remember such things as a waddling turtle, a chipmunk with his pouch full of nuts, a golden trout leaping high on the river—and suddenly I realize what life is, for lichen, turtle, or man—we share together the moving experience that is the ceaseless river of life and we must learn the ritual of this eternal river and not be betrayed by the artificiality of the clock. Clock time is relatively a recent invention, an abstraction. . . . The clock makes the world we live in possible, but we can be betrayed by the clock; perhaps I am more conscious of this fact than most people. If there is to be an ultimate transforming End for me soon, the clock will not be there.

* * * * *

I keep thinking it is an awesome thing to look into the face of the living God. I feel God is turning the screws so I will get into an ultimate position of transition, but I also feel that the centre of the circle is buoying me up, holding me in suspension as though I were in God's hands. And God, terrible and loving, is with me now in His presence.*

Mark Pelgrin, 1919–1956. American teacher, writer.
And a Time to Die.

"Lord, I know not what I ought to ask of Thee; Thou only knowest what I need. . . . I simply present myself before Thee, I open my heart to Thee. Behold my needs which I know not myself. Smite, or heal; depress me, or raise me up; I adore all Thy purposes without knowing them; I am silent; I offer myself in sacrifice; I yield myself to Thee; I would have no other desire than to accomplish Thy Will. Teach me to pray. Pray Thyself in me. Amen."*

François Fénelon, 1651–1715.
French Archbishop of Cambray.

Intercessory Prayer

Intercession is a great and necessary part of Christian Devotion. The first followers of Christ seem to support all their love, and to maintain all their intercourse and correspondence, by mutual prayers for one another. This was the ancient friendship of Christians, uniting and cementing their hearts.

A frequent intercession with God, earnestly beseeching him to forgive the sins of all mankind, to bless them with his providence, enlighten them with his Spirit, and bring them to everlasting happiness, is the divinest exercise that the heart of man can be engaged in. Be daily therefore on your knees, in a solemn, deliberate performance of this devotion, and you will find all little, ill-natured passions die away, your heart grow great and generous, delighting in the common happiness of others, as you used only to delight in your own. This is the natural effect of a general intercession for all mankind.

Though we are to treat all mankind as neighbours and brethren, as any occasion offers; yet as we can only live in the actual society of a few, therefore you should always change and alter your intercessions, according as the needs and necessities of your neighbours or acquaintance seem to require; such intercessions, besides the great charity of them, would have a mighty effect upon your own heart for *there is nothing that makes us love a man so much, as praying for him.* That will give you a better and sweeter behaviour than anything that is called fine breeding and good manners.*

William Law, 1686–1761. English clergyman, mystic.
Serious Call to a Devout and Holy Life.

Meditation on the Interdependence of Mankind

The community of need and interdependence is not a dream; it is not a hope; it is an actual fact however undiscerned by the institutionalized mind. In the hour of his forsakenness the prophet can sink into the folds of this great fellowship and be comforted. By means of it he can leap over the barriers of enmity that separate him from his fellows and hold with them a great friendliness even while they destroy him. For this great fellowship of common need and interdependence, we repeat, is not merely a dream or a hope. It is a present, existing actuality, however hidden from eyes that see not.

One of the great functions of religious worship, both public and private, is to enable a man to grope his way into this community that underlies the mores. Discernment of this community and adaptation to its requirements is one of the chief parts of the practice of religion. The great brotherhood which some religions have fostered, when it is not mere sentimentality, involves some discernment of this interdependence which is so deeply hidden from the custom-bound mind.

Turn away from all other things and contemplate the fact of this unexplored interdependence of men with all its possibilities, which is God.

Strive to attain some deeper insight into this great fact of human interdependence and fellowship wherein God is revealed.

"Ponder in your heart" the social experiences you have had with a view to finding those deeper meanings and integrating objectives which bind men together but which have not yet come into the full light of social recognition. Searchingly examine your own habits and attitudes to discover what hinders you from serving more fruitfully this sacred community.

Formulate as clearly as possible those personal attitudes which are required to connect you creatively with your fellows to the end of reconstructing the established system to meet the needs of human interdependence.

Establish that attitude of mind in which you will be constantly searching through all your associations with others for more complete mutual understanding and cooperation with them, quick to catch every hint that shows the way to better understanding, sensitive to every sign that tells you you have missed the way, patient and long suffering before every rebuff, with a meekness which cannot be humiliated nor angered because it has laid hold on a bond which cannot be broken and which lifts you above the petty pride that is subject to humiliation and anger.

Establish this questioning attitude by some such words as these, repeated many times, "I enter into deep organic creative community with all mankind."*

Henry Nelson Wieman, 1884–.
American philosopher, theologian, educator.
Methods of Private Religious Living.

No, Lord, you do not ask of me anything that is false or beyond my power to achieve. Through your self-revealing and the power of your grace you simply compel what is most human in us to become at long last aware of itself. Humanity has been sleeping—and still sleeps—lulled within the narrowly confining joys of its little closed loves. In the depths of the human multitude there slumbers an immense spiritual power which will manifest itself only when we have learnt how to *break through the dividing walls* of our egoism and raise ourselves up to an entirely new perspective, so that habitually and in a practical fashion we fix our gaze on the universal realities.

Pierre Teilhard de Chardin, 1881–1955.
Priest and Paleantologist.
Hymn of the Universe.

Difficulties of the Beginner

For those of us who have recently begun the practice of religious exercises, or mental prayer (as distinguished from vocal or traditional petitionary prayer) the difficulties seem bewilderingly various. Especially is this so, if the early attempts to meditate have been lightened by the insight or joy which often strengthens the beginner. These difficulties can be placed perhaps in two groups—difficulties arising from outer circumstance, and those springing from one's inner attitude.

Many simple physical adjustments must be made:—the body taught to be relaxed, the hour for prayer chosen wisely so that one is best able to concentrate, the amount and kind of food one eats must be strictly chosen, not on the old basis of one's likes, but on the new one of bodily efficiency. One must learn to relax *toward* the irrelevant noises which seem to fill one's ears, rather than resist them, which serves only to make them roar the louder. The exciting activities and demands of the body, now noticed in the unaccustomed quiet, are to be forgotten. The actual schedule of the day may have to be drastically rearranged to make way for this effort, for it is important to have a margin of time on either side of the hour for meditation to forestall the feeling of breathless self-importance we carry into much of our daily activity. For some people it is a problem to find a solitary, if not a quiet place, where one can be alone or with friends who are meditating too. These adjustments can be grouped together as making up some of the difficulties of outer circumstance or environment.

Harder to banish are the obstacles or difficulties in meditation which spring from one's inner life. Disheartenment over "the years that went in empty sacrifice to mortal things" fills the mind with gloom, amounting almost to despair. Everyone, it seems, goes through this experience. Sometimes, too, it becomes an excuse for not working harder. Suddenly it is clear, "I'm just making this a sideline, all my real interests are out on the counter. Perhaps I really don't want this enough to go on with the discipline." And when this happens one has stumbled on the very stubborn fact of one's own sloth. It is a natural reaction, particularly at those times when the mind seems full of sand, both heavy and dry, or when the mind swarms like a freshly stirred ant hill with thought of everything else but the Reality about which one desires to think.

At other times, over-confidence, the conviction one really belongs among those who may be gifted in prayer, keeps one from making progress. To begin to expect special manifestations of God's grace, to anticipate experiences which one has read about but which belong to a stage far beyond one's own development, is fatal to the real spirit of meditation. If the experts agree on one essential quality of mind and heart, in this work of practicing the Presence of God in prayer, that essential is humility. For, say they all, the real work of prayer is done by God,—our part is to empty the heart of those things which keep Him out. Whatever then comes, if one has been sincere and humbly eager to be fit for His indwelling, will be accepted tranquilly as a necessary part of the process which is to lead us out of our narrow selves into the wideness of God's infinite charity.

So then we learn to pray, not that one's prayer be made easier, but that one's desire for Him be made deeper, not that one can have the gifts one has not earned, but rather, the power to serve Him through each day in every tiny act. We learn that everything we do is insignificant if it points toward ourselves, but strangely significant if it points toward God. With humility and desire and faith in God as infinite and eternal and unchanging in His love and understanding for all his creatures, the difficulties of meditation are seen as part of one's growth. We must all come to terms with Holiness, soon or late. It is for us to decide when.

Elizabeth Hunter, 1893–1972. American.
Written for this anthology.

Insincerity

A temperamental hazard [to progress], if such it can be termed, as high for most honest people as a mountain, is the *insincerity of daily life.* No honest man can pray without a sharp compunction; I pray *this* way, but I live *that* way. The battle is promptly joined between prayer and conduct. Often it is an unequal battle; prayer is killed and buried without obsequies, while conduct lives on uneasy in its unworthiness. Herein is the reason why prayer is tepid and fitful; prayer keeps us from baseness, or baseness keeps us from prayer. Doubt of prayer is sometimes a consequence rather than an origin: we are self-indicted, and then take refuge in alleged perplexities to justify our brokenness. Prayer involves us in a discipline so hard that it resembles surgery. For our wrong does not rest like dust on a smooth surface of life: it cannot be washed away by some ablution of morning and evening prayer. Nor is the wrong separate and distinct: it cannot be picked out by some tweezers-moment of self-criticism.

Prayer is not a vain attempt to change God's will: it is a filial desire to learn God's will and to share it. Prayer is not a substitute for work: it is the secret spring and indispensable ally of all true work—the clarifying of work's goal, the purifying of its motives, and the renewing of its zeal.*

George A. Buttrick, 1892–. American clergyman.
The Christian Fact and Modern Doubt.

Social Pressure

As soon as worldlings perceive that you wish to follow the devout life, they will let fly at you a thousand shafts of their gossip and slander: the more malicious will falsely attribute your change to hypocrisy, bigotry and pretence; they will say that the world has frowned upon you, and that for this reason you turn to God; your friends will hasten to pour out upon you a flood of remonstrances, which in their opinion are very prudent and charitable; you will fall, they will tell you, into a state of melancholy, you will lose credit with the world, you will make yourself unbearable, you will grow old before your time, your domestic affairs will suffer thereby; when one is in the world one must live the life of a person in the world; salvation may be attained without so many mysteries; and a thousand such-like foolish things.

We have seen gentlemen and ladies spend the whole night, and even many nights consecutively, in playing at chess and at cards. Can there be any attention more dull, more melancholy and more dismal than that? And yet worldlings say not a word, friends are not in the least disturbed thereat; but if we make an hour's meditation, or if we are seen to rise a little earlier than usual in the morning, in order to prepare for Communion, everyone runs off to the doctor that he may cure us of melancholy and jaundice. People spend thirty nights in dancing, and not one of them complains of any ill effects; but if they spend one Christmas night in watching, everyone coughs and complains of being ill next day. Who cannot see that the world is an unjust judge; gracious and favourable towards its own children, but harsh and rigorous towards the children of God?

We cannot stand well with the world unless we become one with it. It is impossible for us to satisfy it, for it is too capricious.

Saint Francis de Sales, 1567–1622.
French Archbishop of Geneva.
Introduction to the Devout Life. Trans. Allan Ross.

Immaturities in Devotion

Mundanus is a man of excellent parts, and clear apprehension. He has made a great figure in business; and he is always contriving to carry every method of doing any thing well, to its greatest height. He can tell you all the defects and errors in all the common methods whether of trade, building, or improving land, or manufactures. Thus has Mundanus gone on.

The one only thing which has not received any benefit from his judicious mind, is his devotion: This is just in the same poor state it was, when he was only six years of age, and the old man prays now, in that little form of words, which his mother used to hear him repeat night and morning, without considering how improvable the spirit of devotion is, how many helps a wise and reasonable man may call to his assistance, and how necessary it is, that our prayers should be enlarged, varied and suited to the particular state and condition of our lives.

If Mundanus sees a book of devotion, he passes it by, as he does a spelling-book, because he remembers that he learned to pray, so many years ago under his mother, when he learned to spell.

Now how pitiable is the conduct of this man of sense, who has so much judgment in every thing but that which is the whole wisdom of man?

And how miserably do many people, more or less, imitate this conduct?*

William Law, 1886–1961. English clergyman, mystic.
Serious Call to a Devout and Holy Life.

Advice Regarding Distractions

All day long we go about disguised, to a very large extent hiding our real self that others may not see what we are, and this not seldom to such a degree that the disguise becomes more real to us than our actual self. But when we come to pray, our real self, torn by a myriad interests, our interior mental life, crowded with distractions, surges out into that silent sanctuary wherein we seek the peace of God. 'If we find the door shut, why should we be surprised?'

We must be convinced that little things are often as dangerous in hindering our walk in the path. For instance there is no occasion for us to hear and see, still less to say, half the things which, if they do not lead to sin, yet disturb the peace and calm of the soul. 'Keep thy tongue from evil' and from that idle speaking to which our Lord refers so sternly, for talkativeness and all that it leads to are most harmful to the spiritual life. It is too often the mark of a shallow spirit; indeed, it would seem that the less a man thinks—and thinking is fast dying out—the more he talks. 'Talking,' said Faber, 'is a loss of power,' and it certainly tends to dissipate that sense of the presence of God which is the greatest guard of the soul. Deliberately to choose to be silent at times, to watch and weigh our words when we speak, would accomplish more for many than the pious practices they so much enjoy.

Another sphere in which custody of the sense is necessary, especially in view of our prayer, is that of concentration in the spirit of St. Catherine of Genoa's 'One thing only and one thing at a time.' To pray well demands not merely concentration, but a concentration which has nothing forced or violent about it. St. Francis de Sales never tires of insisting upon the need of calmness and tranquillity in our approach to God. But to have this at our prayer means that we must strive for it outside of our prayer, and one of the greatest aids to this is to learn to do each thing as it comes, as if it were the only thing we had to do, and having done it, or being compelled to leave it to go on to another duty, to do so in the same spirit.

The world of affairs is full of men who are intensely recollected because they are intensely interested in some particular aim or project. They do a thousand things a day, but behind all they do, dominating and influencing all their life, is one supreme thing. They are not always actually thinking of it; they may, indeed, and will at times, be thinking of and doing the common-place things, eating, drinking, playing, that all men do. But always, even if not consciously at the moment, one thing and one alone is supreme and central; for that thing they live; without it, life to them would lose all meaning. They are men of recollection.

And recollection in the spiritual life means precisely the same thing; it is the spirit of the man who is possessed with the reality of God as the true end of all human life. We need a conversion to God, not merely from sin; 'seek the Lord and your soul shall live,' 'for if ye truly seek Me with all your heart ye shall surely find Me,' and to find God is to have found that one absorbing interest before which all else is as naught.*–**

Bede Frost, 1877–. English priest, Church of England.
The Art of Mental Prayer.

Need for I-Thou Relationship

. . . it becomes overwhelmingly important for us *to become detached from our everyday conception of ourselves as potential subjects for special and unique experiences, or as candidates for realization, attainment and fulfillment.* In other words, this means that a spiritual guide worth his salt will conduct a ruthless campaign against all forms of delusion arising out of spiritual ambition and self-complacency which aim to establish the ego in spiritual glory. That is why a St. John of the Cross is so hostile to visions, ecstasies and all forms of "special experience."[18] That is why the Zen Masters say: "If you meet the Buddha, kill him."

Here we must be very circumspect. The "Holy Object" must be destroyed in so far as it is an idol embodying the secret desires, aspirations and powers of the ego-self. On the other hand it is futile and even deadly to simply sweep aside all other idols in order to confirm as absolute and ultimate the idol of an ego-self supposedly endowed with supreme autonomy and able to follow its own omnipotent spiritual whims. This is not spiritual freedom but ultimate narcissism.

Therefore there is a definite place for disciplines based on an I-Thou relationship between disciple and master, between the believer and his God. It is precisely in familiarity with liturgical worship and moral discipline that the beginner finds his identity, gains a certain confidence from his spiritual practice, and learns to believe that the spiritual life has a goal that is definitely possible of attainment. But the progressive must also learn to relax his grasp on his conception of what that goal is and "who it is" that will attain it. To cling too tenaciously to the "self" and its own fulfillment would guarantee that there would be no fulfillment at all.

Thomas Merton, 1915–1968. American Trappist monk.
Zen and the Birds of Appetite.

Reformation of Others

Nothing is more important in the early stages of the spiritual life than to resist that 'temptation of beginners,' the reformation of others. 'Let us look at our own faults, and not at other people's. We ought not to insist on everyone following in our footsteps, nor to take upon ourselves to

[18]Fortunately, religious psychotherapists have become equipped to help persons who experience such psychic phenomena. If properly handled, dreams and visions can be used to great advantage in clarifying religious experience, and in releasing, assimilating and thus integrating unconscious dynamic factors.—Ed.

give instructions in spirituality when, perhaps, we do not even know what it is.' (St. Theresa)

'When people begin to have pleasure in the rest and the fruit of prayer, they will have everyone else be very spiritual also. To desire this is not wrong, but to try to bring it about may not be right, except with great discretion and great reserve, without any appearance of teaching.' She, (St. Theresa), gives an illustration from her own experience, for she had made others endeavour to pray, only to find that they contrasted what she said of the blessedness of prayer with her lack of virtues, in spite of her prayer. 'And thus, during many years, only three persons were the better for what I said to them; but now that our Lord has made me stronger in virtue, in the course of two or three years, many persons have profited.'*

Bede Frost, 1877–. English priest, Church of England.
The Art of Mental Prayer.

The Dark Night of the Soul

Probably the most celebrated of all works dealing with the difficulties (periods of dryness and desolation) met on the religious way is *The Dark Night of the Soul,* written in the sixteenth century by the Spanish mystic San Juan de la Cruz. It describes the benefits and trials of two purgations or Dark Nights. The first Night is described as the purgation of the senses. It is operative through most of the first stage of the spiritual way, becoming more intense as the beginner is being prepared to pass on to the state of proficiency.

These Dark Nights[14] are variously described by different writers[15] and seem to be the common experience of the great mystics. They offer data of special interest to the religious psychologist who wishes to study the Mystic Way and its practices in relation to the release of the creative Self. These data will also be of general interest to all who are in-

[14]The second Night is referred to as *The Cloud of Unknowing* by the anonymous writer of the classic treatise by the same name.—Ed.

[15]See *Mysticism* by Evelyn Underhill for an excellent discussion of difficulties on the Way. Also see the Commentary by Ira Progoff in new trans. of *The Cloud of Unknowing* (Julian, 1957). Also see p. 119; pp. 188–200 of this anthology.—Ed.

tent on following the Way, for to be aware of its hardships helps prevent retarding discouragement.

Although the experience of the first Dark Night is unquestionably inherent in the process of purgation and self-knowledge, there is reason to believe that some of the terrific intensity suffered by the early mystics, especially in the second or Spiritual Night, may have been, in part, due to a too rapid rate of progress, or perhaps to the inconsistencies between an anthropomorphic cosmology and their experience which did not fit the cosmology. The actual Light which they experienced may have been brighter and more vast than the conceptual preparation so that the bright dawn of a new day was like a "Dark Night."

It is believed that the techniques for clarification developed by analytical psychology, if properly handled, can contribute toward an acceleration in the traverse of these Nights of Purgation wherein a transformation of the personality is effected.

Though the writings of St. John of the Cross may present difficulties in the manner of expression, they hold a wealth of insight. We deeply regret that lack of space prevents the inclusion here of the long selections chosen from this great work. The reader is referred to the book itself, *The Dark Night of the Soul* (trans. G. C. Graham, Watkins, 1922, London). See especially the material on The First Dark Night. See pp. 61–83 and 87–105. The reader who has some psychological background is also referred to the lecture by Michael Fordham, M.R.C.P., entitled *Analytical Psychology and Religious Experience,* published by The Guild of Pastoral Psychology, London, Dr. Fordham says of Saint John, "One is tempted to call him a medieval analyst, for mysticism has become almost scientific in his hands. . . ."—Ed.

Two Levels of Interest to Aid in Aridities

One quite general, yet very helpful preparation towards the practice of sobriety in prayer, and hence towards escaping, as far as possible, the acute reactions liable to follow upon such very delightful prayer, is admirably preached and practised by Jean Nicholas Grou. This fine classical scholar, and deeply spiritual writer and leader of souls, urges *the importance of the soul's possession and cultiva-*

tion of two levels and kinds of action and interest—a wholesome, natural interest and action, and a deep supernatural interest and action. The soul will then possess and will cultivate a genuine interest in politics or economics, in language or history, in natural science or philosophy—in these, as part of its bread-winning or as quite freely chosen studies. And we will thus, when in dryness and even in anticipation of it, possess a most useful range of interest to which to turn, as our disporting ground, in relief of the dreariness or the strain of our directly religious life.

Spiritual dryness is indeed inevitable in the life of prayer; we will be much helped to bear these desert stretches, by persistent recognition—hence also, indeed especially, in our times of fervour—of the normality and the necessity of such desolation. We will thus come to treat desolation in religion as we treat the recurrence of the night within every twenty-four hours of our physical existence; or as bodily weariness at the end of any protracted exertion in our psychic life. When desolation is actually upon us, we will quietly modify, as far as need be, the kind and the amount of our prayer—back, say, from prayer of quiet to ordinary meditation, or to vocal prayer—even to but a few uttered aspirations. And, if the desolation is more acute, we will act somewhat like the Arab caravans behave in the face of a blinding sandstorm in the desert. The men dismount, throw themselves upon their faces in the sand; and there they remain, patient and uncomplaining, till the storm passes, and until, with their wonted patient endurance, they can and do continue on their way.

There are generally a weakness and an error at work within us, at such times, which considerably prolong the trouble, and largely neutralise the growth this very trouble would otherwise bring to our souls. The weakness lies in that we let our imagination and sensitiveness be directly absorbed in our trouble. We contemplate, and further enlarge, the trouble present in ourselves, instead of firmly and faithfully looking away, either at the great abiding realities of the spiritual world, or, if this is momentarily impossible for us, at some other, natural or human, wholesome fact or law. And the error lies in our lurking suspicions that, for such trials to purify us, we must feel them fully in their tryingness—that is, we must face and fathom them directly and completely. It ignores the experience of God's saints across the ages, that, precisely in proportion as we can get away from direct occupation with our troubles to the thought and love of God, to the presence of Him Who permits all this, in the same proportion do and will these trials purify our souls.*

Friedrich von Hügel, 1852–1925.
Austrian theologian, author.
The Life of Prayer.

Necessity for Perseverance

Be like the pearl oyster. There is a pretty Indian fable to the effect that if it rains when the star Svâti is in the ascendant, and a drop of rain falls into an oyster, that drop becomes a pearl. The oysters know this, so they come to the surface when that star shines, and wait to catch the precious raindrop. When a drop falls into them, quickly the oysters close their shells and dive down to the bottom of the sea, there to patiently develop the drop into the pearl. We should be like that. First, hear, then understand, and then, leaving all distractions, shut your minds to outside influences, and devote yourselves to developing the truth within you. There is the danger of frittering away our energies by taking up an idea only for its novelty, and then giving it up for another that is newer. Take one thing up and do it, and see the end of it, and before you have seen the end, do not give it up. Those that only take a nibble here and a nibble there will never attain anything. They may titillate their nerves for a moment, but there it will end. They will be slaves in the hands of Nature, and will never get beyond the senses.

Those who really want to be *Yogis* must give up once for all, this nibbling at things. Take up one idea. Make that one idea your life; think of it; dream of it; live on that idea. Let the brain, muscles, nerves, every part of your body be full of that idea, and just leave every other idea alone. This is the way to success, and this is the way great spiritual giants are produced. Others are mere talking machines. If we really wanted to be blessed, and make others blessed, we must go deeper. The first step is not to disturb the mind, not to associate with persons whose ideas are disturbing. But those who take up just a bit of it and a little of everything else make no progress. It is of no use to simply take a course of lessons. To those who are full of *Tamas,* ignorant and dull, —those whose minds never get fixed on any idea, who only crave for something to amuse them—religion and philosophy are simply subjects of entertainment. These are the unpersevering. They hear a talk, think it very nice, and then go home and forget all about it. To succeed, you must have tremendous perseverance.*

Swami Vivekananda, 1863–1902. Hindu mystic, seer.
Raja-Yoga.

CHAPTER VI

Psychotherapy[1]

We need to realise that psychology leads us sooner or later to religious experience, while religion can only be brought home to the individual through essential psychological facts.

MICHAEL FORDHAM

The specific value of psychotherapy is in the revelation of those motives and impulses operating outside the field of consciousness which hold one back from true self knowledge.

FRITZ KUNKEL

Not until one determines to restrict his task to the elimination of his egocentricity, and no longer tries to force an increase of courage and vitality, does the process of self-education get started. The distribution of the parts in the task is something like this: The light is obscured; it is not my problem to light the light (for it is already burning), but my problem is to clear away the obstacles that are obstructing the light. I cannot create light, but I can remove the shade. If a man wished to light the light himself, he would be more vain than ever. If he would wait until the light penetrated the shade by itself, he would be more timid than ever; he would be trying to *escape his responsibilities.* The objective is the untiring work at the removal of the shade and the unerring confidence in the presence of the light.*

Fritz Kunkel, M.D., 1889–1956. American psychiatrist.
God Helps Those.

[1]See "Self-Knowledge," pp. 104–128; See also pp. 155–163. —Ed.

The Relation of Psychotherapy and Religion

It is in the aiding of people to find meaning for their lives that religion and depth-psychology are in partnership. The field of meaning in life is essentially the religious area, but the technique of discovering why persons fail to find meaning—why they suffer hindrances, complexes, irrational fears—is the modern contribution of depth-psychology.

Many modern persons have been unable to quench their thirst for meaning in the stream of organized religion. Numerous reasons could be given for this—the stagnation that results from any large organization, the preaching of dry forms in which the vitality has run dry, the great upheavals in our Western culture of the last century. Whatever the reason, multitudes of modern intelligent people have been unable to find the guidance they wished in conventional religion. They have been told so oppressively often to believe in life and love their neighbors, that the words ring with the cant of mere verbal repetition.

At the threshold of the present century, a new endeavor to understand the human personality sprang up as an answer to a great need. Beginning with Sigmund Freud, this "psychoanalysis" was an attempt to be scientific about the human soul. We cannot achieve health or happiness, Freud pointed out, by the dishonest means of repressing all tendencies that our Victorian moralism finds unpalatable, and we are deceiving ourselves if we think that our arrogant "egos" standing at the thresholds of our minds can arbitrarily decide the great issues of life as the whim strikes them. The new understanding of human motives worked out in Vienna constitutes probably the outstanding discovery of the twentieth century.

The practical application of the knowledge which depth-psychology has discovered was developed through various contributions by Dr. C. G. Jung, who terms his subject "analytical psychology," Alfred Adler, who calls his work "individual psychology," Fritz Kunkel, Otto Rank, and others. The fact that so many of Freud's disciples have dissented from the master, rather than a mutiny of the ranks, was like the independent searching for gold of a number of prospectors—since there was so much gold to be found.

In the past twenty years it has become recognized that most psychological problems are intertwined with religious, and that religious problems have in most cases a very clear psychological aspect. . . . Dr. Jung expresses in vivid and perhaps extreme fashion what psychologists of all sorts are beginning to observe: "Among all my patients in the second half of life—that is to say over thirty-five—there has not been one whose problem in the last resort was not that of finding a religious outlook on life. It is safe to say that every one of them fell ill because he had lost that which the living religions of every age have given to their followers, and none of them has been really healed who did not regain his religious outlook."[2] Dr. Jung goes on to caution us that this has nothing to do with the dogmas of a particular church; it is rather, as this chapter has sought to indicate, the reaching out of the human soul for basic meaning by which it can live.

The psychoanalyst, or consulting psychologist, or whatever he may call himself, is concerned with helping the individual overcome fears and rationalizations and inhibitions so that he can move ahead with success. The neurotic man who refuses to meet people and who holds that all women are demons must first understand the detours in his background that have led him to the impasse—here the sheer technique of analysis comes into its own. But then, having been helped back on the road, he must believe in the worth of love and friendship in order that he may move down the road with courage. . . . So psychotherapy, the technique, points inevitably toward religion, the goal and meaning.

Dr. Adler holds in his last book that we should view life *sub specie aeternitatis* and at the time of his death he was engaged in collaborating with clergymen in work on pastoral psychology. "The best conception hitherto gained," he writes, "for the elevation of humanity is the idea of God."[3]

"It is doubtless true," writes Dr. Menninger, "that religion has been the world's psychiatrist throughout the centuries."[4] One can be coldly scientific in segments of the

[2]*Modern Man in Search of a Soul.*
[3]*Beyond Good and Evil,* p. 208.
[4]*Man Against Himself,* p. 449.

technique of analysis; but the closer the treatment comes to completion, the more the therapist must take into consideration aspects of life which are by no means coldly scientific, such as faith, hope, and love. "The patient needs a world view," Dr. Otto Rank aptly puts it, "and will always need it, because man always needs belief, and this is so much more, the more increasing self-consciousness brings him to doubt."[5]*–**

Rollo May, 1909–. American psychotherapist.
Springs of Creative Living.

Psychotherapy as a Catharsis

To cherish secrets and hold back emotion is a psychic misdemeanour for which nature finally visits us with sickness—that is, when we do these things in private. But when they are done in communion with others they satisfy nature and may even count as useful virtues. It is only restraint practised for oneself alone that is unwholesome. It is as if man had an inalienable right to behold all that is dark, imperfect, stupid, and guilty in his fellow men—for such, of course, are the things we keep secret in order to protect ourselves. It seems to be a sin in the eyes of nature to hide our inferiority—just as much as to live entirely on our inferior side. There would appear to be a sort of conscience in mankind which severely punishes every one who does not somehow and at some time, at whatever cost to his virtuous pride, cease to defend and assert himself, and instead confess himself fallible and human. Until he can do this, an impenetrable wall shuts him off from the vital feeling that he is a man among other men.

This explains the extraordinary significance of genuine, straightforward confession—a truth that was probably known to all the initiation rites and mystery cults of the ancient world. There is a saying from the Greek mysteries: "Give up what thou hast, and then thou wilt receive."

We may well take this saying as a motto for the first stage in psychotherapeutic treatment. The beginnings of psychoanalysis are in fact nothing else than the scientific rediscovery of an ancient truth; even the name that was

[5]*Will Therapy*, p. 135.

given to the earliest method—catharsis, or cleansing—is a familiar term in the classical rites of initiation. The early cathartic method consisted in putting the patient, with or without the paraphernalia of hypnosis, in touch with the hinterland of his mind, hence into that state which the yoga systems of the East describe as meditation or contemplation. In contrast to yoga, however, the aim here is to observe the sporadic emergence, whether in the form of images or of feelings, of those dim representations which detach themselves in the darkness from the invisible realm of the unconscious and move as shadows before the inturned gaze. In this way things repressed and forgotten come back again. This is a gain in itself, though often a painful one, for the inferior and even the worthless belongs to me as my shadow and gives me substance and mass. How can I be substantial without casting a shadow? I must have a dark side too if I am to be whole; and by becoming conscious of my shadow I remember once more that I am a human being like any other. At any rate, if this rediscovery of my own wholeness remains private, it will only restore the earlier condition from which the neurosis, i.e., the split-off complex, sprang. Privacy prolongs my isolation and the damage is only partially mended. But through confession I throw myself into the arms of humanity again, freed at last from the burden of moral exile. The goal of the cathartic method is full confession—not merely the intellectual recognition of the facts with the head, but their confirmation by the heart and the actual release of suppressed emotion.

Carl G. Jung, M.D., 1875–1961. Swiss psychiatrist.
The Practice of Psychotherapy. Trans. R. F. C. Hull.

The Role of "Helper"

Seek a helper. It may seem paradoxical to think of self-education as involving the need of outside help. Yet the fact is, as we have noted, that a helper is sometimes necessary and the most practical thing to do is to seek one. After all, it must be obvious, that even with the aid of the helper much depends upon one's own efforts at self-education.

Some few persons have such a vivid sense of the reality of God that they may find in communion with Him the helper *par excellence*. For most of us, however, the helper must be the human being whose voice we can hear with our ears and whose presence we can sense by touch and sight. This person should be one who is not connected with our pressure. No one can be thought of by an egocentric person as the source of any serious distress involved in pressure and at the same time be accepted as the helper. Much the same situation is involved here as in the case of criticism. One factor in the suffering under pressure is the feeling, conscious or unconscious, that one has been attacked. This feeling is due to the fact the Ego seems to be the Self, and, therefore, pressure exerted on the Ego seems to be a threat to our very existence, and an unkind, inconsiderate, inimical act insofar as we feel that anyone is responsible for it. There is, therefore, a resistance to the pressure and consequent negative reaction to the person. He is felt to be the Black Giant who certainly cannot be trusted as a helper.

This psychology of resistance in all serious cases makes it necessary to seek help from one who is not connected with the pressure. In minor, more or less incidental matters, it may be that one who points out our weakness or gives us some slight degree of hurt may be accepted as the helper, but even in such a case, there are dangerous possibilities.

They are especially significant within the family or between friends. For the natural and inevitable resistance to changing our Ego in any way may develop into antipathy to anyone who indicates that we ought to do so. This, the helper must do. Thus deep resentments and even hatred may spring up between husband and wife or friend and friend if one tries to be the helper for the other. Even though this attitude may be only temporary, as it should be and is, if the crisis turns out well, it is better that no such negative feelings be stirred up among members of the family or friends. As a practical matter it is, therefore, desirable to seek the helper among those not too closely bound to one by family or friendship ties, though in some cases the helper may be found among close relatives and friends.

The helper need not be a psychologist though often such a person is better qualified than others are. Any person of well-developed We-feeling often can serve one most helpfully even though not formally schooled in psychological principles. In our langugage we woud speak of them as comparatively objective persons. Seek such a person.

Sometimes the helper may be a good book which interprets a person to himself somewhat as the helper must, and points out life values clearly and convincingly. This is one reason for the preeminence of the Bible. Its power to speak truth to the human heart, to interpret one to himself, to present life's highest values challengingly is enough in itself to make it The Great Book. Try finding in its pages something of the counsel the helper must give.

Then turn to the pages of biography for the story of well-lived lives, for illustrations of mistakes overcome and lives transformed by objective purposes. This need not be the biography of some famous person, helpful as it may sometimes be. Sometimes it is even more helpful to find in the lives of plain people, like ourselves unknown to fame, illustrations of the possibilities of creative living—of growth into finer and fuller personalities. Even a sound book of fiction may have much the same value in interpreting to us life's values and our own reactions.

Finally, turn for help to the creative philosophers and psychologists who have left the record of their insight into truth and human nature and its needs on the pages of old books or even current magazines. Here, too, one may find the truth he needs—the deeper insight into himself and life's values which are so necessary to him.

After saying all this, it is necessary to add a word of caution. Much that is written in the name of psychology and philosophy is so inaccurate in its facts or unsound in its presentation that it is merely trash. It is, therefore, important to read only material that has stood the test of criticism[6] by those who are qualified to evaluate it.*

Fritz Kunkel, M.D., 1889–1956. American psychiatrist.
and Roy E. Dickerson, 1886–, American author.
How Character Develops.

The Role of Dream Analysis

Doublemindedness harasses the path of all who consciously attempt to follow the religious Way. Man is not only motivated by those factors of which he is aware, but is more often propelled into action by irrational yet potent

[6]See Recommended Reading list, p. 468.

impulses and motives operating outside the field of consciousness. Sigmund Freud, the father of psychotherapy, postulated that there were virtually autonomous systems working against the rest of the psyche, and causing various kinds of personality splits. How can this contradictory doubleness of behavior be eliminated? We can look to psychotherapy as an aid in apprehending these unconscious factors, in understanding their content, in setting free the energy contained in them, and in integrating them into the total personality.

The use of dreams came to be for Freud what he called the "via regia" to the unconscious. For him, of course, dream analysis was based upon the theoretical assumptions he made about the psychic structure, and involved primarily his notions of sexuality. In the development of their own points of view some of Freud's followers departed radically from him. The outstanding of these are C. G. Jung, Fritz Kunkel, Alfred Adler, and Otto Rank. They followed Freud in use of dreams as revelation of material not accessible to consciousness in any other way. But in the symbolism of the dream, the way of interpretation, and the use of the dream in relation to the rest of the personality, they differ widely from him. The discussion which follows is oriented unreservedly toward the point of view of Jung and Kunkel.

One of the major implications of the religious Way is the ability to discriminate between the apparent self and the real self—to recognize those elements within the personality structure that block the needed movement from the periphery of consciousness to the Center, which is of God. Dreams reveal those things that hold one back from true self-knowledge,—i.e., the complexes, inhibitions, fears which imprison part of the libido (life energy), splitting the personality. These elements lie in the unconscious, apparently non-existent, but actually dynamic and often destructive, and often going counter to that which is consciously desired.

The dream images in the unconscious are diverse, arising as they do from different sources and different levels. According to Jung elements in the *personal unconscious* are the result of personal experience, the roots of which lie in long-forgotten childhood experiences, or of experiences repressed, either because they are contrary to accepted development or because they are unpleasant or even unthinkable. The *collective unconscious* is that domain of inherent inner images arising out of the psyche, as part of its very essence, and not dependent on the outer or personal experiences at all. These images form the basis of mythology, and are the common sub-stratum of experience for all men. These deeper images may be influential on behavior. They give rise to moods, fantasies, uncontrollable emotions, irrational desires (as seen from the rational standpoint). Once the complex nature of the unconscious is understood, much that was formerly unclear and unknown becomes clear.

In order to utilize this technique of dream analysis it is advisable to work with a specialist in the field. A skilled and trustworthy analyst or psychotherapist . . . would be cognizant of the limitations as well as the contribution which the psychotherapeutic procedure can make to progression on the religious Way. With the help of an analyst progress in clarification is relatively certain. After some guidance enough understanding can sometimes be obtained to permit one to proceed alone for a time. It is doubtful, however, whether any trustworthy insight into the interpretation of dreams can be obtained unless one begins with an expert. Indeed, the majority of therapists would say that a person can do nothing of value alone in this area and that to try may definitely work harm. They contend that an unskilled person, working alone, cannot understand the symbols in dreams, many of which are hidden and disguised because of their deeper meanings. Furthermore, in dream analysis, as well as in all other phases of psychotherapeutic procedure, resistance to the dream content may occur because what is revealed is often the dark, repressed side which one would rather not acknowledge as part of himself. Any inner resistance hinders a true interpretation of dreams. A wrong interpretation is likely to produce a helpless feeling with a consequent paralyzing effect. However, it must be noted that there are instances on record, both ancient and contemporary, where persons have by themselves gained significant insights through dreams relating to particular problems and their solution. Much exploring remains to be done before any final opinion can be formed on this point.

In summary, then, dream analysis in the hands of a specialist can be of vital importance in its revelation of those unknown factors which, if left hidden, may hinder but if revealed and understood will contribute to progression on the religious Way. Dreams possess creative, dynamic power which can be freed and used when the dream is truly understood and its power assimilated. Dreams also are the symbols of negative forces unless they are brought to consciousness and understood.

Many persons who have worked through analysis in search of the real self can testify that what occurs is similar to the religious experience of conversion. For what is finally touched, if the process goes deeply enough, is the Self, which is God within. When this happens, the basic roots of the person are established within himself as a part of that larger universal framework of which he is a part. He is truly himself, because he is a part of the larger whole. Let it be said that understanding a few dreams does not lead to this, nor does any given period of analysis do so, in and by itself. It is achieved only by those who continue to work throughout their lives, and often through great suffering, to liberate the libido within, and to understand with the heart the deeper unknown parts of Self.*–**

Elizabeth Boyden Howes,
contemporary American Jungian analyst and author.
Sheila Moon,
contemporary American Jungian analyst and author.

The Symbol in Dream-analysis

In Jungian dream-analysis the *symbol* plays a central role. The psychic images, in the dream as in all their other manifestations, are at once reflection and essence of the dynamics of the psyche. Just as, in the case of a waterfall, the waterfall is at once reflection and essence of force itself. They are the real energy-transformers in psychic events. They have at the same time expressive and impressive character, expressing on the one hand internal psychic happenings pictorially, and on the other hand influencing—after having been transformed into images—through their meaningful content these same happenings, thus furthering the flow of the psychological processes. For example, the symbol of the withered Tree of Life, which was meant to convey the idea of an over-intellectualized existence that had lost its natural instinctive basis, would on the one hand express this meaning pictorially before the very eyes of the dreamer, and on the other hand, by thus presenting itself to him, impress him and thereby influence his psychic dynamism in a certain direction. One can continually observe in the course of an analysis how the various pictorial motives determine and lead into one another. In the beginning they still appear in the guise of personal experiences; they bear the characteristics of childhood or other remembrances. As the analysis penetrates to deeper levels, however, they exhibit the outlines of the archetypes ever more clearly, the field becomes dominated ever more definitely by the symbol alone. Symbols can stand for the most varied contents. Natural events can be portrayed symbolically just as well as internal psychological processes. The symbol of "rebirth" stands always, for example, for the fundamental concept of spiritual transformation, whether it occurs as a primitive initiation rite, as a baptism in the early Christian sense, or in the corresponding dream-picture of a present-day individual. Only the way in which this rebirth is attained differs according to the historical and individual situation in consciousness. Just for this reason it is necessary to evaluate and interpret every symbol on the one hand, collectively, on the other, individually, if one will do justice to its actual meaning in any given case. The personal content and the psychological situation of the individual must always remain decisive.

The content of a symbol can never be fully expressed rationally. It comes out of that "between-world of subtle reality which can be adequately expressed through the symbol alone."[1] An allegory is a sign for something, a synonymous expression for a known content; the symbol, however, always implies in addition something inexpressible by rational means. When "Plato, for example, sums up the whole epistemological problem in the parable of the cave, or when Christ presents his concept of the Kingdom of God in parables, these are true and genuine symbols—namely, attempts to express something for which as yet no verbal concept exists." . . . the symbol is best able to give an account of the processes of the totality of the psyche and to influence as well as to express the most complicated and contradictory psychological conditions.*

Jolande Jacobi, 1890–1973. Swiss analytical psychologist.
The Psychology of Jung. Trans. K. W. Bash.

---

[1]*Contributions to Analytical Psychology*, C. G. Jung, pp. 231–232.

The Dream, Its Compensatory Function

The particular truth which personal dreams bring out is directly applicable to the dreamer himself. An apparently grotesque and trivial dream may have a deep importance in showing what the dreamer's immediate difficulty actually is.

For the dream has a compensatory and balancing quality. If the whole conscious attention is concentrated upon one aspect of a problem, the excluded and conflicting aspect becomes active in the unconscious, and the dream, portraying what is going on in the unconscious, reveals the other side which we need to remember in order to evaluate ourselves properly and to see the complete picture. It says, "This, too, is true." It is as though when the conscious is concentrated upon one aspect the unconscious said, "But this is the way things appear down here—you forget about this."

The dream, therefore, gives us a true picture, but often its truth is only comparative, the truth about one aspect which needs to be brought to our attention. Even when the dream startles us by its vivid, pertinent comment we cannot rely on this as the voice of infallible wisdom. We must connect it with our conscious attitude and our outer situation at the time. For we are full of contradictory elements; we can love and hate, fear and trust, desire and reject, and we must remember that both sides are present when we are in a tight place. Only by a comparison of the "affect" of the dream—that is, the degree of emotion aroused by it—with our own conscious attitude can we see that other aspect, and then choose for ourselves the side we will accept, always remembering the other side with which we must reckon. So the dream is continually reminding us of the part which our conscious is forgetting. It does not speak with any absolute authority; it simply gives a true picture of a situation which exists in the unconscious. It speaks truth; but not, as some persons believe, *the* truth. It shows the other side.

The unconscious may with infinite patience repeat a lesson over and over, trying with new images, new pictures, to show the truth. To express a relationship between unconscious images and conscious life is not the same as asserting that the unconscious is purposeful and itself acts with consciousness. The unconscious simply paints the picture, this picture, that picture, as the sea may cast up treasures on any shore; what use we make of these things is entirely our own affair.

In each case the event, whether dream or outer happening, must be accepted as an experience. It is as true with dreams as with life events that the importance of the happening itself is secondary to the importance of what we do with it. The dream does indicate that something has happened in the unconscious, that an event has actually taken place. If we will accept this inner event, experience it, make it part of our consciously lived life, then it becomes a potent factor, it produces change; we go from there to a new grasp, a deeper reality.*

Frances G. Wickes, 1875–1970. American psychotherapist.
The Inner World of Man.

The Activity of the "Shadow"[8] as Revealed by Dreams

Sometimes when one feels that the obstacles of life, even when faced with courage, are insurmountable, one may discover that part of the difficulty is caused by the unsuspected activity of the Shadow.

A result of ignoring the personal Shadow is graphically illustrated by a man's dream. At the time, he was involved in a situation which called for more conscious responsibility and frankness than he was willing to give. A relationship in which he had looked for unalloyed happiness developed unexpected difficulties. He had intuitions of the unpleasant elements at work. The more he tried to ignore these, the more his energies seemed to go from him. Doubt and distrust crept in, and he put the blame for this upon others. He feared to face the situation frankly, desiring to hold his infantile phantasy of perfection.

Then he tried to dismiss his intuitions as disloyal. He tried to reason things out consciously and to argue to himself that it was all unimportant, but he only became confused as to what faults were real and what were projections. He thrust the problem down out of consciousness.

---

[8]That unconscious part of the psyche containing both negative and positive aspects—the repressed (hidden) part which we need to recognize and learn to deal with. See pp. 116–117; 158 of this anthology.—Ed.

But though his attempt was to repress only the negative side, he lost all spontaneity of feeling. Then the dynamic energy of the unconscious seemed to go from him—not only had his feeling gone out, but the creative quality which had been present in his work was no longer at his disposal. At this point, the unconscious came to his aid by painting a dream picture:

"I am on a ship which has become stranded in a strange waste land. I know that we have submerged this country in order to drown out the inhabitants, whom we feared. But now we are attacked by a greater enemy; we are prisoners. Then I realize that if we had not drowned out the inhabitants we might have got help from them, whereas now we are delivered over, helpless, to some unseen but omnipotent tyrant from whom there is no escape."

His own interpretation was, "I have been trying to pretend that all sorts of things which I knew intuitively were wrong in this business either were better not talked about or else were the fault of others involved and that, therefore, I could do nothing about them and had best ignore them. But this has left me high and dry, delivered over to the enemy who, in some strange way, has drained me of my energy both in feeling and in power to work. I feel absolutely unable to get back any enthusiasm for life."

Here the Shadow elements which he tried to drown were the negative distrustful elements in himself which were roused when he was faced with the responsibilities involved in the working out of a difficult reality. In becoming conscious of these, in letting the waters of the unconscious cover them, he projected the whole thing upon other people involved and felt it all was due to the influence of *their* shadows. He feared to test out the truth of his doubts lest he should discover the situation to have no value for himself and he would lose even the illusion of happiness. He would not frankly face the disaster which might result from acknowledging the truth. First he projected all the difficulties upon others, and then he tried to repress these projections as being disloyal. He refused to become aware of the inner voices which were contradicting his conscious decision. So the whole problem was pushed back into the unconscious, where it acted like an ever-increasing magnetic force continually drawing down his energy.

In the end, it made the unconscious assume the proportions of a great inundation which drowned all his spontaneous energy and finally left him helpless, delivered over to one of those greater shadows of the collective unconscious which in the dream appeared as the inescapable tyrant. For, whenever he had pushed down any of his fears, he had really been feeding the Shadow until it had grown to proportions too great for his personal ego-consciousness to meet. It had taken from him the dynamic and creative elements of the unconscious which before fed his creative life.

For if one ignores the personal Shadow, one may be delivered over to the greater enemy. In such a typical human situation as this, for example, a failure to meet the problem may leave one at the mercy of the archetype—here the unseen invincible tyrant. If the archetype succeeds in swallowing the ego, the individual values are disintegrated and one becomes possessed by the unconscious and bereft of energy.

This man was acting in accordance with a generally accepted social standard that the negative and disturbing aspects of a situation should be passed over in a well-bred silence; that unpleasant things are best left out of a discussion; that resentments and anger should be hidden; in fact, that all the realities of the situation should be concealed if they interfere with harmonious adjustment. But realities dwindle when one fears anything which might disturb surface calm, whether these realities are in the outer situation or the inner. Then the difficulties may be projected. The devil is at work in the other fellow. The shadows of others fall across the path and they must be avoided. The outer life narrows, the inner life becomes more shallow. But down below, the Shadow has a good supper.*

Frances G. Wickes, 1875–1970. American psychotherapist.
The Inner World of Man.

The Fantasy and the Transformation of Personality

. . . the scientific credo of our time has developed a superstitious phobia about fantasy. But the real is what works. The fantasies of the unconscious work, there can be no doubt about that. Even the cleverest philosopher can be the victim of a thoroughly idiotic agoraphobia. Our famous scientific reality does not afford us the slightest protection against the so-called unreality of the unconscious. Something works behind the veil of fantastic images, whether we give this something a good name or a bad. It is something real, and for this reason its manifestations must be taken seriously. But first the tendency to concretization must be overcome; in other words, we must not take the fantasies literally when we approach the question of interpreting them. While we are in the grip of the actual experience, the fantasies cannot be taken literally enough. But when it comes to understanding them, we must on no account mistake the semblance, the fantasy-image as such, for the operative process underlying it. The semblance is not the thing itself, but only its expression. . . .

The two opposing "realities," the world of the conscious and the world of the unconscious, do not quarrel for supremacy, but each makes the other relative. That the reality of the unconscious is very relative indeed will presumably arouse no violent contradiction; but that the reality to the conscious world could be doubted will be accepted with less alacrity. And yet both "realities" are psychic experience, psychic semblances painted on an inscrutably dark back-cloth. To the critical intelligence, nothing is left of *absolute* reality.

Of the essence of things, of absolute being, we know nothing. But we experience various effects: from "outside" by way of the senses, from "inside" by way of fantasy. We would never think of asserting that the colour "green" had an independent existence; similarly we ought never to imagine that a fantasy-experience exists in and for itself, and is therefore to be taken quite literally. It is an expression, an appearance standing for something unknown but real. . . .

Continual conscious realization of unconscious fantasies, together with active participation in the fantastic events, has, as I have witnessed in a very large number of cases, the effect firstly of extending the conscious horizon by the inclusion of numerous unconscious contents; secondly, of gradually diminishing the dominant influence of the unconscious; and thirdly of bringing about a change of personality.

This change of personality is naturally not an alteration

of the original hereditary disposition, but rather a transformation of the general attitude. Those sharp cleavages and antagonisms between conscious and unconscious, such as we see so clearly in the endless conflicts of neurotic natures, nearly always rest on a noticeable one-sidedness of the conscious attitude, which gives absolute precedence to one or two functions,[9] while the others are unjustly thrust into the background. Conscious realization and experience of fantasies assimilates the unconscious inferior functions to the conscious mind—a process which is naturally not without far-reaching effects on the conscious attitude.

For the moment I will refrain from discussing the nature of this change of personality, since I only want to emphasize the fact that an important change does take place. I have called this change, which is the aim of our analysis of the unconscious, the transcendent function. [There is a] remarkable capacity of the human soul for change, expressed in the transcendent function. . . .*—**

Carl G. Jung, M.D., 1875–1961. Swiss psychiatrist.
Two Essays on Analytical Psychology. Trans. R. F. C. Hull.

Dangers of Psychotherapy

A peculiar and, for the religious situation, important significance is attached in the present to the art of healing. It must be recalled that with the elemination of the priestly confessional and the loss of its real values the physician stepped upon the scene as a substitute. Yet he was a substitute who could not supply what should have been supplied, a healing process proceeding out of man's central function, that is, out of his religious relations. First of all the separation of body and soul, then the mechanization of the body, then the conception of the psychic as a product of the physical machine—these logical consequences of a rationalistic, atomistic conception of nature, which had been deprived of life and of inwardness, made the healing art more and more a mechanical and technical activity. The separate organs were treated as though they were separate parts of a machine which could be isolated; furthermore, the body was treated, and only the body. Even the science of psychical healing came to be in fact a science of physical healing

[9]Feeling, thinking, intuition and sensation. (See p. 325.)—Ed.

or of the healing of separate organs. It is evident that according to this conception the relation of physician and patient could only be an external, objective and contractual relationship, not one of real community supported by love. Such a relationship corresponds to the fundamental lack of community-love in the spirit of capitalist society. In spite of all principles, it is true, authority upon the one hand and trust upon the other always played an important role and revealed their great significance, particularly in the treatment of psychic disorders. But it was only when the psycho-analytic method became effective after 1900 that more important consequences were realized. This method restores independence to the soul. The depths of the unconscious are explored independently of bodily and organic processes. Naturally such a procedure cannot be used unless the physician can enter sympathetically into the mind of the patient and this requires again that the patient have a personal Eros-attitude toward the physician (the attitude will oscillate between love and hate, and has nothing to do with eroticism, must in fact exclude this). Thus an important analogy to the old confessional relationship has been created. In the one, as in the other, decisive significance attaches to the soul's misery, which is almost always connected with guilt-complexes, to the relief brought by the recognition, verbal expression and the realization of hidden connections and, finally, to the determination to reconstruct the soul. Yet there is a profound difference between the two methods. In the confessional all this takes place in the presence of God. The mind is directed first of all to the eternal and only in the second place toward itself. The things confession is concerned with belong to the very heart of personality, to its freedom and responsibility. The danger of psycho-analysis is that it will deal with these same things from the point of view of natural occurrences and that it will constantly direct the attention of the patient to himself and his temporal existence. Thus the soul's center of gravity may be transferred from the center—from the point of personal responsibility in the presence of the Unconditioned—to the impersonal, unconscious, purely natural sphere. This is the source of the frequently destructive effects of psycho-analysis and the indication that in this instance also the self-sufficient finitude of the psychic has not been actually broken through. Only a priestly man can be a complete psychiatrist. For with him the relation to the patient and the inner activities of the patient have been lifted out of the realm of the subjectivity of the finite into the inclusive life of the eternal.

Paul Tillich, 1886–1965. American theologian, philosopher.
The Religious Situation.

Some Self-Education Procedures

The Religious Function of the Ego

. . . the ego functions religiously when it takes on, as a very conscious act, dedication or commitment to suprapersonal values—when it decides with deliberation to go the way of wholeness. It has been my interest over many years to work not only as an analyst but also as a leader in seminars where this element is particularly stressed. I have come to make the distinction between a strong uncommitted and a weak but committed ego. When with full consciousness such a dedication has been made, it has a profound effect on one's analytical journey, on the relation of the journey to lived life, and on the deeper bringing together of inner and outer values. A patient of mine, who had a fairly weak but very dedicated ego, dreamed that his decision about marriage must be in the context of the will of God. Such a dream would indicate an ego obviously related in a very purposive way to whatever the dreamer calls the "will of God," a will different than that which is in consciousness. When the conscious side takes on this more total attitude it is involved in what I would call the problem of the discipline of the ego, which can be worked at in other ways through analysis. (As an analyst, I obviously believe psychotherapy is the main way for many of us, but I do not believe that in and of itself, analysis necessarily is enough.)

One of the religious functions of the ego is how it chooses to find time or "steal" time (for time always has to be "stolen") to work at transformation. One of the great needs in the field of psychology and religion is to experiment with techniques, procedures, ways of meditation and prayer consistent with our analysis, because these are aspects of a necessary centralizing process. I would stress, as Jung did, that these must meet the needs of the Western psyche, not the Eastern. I have been experimenting with, and have led seminars on, introversion, meditation, and prayer in which Martin Buber's idea of dialogue was emphasized as an inner interaction. Here the "I" relates to elements which must also be seen as "Thou." The dialogue between "I" and an unknown inner "Thou" is a certain form of active imagination, in which the way the ego speaks and other parts of the psyche reply helps us to deepen self-insight. I believe this idea of the dialogue of the ego and the parts has dynamic possibilities. Sometimes two or more elements in a dream can be brought into active interrelatedness. The dialogue should be entered into only after one evokes the central presence of God. This is a profound religious act, and one that is not done too easily nor too often; but it is a creative combination of the human and the divine.*

Elizabeth Boyden Howes. Contemporary Jungian analyst.
Intersection and Beyond.

The Handling of Fantasy Material

The art of letting things happen, action through non-action, letting go of oneself as taught by Meister Eckhart, became for me the key that opens the door to the way. We must be able to let things happen in the psyche. For us, this is an art of which most people know nothing. Consciousness is forever interfering, helping, correcting, and negating, never leaving the psychic processes to grow in peace. It would be simple enough, if only simplicity were not the most difficult of all things. To begin with, the task consists solely in observing objectively how a fragment of fantasy develops. Nothing could be simpler, and yet right here the difficulties begin. Apparently one has no fantasy fragments —or yes, there's one, but it is too stupid! Dozens of good reasons are brought against it. The conscious mind raises innumerable objections, in fact it often seems bent on blotting out the spontaneous fantasy activity in spite of real insight and in spite of the firm determination to allow the psychic process to go forward without interference. Occasionally there is a veritable cramp of consciousness.

If one is successful in overcoming the initial difficulties, criticism is still likely to start in afterwards in the attempt to interpret the fantasy, to classify it, to aestheticize it, or to devalue it. The temptation to do this is almost irresistible. After it has been faithfully observed, free rein can be given to the impatience of the conscious mind; in fact it must be given, or obstructive resistances will develop. But each time the fantasy material is to be produced, the activity of consciousness must be switched off again.

In most cases the results of these efforts are not very encouraging at first. Usually they consist of tenuous webs of fantasy that give no clear indication of their origin or their goal. Also, the way of getting at the fantasies varies with individuals. For many people, it is easiest to write them down; others visualize them, and others again draw or paint them with or without visualization. If there is a high degree of conscious cramp, often only the hands are capable of fantasy; they model or draw figures that are sometimes quite foreign to the conscious mind.

These exercises must be continued until the cramp in the conscious mind is relaxed, in other words, until one can let things happen, which is the next goal of the exercise. In this way a new attitude is created, an attitude that accepts the irrational and the incomprehensible simply because it is happening. This attitude would be poison for a person who is already overwhelmed by the things that happen to him, but it is of the greatest value for one who selects, from among the things that happen, only those that are acceptable to his conscious judgment, and is gradually drawn out of the stream of life into a stagnant backwater.

At this point, the way travelled by the two types mentioned earlier seems to divide. Both have learned to accept what comes to them. . . . One man will now take chiefly what comes to him from outside, and the other what comes from inside. Moreover, the law of life demands that what they take from outside and inside will be the very things that were always excluded before. This reversal of one's nature brings an enlargement, a heightening and enrichment of the personality, if the previous values are retained alongside the change—provided that these values are not mere illusions. If they are not held fast, the individual will swing too far to the other side, slipping from fitness into unfitness, from adaptedness into unadaptedness, and even from rationality into insanity. The way is not without danger. Everything good is costly, and the development of personality is one of the most costly of all things. It is a matter of saying yea to oneself, of taking oneself as the most serious of tasks, of being conscious of everything one does, and keeping it constantly before one's eyes in all its dubious aspects—truly a task that taxes us to the utmost.

A Chinese can always fall back on the authority of his whole civilization. If he starts on the long way, he is doing what is recognized as being the best thing he could possibly do. But the Westerner who wishes to set out on this way, if he is really serious about it, has all authority against him—intellectual, moral, and religious. . . . The individual must devote himself to the way with all his energy, for it is only by means of his integrity that he can go further, and his integrity alone can guarantee that his way will not turn out to be an absurd misadventure.*

Carl G. Jung, M.D., 1875–1961. Swiss psychiatrist.
Alchemical Studies. Trans. R. F. C. Hull.

Active Fantasying consists in letting the mind loose, allowing whatever will to come into consciousness. The difference between this and idle daydreaming is a question of valuation or attitude. The very fact that meaning is attached to the imagery, and that it is recorded and valued, seems to constellate the autonomous activity in a peculiar way. Instead of wayward ephemeral fancies that blow down the wind like thistledown, the images that arise under the influence of value and attention are pregnant and relevant in a high degree. It is not unlike the experience of men who, for years perhaps, have had only the lightest and most trifling relations with women; suddenly, for no discoverable reason, a woman steps out of the condition of ephemeral irrelevance and becomes commandingly relevant. Such a man, we say, has been seized by the love-problem. In much the same way one can be seized by the psyche, the spontaneous, unwilled activity of the mind suddenly assuming a peculiar significance. What makes the woman or the fantasy suddenly relevant? In neither case is it mere accident; indeed, in the psyche sphere there can be no such thing as accident; when reason is in control, we are able to weigh all the factors for or against a certain decision; but in the irrational realm, the event goes of itself without conscious direction, and often with astonishing certainty of aim. But whose aim? Unless we wish to introduce some extra-psychic cause in deference to time-honored tradition, we have to accept the concept of the self as embracing both irrational and rational, unconscious and conscious elements. Only with this conception is it possible to comprehend a subjective aim more far-sighted and more commanding than the deliberate-aiming consciousness. Without this central conception it is, I believe, fundamentally impossible to reach the heart of a dream, or to give vital value to such irrational products as we shall presently discuss.

Active fantasy-production may follow many different routes, according to individual preference. With some subjects the fantasy springs directly out of a dream, and there is an immediate inclination to paint or in some way[10] elaborate the dream-image. Modelling clay or plasticine, painting or drawing, carrying on the dream-scene in waking fantasy, conversing with personification of the unconscious or independent entities, written accounts, poems, dialogues, even dancing and posturing—in fact, any method at all which gives concreteness, independence, plastic vitality to the psychic contents I include under this term as a rule. Those products have little or no aesthetic value; in short, the ideal condition for active fantasying is that of the child, only it must be combined with the purposiveness of maturity.*

H. Godwin Baynes, M.D., 1888–1943. English Jungian analyst.
Mythology of the Soul.

Confessional Meditation[11]

If you repress what you harbor, you will be stifled by your own unlived life. If you express the repressed tendencies, you may destroy and kill. You must find another way to "make terms with your opponent, so long as you and he are on the way to court" (Matt. 5:25, Moffatt). The way out, indeed the only way out, as far as we know, is the way of confession. But the word confession must be understood,

[10]See pp. 316–317 (For extensive practice of Active Fantasy analytic guidance is advisable).—Ed.

[11]The practice of Confessional Meditation should not be attempted too strenuously without further direction such as is found in the final chapters of *In Search of Maturity* by Fritz Kunkel (Scribner).—Ed.

and the method must be used in the right way, according to the structure of the human mind and the special problems of our time. Otherwise, the result will be the opposite of what it should be . . .

We have to revitalize, indeed to recreate, the meaning of the old and colorful word if we can use it at all. And we try to do so by stressing two aspects of its meaning . . .

The first aspect is that the nearer mankind draws to real Christianity the more the Christian can and should confess to the One who was always supposed to be represented by, or present in, the Father Confessor, namely God. A trustworthy friend, a father confessor, if possible an expert in depth-psychology, should be available in case of emergency. But the main part of the task has to be solved by the individual alone by himself in confessional meditation; and that means "in the presence of God." Try to pour out before Him whatever comes to your mind. Be not embarrassed by His presence. Do not refrain from strong words—say "swine" if you mean swine: God knows what you say and what you do not say anyhow. He knows your conscious and your unconscious mind equally. Therefore His presence will help you to discover your "secret sins" and unearth your "buried talents."

Here we reach the second point: our confession has to bring to light the unknown, the unconscious darkness, and the undeveloped creativity of our deeper layers. Confession then becomes research, investigation, discovery. We discover our individual as well as collective drives, too much and too little power, emotional drought and emotional floods, destructive and constructive urges, our animal nature and our vegetal nature. If we can spread out before Him all the hidden roots of our virtues and vices, if we are honest and courageous enough to release before Him the high voltage of our unconscious hatred and love, we may discover that all our power is in the last analysis His power, and that our darkness turns into light because He is both darkness and light.

Expression of what we find within ourselves, honest and reckless expression before the face of the Eternal, assuming responsibility for what we are, even if we are unaware of it, and asking God to help us to master the wild horses, or to revive the skeletons of horses which we dig out during the long hours of our confessions—this is the psychological method of religious self-education. It is a way of bringing to consciousness our unconscious contents, and of establishing control over our hidden powers. It is the way to mature responsibility . . . if you hate your brother, and you pour out all your hatred, remembering at the same time, as much as you can, the presence of God—and your hatred does not change, then you are not sufficiently aware either of the presence of God or of your hatred, and probably of neither. Be more honest, give vent to your emotions. . . . God is there, tell him the truth. . . . You are ten years old now—get up from your chair, don't pretend to be a wise old Buddha, pace the floor, yell, scream, punch the furniture, express yourself until you are exhausted, or until you laugh at yourself. . . . It may take weeks or months for [some problems]; you may have to travel the long way through the whole Old Testament. And finally you will meet the God of the inner storms: "Smoke fumed from his nostrils, and scorching fire from his lips, that kindled blazing coals, as down he came on the bending sky, the storm-cloud at his feet" (Psalm 18:8,9, Moffatt). It is a nightmare more real than anything you have ever seen in the outer world. But it is not yet real enough. The highest reality emerges out of the fire in complete calm. We may realize it for a moment beyond space and time: the center itself. And at last "What is old has gone, the new has come" (II Cor. 5:17, Moffatt). The new is "God's peace that surpasses all our dreams." (Phil. 4:7, Moffatt.)

Thus we combine the old practice of "the presence of God," well known in the tradition of meditation and prayer, with the new practice of depth-psychology, well known in modern literature. The result is "confessional meditation."

Much unconscious, unexpected material will come to light: Forgotten scenes will be recalled, people and relations will appear in a different light. More important, of course, than the accumulation of material is its new evaluation and its application to our future. Grudge will change into compassion, and hatred into love. Destructive tendencies will give way to newly discovered creative capacities. Our unlived life, thus released from its prison, wants to be lived. We are dimly aware, during this time, of the primitiveness and immaturity of our new desires and ideas; yet the same regression which enabled us to unearth the unconscious power now makes it difficult to refrain from its immediate use. No mistake, however, would be worse than this. Confessional meditation without continence, fasting, voluntary privation, is doomed to failure. Express your hatred or love, your greed or envy, before the face of God; but do not express them to the people whom you hate or love. This is the best way to discover more or deeper hatred or love, and to draw nearer to the real center.

Our repressed drives, when they come to consciousness, are primitive, undifferentiated and powerful, like young hippopotami. Not to satisfy them is a heroic task, presupposing some training in the old and almost forgotten art of fasting. Therefore, when you set out on the road of self-education learn how to fast. . . . We talk too much, read too much, write too much; we are too busy satisfying our petty needs. And when you have the first great dream, and, stunned by its appalling colors, would like to tell your friends or husband or wife about it—stop! Fast! Refrain from gossip! If you betray the secrets of the soul no further secret will be entrusted to you. Conscious sacrifice is required, instead of unconscious repression. . . . The child-like imperative "you must not . . ." is replaced by the mature insight "I will not . . ." Thus we may learn to leave "brothers or sisters or father or mother or wife or children or lands or houses" (Matt. 19:29, Moffatt). This conscious sacrifice is what is meant by fasting and plucking out our eye. It is an integral part of confessional meditation.

But the long and winding road of self-education cannot be travelled in seclusion and solitude. It has to be a part of our normal activity. We have to live in the world, and its demands, satisfactions and disappointments are an integral contribution to our psychological research. We should refrain—at least during periods of crisis—from important decisions and from strong emotional reactions towards the outer world. But we should study this world and study our reactions towards it, and even sometimes try, in the sense of an experiment, to do something against our habit-patterns or beyond our usual self-control.

Without the verification in outer life all our inner progress remains questionable. And without the inner experience of new understanding, power and creativity, all our outer improvements would remain a shallow masquerade. The pendulum of religious self-education has to swing back and forth between introvert and extravert experiences, confessional meditation and positive training: this is the best way to avoid the one-sidedness and self-deceptions which always threaten our spiritual development.*–**

Fritz Kunkel, M.D., 1889–1956. American psychiatrist.
In Search of Maturity.

Positive Training

Do something new. The way out of your shell involves enlarging your experience in the direction of greater usefulness and larger productivity. Your Ego includes your ideas about what you cannot do as well as your feelings about your value or worth. These set up limits beyond which you hesitate to venture. Nevertheless the Self seeks expressions of its creative capacities. So again and again you may feel "I don't think I could do that but I could try." We may speak of this as the temptation to productivity, representing the inner urge to growth, the prompting of the Self toward increasing productivity.

It is important to understand the inner meaning of the feeling, "I cannot," which one often has. Of course, there are absolute limits to what one can do. Obviously the lack of wings and the possession of only two hands instead of four impose certain limitations concerning which we must say "I cannot." Apart from incapacities of this type the meaning of the feeling "I cannot" is usually "I must not because I am afraid of what might happen if I did."

Growth in character and the consequent deeper satisfactions are dependent again and again upon discovering this masked fear and facing it. Quite the opposite reaction also needs to be understood in this connection. It is the feeling, "I must." It is the sometimes terrifying feeling that one experiences when he feels impelled to do something that seems virtually impossible yet somehow necessary to one's very existence. . . . Here, too, back of the "I must" is the -100, the fearful thing which one is seeking to escape, this time not by refusing to try the new task but by assuming what may be an impossible one.

Look back of your feeling "I must" for the possible *minus 100* in your life. Do so especially when you feel unhappily urged on. But the "I must" may be, and is at times, the wholesome urge to greater creativity. . . . In such cases there is a deep joy in the impulsion to go on. This is objective living which is by no means free from hardship but always essentially satisfying and even joyous. The egocentric "I must" is darkly dyed with fear and unhappiness.

In all sound efforts to do something new, it is important to remember the principle of the small steps. When you look ahead to the new experience that you need to widen your world and take you beyond your former limits, do not think of some quick and easy journey to new realms, for that is the egocentric wish for quick triumph. It tends to defeat your own ends, especially in those situations in which your reaction is "I cannot." If, feeling thus, you try to reach your goal by one giant step, you will, of course, fail, and then you will say to yourself and others, "I was right. I thought I could not and now I know it. I tried and I failed as I thought I would."*

Fritz Kunkel, M.D., 1889–1956. American psychiatrist,
and Roy E. Dickerson, 1886–, American author.
How Character Develops.

. . . we seldom get rid of an evil merely by understanding its causes . . . and for all our insight, obstinate habits do not disappear until replaced by other habits. But habits are won only by exercise, and appropriate education is the sole means to this end. The patient must be *drawn out* of himself into other paths, which is the true meaning of "education," and this can only be achieved by an educative will . . .

. . . no amount of confession and no amount of explaining can make the crooked plant grow straight; it must be trained upon the trellis of the norm by the gardener's art.*–**

Carl G. Jung, M.D., 1875–1961. Swiss psychiatrist.
The Practice of Psychotherapy. Trans. R. F. C. Hull.

You Who Fear Change

You who fear change are like these sheep that turn
Back from cold mountain creeks, and drink
Only in small familiar pools, or suck
Green milk of these marshy ponds that lie
Round and unmoving in a valley's palm.
O slow and complacent muzzles, does it mean

Nothing to you that dust and drouth
Shrivel the little pools, and dung
Stains the warm stagnant water where the steers
Follow your little pathways to this pond?

Time fouls still water and slime lies
Mucous and soft above all ponds.
The lake by living springs unfed
Shrinks to a caking slough.
Blind is that shepherd who would lead his sheep
Back to these steer-trampled waters!

Josephine W. Johnson, 1910–. American novelist, poet.
Year's End.

Participation in the Creative Process

One can often help cultivate the needed changes—seek "the cold mountain creeks"—by exposing himself more consciously to the creative process, as it is to be discovered through the various forms of art, music, poetry, dancing, writing, as well as through nature, work (see p. 378), personal relationships and worship. It is up to each person to find the way through to his own creativity, to explore and experiment, and to recognize the relation of such exploration to the whole religious process.

Repressed sides of the personality that need recovering: undeveloped potentials which await release: indeed the whole of man's being with its innate yearning for contact with the Creative Source, motivates such experiment.

Brief glimpses are given here into some of the ways to cultivate the new awarenesses. The reader will find suggestions for follow-up study in the Recommended Reading list at the end of the book.

Perhaps it should be noted in passing that a wise and individual choice of any of the techniques—such as are described in the whole of Part Two of this book—can better be made if one has some knowledge of how he conducts his life; if he senses, for instance, in what situations he feels "at home" and effective, and in which ones he feels lame, vulnerable, and incomplete. Clues gained in this way point up the needed emphases in all one's exploratory efforts. They can lend guidance to one's practice of prayer and meditation (choice of subject matter, etc.). They also can throw light on the kind of "Fellowship" (Chapter VII) one seeks (an overly extraverted person needing intimate group experience and retreats alone, perhaps, etc.). The implications of such discovery can certainly have bearing on one's choice of "Action" (Chapter VIII)—on the new habit patterns one seeks to develop—as well as on the kinds of creative activity into which one moves.

It is interesting to note that from Plato on, men have sought from time to time to clarify the fourfold way in which reality is approached and perceived. Jung has contributed greatly toward this understanding through his observation of what he terms the "four functions"[12] in both their introverted and extraverted aspects. He divides the major functions into thinking (logical judgment) and its logical counterpart, feeling (value judgment); intuition (imaginative perception) and its opposite, sensation (factual perception—practical "know-how"). Though every individual is endowed with all four functions, there seems always to be one which is the most readily available to consciousness while the others tend to remain undeveloped or are repressed entirely. Since the use of each one is needed in the conduct of life, an understanding of personality types and the various ways in which they are expressed has tremendous relevancy to one's progression on the Way—to the response one gives to that clarion call to wholeness, "Thou shalt love the Lord thy God with all thy heart, with all thy strength, with all thy mind, and with all thy soul"—and to the ability one achieves in fulfilling the whole of love's great trinity—love of God, of self and of neighbor.

The selections which follow provide hints of some of the ways in which one can supplement his own limited experience and come more fully to perceive and participate in

---

[12]See *Types of Personality* by C. G. Jung. For a good summarization of Jung's findings in this area see *Experiment in Depth* by P. W. Martin (Pantheon, 1955), Chap. II. There are new clinical tests being perfected (one, the Briggs-Meyer Type Index Test) by which functional types can be ascertained fairly accurately. Such tests will prove valuable in vocational analysis as well as in "Self-knowledge" from the standpoint considered in this book. Coupled with other projective techniques (such as the Rorschach test) they can throw a great deal of light on one's undeveloped potentials.

aspects of reality which heretofore may not have been accessible to him.

CREATIVE PERCEPTION OF REALITY

Art is always visionary. Art always disturbs present realities, however satisfactory they may seem to the rest of the world.

Ben Shahn, 1898–1969. American painter.
Conversations with Artists by Selden Rodman.

The greatest art enlightens the conscious mind as well as the unconscious.

Jacques Lipschitz, 1891–. Polish sculptor.
Conversations with Artists by Selden Rodman.

Creative imagination is given to everyone, but most men do not realize that they possess it. Not everyone has the imagination of a truly gifted artist, but all have it to the extent that they are able to relate to the creative life force, and allow it to flow through them. Not all men are creators, but the ideal beholder must also engage in the creative act, if he sincerely wishes to participate in the experience of the one who created the work of art.

This participation requires a very special effort, one which most men are not willing to make. They expect, even demand, that a work of art speaks to them immediately. Make no mistake—art is not a direct means of communication. It speaks indirectly. You hear it with an inner ear and perceive it with a third eye. It does not reach your intellect, first, as does the written word. You have to prepare yourself to receive it. In this sense, the pleasure experienced through an appreciation of the plastic arts is like that derived from poetry. When, at last, you begin to sense its meaning, you realize you are in contact with some force, higher than yourself.

The true lover of art experiences something of the same elevated emotion that the artist felt during the moment of creation. This is one of the symbolic functions of the artist —to act as a medium in communicating a message to those who may be less sensitive, and thus less able to receive their own messages.

Pegot Waring, 1909–. American sculptor.
Speak with Granite Tongues.

I discovered that there were a multitude of ways of perceiving, ways that were controllable by what I can only describe as an internal gesture of the mind. It was as if one's self-awareness had a central point of intensest being, and this core of being could be moved about at will. . . .

The first hint that I really had the power to control the way I looked at things happened in connexion with music. . . . I lost myself in a Schubert Quartet partly by ceasing all striving to understand it, partly by driving off intruding thoughts, and partly by feeling the music coming up inside me, myself a hollow vessel filled with sound. . . . Gradually I found, that though I could not listen by direct trying I could make some sort of internal gesture after which listening just happened. Sometimes I seemed to put my awareness into the soles of my feet, sometimes to send something which was myself out into the hall, or to feel that I was standing just beside the orchestra . . . close to the music. Sometimes it closed over my head, and I came away rested and feeling light-limbed.

At this time also I began to surmise that there might be different ways of looking as well as of listening. One day I was idly watching some gulls as they soared high overhead. I wás not interested, for I recognized them as "just gulls," and vaguely watched first one and then another. Then all at once something seemed to have opened. Idle boredom with the familiar became a deep-breathing peace and delight. My whole attention was gripped by the pattern and rhythm of their flight.

. . . I had been brought up to believe that to try was the only way to overcome difficulty. . . . So if ping-pong was difficult, one must try. The result was a stiff body, full of effort, and a jerky swipe at the ball, until someone said: "Play with a loose arm," and I tried, unbelieving. At once the ball went crisply skimming the net to the far court, not once only, but again and again, as long as I could hold myself back from meddling. What surprised me was that my arm seemed to know what to do by itself, it was able to make the right judgements of strength and direction quite without my help. . . .

My next discovery about movement was while darning stockings. I was usually clumsy-fingered, fumbling and impatient to be finished, but slow because I did not find the task interesting. . . . Now I found I could make some internal act while darning my stocking, an act of detachment by which I stood aside from my hand, did not interfere with it, but left it to put in the needle by itself. At first I found great difficulty in restraining my head from trying to do my hand's work for it, but whenever I succeeded the results startled me; for at once there came a sense of ease and I was able to work at maximum speed without any effort. . . .

I was reminded of that little one-celled animal which can spread part of its own essence to flow round and envelop within itself whatever it wants for food. This spreading of some vital essence of myself was a new gesture . . . like a spreading of invisible sentient feelers, as a sea anemone spreads wide its feathery fingers. . . .

One day I stopped in front of a Cezanne still-life—green apples, a white plate and a cloth. Being tired, restless, and distracted by the stream of bored Sunday afternoon sight-seers drifting through the galleries, I simply sat and looked, too inert to remember whether I ought to like it or not. Slowly I became aware that something was pulling me out of my vacant stare and the colours were coming alive, gripping my gaze till I was soaking myself in their vitality. Gradually a great delight filled me. . . . It had all happened by just sitting still and waiting. . . .

If just looking could be so satisfying, why was I always striving to have things or to get things done? Certainly I had never suspected that the key to my private reality might lie in so apparently simple a skill as the ability to let the senses roam unfettered by purposes. I began to wonder whether eyes and ears might not have a wisdom of their own. *–**

Joanna Field, contemporary English analyst and author.
A Life of One's Own.[13]

Entering into the Experience of the Inner Image

A leaven of humility, a receptivity, a trust in the forces of life within the psyche; a willingness to let life live, to generously consider the possibility that this voice, so alien to our conscious ego edicts, may have a message for us; all this makes us open to the magic of the suggestive image.

[13]This book, first published in 1934, is an account of the author's attempt to come to self-knowledge on her own, long before she became an analyst.—Ed.

The mood or feeling which is too inarticulate to find expression in words may evoke an image which in abstract or impersonal form says the unsayable and so reveals the nature of the force within the psyche that has exerted such magnetic power.

A little child of seven wrote:

"The tree said, 'I am lonely, I am lonely.' And it whispered it, and then it got frightened and called out loud, 'I am lonely.' And that was the big lonely wind, and I heard it and I was lonely too."

Another child painted a picture of three bare trees, stark, desolate in the wind, gray lines bent almost to touch the bleak hillside.

"Have you ever seen trees look like that?" she was asked.

"No, but I have seen them feel like that."

Both these children had entered into the experience of loneliness, had known its terror. To the one came the desire to express this inner knowledge in the visual image. She knew the feeling of the wind-swept tree. Because she had let the feeling move within her, she could let it form itself on paper. She was too young to say, "There are forces greater than I. They are like the storm, one can only bow before them and wait." But the picture said it. *It* was as old as she was young.

The other child heard the *voice* of loneliness. She, too, became one with the solitary tree and so knew what the wind was saying and, in that experience of lonely listening, she conceived the creative image, the wind as the voice of loneliness, and she wrote what she heard as poignantly as did the poet Yeats:

"The wind blows out of the gates of day
The wind blows over the lonely of heart."

But we do not wish to penetrate the heart of loneliness. We turn from the dark doorway and turn on the radio or busy ourselves with trivial busyness. For Satan finds some deadening task for busy hands to do. Anything to evade the primal experience! But the ability and willingness to enter into experience, honestly appraising it, finding its value in outer life and courageously exploring its inner meaning to us, is the attitude that sets free creative energy and makes life move within us.

By the act of creation, which embodies idea or emotion in the form in which it arises within us, a pathway of communication with others is opened. This child who was too isolated and too inarticulate to ask for the help she needed, reached out unconsciously through the impersonal expression of her need. These words spoke to an adult, who had also known loneliness, and through the communication so established, the creation of a new relatedness took place. For the creative spirit moves from form to form, from creature to creature, creating and re-creating. This newly created feeling also found form in pictorial words. When loneliness had been dispelled, this same child wrote:

"The sun shone and the brook danced, and it danced, and it danced, and danced, and it danced and it danced."

Again the child entered into experience, this time expressing a joy, a motion. a rhythm like the beating of a drum. Primitives also know the power of the rhythmic beat to evoke a force that seems to rise from inner depths, or from the earth itself. The rhythm sets the feet to dancing but also evokes a rhythmic movement within the spirit which stirs latent power. Energy is activated through rhythmic repetition in which both body and spirit yield themselves to the expression of a force derived from the primordial reservoir.

"The earth is my home
It is powerful
Water speaks in foam
It is powerful
There sits a hill
It is powerful
I go now to kill
I am powerful."

This war song is used to energize the individual with collective strength which he dedicates to the tribe. It is the invocation of the powers of darkness that dwell within each one of us. Is it so different from our personal or national invocations which we use to stir us to strife? In contract is the chant which evokes beauty as companion to the spirit:

"As I walk, as I walk
The universe is walking with me
Beautifully—it walks before me
Beautifully—on every side
As I walk—I walk with Beauty."

Potent images call to inner power. To the Indian the primary goal of creative energy is the creation of energy within the individual. This is why an Indian will work with complete absorption and with utter concentration upon a sand-painting which must be destroyed as the sun sets. He knows his work, as a concrete product, will vanish with the single day but the healing that it has accomplished will live again, a re-creation, and all who have participated in this ceremony will have shared in the creation and rebirth of power. Here the creative power works not through original creation, but through exact and patterned imitation, a meticulous obedience to ordained ritual, and the image which is held in the contemplation of the worshipper works potently within him. Here obedience is not repression but dedication and control. It is therefore not in opposition to, but in service of, creativity. The sand-painter's personal achievement is swallowed up in identification with the healing power of the god. He transmits power through obedience. The measure of the healing is proportionate to the spiritual participation of those who take part, either actively or through receptivity. In all such experiences the whole being is in a state of heightened receptivity, of intuitive awareness and of desire. For creative energy must submit to discipline and hard work, but its source is *desire*. As Yeats said, "Keep in your minds some images of magnificence, keep in your hearts some desires that can live in Paradise."*

Frances G. Wickes, 1875–1970. American psychotherapist.
"The Creative Process."

THE CREATIVE PROCESS AS CREATIVE ACT

The soul of Man must quicken to creation.
Out of the formless stone, when the artist united
himself with stone,
Spring always new forms of life, from the soul of
man that is joined to the soul of stone;
Out of the meaningless practical shapes of all that
is living or lifeless
Joined with the artist's eye, new life, new form,
new colour.
Out of the sea of sound the life of music,
Out of the slimy mud of words, out of the sleet
and hail of verbal imprecisions,

Approximate thoughts and feelings, words that
    have taken the place of thoughts and feelings,
There spring the perfect order of speech, and the
    beauty of incantation.

LORD, shall we not bring these gifts to Your service?
    Shall we not bring to Your service all our powers
For life, for dignity, grace and order,
And intellectual pleasures of the senses?
The Lord who created must wish us to create
And employ our creation again in His service
Which is already His service in creating.
For Man is joined spirit and body,
And therefore must serve as spirit and body.
Visible and invisible, two worlds meet in Man;
Visible and invisible must meet in His Temple;
You must not deny the body.

  Now you shall see the Temple completed:
After much striving, after many obstacles;
For the work of creation is never without travail;
The formed stone, the visible crucifix,
The dressed altar, the lifting light,

  Light

  Light

  The visible reminder of Invisible Light.

T. S. Eliot, 1888–1965. English poet.
Choruses from "The Rock."

Many are the instruments through which the soul seeks utterance: form and color of paint or clay; hewn stone; strings plucked or hammered; breath blown through reed or brass; chords vibrating in a human throat; and earliest of all primeval instruments—the whole human body itself.

Peggy Baum Gerry,
contemporary American teacher and analyst.

"The body—and sex—are our first and our last living realities. Our soul is contained in them. We must love and respect them."[14] . . . To master the stuff he is made of—not to beat it into a repressed subjection, not to make it into a singular god to be worshiped—is what man needs to do as he lives his wholeness in body as well as in spirit."*–**

Elizabeth Boyden Howes,
contemporary American Jungian analyst.
Sheila Moon,
contemporary American Jungian analyst and writer.
Man the Choicemaker.

Through Movement

It is astonishing how many people are almost completely unaware of themselves physically. The wonderful joy in movement, which children have, has been lost. Movement has become a means to an end, usually a rational and purposeful end, and takes place automatically in response to hundreds and hundreds of mental images of going someplace and doing something.

[Yet] the kinesthetic sense is just as valuable as the five which inform us of the physical world about us. But if this sense is never developed, or seldom used, it becomes unconscious and one is in the situation I can only call living in the head, which fact the body faithfully reflects, since it must move, by acquiring a whole series of distortions, short circuits, strains and mannerisms accumulated from years and years of being assimilated to mental images of choice, necessity, value and appropriateness.

There is an interesting reflection in connection with this. In our time there is a widespread repression of all physical emotion, that is, all bodily expression of joy, grief, anger, affection, fear, and yet an equally widespread fascination with the body's appearance and function. We are embarrassed and irritated when confronted by any form of physical intensity in our personal lives. Joy in the voice and face is all right, grief in the voice and face is understandable, anger in the voice and face will pass, but an exuberant enveloping arm thrown around our shoulders, the sight of a body rocking back and forth with grief, the sudden eruption of a stamped foot or a book slammed violently down on a table, all upset us. Could it be that the body *is* the unconscious and that in repressing and, more important,

---

[14]Linda Fierz-David, unpublished notes.

disregarding the spontaneous life of the sympathetic nervous system, we are enthroning the rational, the orderly, the manageable, and cutting ourselves off from all experience of the unconscious, and therefore of the instincts? . . . The less the body is experienced, the more it becomes an appearance; the less reality it has the more it must be undressed or dressed up; the less it is one's own known body, the further away it moves from anything to do with one's *self.*

The kinesthetic sense can be awakened and developed in using any and all kinds of movement, but I believe it becomes *conscious* only when the inner, that is, the subjective connection is found, the sensation of what it feels like to the individual, whether it is swinging, stretching, bending, turning, twisting, or whatever. People can learn movement in a variety of ways; they are not necessarily enabled to feel it when they do so—it is the concrete, specific awareness of one's own act of moving which is so satisfying. The usual physical culture courses work with the body as object, not as subject; and while a general release takes place, there is no corresponding experience of the personal identity, its quality and its movement. This seems to mean that something more is needed than simply body mechanics, that the feelings hidden in the body, the source of all its movement, must be involved.

Working from this standpoint[15] movement becomes an initiation into the world of the body as it actually is, what it

[15]We suggest in addition that a number of fine teachers use the unusually effective gindler method for an inner and individual approach to Movement, Dance, and Body Awareness. Far from being a "fad," such work is coming to be recognized more and more as a helpful and needed counterbalance to the mechanized and split-off quality of modern life. It can be especially valuable for the overly practical person, as well as for the intuitively oriented one who tends to live in the realm of ideas ("head in the sky"). It can be advantageous in establishing a firmer sense of individual identity (ego structure) and often contributes to a deeper "coming to oneself." See *Sensory Awareness and Total Functioning* by Charlotte Selver, Gen. Semantics Bulletin, 1957. This article has been reprinted in *Catalogue of the Ways People Grow* by Severin Petersen (paperback, Ballantine Books, 1971).—Ed.

can do easily, with difficulty, or not at all. And it also can be a serious discovery of what we are like—for we are like our movement.*–**

Mary Whitehouse,
contemporary American writer, movement-therapist.
From a lecture, "The Tao of the Body."

In work both with individuals and with groups one of the most easily usable [and safe][16] methods of relating to the body is *moving to music*. *Not* dancing, *not* gymnastics, but moving to music. The music chosen can be of an infinite variety, but it is well to choose the kind that will best cut through whatever the day has held of tension, or depression, or hurry, or dullness. Primitive drums or other music having a definite and full beat often can set the body free from its mechanical tightness. Joyful music can cut through physical lethargy. Romantic composers can lead away from the sterile intellect, whereas classical composers can often help still the ravages of negative emotions. This is an area where each person must experiment freely with all kinds of music and all kinds of body movements until he learns what will most help in bringing his psyche and his body into friendly relationship. Moving to music is a method that can be used alone or in the company of others. When with others—whether with members of the family or with friends—it is important that there be no watchers . . . for inhibitions about bodily movements are so great that one inevitably either tightens up or begins to "perform." When the method is used by an individual, there are no ground rules. Pick your music. Move. In a dark room by candlelight. In sunlight. And in whatever way your own body and psyche tell you.

Elizabeth B. Howes and Sheila Moon.
Man the Choicemaker.

A dancer is a dealer in symbols. His responsibility is to objectify and make meaningful the fruits of his experience, poetically and symbolically. . . . The dance derives from feeling, intuition, the irrational; and as the instrument in the dance is the human personality, there is, perhaps, an

[16]"Safe" i.e., without a qualified teacher of body movement at hand.

unusually close access to the unconscious. But the artist, far from knowing the whole of what he has wrought, will constantly discover new meaning in every work evolved through the opening doors of self-perception.*

Tao Strong, contemporary American dancer, choreographer.

Music and rhythm find their way into the secret places of the soul.

Plato, 427?–347 B.C. Greek philosopher.

Dance as a Primary Expression of Man

The dance was, in the beginning, the expression of the whole man, for the whole man was religious. Just as in our prayer books there are divine services for all the great fundamental acts of life—for birth, for marriage, for death—as well as for the cosmic procession of the world as marked by ecclesiastical festivals, so also it has ever been among primitive peoples. But, instead of praying for them, they danced for them the fitting dance which tradition had handed down. . . . The gods themselves danced—so many people held; and to dance is therefore to imitate the gods, to work with them, perhaps to persuade them to work for us. . . .

You cannot find a single ancient mystery in which there is no dancing; in fact most people say of the devotees of the Mysteries that "they dance them out." This is not more pronounced in early Christianity, and among the ancient Hebrews who dance before the ark, than among . . . the Shamans in the remote steppes of Siberia who still have their ecstatic religious dances; and the Turkish dervishes, who still combine dance with song and prayer, as a regular part of devotional service. . . . Even in more modern times an ancient Cornish carol sang of the life of Jesus as a dance, and represented him as declaring that he died in order that man "may come unto the general dance." . . . The very idea of dancing had a sacred and mystic meaning to the early Christians.

But it is in the sphere of pantomimic dancing crystallised into ritual, rather than in the sphere of ecstatic dancing, that we may to-day in civilization mainly witness the survivals of the dance in religion. . . . Yet genuine dancing seems also to have been frequently introduced into Christian worship. In English cathedrals dancing went on until the fourteenth century. At Paris, in France, the priests danced in the choir at Easter up to the seventeenth century. In Spain religious dancing took the firmest root and flourished the longest, and at the present day, a dancing company on the festival of St. Roch dance into the church in fanciful costumes with tambourines, up to the steps of the high altar, immediately after Mass.[17]

Dancing has been so essential, so fundamental, a part of all vital and undegenerate religion, that, whenever a new religion appears, a religion of the spirit and not merely an anaemic religion of the intellect, we should ask of it the question of the ancient Bantu: "What do you dance?"—**

Havelock Ellis, 1859–1939. English social scientist and writer.
The Dance of Life.

Praise the Lord! . . .
Praise him with the trumpet sound;
praise him with lute and harp!
Praise him with timbrel and dance;
praise him with strings and pipe!
Praise him with sounding cymbals;
praise him with loud clashing cymbals!
Let everything that breathes praise the Lord!
Praise the Lord!*

Psalm 150:1–6.
Old Testament. Revised Standard Version.

Through Art

The soul is asking for a home again. The mind rebels against its own emptiness. The hands, those precious wonderful instruments, ask for some creative occupation.

Fritz Eichenberg, 1901–. American artist.
Art and Faith.

---

[17]There is evidence of a revival in Protestant worship of "pantomimic dancing" (ritual) and also of more interest in interpretative dance expression as an integral part of worship. See *The Art of the Rhythmic Choir* by Margaret Palmer Fisk (Harper 1950).—Ed.

Part of our business as adults is to learn to see as the artist-self within us sees. Each of us must find this lost side of ourselves, then feed it and encourage it as if it were an actual child that we love.*–**

Mildred Tonge, contemporary American artist and teacher.
A Sense of Living.

The full realization and active expression of the potentialities peculiar to each one of us as individuals, is, I believe, the greatest contribution to public welfare any one can make. It is a question whether we contribute anything to the benefit of humanity that is not, to some extent, invalidated by unconscious and unrealized trends within our own nature, unless some degree of self-realization has been achieved, unless we have begun to discover that the "factors" affecting human life and society are active elements in our selves. . . .

The problem of our day is, not so much to establish peace in the world, or to achieve peace as individuals, as it is the problem of making the conflict which breaks forth everywhere about us, creative and productive. One way is to experience the conflict within one's self. Individual man in himself then becomes the battlefield, instead of the outside world. The end of fighting on the battlefield is often, for the individual, the beginning of the conflict within. On this inner, individual basis, experiencing the conflict can be creative. Art is a more productive form of expression than war.

In clay modelling for instance, we can have the experience of allowing something within the self to do the work, to determine the nature and meaning of the forms, instead of trying to do it by means of conscious thought and conscious effort. One can then become the instrument of that which rises within and requires expression. Probably there is in every one this constant stream of inner dynamic, rising toward consciousness. Things begin to happen in our outward lives and in our expression in clay or paint when we manage to make contact with that stream and learn to let ourselves be activated by it; when we learn, so to speak, to dip into this stream to refresh and revitalize our ideas, to renew our primeval images. That stream is a tributary of the great Collective Unconscious. By following it back or inward, we are led to the original storehouse of human culture, to that ancient, mystical garden from which the symbols arise.*

Sherry Peticolas, 1904–1956. American sculptor.
From a lecture, "Art for Non-professionals."

Experimental Modeling and Painting

There are important differences between the results of art activity for non-professionals and what we usually call art. It is not intended for exhibition, to demonstrate talent, to earn a living or to establish a career. The results often have value and meaning similar to the work of professional artists but they differ in the purpose for which they were done. . . .

Work produced is intended primarily for the benefit of its creator and its value is considered in relationship to the individual. Each person is encouraged to find the pattern or image for what he does from within himself. . . . Often a newcomer to a group of this kind is quite disconcerted to discover that there is nothing to copy, no model to follow. . . . Yet we notice in work done from the inner image a validity that is self-sustaining, a difference in vitality, in contrast to things done from more conscious or external patterns. . . .

Experimental modeling is not for everyone. Some find painting more responsive and expressive for them. . . . Clay, unlike painting and drawing, requires some realization of form-in-the-round. These limitations impose a kind of discipline of the material upon the work, which some people find more stimulating than the relatively unlimited and more quickly achieved effects of painting and drawing. . . . But there are times when even those who have the most ready access to their inner images find the clay unwilling and unresponsive. . . . It often seems as if it were possessed by a will of its own and refuses to cooperate with the modeler, unless he is willing to go with it. . . . Surprising things can happen as a result of this following where the clay leads. . . . Sometimes the unsuspected resource through such experimentation that is discovered is so rich, so active and rewarding that it may lead to definite changes in the individual's way of life. . . .

It isn't a question of how much talent[18] a person has. . . . A meaningful work of art is not something we make. It is something that happens. Great things can happen to the average person as well as to the talented. We have to provide the time and place for it to happen and the human effort that gives it expression.*–**

Sherry Peticolas, 1904–1956. American sculptor.
From a lecture, "Art for Non-professionals."

Keeping a Journal

There are ways a person can work alone. One method is to keep a notebook in which he writes down, during times he has kept for himself, answers to (or at least struggles with) such questions as:

What are the excuses I give myself, or hear from others, for not working at this journey? ("I can't do it well enough." "There isn't time." "I keep having headaches.") Each has his own sort of excuse. For every excuse, try to see what would happen if it were faced and worked through.

What kinds of people bother me the most—keep me from concentrating? (Whining people, argumentative people, noisy people, strong people, weak people, and so on and on.) Try to discover whether the negative qualities they have may also be in yourself. If so, they must be acknowledged before they can be harnessed creatively. They may have come from childhood experiences with parents and siblings, experiences never resolved.

When I am thrown into a depressed mood because of the shattering of an [egocentric] image,[19] what is my first response? ("I never have any luck!" "Why don't people leave me alone?" "I'll show them next time!") But is life merely a series of events, lucky and unlucky, meaningful and meaningless, strung together from birth to death? Perhaps my life is something different, something in which I have in fact participated as I move in the direction of a goal not always known, but there. What would I learn if I would stop

[18]See *The New Art Education* by Ralph Pearson (Harper, 1953).—Ed.

[19]See pp. 183–184 of this anthology for discussion of egocentric images.

and ask myself the question that the Lord God asked Adam—"Where are you?" To write the answers to this question, from time to time, as a kind of personal history, can bring unexpected healing.

Another way of working at resistances and regressions is to write as graphic a description as possible of (1) what kind of a person my parents wanted me to be, (2) what kind of a person I believe I am, and (3) what kind of a person would be the opposite of (1) or (2). Comparisons of (2) with (3) can give further clues about self-images and other-images, with (3) very often holding the key to patterns of resistance and regression because it describes what threatens. For example, a man who had always been in full and rational control of himself thoroughly disliked people who cried. His parents had always rewarded unemotional objectivity. At the time of the funeral of the assassinated President John F. Kennedy, he wept uncontrollably. Persons (1) and (2) in him were engulfed by person (3)—with the result that eventually the man began to honor and to utilize his buried feelings.

Try to list which of the following you use to "escape from freedom": altruism; pseudo generosity; doing good for others, but with, hidden behind it, hostility and self-pity; busy-ness; pressures from outside and clamor from inside; sense of worthlessness, "little-old-me-ness"; independence that is arrogance; attachment to physical symptoms. If you are willing to look at some of these escape devices and acknowledge them, you have taken one more step toward essential reality.

When we come to the matter of distractions, we need to recognize that they are basically expressions of regression and/or resistance—that is to say, we use distracting things unconsciously to justify regressive and resistant responses. We say: "Well, I couldn't collect myself today. People kept telephoning and asking me to do things." Or we say, "If it weren't for those noisy neighbors, I might be able to write in my journal." In both cases we want to be distracted. At the same time, there are distractions that contain in themselves potentials for healing. For example, a man who has been working intensely to master a certain technique of meditation was continually being distracted by the image of a clown dancing. As soon as he followed the distraction rather than the meditation, he was led toward a long-buried and much-needed sense of humor. So there is a critical problem of discrimination involved. When should a distraction be pushed away as a negative and regressive pull, and when should it have its way so it can lead into a new place? The question can always be asked as to whether the distraction seems to be serving egocentric patterns or whether it seems to be speaking for a "dark brother," some unknown and/or lost part such as the clown image was for the man described above.

Only slowly do we learn to communicate with the inner parts of ourselves, only slowly do we learn to listen. Resistances raised because of shadow[20] figures can be almost as unconquerable as the shadow itself, and often only the most patient, perseverant, and creative use of meditative techniques and/or analysis can deal with them.*–**

Elizabeth Boyden Howes, contemporary Jungian analyst.
Sheila Moon, contemporary Jungian analyst and writer.
Man the Choicemaker.

"Reflections on Writing"

Writing, like life itself, is a voyage of discovery. The adventure is a metaphysical one: it is a way of approaching life indirectly, of acquiring a total rather than a partial view of the universe. The writer lives between the upper and lower worlds: he takes the path in order eventually to become that path himself.

I began in absolute chaos and darkness, in a bog or swamp of ideas and emotions and experiences. Even now I do not consider myself a writer, in the ordinary sense of the word. I am a man telling the story of his life, a process which appears more and more inexhaustible as I go on. Like the world-evolution, it is endless. It is a turning inside out, a voyaging through X dimensions, with the result that somewhere along the way one discovers that what one has to tell is not nearly so important as the telling itself. It is this quality about all art which gives it a metaphysical hue, which lifts it out of time and space and centers or integrates it to the whole cosmic process. It is this about art which is "therapeutic": significance, purposelessness, infinitude.

---

[20]For definition and discussion of the "shadow" see pp. 118–119 and pp. 308–310 of this anthology.

From the very beginning almost I was deeply aware that there is no goal. I never hope to embrace the whole, but merely to give in each separate fragment, each work, the feeling of the whole as I go on, because I am digging deeper and deeper into life, digging deeper and deeper into past and future. With the endless burrowing a certitude develops which is greater than faith or belief. I become more and more indifferent to my fate, as writer, and more and more certain of my destiny as man.

Henry Miller, 1891–. American writer.
The Wisdom of the Heart.

Odd how the creative power at once brings the whole universe to order.

Virginia Woolf, 1882–1941. English novelist.
A Writer's Diary.

THROUGH NATURE

To see a World in a Grain of Sand,
And a Heaven in a Wild Flower,
Hold Infinity in the palm of your hand,
And Eternity in an hour.

William Blake, 1757–1827. English poet, artist, mystic.
Auguries of Innocence.

"The men where you live," said the little prince, "raise five thousand roses in the same garden—and they do not find in it what they are looking for."

"They do not find it," I replied.

"And yet what they are looking for could be found in a single rose, or in a little water."

"Yes, that is true," I said.

And the little prince added:

"But the eyes are blind. One must look with the heart."**

Antoine de Saint-Exupéry, 1900–1945.
French airman and writer.
The Little Prince. Trans. Katherine Woods.

Once, exploring the night beach, I surprised a small ghost crab in the searching beam of my torch. He was lying in a pit he had dug just above the surf, as though watching the sea and waiting. The blackness of the night possessed water, air, and beach. It was the darkness of an older world, before Man. There was no sound but the all-enveloping, primeval sounds of wind blowing over water and sand, and of waves crashing on the beach. There was no other visible life—just one small crab near the sea. I have seen hundreds of ghost crabs in other settings, but suddenly I was filled with the odd sensation that for the first time I knew the creature in its own world—that I understood, as never before, the essence of its being. In that moment time was suspended: the world to which I belonged did not exist and I might have been an onlooker from outer space. The little crab alone with the sea became a symbol that stood for life itself—for the delicate, destructible, yet incredibly vital force that somehow holds its place amid the harsh realities of the inorganic world. . . .

Looking out over the cove I felt a strong sense of the interchangeability of land and sea in this marginal world of the shore, and of the links between the life of the two. There was also an awareness of the past and of the continuing flow of time, obliterating much that had gone before, as the sea had that morning washed away the tracks of the bird. . . .

There is a common thread that links these scenes and memories—the spectacle of life in all its varied manifestations as it has appeared, evolved, and sometimes died out. Underlying the beauty of the spectacle there is meaning and significance. It is the elusiveness of that meaning that haunts us, that sends us again and again into the natural world where the key to the riddle is hidden. It sends us back to the edge of the sea, where the drama of life played its first scene on earth and perhaps even its prelude; where the forces of evolution are at work to-day, as they have been since the appearance of what we know as life; and where the spectacle of living creatures faced by the cosmic realities of their world is crystal clear.*

Contemplating the teeming life of the shore, we have an uneasy sense of the communication of some universal truth that lies just beyond our grasp. What is the message signaled by the hordes of diatoms, flashing their microscopic lights in the night sea? What truth is expressed by the legions of the barnacles, whitening the rocks with their habitations, each small creature within finding the necessities of its existence in the sweep of the surf? And what is the meaning of so tiny a being as the transparent wisp of protoplasm that is a sea lace, existing for some reason inscrutable to us—a reason that demands its presence by the trillion amid the rocks and weeds of the shore? The meaning haunts and ever eludes us, and in its very pursuit we approach the ultimate mystery of Life itself.

Rachel Carson, 1907–1964. American author.
The Edge of the Sea.

All that summer, I had worked in a sort of animal content. Autumn had now come, late autumn, with coolness in the evening air. I was plowing in my upper field . . . and it was a soft afternoon with the earth turning up moist and fragrant. I had been walking the furrows all day long. I had taken note, as though my life depended upon it, of the occasional stones or roots in my field; I made sure of the adjustment of the harness; I drove with peculiar care to save the horses. With such simple details of the work in hand I had found it my joy to occupy my mind. Up to that moment the most important things in the world had seemed a straight furrow and well-turned corners—to me, then, a profound accomplishment.

I cannot well describe it, save by the analogy of an opening door somewhere within the house of my consciousness. I had been in the dark; I seemed to emerge. I had been bound down; I seemed to leap up—and with a marvellous sudden sense of freedom and joy.

I stopped there in my field and looked up. And it was as if I had never looked up before. I discovered another world. It had been there before, for long and long, but I had never seen nor felt it. All discoveries are made in that way; a man finds the new thing, not in nature but in himself.

It was as though, concerned with plan and harness and furrow, I had never known that the world had height or color or sweet sounds, or that there was *feeling* in a hillside. I forgot myself, or where I was. I stood a long time motionless. My dominant feeling, if I can express it, was of a strange new friendliness, a warmth, as though these hills, this field about me, the woods, had suddenly spoken to me and caressed me. It was as though I had been accepted in membership, as though I was now recognized, after long trial, as belonging here.*

David Grayson. 1870–1940. United States commissioner.
Adventures of David Grayson.

Live in simple faith . . .
Just as this
Trusting cherry
Flowers, fades, and falls.

Issa, 1763–1827. Japanese poet.
Japanese Haiku.

Solstice

"Starlight, star bright"
in sky of blackenameled bone,
ice-sharp,
carving the earth in tense annunciation,
and dissolving time
into snowflakes multiple and breathless,
come straightway
over reluctant thresholds of hearts
into the weary window of the world.

"First star. . . ."
first as each mystery is always a beginning
eternally for the first time,
sing your white song to all beasts,
including man,
who are lost in leafless places, and sorrowing;
sing from the feathered cedar
a lullaby to foundling peace.

"I wish I may. . . ."
How do I wish? How do I wish?
With love, with love,
turning the dark corner of the year
to walk into quivering flocks of sheep,
to look into the soft eyes of a lonely mouse,
to touch the downy-breasted owl,
and to see, nimbused in small starlight,
naked hope as a child come home.

"Haye the wish I wish tonight."
What do I wish?
That the dark sky shall comprehend
and wrap itself in silence,
that all aching mortality
fall to its knees
before such minor miracles as stars,
a handful of fire to warm a room,
the inexpressible alleluia of birth,
and the frail, imperishable body of love.

Sheila Moon,
Contemporary American analytical psychologist, poet.

THROUGH RELATIONSHIP

Without the conscious acknowledgment and acceptance of our kinship[21] with those around us there can be no synthesis of personality.

Carl G. Jung, M.D., 1875–1961. Swiss psychiatrist.
The Practice of Psychotherapy. Trans. R. F. C. Hull.

Psychological development for Western people, whether men or women, cannot progress very far apart from relationship. We have not the ability to go deeply into self-knowledge through introversion uncontrolled by close contact with another human being. In the Orient many well-elaborated systems of self-culture as, for instance, the various yoga systems have been developed, which are based on solitary introversion, though even there the disciple is usually in close relation to a teacher who guides and controls the work. But for us in the Occident, something beyond analysis of the psyche through introversion is needed for real inner development. Introversion is, of course, enormously valuable, especially when it is guided and checked by one experienced in these things—here we call such a one an analyst. But the resulting development must be tested against a reality of its own kind—in other words,

[21]Dr. Jung places "kinship libido" in the category of an instinct—an irreplaceable need, such as the early Christian communities satisfied.—Ed.

a psychological relationship is absolutely necessary for psychological development.

M. Esther Harding, M.D., 1888–1971. American psychiatrist.
The Way of All Women.

Relationship reflects the stage of development of the participants. But just as an improved capacity to relate is one outcome of a greater development, so also development itself may be accelerated by sincere work on relationships and the unconscious factors which influence them.

Individuation[22] cannot take place in a vacuum. As Dr. Jung once said, "The hermit either will be flooded by the unconscious or he will become a very dull fellow." Life must be lived to the full if it is to change anyone for the better. It is possible to develop a certain amount of consciousness in relation to things and inanimate nature, and even more in relation to animals, where feeling may be strongly touched. But only another human being can constellate so many sides of ourselves, can react so pointedly, and can bring to consciousness so much of which we had been unaware. And because of the real values involved, and the consequently deep desires, the heat of emotion is raised high enough to produce the transformation more readily and more often in relationship than in almost any other experience of life.

Eleanor Bertine, M.D., 1888–1968. American psychiatrist.
Human Relationships.

Because of its unconsciousness, the beginning of a relationship may be as naïve as kittens at play, but if it is to become a real relatedness, it will require some serious effort. And this effort must not be the attempt only to be nice and kind to the other person, but to understand both him and oneself, and especially the unconscious images that each brings to life in the other. The objective is to clear a bridge, freed from both egocentric distortion and compulsive overadaptation, across which free communication may pass and so permit two simple human beings to experience themselves, each other and the maximum current of life that belongs in the situation between them. In this way love

[22] See pp. 61–65 of this anthology.—Ed.

and meaning unite in a life experience which is not only personal, but also, in a deeper sense, truly religious.

From all of this it may be realized how immensely important, even how essential, a part human relationships play in the development, not only of a satisfactory outer experience or the reverse, but quite as much of an inner life of vitality and significance. Knowledge of the Self[23] consists not at all of the conclusions formed in an autoerotic introspection, but of coming to terms with inner forces which we do not invent but discover in a moving experience. So it is through conscious relatedness with a fellow man that we may realize the Self. And with a reciprocal action the Self alone makes real relatedness possible. Or as Jung has said, "redeemed love is the extraverted aspect of individuation."

Eleanor Bertine, M.D., 1888–1968. American psychiatrist.
Human Relationships.

The Love Relationship as Challenge to the Whole Man

It is no more possible to make life easy than it is to grow a herb of immortality. The force of gravity can be overcome only by the requisite application of energy. Similarly, the solution of the love problem challenges all our resources. Anything else would be useless patchwork. Free love would be conceivable only if everyone were capable of the highest moral achievement. The idea of free love was not invented with this aim in view, but merely to make something difficult appear easy. Love requires depth and loyalty of feeling; without them it is not love but mere caprice. True love will always commit itself and engage in lasting ties; it needs freedom only to effect its choice, not for its accomplishment. Every true and deep love is a sacrifice. The lover sacrifices all other possibilities, or rather, the illusion that such possibilities exist. If this sacrifice is not made, his illusions prevent the growth of any deep and re-

[23]"Self" as "the focal point of the psyche in which God's image shows itself most plainly and the experience of which gives us the knowledge, as nothing else does, of the significance and nature of our likeness to God."—Jolande Jacobi.

sponsible feeling, so that the very possibility of experiencing real love is denied him.

Carl G. Jung, M.D., 1875–1961. Swiss psychiatrist.
Civilization in Transition. Trans. R. F. C. Hull.

In the recognition that man does not live to himself alone even in his most individual and personal acts—not even in his relation to the one person in all the world whom he loves—in this recognition the truly religious spirit is born. The most precious things of life do not belong to us personally. In our most intimate acts, our most secret moments we are *lived* by Life. Again and again we are reminded that in the daily contact with one we love our little personal egos must be surpassed, only so can we take our place in the stream of life and submit ourselves to that supra-personal value which alone can give significance and dignity to the individual.

M. Esther Harding, M.D., 1888–1971. American psychiatrist.
The Way of All Women.

Every particular thou is a glimpse through to the eternal Thou.

Martin Buber, 1878–1965. Israeli theologian and mystic.

THROUGH PRIVATE AND COMMUNAL[24] RITES

. . . in the (Indian) sand painting, the spirit of reverence can endow ritualistic imitation with a subtle creative meaning. Not a grain of sand can be allowed to follow the individual creative impulse of the sand painter, but a subjective creation takes place. The ancient rituals, dances, chants, the temple ceremonies may re-incarnate the holy spirit within man, or may be only a formal non-creative obedience to the letter of the law.

These rites, both private and communal, which establish communion between man and the Great Spirit above, or the earth forces below, are directed toward the winning and controlling of power and toward bringing man into contact with that stream of creative energy which can make him more vitally alive. So, devotional rites prepare a pathway

[24]See pp. 362–365.—Ed.

through the jungle of unconsciousness for the god of creativity to enter.

Frances G. Wickes, 1875–1970. American psychotherapist.
"The Creative Process."

Ceremonies are the outward expression of inward feeling.

Laotzu, sixth century B.C. Chinese philosopher.

All our external religious activities—services, communions, formal devotions, good works—these are either the expressions or the support of the inward life of loving adherence. We must have such outward expression and supports, because we are not pure spirits but human beings, receiving through our senses the messages of Reality. But all their beauty is from within: and the degree in which we can either exhibit or apprehend that beauty depends on our own inward state.

Evelyn Underhill, 1875–1941. English writer, mystic.
Concerning the Inner Life.

Particular sacraments are meant to teach us that all life is sacramental, every deliberate act should be, in a sense, the outward sign of inward grace. A sacrament is more than a symbol. A symbol leads us from the lower to the higher; a sacrament brings us back again to earth, but infuses a heavenly meaning and divine potency into common things and actions.*

W. R. Inge, 1860–1954. English philosopher and divine.
Personal Religion and the Life of Devotion.

If the Church has emphasized the function of art in her public prayer, it has been because she knew that a true and valid aesthetic formation was necessary for the wholeness of Christian living and worship.[25] The liturgy and the chant and Church art are all supposed to form and spiritualize man's consciousness, to give him a tone and a maturity without which his prayer cannot normally be either very deep or very wide or very pure.

There is only one reason why this is completely true; art is not an end in itself. It introduces the soul into a higher spiritual order, which it expresses and in some sense explains. Music and art and poetry attune the soul to God

[25]See pp. 326–362.—Ed.

because they induce a kind of contact with the Creator and Ruler of the Universe. The genius of the artist finds its way by the affinity of creative sympathy, or co-naturality, into the living law that rules the universe. This law is nothing but the secret gravitation that draws all things to God as to their center. Since all true art lays bare the action of this same law in the depths of your own nature, it makes us alive to the tremendous mystery of being, in which we ourselves, together with all other living and existing things, come forth from the depths of God and return again to Him.

Thomas Merton, 1915–1968. American Trappist monk.
No Man Is an Island.

Holding to the Deep Centre

A man may have the most marvellous dreams and visions, but get nowhere with them. Conversely, a man who has never looked at a dream, never had a vision, never heard a voice, may nevertheless have a firm hold upon the deep centre: and it is the hold upon the deep centre that matters, not the methods. But put to their right use, the dreams, visions, voices of the constructive technique,[26] and the transforming symbols so channelled into consciousness, constitute the surest means of access to the "germinal higher part" for the man or woman who persists.

It is the great strength of the Society of Friends that their Meeting for Worship to some extent brings together all four of these approaches. In form, the Meeting consists of a handful of men and women, often less than a score, rarely exceeding fifty or a hundred, who sit together for about an hour, for the most part in silence, in an ordinary room or hall. The silence is broken only if someone in the Meeting feels "called to the ministry." When this happens, the one so stirred normally speaks, for some few minutes perhaps, often less, of something that has come to him out of

[26]Techniques supplementary to the reductive technique (used in psychoanalysis) developed by C. G. Jung to foster conscious co-operation with the unconscious—especially appropriate for the normal person who, under skilled guidance of an analyst, is making the "experiment in depth" as a part of the religious Way. See the author's text. Also see Chapter VI, "Psychotherapy," in this anthology.—Ed.

the silence. He may be followed by one or two others, equally brief, typically taking up the same thread and continuing it.

When it is successful (which, needless to say, is not always) the Quaker Meeting for Worship is indubitably a method by which the deep centre is experienced and the experience transmitted. How this comes about is at present a matter of surmise rather than knowledge. Partly, no doubt, it is due to the concerted seeking in silence. Since there is little to distract attention, the libido is free for inward exploration, for the discovery of the Kingdom. Partly it is attributable to the fact that in such Meetings there may be at least one or two present—possibly a number—who in their lives have gone over to the deep centre. These, as it were, can help to "take the meeting down." It is not only in speech, but also in the silence, that Plato's "light from a leaping flame" can pass. Partly it may derive from the fellowship-in-depth of a "gathered" Meeting. This sense of togetherness is a characteristic feature. In a Meeting that has "centred down" there is simultaneously the feeling of the most complete unity and the most complete individuality. Equally characteristic is the ministry itself. The call that comes to speak in the Meeting for Worship is experienced (at least by some) as wholly different in kind from ordinary speaking, being marked by a trepidation, a pounding of the heart, a feeling akin to dread, even to people thoroughly habituated to public address. At its best, as in George Fox's day, the ministry has the character of the transforming symbol, bringing to the common fund words and images which make possible a new direction of energy. The fact that, whether or not he speaks, everyone in a Quaker Meeting has responsibility for the ministry, is perhaps the most potent factor of all. In a Meeting where no word is said there is still this silent concentration of responsibilities, which in the end may be more effective than any speech.

By whatever means the deep centre is discovered, the great and abiding problem is to hold to it. Repeatedly there is a regression to the ego-centred condition. Repeatedly some earlier attitude comes up and for a while we are that attitude. It needs only a word or a thought or a situation to arise, and we are caught again in some entrenched habit of the past. By tracking down the wrong attitude something can be done towards correcting it. But in the end, the only means by which consciousness can hold to the deep centre is by the continuous discovery and re-discovery that any other way of life has become impossible. The man who passes beyond the ego-centred, archetypally-impelled[27] life to the life lived in depth, is committed.

P. W. Martin, 1893–. English social scientist.
Experiment in Depth.

Reciting scriptures . . .
Strange the
Wondrous blue I find
In morning glories.

Kyoroku, 1656–1715. Japanese Poet.
Japanese Haiku.

---

[27]The word "archetypal" refers to those patterns of psychological functioning latent in the collective unconscious (see pp. 156; 306). They are universal in content and meaning; and are as powerful in the psychological realm as are instincts in the physiological realm.—Ed.

CHAPTER VII

Fellowship

The first, easiest and most obvious assistance toward an individual's private efforts is the simple association with others making the same attempt.

ANONYMOUS

Intimate Fellowship

Fellowship too [as well as prayer] is a lesson in receptivity. Its discipline of silence is not less rigorous because it is incidental to the business and enjoyments of daily living. Without such silence it would relapse into mere noisy sociability. There is a seeking out of the best in others, of that which is most ultimate in them, and exposing oneself to it, to learn from it and be made over by it, which brings friendship very close to the mood of prayer. It runs also the same risk of romantic subjectivism. It is all too easy to use one's friends as a pleasant retreat from the facts of one's own failure or of the world's iniquity, build up with them little gardens of Epicure and wall out the dirt and distress of the real world outside.

But the distinctive thing about fellowship is its lesson of self-subordination. Confronted with the problem of self-assertiveness, prayer takes it out by the horns and simply bids the self be stilled and quiescent, while it seeks directly the great reality of God. Fellowship cannot take quite so radical a way. My self is precisely that which I must bring to my friends, with which I must approach them, and through which I must present whatever contribution I have to make. I cannot suppress it. I must find the place within the relationship which it can legitimately fit, and let it grow into it. Any friendship—between two or between a hundred—entails a new emergent unity, where each of the constituent selves is far more in its functional oneness with the rest than it ever was in its apartness.

That greater self demanded by the relation is the self which I can and must try to be; if it is a definite possibility which invites growth, demands readjustment, has power of inspiration and criticism. And I find that greater self just in so far as I am willing and able to lose myself—the isolated, unrelated self—in the organic unity of the prospective togetherness. In that process of losing, to find myself, I get the most effective working correction and expansion of the content of my idea of God.

Take the marriage bond, for instance. To enter it is to find whole new realms of understanding, of loyalty, of forgiveness, of patience, of appreciation, of trust. One's earlier notion of the good grows with the harvest of this new experience; it is corrected, enlarged, enriched. It is the same good, the same God, whom one still serves and celebrates, but it covers now a new dimension of experience and vibrates with new meanings. Every relationship[1] brings the same enrichment. If one be only sensitive to the needs of each new situation, if one be willing to cut loose from one's old moorings and meet each new association with all the eagerness and humility of faith, one will live to follow the Unknown God in an ever deepening acquaintance, a steady process of discovery and growth.

Gregory Vlastos, 1909–. Canadian professor of philosophy.
The Religious Way.

Group Fellowship

No man can live this religious life alone. He must have the fellowship of others who are trying to live in this way. This is so because the human personality above all things is a social entity. It is created by association and shaped by association. Interchange of thought and feeling with other persons is the very breath of life of personality. As the organism must breathe to live, so the human personality must communicate to live.

The most potent group in which to foster the distinctively religious way of living is small in number. It should range from two or three or four up to twelve or fifteen, although the last number is too large except in rare cases. Jesus Christ chose twelve and that seems to have been too many by one. The number must be few enough to permit

[1]See pp. 347–350 of this anthology.—Ed.

personalities to interact freely and know one another deeply, at least in respect to the nature of their ruling loyalty. One of the purposes of such a fellowship is to make inhibitions to dissolve away, the dark areas of personality to be illuminated, and the individuals to become translucent to one another.

Our civilization is one in which people, as a usual thing, do not know one another beyond superficial levels. Consequently we are constrained, concealed, unconfessed; at best suave and smooth and efficient, with an oily ease in getting about and dealing with people. But the depths of personality are never exposed. Human personality cannot grow and flower in such dark crypts of social concealment. It must have the sunshine and rain of understanding and sympathy. Psychic madness, social revolution, and international conflict rise higher and higher as long as this personal isolation continues with its competitive attitude toward all comers.

In forming a fellowship to save personality from these evils the individuals should be selected with great care. A single wrong choice will ruin it. If it is found that there is some one who cannot interact fittingly, the group should disband and another be formed at some later time. Individuals selected should be ready to practice the method we have described. This exclusiveness is not selfish, for the main purpose of such a group is to release power to transform personalities and change the social order in the interests of greater community among all.

It is important to note that such groups often arise spontaneously. Many people are already members of such a group without knowing it. Such fellowships grow up like wild native plants. All we need do is to learn the disciplines required for fostering their growth that they may be more luxuriant and productive. However, we may be reaching a stage in our civilization where they must be consciously fostered, else they will not grow.

Members of the group should strive for most complete openness toward one another in relation to what is most important in their lives and in relation to the difficulties in their respective personalities which interfere with their ruling devotions. They should work out together a body of convictions they can share concerning what is most worthful. Deep communion and most complete openness between the members will make for spontaneity and freedom in dealing with all personalities and situations and provide for richer growth of all the connections of value.

Occasionally each member of a group should seek out among the members some friend whose love and ruthless honesty and insight he can trust. He should expose himself to the criticism of that other, for only the penetrating gaze of such a friend who shares devotion in this peculiar way of life can reveal to one the defects and obstacles which interfere with growth. However, not all persons are equipped to pass judgment upon another in this way, even when they are most sincere and loving. They do not know enough about life and personality. Hence there should be some criteria by which to determine who is able to render this service and who is not. On the other hand, it should be noted that even a mistaken judgment about oneself made in all sincerity by another may be very illuminating if one can take it objectively and discover the error in it. The discovering of the error in the judgment about oneself made by another, will often reveal truth about oneself that could not otherwise be detected.

The group should worship together, although the practice may not go by that name and should assume the form best fitted to their needs. It may be Quaker silence, or singing together, or reading together great prose or poetry or biography. Such practice helps to illumine the direction and meaning of their lives, unite them in their controlling loyalty, purge them of inhibitions, fixations, conflicts, and disturbing attachments. It widens their horizons, purifies their motives, quickens their devotion.

Such a group as we have described is a source of spiritual power. It is out of such power-groups that all the great world transforming religious movements have arisen. The early Christian groups, the Franciscan and Jesuit groups, the early Quaker and Methodist groups, are examples.

In a time like ours the only way that a new and transforming religious movement can be started is through creative fellowships such as we have tried to describe. He who lives in the peculiarly religious way must have the support of such a group. The devitalizing, competitive, atomistic social order is all around him. It will suffocate or crush or desiccate the devoted life within him unless he has the support and nourishment of such a cell of spiritual renewal and power.*

Henry Nelson Wieman, 1884–1973.
American philosopher, theologian, educator.
The Growth of Religion.[2]

God can show Himself as He really is only to real men. And that means not simply to men who are individually good, but to men who are united together in a body, loving one another, helping one another, showing Him to one another. For that is what God meant humanity to be like; like players in one band, or organs in one body.

Consequently, the one really adequate instrument for learning about God is the whole Christian community, waiting for Him *together*. Christian brotherhood is, so to speak, the technical equipment for this science—the laboratory outfit.

C. S. Lewis, 1898–1963. English professor, author.
Beyond Personality.

Personal and Group Retreats

Where Goethe is said to have cried when dying, "Light, light, more light!" and Miguel Unamuno, the Spanish prophet of the last generation, has responded with his, "No —warmth, warmth, more warmth! for we die of cold and not of darkness . . ."; we today seem driven to plead for "Air, air, more breathing space, for we die by the outbreathing of our own poisons." We have more light, more knowledge and more widely disseminated knowledge than Goethe or the Encyclopedists ever dreamed of possessing. We have warmth and passion enough and to spare behind the political and social ideologies of our time. We seem almost to be broiled in a surfeit of this light and warmth as though we had been strapped under a sun lamp and could not pull away. Yet the lungs of our spirit fail us in this self-poisoned air where we breathe and rebreathe the projections of our own fear and greed and provincialism. . . .

In nearly every previous crisis of Western civilization some group of men or women, haunted by the invisible drawing power of the figure of Jesus Christ . . . have

[2]Part I by Walter Marshall Horton, Part II by Henry Nelson Wieman.

stepped back from what the world regarded as active life in order to listen to the [inner voice]. . . . Their work has later been hailed by many as having pried open a window . . . and set blowing a draught of new air that helped to shape the period that followed.

There is no single . . . reason or pattern or date for these movements of withdrawal. Some have carried them out quite alone, on their own responsibility, and as a subjective necessity. They [may] have simply shut up their house in fourth century Alexandria or turned it over to their family or given it to the poor, and have gone out into the desert, as some fifty thousand others were to do. . . . Perhaps they have given others no better reason for what they have done than a New Jersey solitary who insisted that he had come away for no other purpose than "to balance the budget." . . .

Most of these solitary ventures turned into corporate measures before they had been in existence for many years, for the deepest search nearly always draws men together. . . . Many of these withdrawals have been for life. Others have been for shorter periods.

It does not call for an especially intensive knowledge of the Bible itself to note that the record is sprinkled through and through with identical instances of such withdrawal whether it was in the life of Jesus or Paul or in such figures of the Old Testament as Moses, Isaiah, Amos or Elijah.

Are these withdrawals for a day or a week or a month or a lifetime to be written off as loss of nerve? Are they social treasons? Are they life-flight? Or are these men and women . . . engaged in opening transoms into the world of their time? Are they encircling their world once again with breathable atmosphere, with fresh purpose, with a deeper sense of inward community, with an invisible sense of direction—and all of this quite as a by-product of their personal search for integrity?

To answer this final question affirmatively means to be concerned about encouraging such a recovery of breathing space for our time. . . .

There are signs in our own day of some reappearance of this same spontaneous, unorganized, radically experimental seeking that has characterized past crises. Many of these contemporary attempts are little more than desperate lunges away from what they know is intolerable. . . .

There are other withdrawals that follow old and tried

practice and give much ground for hope. But it is a rare situation that does not call for newly adapted instruments. . . .

The very nature of the retreats that are planned for the future must be re-cast. They must reveal a new kind of leadership, a new kind of therapy, a fresh form of ordering. They must be newly constructed experiments which do not deny what is true and what has gone before, but which reshape or rub clean old forms in order to make them usable electrodes for the conduct of power to the peculiarly anguished needs of our own time.*

Douglas V. Steere, 1901–.
American author, professor of philosophy.
Time to Spare.

The Individual in the Community

Dr. Jung is reported to have said that groups should be shunned because "consensus is unavoidable." On the other hand he has said that "individuation cannot take place in a vacuum." The problem then is how to work with people in any kind of real community and not fall either into over-uniformity or into the chaos of each person autonomously "doing his own thing." The ability to find the balanced attitude here is surely one of the fruits of the Way.

A distinction should be made between "group" and "community." The former tends in one way or another towards conformity, loss of individuality, and can fall into a "participation mystique." The "community," whether as a permanent living situation or as a temporary one working towards an objective goal, is marked by each person taking full responsibility for his own personality and yet cooperating with other members in whatever way they have to offer. Each person in such a community must avoid being "psychologically infectious," in the meaning of Eric Neumann. Each must see himself as clearly as possible and be able to "hear" what others tell him. He must also be able to speak to others with whatever truths he sees. In this sense the community is based on the deeper element of the search of every member for the real Self. This gives a common ground but allows for individual differences. It is not easy to achieve but it is possible.

Where this objective prevails the work undertaken, whatever its nature, will on the whole be done earnestly, efficiently and lovingly. Each person will make his full contribution and at the same time be willing to step aside for others who are more capable of certain tasks. He will also set aside his fear of awkwardness or inefficiency in tasks which he needs to do wherein he is not especially efficient.

The key words are: *consciousness, responsibility* and *purposiveness,* and these can only be attained within a community that shares the conviction that "he who loses his life shall find it." This is possible if a person sees the commitment of his ego to self-knowledge in the most inclusive sense. It involves ruthless honesty about his own egocentricity and shadow. The real Self, or Center, when touched gives an objective perspective on the values that transcend individual selves. In fact, this very process helps the individuation of each. The rhythm between activity with others and time for work alone fits into the needed pattern of "withdrawal and return." Both are constantly necessary.

As has been said earlier, this applies to communities permanently withdrawn from the world, as well as to communities temporarily drawn together for specific aims, whether of a psychological, spiritual or practical motivation.

When any community is devoted to the vitality of the Center of and beyond each individual, there will be no danger of damaging consensus, for the particular "color" of the Center as it expresses itself through each personality will contribute richness to the whole. This will bring relatedness and cooperation, not consensus.**

Elizabeth Boyden Howes, contemporary Jungian analyst.
Written for this anthology.

Corporate Worship

Central as is the relationship between the separate individual and God, each man needs an experience of life in the great family of God if he is to grow to understand the real nature of that love and the real character of his response to that love, to say nothing of growing to understand and to live creatively with his fellows.

For the past fifteen years I have lived among students and intellectual people both in this country and abroad. And I have seen the pain and the blocking of inner growth that has come to people who have known the religious life, for the want of fellowship and of active participation in the corporate worship and family life of some religious group.

Critical as this generation is, and may be justified in being, of the existing forms of religious fellowship, it can no longer be content with the emphasis of men such as William James, who interpreted religion as an individual affair that had little to do with its group expressions, or even with Henri Bergson, for whom the corporate side of religion can never be other than a static element. This Olympian aloofness of "sitting like God, holding no form of creed but contemplating all" and feeling above active participation in corporate worship has flatly failed to help its defenders to grow in the religious life.

The role that actual participation in corporate religious worship plays in nurturing the life of us halting ones has too long been obscured.[5] Augustine's regular attendance on the church celebrations and the sermons of Bishop Ambrose in Milan played no small part in preparing him for that scene in the garden where he consciously yielded to the Christian way. Only in vital action, whether it be symbolic or direct, does thought ripen into truth, and the modern mind would do well not to confuse religion with a state of consciousness. "Thou art man," *The Imitation of Christ* gently reminds us, "and not God; Thou art flesh and no angel." And Pascal saw that this flesh must be disciplined not alone by thoughts but by acts of love and by corporate acts of worship. "For we must not misunderstand ourselves; we are as much automatic as intellectual; and hence it comes that the instrument by which conviction is attained is not [rationally] demonstrated alone." We become what we do.

It is almost impossible to avoid a self-centered religion when one has no active regular share in the corporate worship of a larger religious fellowship. This is particularly true of those who are not engaged in manual work. There is the subtle temptation to become one of those who mistake being "agin" the group, being otherwise-minded, for following the dictates of conscience. Eccentricity, the sense of martyrdom, and an almost total absence of that precious element of "creatureliness," of humility in one's religious

[5]See pp. 351–353 of this anthology. See also *Worship* by Evelyn Underhill (Harper, 1937).—Ed.

life as one of the great family of fellow creatures offering up their lives before the great Father—these frequently accompany this reluctance to share in corporate worship. Friedrich von Hügel used to tell of the sense of common need and of common love that came to him as he prayed through his rosary or listened to the mass while kneeling next to some Irish washerwoman. For this woman and millions of others, whatever their place in man's petty order of rank, would that very day perform the same act of love and devotion before a Father in whose loving regard each was of equal worth.

It is this vivid sense of creatureliness and the felt attitude of the creature towards the creator that many have declared to be the central experience of worship or devotion and the very secret source of the religious refreshment at the base of their lives. For in this sense of creatureliness, the springs of the only enduring center of equality between men are forever being renewed. Here is the heart of a social gospel that is eternal. Here each is visited with a sense that he, in his need, is one and only one among other needy ones; that he is one among the many who have come to offer up their adoration and aspiration; that he is responsible for all and can never wrench loose from that responsibility. Howard Brinton has expressed the effect of this approach to the center in the fellowship of worship by the figure of the spokes of a wheel. The nearer the spokes of the wheel are to the center, the nearer they are to each other.

Corporate worship, however, does much more than to induce creatureliness and to strengthen the bonds of the divine family. The regular participation in corporate worship nurtures the tender insight of private prayer and helps to give it a stalk, a stem, a root, and soil in which to grow. Without its strengthening power of believing in your conviction, you may be overcome by the general attitude of the world in which you live or by the same attitude that is being pressed upon you from within by the vast residue of fear-carcasses that the mind and habits are still laden with and that have not yet been cleared away. Not only in the tender beginning, but at every point in the life, we need this fellowship of corporate worship. For again and again, dry times and doubt and conflict level the fragile house of our faith and compel us to rebuild it on deeper foundations. At times the fellowship seems the only cord that holds us.

We need corporate encouragement to recall and be rededicated to that deep citizenship to which our lives stand pledged. To scorn such reminders and to claim all days as sabbaths and all places as equally holy may mean that one has reached a high sense of spiritual freedom. But it may also mean that one is approaching indifference. This corporate ceremonial communion in any Christian group that is more than occasional in its character carries a sense of historical continuity with a great spiritual tradition. You do not begin this quest nor will it end with you. It has been lived in the world of space and time by others who have gone before. Their lives have irrefutably proved and tested it and lifted it above the realm of speculative ideals and theories. In such corporate worship you become a working member of that great community and you enter the vast company of souls whose lives are opened God-ward. Your life takes on a new perspective in this great communion of the church invisible.

Douglas V. Steere, 1901–.
American author, professor of philosophy.
Prayer and Worship.

Therapeutic Value of Religious Fellowship

My experience convinces me that religious group psychotherapy in right hands and under proper conditions has a great contribution to make to neurotic healing. Worship has a double function to perform for these patients: firstly, it gives the patient some insight into his own personality faults; in this way worship is psycho-diagnostic: secondly, worship makes available the power, the ability, the means by which these faults, in measure at least, can be corrected; in this way worship is therapeutic.

The healing effect of worship is greatly assisted by the warm fellowship that invariably springs up between the members of a worshipping group. I have been interested to observe the gradual and progressive spiritual evolution and healing of some of my patients who have been persuaded to join such groups.

In many cases. however, expert psychological treatment is a necessary preliminary. Sometimes that treatment seems to fail because it is not carried on beyond the critical point at which insight is reached and true healing commences.

The analyst "dissolves" a sentiment or analyses a complex: if he does not restore the functional efficiency of the analyzed mental organisation, he may leave the patient worse than he found him, like the "house swept and garnished." In so far as the analyst proceeds to synthesis, he is a spiritual healer: if he be a spiritual healer, why does he not make use of the most powerful means of psycho-synthesis, namely, worship? Again, why do we cling to the notion that the healing relationship between doctor or psychologist and patient is essentially or solely a person-to-person relationship? How can a solitary person heal a socially-caused or a socially-conditioned illness? Nearly all neuroses and psychoses manifest themselves as faults in human relationships. Only a social, a group-to-person relationship, can heal such faults. To tell the neurotic to "go and make friends" is silly: that constitutes his problem. We must provide for him a group of friends, who will accept him with all his faults and will help him to resolve his difficulties by understanding him, by encouragement and by example. I believe that these needs can only be provided by a worshipping group and by the life of fellowship and friendship that surrounds it. It seems to me, therefore, that the Church can become, if it will, the group physician of the future.

Much has been written, especially by Freudians, about "transference" and the difficulties that occasionally arise in connection with it. The resolution of the "transference" should always be its sublimation—or so I think. Every psychotherapist should be able to point, as John the Baptist pointed to Jesus, to One who is greater than the psychologist. During worship a transference is established between the worshipper and Christ. During worship child-dependence is replaced by mature competence and by co-operation with others in the fellowship. Until this has been achieved, treatment has not been completed, even if it has been ended.*

Howard E. Collier, M.D., 1890–1953. English physician.
The Place of Worship in Modern Medicine.[6]

CHAPTER VIII

Action[1]

Enlarging insight depends on expansion due to exercise; vision on action, on acting up to the limit of what has been glimpsed.

ANONYMOUS

You must lay aside with your former habits your old self which is going to ruin. . . . You must adopt a new attitude of mind, and put on the new self which has been created in likeness to God.

SAINT PAUL[2]

We must alter our lives in order to alter our hearts, for it is impossible to live one way and pray another.

WILLIAM LAW

Worship and Work

Commitment does not stop with contemplation. It seeks issue in work. For the God discovered thus is a God at work, reconciling the world to Himself. And those who worship in spirit and truth find themselves called to a ministry of reconcilation. A world unfinished and broken is to be made whole. Worship sends us out to work. But work in turn, through frustration or consummation, may continually tend again toward worship, wherein illumination and

[1]See Chap. XI under "In Influence and Action."

[2]Trans. E. J. Goodspeed.

renewal are to be found. Such, in part, is man's way toward God.*

Robert Lowry Calhoun, 1896–.
American theologian, educator.
God and the Common Life.

Doing as the Completion of Knowing

Knowledge is the beginning of practice; doing is the completion of knowing. Men of the present, however, make knowledge and action two different things and go not forth to practice, because they hold that one must first have knowledge before one is able to practice. Each one says, "I proceed to investigate and discuss knowledge; I wait until knowledge is perfect and then go forth to practice it." Those who to the very end of life fail to practice also fail to understand. This is not a small error, nor one that came in a day. By saying that knowledge and practice are a unit, I am herewith offering a remedy for the disease.*

Wang-Yang-Ming, 1472–1529. Chinese philosopher.
Works of Wang-Yang-Ming. Trans. Henke.

The method of investigation by which we test our religious insights requires that we become clearly and deeply conscious of what we are doing and what mankind is doing for or against the process of integration which is at work in the world. It consists in bringing the whole of human life so far as possible under the searchlight of observation with a view to seeing how well adjusted it is, and how it can be better adjusted, to the value-making process of the world. In religious experience one gets a new impulse toward some new way of living; in religious method one observes the working of that impulse and of all other impulses and habits to discover whether they lead to richer integrations. Another function of religious method is to bring to practical fruition the new possibilities for good which are opened by the way of life, discovered through religious experience.

This phase might be called the practical and constructive. It is the endeavor to reconstruct customs, institutions, personal attitudes and physical conditions in such a way that they will foster the most inclusive and intimate mutual support between individuals and groups of men, and between men and the rest of the world. It is the tremendous effort to remake this world into a home for men and to remake men so that they can live in it like brothers. Great work awaits the doing; but men have not the courage for it, they have not the energy and poise and insight and passion for it, unless religion supplies them. Historically religion has provided this equipment of personality for great achievement and can do it again if the right methods of religious living are known and practiced.*

Henry Nelson Wieman, 1884–1973.
American philosopher, theologian, educator.
Methods of Private Religious Living.

Prayer is Preparation for "Action"

Prayer is not escape from reality and from action; it is the source of strength and insight for action. It is the only preparation for sound action.

Prayer is not the pleading to be saved suffering; it is the pleading that one will be spared no suffering which is necessary to achieve the end one desires: unity with God and co-consciousness with all men.

Prayer expresses itself fundamentally in the two great Christian attitudes toward life: gratitude and contrition. Gratitude springs from a sacramental view which sees the earth and the creatures of it as the whole creation of God and stands in awe and wonder before the majesty of God's handiwork. Contrition springs from man's recognition of his failure to act on that fact, recognition of his constant effort to make himself God and the center of life, instead of giving central place to God, Author of all creation.

Out of this dialectic springs a synthesis which is the unity of the self in resolution so to act that this creation of God's may be made more pleasing in the sight of God; that man may be made again in the image of God.

There is danger that prayers such as "Grant us brotherhood" may become substitutes for positive action toward creation of brotherhood in the world. It is a trick of the human spirit to turn to abstract worship of something which man will not pay the price to achieve—so vicariously he enjoys the fruits of it in an idealistic worship of something of which the realities of the world make a mockery.

Kneeling alone in a dark garden in an ultimate crisis of his life, Jesus said, "Father, may this cup pass from me." But that was not the end of his prayer. Had he—as we so often do—proceeded to rationalize the ways in which an answer might come; the course of human history might have been different. Instead, he carried that prayer—a legitimate cry of the human spirit—on to the absolutely essential conclusion, "Nevertheless not as I will but as thou wilt." And his action, following that prayer, has changed the pattern of human history.

Rose Terlin, contemporary American editor, writer.
Prayer and Christian Living.

The Relation Between Action and Insight

It is not easy for man so to change himself. As we have seen, it is one of the most tragic facts about ourselves that we have always imagined that it was easy, but of no great profit, to change one's own nature, and hard, but immensely valuable, to change outer nature. Detailed examination of the problem is now showing us the reverse to be the truth. Our construction of fact (what we call the outer universe) and ourselves we see as tied together in an intense interlock. We can change the world we see, but only in proportion as we have the self-control and courage to let go of the present current construction. For it is not possible, without mental disaster, for anyone to see with equal clearness two mutually exclusive worlds at once. There can never be for a living creature more than one full reality at one time.

We must remember how much even the best of us cling to the present picture of things. The world made by greed and fear suits most people so well that to suggest that it is brutal and in the end will prove disastrous is to awake even more fear and resentment. They will endure agonies rather than leave it. However much they complain, in all who are still ruled by fear and greed there is no real wish for any other sort of world.

The third ethic can therefore have one aim and one only: to set men free of fear and greed. And, because of the reciprocity of ethics and cosmology, vision and action, the consequence of living up to this ethic can be nothing less than the emergence into our sight of an objective world in which greed and fear are steadily diminishing elements.

This is the fundamental discovery of the third cosmology and its fundamental difference from the only other two cosmologies which have preceded it. Here is a cosmological-ethical revolution: man makes the universe; he has made its nightmare, arbitrary quality (of polytheism), its inaccessible righteousness (of monotheism), its blind, inhuman necessitarianism (of mechanism). Each of these cosmologies has been a part picture of an aspect of his nature. He has only been able to see in outer nature what confirms and answers to his inner nature. The invisible replies and materializes in the form in which it is summoned and imagined.

But man can only remake the present crumbling picture of the universe into one which will not be a pure chaos but an answer to his higher emergent, super-individual nature, if he will behave continually in such a super-individual way. The growth of the cosmology waits on the growth in the ethic; enlarging insight depends on the expansion due to exercise; vision on action, on acting up to the limit of what has been glimpsed.

Therefore man does not and cannot wait on an external God so that that God may remake the universe in order that, when this has been safely accomplished, man may get on with his noble behavior, his idealistic activity, his saintly conduct. Man is more than God's vice-regent. He is the creative power's vice-creator, for he may make any universe up to the standard of which he is prepared to live. Absolute freedom from the individual self approaches absolute creative power. For as man dares act (this is the fact of creative faith), his apprehension-construction grows and he sees not subjectively but objectively a new reality. For he brings into being that which he has so dared to desire. His desire (equal to the creative desire of animal need which created out of energy-radiation another world of common sense and appetite) creates out of that same energy-radiation another world, a nobler world, but a world as firm as the world of common sense, because constructed and cemented by a desire as strong. The one fundamental objective fact is that the energy-radiation will sustain and substantiate any construction creative desire calls upon it to support and fulfill.

The Kingdom of God is not imminent but immanent; it is not "among you," about suddenly to break like a thunderstorm, but "within you," ready to be expressed the moment you understand your latent, common nature and how you must and can transcend your individuality, your egotism, which makes the world the obstacle it proves to-day to be to you.*

Gerald Heard, 1889–1971.
English author, religious philosopher.
The Third Morality.

The Christian life is a journey. Jesus said, "They who do the will of my Father shall know. . . ." And St. Gregory, "Whosoever would understand what he hears, must hasten to put into practice what he has heard. . . ."

Therefore do not wait for great strength before setting out, for immobility will weaken you further. Do not wait to see very clearly before starting: one has to walk toward the light. Have you strength enough to take this first step? Courage enough to accomplish this little tiny act of fidelity or of reparation, the necessity of which is apparent to you? Take this step! Perform this act! You will be astonished to feel that the effort accomplished, instead of having exhausted your strength, has doubled it, and that you already see more clearly what you have to do next.*

Philippe Vernier, 1909–. French Protestant minister.
With the Master. Trans. Edith Lovejoy Pierce.

Action of the Unskilled Person Versus the Expert

We ought to learn how to keep a free mind in all we do, but it is rare that an untrained person can do this, so that neither circumstances nor jobs bother him. It requires great diligence. Expert attention is necessary. To be aware of God at all times and to be enlightened by him equally under all circumstances, there are two special requirements. First: be spiritually quite private, guarding the mind carefully against irrelevant ideas, so as to keep them out and not deal in them, giving them no place in your life. The second has to do with the mind's own inventions, whether spontaneous in the mind or representing some object, or whatever their nature. Do not be dissipated in such ideas lest you become lost in the crowd of them. For these two requirements, for this goal, one must focus all his mental powers and train his mind, for he will need to have his wits about him.

You may say: "But when a person has a job to do, he must give attention to it and thus concentrate on external things, for it takes an idea to make a job possible." And that is quite true, but the reference of ideas to things does not belong to the objective world as far as the spiritual (subjective?) man is concerned, for all things are to him simply channels of the divine and spiritual.

And this viewpoint is possible only through discipline and the training of the intellect to the ways of God, and, doing this, a man will become, in time, divine within. The mind does not get as close to anything as God does, nor is it so germane to things, nor do they require its presence (as they require God). Thus, there is no need for the mind to turn elsewhere (than to God).

It would be fatal for an undisciplined and unskilled person to try to do what an expert may do, and, what is more, he would get nowhere by trying. Only when he has been thoroughly weaned away from things and things are alien to him—only then may a man do as he pleases with things, free to take them or leave them with impunity.*

Meister Johannes Eckhart, 1260–1327.
German scholar, mystic.
Meister Eckhart. Trans. R. Blakney.

Creative personalities when they are taking the mystic path which is their highest spiritual level, pass first out of action into ecstasy and then out of ecstasy into action on a new and higher plane. In using such language we describe the creative movement in terms of the personality's psychic experience. In terms of his external relations with the society to which he belongs we shall be describing the same duality of movement if we call it withdrawal and return. The withdrawal makes it possible for the personality to realize powers within himself which might have remained dormant if he had not been released for the time being from his social toils and trammels . . . but a transfiguration in solitude can have no purpose, and perhaps even no meaning, except as a prelude to the return of the transfigured personality into the social milieu out of which he had originally come: a native environment from which the human social animal cannot permanently estrange himself without repudiating his humanity and becoming, in Aristotle's phrase, "either a beast or a god." The return is the essence of the whole movement as well as its final cause.*–**

Arnold J. Toynbee, 1889–. English historian.
A Study of History.

Seen with the eyes of the social historian, the three years' activity as a social revolutionary is the life of Jesus in its impact upon human history. What makes it unique is the scope of the vision it embodies, and his profound insight into the conditions demanded for its accomplishment. The teaching of Jesus is not something separable from his life; it is the expression of the understanding which grew out of his life. Theory and practice are there completely unified. The one interprets and expounds the other. It is the fusion of insight and action that makes the life of Jesus the religious life *par excellence,* though it is far from being the kind of life that nowadays would be so described.

John Macmurray, 1891–.
Scottish professor of philosophy.
Creative Society.

ACTION AS A TECHNIQUE

Not *Karma,* mere action, but *Karma Yoga,* union with God through action, is the essence of the teaching of the *Gita.* . . .

Not sacrifice for humanity, but service to humanity as a sacrifice unto God, whose image we learn to see in man, is the true ideal. Not political activities undertaken with a selfish motive, but duties performed as worship of God; not merely family life and the performance of the ordinary domestic duties, but a life of non-attachment in the midst of these duties, combined with the knowledge of the nature of one's immutable, eternal Self,—this is the real message of the *Bhagavad Gita.* In short, temporal life and spiritual values stand in a relation of harmony—one divine life, as the *Gita* tells us.*

Swami Prabhavananda, 1893–.
Monk of Ramakrishna Mission.
Vedic Religion and Philosophy.

To work alone thou hast the right, but never to the fruits thereof. Be thou neither actuated by the fruits of action, nor be thou attached to inaction.

O Dhananjaya, abandoning attachment and regarding success and failure alike, be steadfast in Yoga and perform thy duties. Evenmindedness is called Yoga.

O Dhananjaya, work (with desire for results) is far inferior to work with understanding. Therefore seek refuge in the Yoga of understanding. Wretched indeed are those who work for results.

Being possessed with this understanding, one frees one's self even in this life from good and evil. Therefore engage thyself in this Yoga. Skillfulness in action is called Yoga.

The wise, possessed with knowledge, abandoning the fruits of their actions, become freed from the fetters of birth and reach that state which is beyond all evil.

The "New Testament" of Hindu Scriptures, first century B.C.
Bhagavad-Gita, Trans. Swami Paramananda.

To discover the Kingdom of God exclusively within oneself is easier than to discover it, not only there, but also in the outer world of minds and things and living creatures. It is easier because the heights within reveal themselves to those who are ready to exclude from their purview all that lies without. And though this exclusion may be a painful and mortificatory process, the fact remains that it is less arduous than the process of inclusion, by which we come to know the fulness as well as the heights of spiritual life. Where there is exclusive concentration on the heights within, temptations and distractions are avoided and there is a general denial and suppression. But when the hope is to know God inclusively—to realize the divine Ground in the world as well as in the soul, temptations and distractions must not be avoided, but submitted to and used as opportunities for advance; there must be no suppression of outward turning activities, but a transformation of them so that they become sacramental. Mortification becomes more searching and more subtle; there is need of unsleeping awareness and, on the levels of thought, feeling and conduct, the constant exercise of something like an artist's tact and taste.

Aldous Huxley, 1894–1963. English writer, literary critic.
The Perennial Philosophy.

It is well to remember that even in the holiest undertakings, what God requires of us is earnest willing labour, and the use of such means as we can command; but He does not require success of us: that depends solely upon Himself, and sometimes in very love for us He refuses to crown our best intentions with success.

Jean Nicolas Grou, 1731–1803. French Catholic priest.

Beginning Steps in We-Activity

Expose yourself to situations in which you are stirred by genuine understanding and sympathy, in which you feel a desire to cooperate with and help another regardless of material or other reward than your inner We-feeling satisfaction. Learn from first-hand observation something of the life of those less-favourably situated than you are. Seek an opportunity for some volunteer service to the sick, the needy, the oppressed. Visit some shut-in and read aloud awhile or otherwise share his load. Find a way to understand better the unhappiness of someone oppressed by racial prejudice or social injustice. Look for the shy person to whom you can be friendly. Give a lift to your tired fellow-worker. Let your imagination lead you into some We-feeling response to those far away—perhaps the starving men in Europe, in Asia or the flood victim in your own country. These are but a fraction of the possibilities which may be discovered.

In all cases focus your thinking upon the sense of We-feeling experienced in your deed. Do not be dismayed by discovering a certain amount of egocentricity in any act. Avoid that which gives you chiefly a feeling of pride, or superiority or the pleasure of talking about your generosity or so-called unselfishness. Such reactions are not We-feeling, but only egocentric, + 100 emotions. Do whatever stirs the chords of genuine We-feeling. Seek to set them vibrating more and more until they become the dominating or sole satisfactions in your experience.*–**

Fritz Kunkel, M.D., 1889–1956, American psychiatrist,
and Roy E. Dickerson, 1886–, American author.
How Character Develops.

True Work Defined

You should work like a *master* and not as a *slave;* work incessantly, but do not do slave's work. Do you not see how everybody works? Nobody can be altogether at rest; ninety-nine percent of mankind work like slaves, and the result is misery; it is all selfish work. Work through freedom! Work through love! The word "love" is very difficult to understand; love never comes until there is freedom. There is no true love possible in the slave. If you buy a slave and tie him down in chains and make him work for you, he will work like a drudge, but there will be no love in him. So when we ourselves work for the things of the world as slaves, there can be no love in us, and our work is not true work. This is true of work done for relatives and friends, and is true of work done for our own selves. Selfish work is slave's work; and here is a test. Every act of love brings happiness; there is no act of love which does not bring peace and blessedness as its reaction. Real existence, real knowledge, and real love are eternally connected with one another, the three in one: where one of them is, the others also must be; they are the three aspects of the One without a second—the Existence-Knowledge-Bliss. When that existence becomes relative, we see it as the world; that knowledge becomes in its turn modified into the knowledge of the things of the world; and that bliss forms the foundation of all true love known to the heart of man.

Swami Vivekananda, 1863–1902. Hindu mystic, seer.
Karma-Yoga.

Can we be believed?—and once more this amounts to the same—we have known workmen who really wanted to work. No one thought of anything but work. We have known workmen who in the morning thought of nothing but work. They got up in the morning (and at what an hour), and they sang at the idea that they were off to work. At eleven o'clock they sang on going off to eat their soup. Work for them was joy itself and the deep root of their being. And the reason of their being. There was an incredible honor in work, the most beautiful of all the honors, the most Christian, perhaps the only one which stands of itself. That is why I say, for example, that a freethinker of those days was more Christian than a devout person of our day. Because nowadays a devout person is perforce a bourgeois. And today, everyone is bourgeois.

We have known an honor of work exactly similar to that which in the Middle Ages ruled hand and heart. The same honor had been preserved, intact underneath. We have known this care carried to perfection, a perfect whole, perfect to the last infinitesimal detail. We have known this devotion to *l'ouvrage bien faite,* to the good job, carried and maintained to its most exacting claims. During all my childhood I saw chairs being caned exactly in the same spirit, with the same hand and heart as those with which this same people fashioned its cathedrals.

Those bygone workmen did not serve, they worked. They had an absolute honor, which is honor proper. A chair rung had to be well made. That was an understood thing. That was the first thing. It wasn't that the chair rung had to be well made for the salary or on account of the salary. It wasn't that it was well made for the boss, nor for connoisseurs, nor for the boss' clients. It had to be well made itself, in itself, for itself, in its very self. A tradition coming, springing from deep within the race; a history, an absolute, an honor, demanded that this chair rung be well made. Every part of the chair which could not be seen was just as perfectly made as the parts which could be seen. This was the self-same principle of cathedrals.

There was no question of being seen or of not being seen. It was the innate being of work which needed to be well done.

All the honors converged towards that honor. A decency and a delicacy of speech. A respect for home. A sense of respects, of all the respects, of respect itself. A constant ceremony, as it were. Besides, home was still very often identified with the work-room, and the honor of home and the honor of the work-room were the same honor. It was the honor of the same place. It was the honor of the same hearth. What has become of all this? Everything was a rhythm and a rite and a ceremony from the moment of rising in the early morning. Everything was an event; a sacred event. Everything was a tradition, a lesson; everything was bequeathed, everything was a most saintly habit. Everything was an inner elevation and a prayer. All day long, sleep and wake, work and short rest, bed and board, soup and beef, house and garden, door and street, courtyard and threshold, and the plates on the table.

Laughing, they used to say, and that to annoy the priests, that *to work is to pray* and little did they know how true that was.

So much of their work was a prayer, and the work-room an oratory.*

Charles Péguy, 1873–1913. French writer.
Charles Péguy. Trans. A. and J. Green.

"The Cause"

There are some individuals who have achieved a remarkable objectivity, whose personal influence is widely and constructively felt, but who have not been known as "religious" persons. How does one explain them?

In many cases they have achieved their freedom of spirit through devotion to a cause. One is therefore challenged to make a clear evaluation of "devotion to a cause" as it contributes to the development of the mature individual.

Within most worthy causes there are obviously elements of value. It is probably true that the degree to which a person yields himself in devotion to these elements, to that extent will his selfish motives be modified, at least temporarily. If the devotion is sustained over a long period, more permanent changes in character are likely to occur, for sustained devotion requires inner discipline. That there have been men and women who have yielded to such discipline is well evidenced by their lives, and in some cases by their own writings. Of these someone has written: "It is a strange fact that certain men, who have spent long periods of their lives in lonely prison cells, men who are not Christians,[8] nevertheless have written some of the profound truths which also are found in Christianity. I think of the letters of Rosa Luxemburg and of Eugene Debs and of the autobiography of Angelo Herndon. . . .

"When offered the opportunity to run away rather than risk return to the Georgia chain-gang and to possible death, Angelo Herndon said, 'I cannot run away. There is too much at stake. If I run away and you run away, and every one else who loves freedom and truth runs away, who will be left to fight the good battle? I am not afraid. Death itself is not the greatest tragedy that could happen to a man. Rather, the greatest tragedy is to live placidly and safely and to keep silent in the face of injustice and oppression.' Those words—amazing ones for this boy of nineteen—indicate the kind of insight which comes to people who spend long hours alone and who are committed to a high cause."

---

[8]One is immediately reminded of Jawaharlal Nehru and Mohandas K. Gandhi whose years of imprisonment turned into benefit for all of India.

However, there are grave dangers in the "Cause" as a way of growth, for the degree to which a cause is partial and limited, and therefore non-universal, and blocking to the good of the whole, to that degree will the devotee also tend to be limited and lacking in wholeness. Also should the activity in service of the cause be based on the policy that the end justifies the means, a distortion in the character of the participant, as well as in the end served, is bound to occur.

One, therefore, needs to be warned against any cause as a sufficient-in-itself method for the transformation of personality. One certainly needs to be reminded that the beginner on the religious Way has little or no insight that would contribute vitally to any major cause. He had best limit his activity to areas commensurate with his stage of progress. It is important also to be aware that most ordinary, uninspired activity may in itself become an escape device.

In spite of these warnings the role of action in bringing man to his highest fulfillment must not be underestimated. Without action up to the height of insight there can be no growth of insight. God may become very real in "action," and action and meditation have been found to be both complementary and indispensable to one another.

Anonymous.
Written for this anthology.

Discrimination in "Doing Good to Others"

One may be so preoccupied with the desire to be of use to society that one loses the opportunity to do what one was best fitted to perform. If we fail thus in effectiveness it is because we have not been free to be honest with ourselves. We have been distracted by that too urgent and insistent demand to note the social consequences, immediate or remote, of our enterprises. We have been nagged into diminishing the scope of our effort from the breadth of its original disinterestedness to suit some narrow utilitarian requirement.

The work of doing good to others over its whole range from the simplest alleviation of human misery to the missionary ambition of saving souls, is notoriously a difficult and, for the most part, a thankless task. The reasons for this are many, but some of them spring from the essential nature of the relationship involved between the doer and the recipient of good. It is with these that we are concerned.

"If I knew for a certainty," wrote Thoreau, "that a man was coming to my house with the conscious design of doing me good, I should run for my life as from that dry and parching wind of the African deserts called the simoom, which fills the mouth and nose and ears and eyes with dust till you are suffocated, for fear I should get some of his good done to me,—some of its virus mingled with my blood."

We may say that the successful reformers are those who are seeking not so much to "make people good" as to share an enthusiasm. The change they may work in others is a by-product of some disinterested devotion. I am justified in attacking my neighbour's meanness or duplicity only in so far as I am manifestly inspired by a love of generosity and integrity. My efforts can then be interpreted as an attempt to recall him to his ideal and mine. I do not plan his voyage, I merely propose to correct his compass. I am like the man in Plato's Allegory of the Cave who knew that his chief task was to turn the prisoners round so that they could face in the direction of the sun. The sun would do the rest.*

Charles A. Bennett, 1885–1930. English philosopher.
Philosophical Study of Mysticism.

Who are you who go about to save them that are lost?
Are you saved yourself?
Do you not know that who would save his own life must lose it?
Are you then one of the "lost"?
Be sure, very sure, that each one of these can teach you as much as, probably more than, you can teach them.
Have you then sat humbly at their feet, and waited on their lips that they should be the first to speak—and been reverent before these children—whom you so little understand?
Have you dropped into the bottomless pit from between yourself and them all hallucination of superiority, all flatulence of knowledge, every shred of abhorrence and loathing?
Is it equal, is it free as the wind between you?

Could you be happy receiving favors from one of the most despised of these?

Could you be yourself one of the lost?

Arise, then, and become a savior.

Edward Carpenter, 1844–1929. English author, poet.
Towards Democracy.

PART THREE

The Outcomes

God does not work in all hearts alike but according to the preparation and sensitivity he finds in each.

MEISTER ECKHART

Endowments vary, but the Spirit is the same, and forms of service vary . . . but God who produces them all in us all is the same. Each one is given his spiritual illumination for the common good.

SAINT PAUL

In the world to come I shall not be asked, "Why were you not Moses?" I shall be asked, "Why were you not Zusya?"

RABBI ZUSYA

CONTENTS
Part Three

INTRODUCTION

This section presents descriptions of some of the outcomes experienced by those who proceed along the Way. The purpose of these descriptions is to make vivid the second half of Jesus' paradoxical statement, "He who will lose his life shall perserve it." They give content to the "Life" that is to be preserved.

The reader is warned not to anticipate any particular "set" of outcomes for himself or for any other person. This is of highest importance, for any striving for particular results blocks progression and causes needless discouragement. Many factors enter into determining the particular emphasis which the transformation will take in each person. Biological endowment, temperamental equipment, and the degree of early psychic conditionings influence the rate of progress and determine the particular characteristics manifest for each person as he progresses.

The only tenable hope, therefore, that one who has started on the Way can have concerning outcomes, is faith that with an increase of devotion, a gradual release from unconscious hamperings, and perseverance, there will come a reorientation around the new Center—a reorientation that assures a gradual discovery of the new, the maturing, the "real" self and a gradual leave-taking of the old, the immature, the "false" self. Every step of the way to fulfillment offers its own highest reward—that of a deepening sense of coming ever closer to the end for which one was created. Having left behind his strangulated self, man achieves the kind of awareness wherein he finds himself at home in his inner depth, at one with all mankind, and possessed of an indwelling love which spontaneously ministers to all.

It is hoped that the words of men and women who have

in varying degrees gone this way before will serve as a compelling factor to the reader to make "the choice" that "is always ours"—if he has not already done so; and to follow through as deep and as far as endowment, effort, and "grace" will permit, so that he will eventually find the full treasure open before him.

CHAPTER IX

Inward Renewal

The living water wells up from the depths and flows gaily through the new-born man.

J. MIDDLETON MURRY

Self realization has ceased to be looked upon as self fortification.

HENRY BURTON SHARMAN

There are things—
"Which no eye ever saw and no ear ever heard,
And never occurred to the human mind,
Which God has provided for those who love Him."

I CORINTHIANS[1]

THE GOLDEN AGE IS IN MY HEART TODAY

Who are you, any one, who can remain unmoved when the Light breaks upon you?
Who can say it does not concern him?
Who can say it is just as well not to see as to see?
Who can ever be the same child or woman or man again after the Day has broken?
Who can admit there is anything else in the world, after this has come to the world?
I brushed all obstructions from my doorsill and stepped into the road;
And though so many cried to me, I did not turn back;

[1]Trans. E. J. Goodspeed.

And though I was very sorrowful having to leave so many friends behind, I did not turn back;
And though the ground was rough and I was overtaken by fierce storms, I did not turn back;
For when the soul is once started on the soul's journey, it can never turn back. . . .
Can you now go on with your old life as if nothing had happened;
The whole universe has happened;
All your forgotten kinship to the people has happened;
All the terrible thirst for justice has happened;
And all sad things have happened in gladness at last;
And all things out of place have happened in place at last;
And all old enmity has happened in friendship at last;
The golden age is in my heart today.

Author unknown.

Slowly on You, too, the meanings: the light-sparkles on water, tufts of weed in winter—the least things—dandelion and groundsel.

Have you seen the wild bees' nest in the field, the cells, the grubs, the transparent white baby-bees, turning brown, hairy, the young bees beginning to fly, raking the moss down over the disturbed cells? the parasites?

Have you seen the face of your brother or sister? have you seen the little robin hopping and peering under the bushes? have you seen the sun rise, or set? I do not know —I do not think that I have.

When your unquiet brain has ceased to spin its cobwebs over the calm and miraculous beauty of the world:

When the Air and the Sunlight shall have penetrated your body through: and the Earth and Sea have become part of it:

When at last, like a sheath long concealing the swelling green shoot, the love of learning and the regard for elaborate art, wit, manners, dress, or any thing rare or costly whatever, shall drop clean off from you;

When your Body—for to this it must inevitably return—is becoming shining and transparent before you in every part (however deformed);

Then (O Blessed One!) these things also transparent,

possibly shall surrender themselves—the least thing shall speak to you words of deliverance.

Edward Carpenter, 1844–1929. English author, poet.
Towards Democracy.

From the Wilderness

He who was a river into the wilderness
Is now come back from misery to bless
The hounding spirit.
He who was rich and now so seeming poor
Owns an inheritance which was not his before—
Even his self.

This was the gift from the dark hour which thrust
Him forth to solitude;
Which laid him in a grave while yet the dust
Was under him; while yet the blood
Water'd the withering march 'twixt sense and sand.

He knew the hour of nothingness when the hand
Is empty, and empty is the heart;
And the intelligence, with its keen dart
Of reasonable speech, slays its own pride.

'Twas thus he died;
Suffering his solitary hour beyond the world of men:
And it was thus, alone, he found the flower
Of his own self;
Which yet had been only a flower of stone
Had he not brought it back into the world again.

William Soutar, 1898–1943. Scottish poet.

I am like a child who awakes
At the light, so safe and so sure,
Free from night's fears when dawn breaks,
In Thee I am ever secure.
There are times when doubts over me steal
But I know Thou are there and awake.
Thou art—and art—and I feel
No surging of aeons can shake

Thee—Life is a ring, I have found—
I am child, boy, man, more—I learn
The circle is rich, the full round
Complete in its perfect return.

I thank Thee, Thou deep force that falls
Imperceptibly on me, to grace
My working day on the hard lands,
To smooth it—as back of dim walls
And like a far-off Holy Face
Thy radiance shines on my dark hands.

Rainer Maria Rilke, 1875–1926. German poet.
Rainer Maria Rilke Poems. Trans. Jessie Lemont.

I waited patiently for Jehovah;
And he inclined unto me, and heard my cry.
He brought me up also out of a horrible pit, out of the miry clay;
And he set my feet upon a rock, and established my goings.
And he hath put a new song in my mouth, even praise unto our God:
Many shall see it and fear,
And shall trust in Jehovah.
Blessed is the man that maketh Jehovah his trust,
And respecteth not the proud, nor such as turn aside to lies.
Many, O Jehovah my God, are the wonderful works which thou hast done,
And thy thoughts which are to us-ward:
They cannot be set in order unto thee;
If I would declare and speak of them,
They are more than can be numbered.
Sacrifice and offering thou hast no delight in;
Mine ears hast thou opened:
Burnt-offering and sin-offering has thou not required.
Then said I, Lo, I am come;
In the roll of the book it is written of me:
I delight to do thy will, O my God:
Yea, thy law is within my heart.

Psalm 40:1–8.
Old Testament.

I never lose heart. Though my outer nature is wasting away, my inner is being renewed every day.

Saint Paul, first century Christian Apostle.
New Testament. Trans. E. J. Goodspeed.

When one takes God as He is, divine, having the reality of God within him, God sheds light on everything. He will be like one athirst with a real thirst; he cannot help drinking even though he thinks of other things. Wherever he is, with whomsoever he may be, what ever his purpose or thoughts or occupation—the idea of the Drink will not depart as long as the thirst endures; and the greater the thirst the more lively, deep-seated, present, and steady the idea of the Drink will be. Or suppose one loves something with all that is in him, so that nothing else can move him or give pleasure, and he cares for that alone, looking for nothing more; then wherever he is or with whomsoever he may be, whatever he tries or does, that Something he loves will not be extinguished from his mind. He will see it everywhere, and the stronger his love grows for it the more vivid it will be. A person like this never thinks of resting because he is never tired.*

Meister Johannes Eckhart, 1260–1327.
German scholar, mystic.
Meister Eckhart. Trans. R. Blakney.

Two people who lived their lives deeply and consciously often come to my mind, and I am struck both by their dissimilarity and by their inherent likeness. One was a great physician and scientist, the other a washerwoman in a frontier town. The dissimilarity lay in circumstances and outer opportunity, in gifts and natural ability. The similarity lay in their attitude towards experience; in their ability to live deeply in whatever came to them, and to see the true drama of life as something not produced by circumstance or Fate, but by the inner relation to events. In each of them one felt as the dominant quality, a life wisdom which, while drawn from the daily experience, yet penetrated deeper to a level where the inner being of the spirit was revealed and the moment became a part of a greater reality. In each the judgment of an act was tempered by a form of charity which, always acknowledging its own limitations, was willing to give to others an understanding that helped to cast out fear, so that bewildered people could see themselves more clearly and, through this understanding, accept themselves.

One of these two people, operating in the world of science, contributed not only to the healing of individual lives, but also to the greater knowledge of mankind; the other, operating in a small pioneer town, contributed new courage and understanding to the lives of many. In both were present an almost fierce integrity and self-scrutiny, which, turned upon their own acts, gave them clarity of vision in judging the acts of others. In thinking of them, I have often remembered the parable of the talents and the judgment of "Well done, thou good and faithful servant"—a judgment as right for the possessor of two talents as for the one to whom ten had been given.

To each of these people the word "individual" can be applied, for the individual is one who, from the chaos of inner confusion and the assault of outer reality, separates that undefinable nucleus which makes him a unique being. This individual self may be very simple or infinitely complex—the essential quality is the acceptance of its own reality and its own true relation to life. Such people remind us of trees whose roots are deep in the earth, their life is a process of growth, their nature a maturing of some central germ, they are deeply themselves. They are also more than themselves because they are rooted in universal form. We may find them in any walk of life, for their reality is not dependent upon outer circumstances but upon the fact that in some way they have always maintained their connection with themselves, and in the various experiences of life have accepted their own responsibility and have looked for the meaning behind each personal experience.

Perhaps we could best describe these people by saying that they do not accept life ready-made, as does the ordinary person. Whether their thoughts are brilliant or simple, they are their own; whether their taste is crude or subtle it expresses something that they wish to express. Whatever they create in life, whether it be a philosophical theory, a work of art, or a human relation, it is their own creation, not something which they have taken over from outside. It is perhaps this creative quality in them which makes them stand apart.*

Frances G. Wickes, 1875–1970. American psychotherapist.
The Inner World of Man.

All my writings may be considered tasks imposed from within; their source was a fateful compulsion. What I wrote were things that assailed me from within myself. I permitted the spirit that moved me to speak out. I have never counted upon any strong response, any powerful resonance, to my writings. They represent a compensation for our times, and I have been impelled to say what no one wants to hear. For that reason, and especially at the beginning, I often felt utterly forlorn. I knew that what I said would be unwelcome, for it is difficult for people of our times to accept the counterweight to the conscious world. Today I can say that it is truly astonishing that I have had as much success as has been accorded me—far more than I ever could have expected. I have the feeling that I have done all that it was possible for me to do. Without a doubt that life work could have been larger, and could have been done better; but more was not within my power.

Carl G. Jung, M.D., 1875–1961. Swiss psychiatrist.
Memories, Dreams, Reflections.

To have learned through enthusiasms and sorrow what things there are within and without the self that make for more life or less, for fruitfulness or sterility; to hold to the one and eschew the other; to seek, to persuade, and reveal, and convince; to be ready to readjust one's values at the summons of a new truth that is known and felt; to be unweary in learning to discriminate more sharply between the false and the true, the trivial and the significant, in life and in men and in works; to be prepared to take a risk for the finer and the better things,—that is perhaps all we can do. Yet somehow as I write, the words "perhaps all we can do" seem a very meager phrase. The endeavor to be true to experience strikes me at this moment as the most precious privilege of all. To have found a loyalty from which one cannot escape, which one must forever acknowledge. No, one cannot ask for more.*

John Middleton Murry, 1889–1957. English author, critic.
To an Unknown God.

Blessed is the man who trusts in the Lord,
To whom the Lord is his confidence!
He shall be like a tree planted by waters,
That sends out its roots to the stream;
And is not afraid when heat comes,
For its leaves remain green;
Nor is anxious in a year of drought,
For it ceases not to bear fruit.

Jeremiah 17:5–8.
Old Testament. Trans. Alex R. Gordon.

The Snow-Blind

As men who once have seen
White sun on snow, white fire on ice,
And in a wide noon, shadowless,
Gone blind with light,
So these men walk who once have seen
God without veils—the mind's
Momentary and blinding birth of sight.
To them henceforth we are but shape and shadow;
Fog-forms, hands moving in the mist,
Our houses dark, our halls are winding tunnels,
Our little triumphs less than little straws
Balanced above a sparrow's nest.
And from that hour we call them dangerous men and
Strange,
Bigoted, fierce, loud croakers of a dream,
Anarchists, atheists, we say
Who walk, eyes stretched as blind men walk
But ask no man the way.

Josephine W. Johnson, 1910–. American novelist, poet.
Year's End.

John Woolman, a member of the Philadelphia Yearly Meetings of Ministers, was deeply revered—a Friend of "great weight." Among other things he was known for his consistency in refusing to benefit from the slave system. One of the measures he found necessary was to wear bleached clothing since the import of dye was involved in the slave trade.

In 1740, impelled by a special "concern," he undertook a month-long sea voyage to England. It was made unusually difficult because he felt obliged to travel steerage in order to maintain his integrity regarding special privilege. His report of the conditions in steerage did much to awaken the Colonies regarding the heretofore almost unknown misery of the sailors of that day. This uncomfortable and hazardous journey to England was matched by an equally trying experience which occurred soon after his arrival. It is related by Janet Whitney as follows.—Ed.

The London Yearly Meeting of Ministers and Elders was the most august body in Quakerdom. [John Woolman of course was a member of the equivalent body in Philadelphia, and a very important member.]

The ministers and elders had been in session about half an hour. There they sat, rank after rank of respectable men. . . . Parliament itself perhaps could hardly offer a more solidly well-to-do group. They conformed sufficiently to the fashion to avoid being conspicuous, and would pass in any company.

Into this dim and dignified assembly there suddenly entered a most extraordinary apparition. "His dress was as follows—a white hat, a coarse raw linen shirt, without anything about the neck, his coat, waistcoat and breeches of white coarse woolen cloth with wool buttons on, his coat without cuffs, white yarn stockings, and shoes of uncured leather with bands instead of buckles, so that he was all white."

A slight stir of horror went over the meeting as this figure advanced confidently to the Clerk's table and laid down his certificate. . . . Well, one never did quite know what was coming from America. But this was the worst ever seen yet. . . . They dreaded to have him go about the country with a minute and have him pointed at by other people as a "Quaker." After a brief, hostile pause, Dr. John Fothergill rose and expressed, in his cold and careful phrases, the feeling of the meeting. He suggested that perhaps the stranger Friend might feel that his dedication of himself to his apprehended service was accepted, without further labor, and that he might now feel free to return to his home.

The stunning humiliation of that blow sank home in a silence that could be felt. Such a sharp public rejection of any visitor, unheard, was without precedent. The man in white started, as if unable to believe his ears, and then sat with his face covered. Those near him were aware that tears were wrung from him in the agony of that discomfiture.

Practised in silence, the meeting waited. Most of the London Friends expected one of two things—either an unseemly outburst from this wild man, or slinking departure. . . . The silence prolonged, while Woolman sought deep within himself, first for control, then for wisdom.

At last he rose, and removed his hat. Then, speaking . . . with pain, but with assured dignity . . . he said with the utmost brevity that he could not feel himself released from his prospect of labor in England, but he could not travel in the ministry without the unity of Friends. While that unity was withheld he did not feel easy to accept hospitality, or be of any cost to them. He had the good fortune to be acquainted with a mechanical trade, and while the impediment to his services continued, he hoped Friends would be kindly willing to employ him in such business as he was capable of, that he might not be chargeable to any.

He sat down, and in spite of themselves they were impressed. They were unable to proceed with business. . . . The silence continued unbroken, but the quality of it was different for that greatest enemy of love, scorn, was no longer present. And as they sat in quiet John Woolman was subtly aware of the difference.

That long silence shaped itself into an invitation. A smaller man might have refused that opportunity out of pique and wounded feelings. A weaker man might have refused it from a self-conscious feeling that to speak now would seem to give a demonstration in support of his credentials. But Woolman had lived in the world for fifty-two years, and such feelings, if he had ever had them, he had long outgrown. Although his reception had shocked him profoundly, he was now bowing his heart to accept it as a discipline of some sort—a lesson in humility or what not—from a higher Hand than theirs. . . . The stranger again rose to his feet, removed his hat, and with his brow serene and lifted, he threw away the personal difficulty that had been between himself and them and spoke to them as to Burlington or New Haven or Philadelphia, in the love of God and the "pure life of truth."

When he had ceased, they sat still awhile more; and then Dr. Fothergill rose and begged John Woolman's pardon in a voice that was husky, and urged the meeting's endorsement of his minute, which was unanimously accorded.

The diary of Elihu Robinson reads: "*5th day*. Our Frd Jno Woolman from Jersey made some pertinent remarks in this Meeting as in many others, and tho ye Singularity of his Appearance might in some Meetings Draw ye Attention of ye Youth and soon cause a change of Countenance in some, Yet ye Simplicity, Solidity and Clearness of many of his remarks made all these vanish as Mists at ye Sun's rising—he made sevl beautiful remks in this Meeting with respt to ye benifit of true Silence and how Incense ascended on ye oppening of ye Seal and there was Silence in heaven for ye space of half an hour."*–**

Janet Whitney, 1894–. English writer.
John Woolman: American Quaker.

He broke fresh ground—because, and only because, he had the courage to go ahead without asking whether others were following or even understood. He had no need for the divided responsibility in which others seek to be safe from ridicule, because he had been granted a faith which required no confirmation—a contact with reality, light and intense like the touch of a loved hand: a union in self-surrender without self-destruction, where his heart was lucid and his mind loving. In sun and wind, how near and how remote.

Dag Hammarskjöld, 1905–1961.
Secretary General of United Nations.
Markings.

Men of stamina, knowing the way of life,
Steadily keep to it;
Unstable men, knowing the way of life,
Keep to it or not according to occasion;
Stupid men, knowing the way of life
And having once laughed at it, laugh again the louder.
If you need to be sure which way is right, you can tell by
their laughing at it.
They fling the old charges:

'A wick without oil,'
'For every step forward a step or two back.'
To such laughers a level road looks steep,
Top seems bottom,
'White appears black,'
'Enough is a lack,'
Endurance is a weakness,
Simplicity a faded flower.
But eternity is his who goes straight round the circle,
Foundation is his who can feel beyond touch,
Harmony is his who can hear beyond sound,
Pattern is his who can see beyond shape:
Life is his who can tell beyond words
Fulfillment of the unfulfilled.

Laotzu, sixth century B.C. Chinese philosopher.
The Way of Life. Trans. Witter Bynner.

My brother has served two years in prison, myself one. We have won a place of trust in the lives of many other prisoners, especially the young. We endured the oppressive and sterile prison atmosphere, with what grace and good humor we can summon. The experience is salutary—for me, in spite of everything; it is a privilege I could not have dared count on even a few years ago, something like landing in the uncharted other side of the moon . . . One survives in either of two ways. He accepts his definition as a loser who may now improve his score by becoming an idler, a loner, an informer. Or he takes his powerlessness as a cue to create new forms of power, within and around him; keeping his mind alert to oppose injustice, confronting his own cowardice and that of others with the example of great prisoners—Socrates, Jesus, Paul, Gandhi, Bonhoeffer, Cleaver. Taking the worst in stride, the atmosphere charged with threats of violence, intrigue, despair; descending into hell. At the mercy of an authority validated only by the clank of weaponry and a profound contempt for goodness. Realizing a prisoner is supposed to pay, day after day, a tribute to the power of death in this world. Refusing to pay, to submit, to go under.

So Philip and I live; we work and pray, undergo bad days and good. We fail in charity and patience; and try again. We taste on our tongues the fate of prisoners, a taste both poisonous and healing. We wake in the morning; the first thought in our minds, like a needle in the flesh, is that we are in prison. Lights go out at night, the doors clang shut, we lie in the law's power, its hand closes like a fist. All day the guards, the blare of loudspeakers, the affront of being numbered and counted like cattle—these rub like a salt in the exposed tissue; a sardonic commentary on the land of the free. What rhyme or reason can there be in a system which is in principle antihuman, irrational?*

Daniel Berrigan, S.J., 1921–. Teacher and poet.
America Is Hard to Find.

If we had not the history to confirm the fact, it would be almost impossible to believe that a priest like Abbe Vianney—so austere, so humble, so surrounded by the veneration of all who were witnesses of his extraordinary holiness—could fall a victim to hatred and calumny. But he was to pass through this supreme ordeal which God reserves for the final purification of His servants.

Even good priests wrote to M. Vianney in insolent and abusive terms. "A man who knows so little theology as you ought never to sit in the confessional!" was the opening sentence of one of these letters. And the Curé of Ars, who was forced to leave unanswered hundreds of letters full of reverent entreaty, found time to answer this rude missive, and to thank the writer. "Oh, how I ought to love you, my dear and much respected brother!" he exclaims: "you are one of the few who know me thoroughly. Help me, therefore, to obtain the favor I have been so long seeking—namely, to be replaced in my position here, which I am indeed unworthy to occupy on account of my ignorance; and that I may be free to withdraw into a corner and weep over my sins."

Once a friend exclaimed to him, indignantly: "Such calumnies could only be invented by the most perverted of men!" But the holy man answered gently: "Oh, no, they are not perverted; they are not wicked at all; it is simply that they found me out and know me better than others!" But when his friend retorted, "M. le Curé, how could they reproach you with having led a bad life?" the servant of God replied with a sigh: "Alas! my life has always been bad. I led in those days the kind of life I am leading now. I was always good for nothing." And so it was all through the trial: to unreasonable hate and devilish rancor he opposed the meekness and charity of an angel.

In after years a brother priest, who had been witness of the persecution he had undergone, asked M. Vianney if it had not troubled the peace of his soul. "What!" cried the servant of God, while a heavenly smile shone upon his face, "the cross trouble the peace of my soul! Why, it is the cross that gives peace to the world! It is the cross that must bring it into our hearts. All our misery comes from our not loving it."

The Curé of Ars was spared, it is true, in this crisis that trial which adds such unutterable anguish to every other pain: he was not deprived of the sense of divine consolation. Another person, in alluding to this time of trial, asked him if he remembered having ever been so unhappy under any other affliction. He replied: "I was not unhappy under it at all. I was never so happy in my life."

During the eight years that slander and hate were let loose upon him the conversions and extraordinary spiritual graces obtained at Ars increased beyond all calculation.*

Kathleen O'Meara, 1839–1888. Irish biographer.
Curé of Ars.

We live happily indeed, not hating those who hate us! among men who hate us we dwell free from hatred! We live happily indeed, free from ailments among the ailing! among men who are ailing let us dwell free from ailments!

We live happily indeed, free from greed among the greedy! among men who are greedy let us dwell free from greed!

We live happily indeed, though we call nothing our own! We shall be like the bright gods, feeding on happiness!

Victory breeds hatred, for the conquered is unhappy. He who has given up both victory and defeat, he, the contented, is happy.

Attributed to Gautama Buddha, 600 B.C.
The Dhammapada. Trans. F. Max Müller.

I am going to say to you that a human being can live without complaint in an ice-house built for seals at a temperature of fifty-five degrees below zero, and you are going to doubt my word. Yet what I say is true. Father Henry lived in a hole dug out by the Eskimos in the side of a hill as a place in which to store sealmeat in summer. The earth of this hill is frozen a hundred feet down, and it is so cold that you can hardly hold your bare hand to its surface.

An Eskimo would not have lived in this hole. An igloo is a thousand times warmer, especially one built out on the sea over the water warm beneath the coat of ice. I asked Father Henry why he lived thus. He said merely that it was more convenient, and pushed me ahead of him into his cavern.

If I were to describe the interior, draw it for you inch by inch, I should still be unable to convey the reality to you. From the door to the couch opposite measured four and one half feet. Two people could not stand comfortably here, and when Father Henry said Mass I used to kneel on the couch.

The couch was a rickety wooden surface supported in the middle by a strut, over which two caribou hides had been spread. On these three planks forming a slightly tilted surface, Father Henry slept.

No white man has anything to boast of in the Arctic, but Father Henry no longer had the little with which he had started. Whatever he had possessed on first coming out here was to him part of a forgotten past, and he referred to it as "all those things." It had helped in the beginning, but now "all that" was superfluous.

(He) lacked every object known to the civilization of the white man. "Those things make no sense here,"—and with that phrase he disposed of the subject. When I unpacked my gifts for him, rejoicing in advance over the delight they would give him, he stood by shaking his head. He took them and put them to one side, saying absentmindedly, "Very kind, very kind." His thanks were an acknowledgment of the intention: the gifts themselves had no meaning for him, no value.

When he heard confession from one of the natives, his box was the outer passage and the scene took place under the vitreous eyes of the frozen seal. In this virtual darkness, at fifty degrees below, the two men would kneel and murmur together.*

I had been with him several days when I began to see that something was on his mind.

"Come," I said, "What is it? You have something on your mind." It must really have been preying on him for he made no attempt to evade me.

"Ah, well," he said, "You see for yourself how it is. Here you are, a layman, enduring these privations, travelling 'tough' "—another locution of the North—"depriving yourself of your only cheese for me. Well, if you do these things, what should I, a religious, be doing?' I stared at him. A religious, indeed! What a distance that one word suddenly placed between him and me! This man was animated and kept alive by something other than the power of nature. Life had in a sense withdrawn from him, and a thing more subtle, mysterious, had taken its place. He was doubly superior to me, by his humility and by his mystical essence as priest. "I am of the most humble extraction," he had said to me. He was a Norman peasant, and it came to me suddenly that if he had chosen to live in this seal-hole instead of an igloo, his choice had been motivated in part by the peasant.instinct to build his own sort of farmstead, even here in the Arctic. He was a direct, simple, naked soul dressed only in the seamless garment of his Christianity.

By grace of that garment, his flesh was as if it were not. When I said, for example, "It is not warm this morning," he would answer mechanically, "No, it is not warm"; but he did not feel the cold. "Cold" was to him merely a word; and if he stopped up the door, or livened up the lamp, it was for my sake he did it. He had nothing to do with "those things," and this struggle was not his struggle: he was somewhere else, living another life, fighting with other weapons. He was right and I was wrong in those moments when I rebelled against his existence and insisted rashly that he "could not live like this." I was stupid not to see, then, that he truly had no need of anything. He lived, he sustained himself, by prayer. Had he been dependent only upon human strength he would have lived in despair, been driven mad. But he called upon other forces, and they preserved him. Incredible as it will seem to the incredulous, when the blizzard was too intense to be borne, he prayed, and the wind dropped. When, one day, he was about to die of hunger—he and the single Eskimo who accompanied him—he prayed; and that night there were two seal in their net. It was childish of me to attempt to win him back to reality: he could not live with reality.

I, the "scientist," was non-existent beside this peasant mystic. He towered over me. My resources were as nothing compared to his, which were inexhaustible. His mystical vestment was shelter enough against hunger, against cold, against every assault of the physical world from which he lived apart. Once again I had been taught that the spirit was immune and irresistible, and matter corruptible and weak. There is something more than cannon in war, and something more than grub and shelter in the existence of this conqueror of the Arctic. If, seeing what I have seen, a man still refused to believe this, he would do better to stay at home, for he had proved himself no traveller.*

Gontran de Poncins, 1900–. French scientist, author.
Kabloona.

The True Man

What is meant by "The True Man"? The True men of old did not reject (the views of) the few; they did not seek to accomplish (their ends) like heroes (before others); they did not lay plans to attain those ends. Being such, though they might make mistakes, they had no occasion for repentance; though they might succeed, they had no self-complacency. Being such, they could ascend the loftiest heights without fear; they could pass through water into fire without being burnt; so it was that by their knowledge they ascended to and reached the Tao. The True men of old did not dream when they had slept, had no anxiety when they awoke, and did not care that their food should be pleasant. Their breathing came deep and silently. The breathing of the true man comes (evenly) from his heels, while men generally breathe (only) from their throats. When men are defeated in argument, their words come from their gullets as if they were vomiting. Where lusts and desires are deep, the springs of the Heavenly are shallow. The True men of old knew nothing of the love of life or the hatred of death. Entrance into life occasioned them no joy; the exit from it awakened no resistance.

Laotzu, sixth century B.C. Chinese philosopher.
Texts of Taoism. Trans. J. Legge.

CHAPTER X

Outward Creativity

Wherever the spirit of the Lord is, there is freedom.

SAINT PAUL

Only those who are their absolute true selves in the world can fulfill their own nature; only those who fulfill their own nature can fulfill the nature of others; only those who fulfill the nature of others can fulfill the nature of things; those who fulfill the nature of things are worthy to help Mother Nature in growing and sustaining life; and those who are worthy to help Mother Nature in growing and sustaining life are the equals of Heaven and Earth.

ASCRIBED TO TSESZE[1]

Between Individuals

IN PERSONAL RELATIONSHIPS

Love and Freedom

The night was luminous. They could see from the hill road the earth, wrinkled with hill and hollow, lying like a vast sleeping creature. The lakes in the hollows glowed like dim moonstones. Paul and his companion did not speak. They who were closer to each other than any in the world besides were yet free, and could take lonely journeys in

[1]*The Golden Mean of Tsesze*. Trans. Ku Hungming and Lin Yutang.

soul sure that they would not lose the way back to each other. They stood for a while at the crest of the hill road. It was there the Avatars had met and gone on their radiant journey together. In that pause of quietness Paul became aware that the years had changed him, that he had come to be within that life which as a boy he had seen nodding at him through the transparency of air or earth. For many years he had peered through the veil but he himself, except for moments which were so transient that he was hardly aware of them until they were gone, had been outside the heavenly circle. Now something was living and breathing in him, interpenetrating consciousness, a life which was an extension of the life that breathed through those dense infinitudes. He could not now conceive of himself apart from that great unity. He knew he was, however humbly, one of the heavenly household. In that new exaltation the lights above, the earth below, were but motions of a life that was endless. He almost felt the will that impelled the earth on which he stood on its eternal round. Through earth itself as through a dusky veil the lustre of its vitality glowed. It shimmered with ethereal colour. Space about him was dense with innumerable life. He felt an inexpressible yearning to be molten into that, into all life. He thought of that great adventure he and his friends were beginning, and what transfigurations in life and nature it would mean. What climbing of endless terraces of being! He knew out of what anguish of body and soul, through what dark martyrdoms, come the resurrection and the life, but he thought of these in peace. At last he came back to earth and to his companion. She was still brooding as he had been, her face lifted up to the skies, intent on the same depths. She was unconscious of the one by her side, and at that moment he loved her more in forgetting than in remembering him.

George William Russell, 1867–1935. British poet.
The Avatars.

Love is letting-be, not of course in the sense of standing off from someone or something, but in the positive and active sense of enabling-to-be. When we talk of "letting-be," we are to understand both parts of this hyphenated expression in a strong sense—"letting" as "empowering," and "be" as enjoying the maximal range of being that is open to the particular being concerned. Most typically, "letting-be" means helping a person into the full realization of his potentialities for being; and the greatest love will be costly, since it will be accomplished by the spending of one's own being.

John Macquarrie, 1919–. Scottish theologian.
Principles of Christian Theology.

Personal Versus Purposeful Relationships

There are two very different ways in which we can enter into relations with our fellows. We can, in the first place, associate with others in order to achieve some purpose that we all share. Out of this there springs a life of social cooperation through which we can provide for our common needs, and achieve common ends. We may define this social life in terms of purposes. That is its great characteristic. There is in this field always a reason beyond the mere association for associating and cooperating in that particular way. Because of this we cannot enter into this form of relationship with the whole of ourselves as complete persons, because the purpose is always only one of our purposes. There are others which cannot be achieved by that particular association. We cannot, therefore, live a personal life on the basis of such relationships. The whole complex of activities which are generated in this way is what we mean usually by society or by social life. But there is a second way in which we can enter into relationships with one another. We may associate purely for the purpose of expressing our whole selves to one another in mutuality and fellowship. It is difficult to find a word to express this kind of relationship which will convey its full meaning, not because there are no words, but because they have all been specialized and degraded by misuse. Friendship, fellowship, communion, love, are all in one way or another liable to convey a false or partial meaning. But what is common to them all is the idea of a relationship between us which has no purpose beyond itself; in which we associate because it is natural for human beings to share their experience, to understand one another, to find joy and satisfaction in living together; in expressing and revealing themselves to one another. If one asks why people form friendships or love one another, the question is simply unanswerable. We can only say, because it is the nature of persons to do so. They can only be themselves in that way. It is this field of human relations which constitutes what we call the personal life, and that is the right name for it. Because that is the only way in which we can live as persons at all, the only form of human life in which we can be our whole selves or our essential selves without self-suppression and self-mutilation. . . .

If two people are associated merely for what they can get out of one another it obviously is not a friendship. Two people are friends because they love one another. That is all you can say about it. If the relationship had any other reason for it we should say that one or the other of them was pretending friendship from an ulterior motive. This means in effect that friendship is a type of relationship into which people enter as persons with the whole of themselves. This is the characteristic of personal relationships. They have no ulterior motive. They are not based on particular interests. They do not serve partial and limited ends. Their value lies entirely in themselves and for the same reason transcends all other values. And that is because they are relations of persons as persons. They are the means of living a personal life. . . .

When two people become friends they establish between themselves a relation of equality. There is and can be no functional subservience of one to the other. One cannot be the superior and the other the inferior. If the relation is one of inequality, then it is just not a personal relationship. But once a personal relationship is established the differences between the persons concerned are the stuff out of which the texture of their fellowship is woven. And provided the equal relationship is maintained, it is precisely the differences that enrich the relationship. The greater the fundamental differences between two persons are the more difficult it is to establish a fully personal relation between them, but also the more worth while the relation will be if it can be established and maintained. All great things are difficult, and this is the greatest of all.*

John Macmurray, 1891–. Scottish professor of philosophy.
Reason and Emotion.

But of deep love is the desire to give
More than the living touch of warmth and fire,
More than shy comfort of the little flesh and hands;

It is the need to give
Down to the last dark kernel of the heart,
Down to the final gift of mind;
It is a need to give you that release which comes
Only of understanding, and to know
Trust without whimpering doubt and fear.

Josephine W. Johnson, 1910–. American novelist, poet.
From the poem "September."

IN MARRIAGE

To love means to decide independently to live with an equal partner, and to subordinate oneself to the formation of a new subject, a "we." This depends neither upon thinking nor upon feeling, but upon the resolution of two subjects to accept life's most difficult task, the creation of a double subject, a "we," with complete disregard for egocentricity, all prejudices, training formulas, and drives. He who has enough courage so to love finds in living with his partner the strongest positive experience imaginable—the appearance of super-personal purposes. He exchanges that part of his egocentricity which he renounces for a part of the great clarification which awaits all of us. And life reveals to him part of its meaning.

Fritz Kunkel, M.D., 1889–1956. American psychiatrist.
Let's Be Normal.

A mutual sexual attraction is no proper basis for a human relationship between a man and a woman.[2] It is an organic thing, not personal. What, then, is a proper basis? Love is, between any two persons. Love may or may not include sexual attraction. It may express itself in sexual desire. But sexual desire is not love. Desire is quite compatible with personal hatred, or contempt, or indifference, because it treats its object not as a person but as a means to its own satisfaction. That is the truth in the statement that doing what we want to do is not the same as doing what we ought to do.

But notice this—that mutual desire does not make things any better. It only means that each of two persons is treat-

[2]See *Creation Continues* by Fritz Kunkel, M.D., and *The Way of All Women* by M. Esther Harding, M.D. See Recommended Reading List.—Ed.

ing the other as a means of self-satisfaction. A man and a woman may want one another passionately without either loving the other. This is true not merely of sexual desire but of all desires. A man and a woman may want one another for all sorts of reasons, not necessarily sexual, and make that mutual want the basis of marriage, without either loving the other. And, I insist, such mutual desire, whether sexual or not, is no basis of a human relationship between them. It is no basis of friendship. It is the desire to obtain possession of another person for the satisfaction of their own needs, to dare to assert the claim over another human being—"You are mine!" That is unchaste and immoral, a definite inroad upon the integrity of a fellow human being. And the fact that the desire and the claim are mutual does not make a pennyworth of difference. Mutual love is the only basis of a human relationship; and bargains and claims and promises are attempts to substitute something else; and they introduce falsity and unchastity into the relationship. No human being can have rights in another, and no human being can grant to another rights in himself or herself. That is one of the things of which I am deeply convinced.

Now take another point. There is only one safe-guard against self-deception in the face of desire, and that is emotional sincerity, or chastity. No intellectual principle, no general rule of judgment is of any use. How can a man or woman know whether they love another person or merely want them? Only by the integrity of his or her emotional life. If they have habitually been insincere in the expression of their feelings, they will be unable to tell. They will think they love when they only want another person for themselves. What is usually known as "being in love" is simply being in this condition. It blinds us to the reality of other people; leads us to pretend about their virtues, beauties, capacities, and so forth; deprives us of the power of honest feeling and wraps us in a fog of unreality. That is no condition for any human being to be in. If you love a person you love him or her in their stark reality, and refuse to shut your eyes to their defects and errors. For to do that is to shut your eyes to their needs.

Chastity, or emotional sincerity, is an emotional grasp of reality. "Falling in love" and "being in love" are inventions of romantic sentimentality, the inevitable result of the deceit and pretence and suppression from which we suffer. Love cannot abide deceit, or pretence or unreality. It rests only in the reality of the loved one, demands the integrity of its object, demands that the loved one should be himself, so that it may love him for himself.

In the second place, between two human beings who love one another, the sexual relationship is one of the possible expressions of love, as it is one of the possible co-operations in love—more intimate, more fundamental, more fraught with consequences inner and outer, but essentially one of the expressions of love, not fundamentally different in principle from any others, as regards its use. It is neither something high and holy, something to venerate and be proud of, nor is it something low and contemptible, to be ashamed of. It is a simple ordinary organic function to be used like all the others, for the expression of personality in the service of love. This is very important. If you make it a thing apart, to be kept separate from the ordinary functions of life, to be mentioned only in whispers; if you exalt it romantically or debase it with feelings of contempt (and if you do the one you will find that you are doing the other at the same time; just as to set women on a pedestal is to assert their inferiority and so insult their humanity): if you single out sex in that way as something very special and wonderful and terrible, you merely exasperate it and make it uncontrollable. That is what our society has done. It has produced in us a chronic condition of quite unnatural exasperation. There is a vast organisation in our civilization for the stimulation of sex—clothes, pictures, plays, books, advertisements and so on. They keep up in us a state of sexual hypersensitiveness, as a result of which we greatly overestimate the strength and violence of natural sexuality. The most powerful stimulant of sex is the effort to suppress it. There is only one cure—to take it up simply, frankly and naturally into the circle of our activities; and only chastity, the ordinary sincerity of the emotional life, can enable us to do so.

Sex, then, must fall within the life of personality, and be an expression of love. For unlike all our other organic functions it is essentially mutual. If it is to be chaste, therefore, it must fall within a real unity of two persons—within essential friendship. And it must be a necessary part of that unity. The ideal of chastity is a very high and difficult one, demanding an emotional unity between a man and a woman which transcends egoism and selfish desire. In such a unity sex ceases to be an appetite—a want to be satisfied—and becomes a means of communion, simple and natural. Mutual self-satisfaction is incompatible with chastity, which demands the expression of a personal unity already secured. Indeed, it seems to me, that it is only when such a unity in friendship has reached a point where it is shut up to that expression of itself that it is completely chaste. How can two people know that their love demands such an expression? Only through a mutual chastity, a complete emotional sincerity between them. That alone can be the touchstone of reality. And the law of reality in the relationship of persons is this: " 'the integrity of persons is inviolable.' You shall not use a person for your own ends, or indeed for any ends, individual or social. To use another person is to violate his personality by making an object of him; and in violating the integrity of another you violate your own." In all enjoyment there is a choice between enjoying the other and enjoying yourself through the instrumentality of the other. The first is the enjoyment of love, the second is the enjoyment of lust. When people enjoy themselves through each other, that is merely mutual lust. They do not meet as persons at all, their reality is lost. They meet as ghosts of themselves and their pleasure is a ghostly pleasure that cannot begin to satisfy a human soul, and which only vitiates its capacity for reality.*

John Macmurray, 1891–. Scottish professor of philosophy.
Reason and Emotion.

CHAPTER XI

Outward Creativity

(continued)

Every individual is involved in interaction with his fellows which reaches down to the innermost recesses of his private life. Hence social and private religious living are identical.

HENRY NELSON WIEMAN

We may risk a generalization and say that at any given moment of history it is the function of associations of devoted individuals to undertake tasks which clear-sighted people perceive to be necessary, but which nobody else is willing to perform.

ALDOUS HUXLEY

Between the Individual and Society

IN ATTITUDE

Interdependence

No man is an Iland, intire of itselfe; every man is a peece of the Continent, a part of the maine; if a Clod bee washed away by the Sea, Europe is the lesse, as well as if a Promontorie were; as well as if a Mannor of thy friends or of thine owne were; any man's death diminishes me, because I am involved in Mankinde; And therefore never send to know for whom the bell tolls; It tolls for thee.

John Donne, 1573–1631. English poet, divine.
Devotions upon Emergent Occasions.

The constructive critic maintains organic fellowship with other members of society even when maladjusted to them at the level of the mores; for he lives in vital conscious membership in the community of interdependence and need. This establishes a bond between him and others which is stronger and deeper than that of the mores. It is a bond which makes him meek before the lowly and fearless before the mighty: for he knows his need and their need is the same and that all men are helpless without one another. Full consciousness of this interdependence saves him in three ways. It enables him to keep his mental balance even when opposed to the mores of his fellow men; it gives him guidance and inspiration for the reconstruction of the social system; it comforts and sustains him by a great fellowship. Even when men in their blindness and misunderstanding have cast him out, he knows he has not lost them from this fellowship. Furthermore this community cheers and sustains him because it is the promise and potency of that richer, better life and more adequately organized society for which he works.

Henry Nelson Wieman, 1884–1973.
American philosopher, theologian, educator.
Methods of Private Religious Living.

It is the duty of us who are strong to put up with the weaknesses of those who are immature, and not just suit ourselves. Everyone of us must try to please his neighbor, to do him good, and help in his development.

Saint Paul, first century Christian Apostle.
New Testament (Rom. 15:1—2). Trans. E. J. Goodspeed.

A sound man's heart is not shut within itself
But is open to other people's hearts:
I find good people good,
And I find bad people good
If I am good enough;
I trust men of their word,
And I trust liars
If I am true enough;
I feel the heart beats of others
Above my own
If I am enough of a father,
Enough of a son.

Laotzu, sixth century B.C. Chinese philosopher.
The Way of Life, Trans. Witter Bynner.

He turns pure Spirit. Utter joy
Creeps on to tranquillize
His mind who seeks such discipline,
While sin with passion dies.

Sin vanishes for him who clings
To training such as this;
At one with Spirit, he attains
With ease and endless bliss.

He sees himself in every life,
Sees every life that lives
Within himself; and so to all
A like emotion gives.

The "New Testament" of Hindu Scriptures, first century B.C.
Bhagavad-Gita. Trans. A. W. Ryder.

To consider mankind otherwise than brethren, to think favors are peculiar to one nation and exclude others plainly supposes a darkness in the understanding. For, as God's love is universal, so where the mind is sufficiently influenced by it, it begets a likeness of itself, and the heart is enlarged towards all men.

John Woolman, 1720–1772. American Quaker.
Journal.

My idea of nationalism is that my country may become free, that if need be the whole of the country may die, so that the human race may live. There is no room for race hatred here. . . . I do want to think in terms of the whole world. My patriotism includes the good of mankind in general. . . . Isolated independence is not the goal of the world States; it is voluntary interdependence. The better mind of the world desires today not absolutely independent States, warring one against another, but a federation of friendly, interdependent States. The consummation of that event may be far off. I want to make no grand claim for our country. But I see nothing grand or impossible about our expressing our readiness for universal interdependence rather than independence. I desire the ability to be totally independent without asserting the independence.*

Mohandas K. Gandhi, 1869–1948. Indian statesman, mystic.

LOVE

Imagine a circle and in the middle of it a center; and from this center forthgoing radii-rays. The farther these radii go from the center, the more divergent and remote from one another they become; conversely, the nearer they approach to the center, the more they come together among themselves. Now suppose that this circle is the world: the very middle of it, God; and the straight lines (radii) going from the center to the circumference, or from the circumference to the center, are the paths of the life of men. And in this case also, to the extent that the saints approach the middle of the circle, desiring to approach God, do they, by doing so, come nearer to God and to one another . . . Reason similarly with regard to their withdrawing—when they withdraw from God, they withdraw also from one another, and by so much as they withdraw from one another do they withdraw from God. Such is the attribute of love; to the extent that we are distant from God and do not love Him, each of us is far from his neighbour also. If we love God, then to the extent that we approach to Him through love of Him, do we unite in love with our neighbors; and the closer our union with them, the closer is our union with God also.

Abba Dorotheus, seventh century. Eastern Orthodox mystic.

If anyone says, "I love God," and yet hates his brother, he is a liar; for whoever does not love his brother whom he has seen cannot love God whom he has not seen. This is the command that we get from him, that whoever loves God must love his brother also.

I. John 4:20–21.
New Testament. Trans. E. J. Goodspeed.

Duty versus Love

The substitution of duty for a living creative love has drained all meaning from the precept "bear ye one another's burdens." The law of Christ was a law of joyous giving and receiving in human relationships. Here we see the danger of letting a living word crystallize into a Mosaic law. Every sacrifice must be newborn of a fresh and creative impulse. Wherever one sacrifices life for another through a desire for self-righteousness or for sterile duty, there are piled up conscious virtue and buried resentment which leave one with a sense of loss and futility instead of a revivifying feeling of attainment. Where the sacrifice is consciously accepted because of a realization of new values, deeper relationships, greater consciousness, fuller life, the result is a release of energy.

Frances G. Wickes, 1875–1970. American psychotherapist.
The Inner World of Childhood.

It is easy for us to love those close to us—"What father among you, if asked by his son for a loaf will hand him a stone?" Even the evil behave differently from that. The point which Jesus makes about love is its inclusiveness—inclusive of those who think differently from you, belong to a different class (especially those regarded as social outcasts), the people of different race from you. These are the ones with whom we are to deal as equal with ourselves.

But how can we? It is one of the most arresting facts about the love preached in the Bible that it is not something which can be manufactured. We cannot make ourselves love. How then are we able to behave like this, or is the impossible asked of us? Love, like peace, is a *product,* a *result* in the Bible. Peace is the product of justice; love is the result of an identification—the identifying of our wills with the will of God, and our fate with that of all men, however obscure, fallen and needy. To love God with the totality of devotion called for by Jesus is to commit one's self to God and his purpose. To love your neighbor as yourself is to stand equal, with no claims of special privilege, with every living creature. Hence Jesus' shocking behaviour in eating and drinking with publicans, harlots, and those racially unacceptable as equals in the best Jerusalem society. The point about the story of the Good Samaritan which must have been very surprising and challenging to its hearers was that a Samaritan, who was racially and religiously an outcast, was more acceptable in the sight of God than a priest or Levite, because he behaved toward an unknown person as if he were a member of his own family. Unfortunately, we have tended to interpret the story in Christian circles as meaning that to love is to help the needy. The fact that the Jews had a magnificent system of helping their own needy, would have robbed such a statement of any point. Nor does it explain Paul's statement that if you give everything you have in charity, it avails you nothing unless you have love. . . .

Interdependence, the acknowledgment that we all desperately need each other, is one of the most important contributions Christianity has to make to social and economic problems. In his letter to the Corinthians, Paul says (in the part immediately preceding his statement about love): "If the foot were to say 'because I am not the hand I do not belong to the body,' that does not make it no part of the body. If the ear were to say, 'because I am not the eye, I do not belong to the body,' that does not make it no part of the body. If the body were all eye, where would hearing be? . . . The eye cannot say to the hand, 'I have no need of you,' quite the contrary." (I Corinthians 12:15-21). We are inescapably all members of one another.

This is love—not saving your own skin, but hungering and thirsting after righteousness; knowing that you cannot have real security yourself while others are insecure.*

Rose Terlin, contemporary American editor, writer.
Christian Faith and Social Action.

If you love only those who love you, what merit is there in that? For even godless people love those who love them. And if you help only those who help you, what merit is there in that? Even godless people act in that way. And if you lend only to people from whom you expect to get something, what merit is there in that? Even godless people lend to godless people, meaning to get it back again in full. But love your enemies, and help them and lend to them, never despairing, and you will be richly rewarded, and you will be sons of the Most High, for he is kind even to the ungrateful and the wicked. You must be merciful, just as your Father is.

Jesus of Nazareth.
New Testament (Luke 6:32–36). Trans. E. J. Goodspeed.

The cynic, who goes into the world determined to trust men no further than he can see them and to use them as pawns in his own game, will find that experience confirms his prejudice; for to such a man men will not shew the finer sides of their nature. The Christian, who goes into the world full of love and trust, will equally find that experience confirms his "prejudice," for to him men will shew the finer and more sensitive sides of their nature, and even where there was no generosity his love and trust will, at least sometimes, create it. But though each finds his view verified, the latter has the truer view, for he sees all that the other sees and more beside.

William Temple, 1881–1944. Archbishop of Canterbury.
Readings in St. John's Gospel.

Let a man overcome anger by love, let him overcome evil by good; let him overcome the greedy by liberality, the liar by truth!

Attributed to Gautama Buddha, 600 B.C.
The Dhammapada. Trans. F. Max Müller.

If one forsakes love and fearlessness,
forsakes restraint and reserve power,
forsakes following behind and rushes in front,
He is dead!

For love is victorious in attack,
And invulnerable in defense.
Heaven arms with love
Those it would not see destroyed.

Laotzu, sixth century B.C. Chinese philosopher.
The Book of Tao. Trans. Lin Yutang.

SENSITIVITY

But if someone who is rich sees his brother in need and closes his heart against him, how can he have any love for God in his heart? Dear children, let us love not with words or lips only but in deed and truth.

I John 3:17–18.
New Testament. Trans. E. J. Goodspeed.

Perhaps it is easy for those who have never felt the stinging darts of segregation to say, "Wait." But when you have seen vicious mobs lynch your mothers and fathers at will and drown your sisters and brothers at whim; when you have seen hate-filled policemen curse, kick and even kill your black brothers and sisters; when you see the vast majority of your twenty million Negro brothers smothering in an airtight cage of poverty in the midst of an affluent society; when you suddenly find your tongue twisted and your speech stammering as you seek to explain to your six-year-old daughter why she can't go to the public amusement park that has just been advertised on television, and see tears welling up in her eyes when she is told that Funtown is closed to colored children, and see ominous clouds of inferiority beginning to form in her little mental sky, and see her beginning to distort her personality by developing an unconscious bitterness toward white people; when you have to concoct an answer for a five-year-old son who is asking: "Daddy, why do white people treat colored people so mean?"; when you take a cross-country drive and find it necessary to sleep night after night in the uncomfortable corners of your automobile because no motel will accept you; when you are humiliated day in and day out by nagging signs reading "white" and "colored"; when your first name becomes "nigger," your middle name becomes "boy" (however old you are) and your last name becomes "John," and your wife and mother are never given the respected title "Mrs."; when you are harried by day and haunted by night by the fact that you are a Negro, living constantly at tiptoe stance, never quite knowing what to expect next, and are plagued with inner fears and outer resentments; when you are forever fighting a degenerating sense of "nobodiness"—then you will understand why we find it difficult to wait. There comes a time when the cup of endurance runs over, and men are no longer willing to be plunged into the abyss of despair. I hope, sirs, you can understand our legitimate and unavoidable impatience.

Martin Luther King, 1932–1968. American minister.
From a letter written in the Birmingham jail.
Why We Can't Wait.

And yet, the life of an honest man must be an apostasy and a perpetual desertion. The honest man must be a perpetual renegade; the life of an honest man must be a perpetual infidelity. For the man who wishes to remain faithful to truth must make himself continually unfaithful to all the continual, successive, indefatigable renascent errors.

And the man who wishes to remain faithful to justice must make himself continually unfaithful to inexhaustibly triumphant injustices.

Charles Péguy, 1873–1913. French writer.
Charles Péguy. Trans. A. and J. Green.

Oppressed people cannot remain oppressed forever. The yearning for freedom eventually manifests itself, and that is what has happened to the American Negro. Something within has reminded him of his birthright of freedom, and something without has reminded him that it can be gained. Consciously or unconsciously, he has been caught up by the *Zeitgeist*, and with his black brothers of Africa and his brown and yellow brothers of Asia, South America and the Caribbean, the United States Negro is moving with a sense of great urgency toward the promised land of racial justice. If one recognizes this vital urge that has engulfed the Negro community, one should readily understand why public demonstrations are taking place. The Negro has many pent-up resentments and latent frustrations, and he must release them. So let him march; let him make prayer pilgrimages to the city hall; let him go on freedom rides—and try to understand why he must do so. If his repressed emotions are not released in nonviolent ways, they will seek expression through violence; this is not a threat but a fact of history. So I have not said to my people: "Get rid of your discontent." Rather, I have tried to say that this normal and healthy discontent can be channeled into the creative outlet of nonviolent direct action. And now this approach is being termed extremist.

But though I was initially disappointed at being categorized as an extremist, as I continued to think about the matter I gradually gained a measure of satisfaction from the label. Was not Jesus an extremist for love: "Love your enemies, bless them that curse you, do good to them that hate you, and pray for them which despitefully use you, and persecute you." Was not Amos an extremist for justice: "Let justice roll down like waters and righteousness like an ever-flowing stream." Was not Paul an extremist for the Christian gospel: "I bear in my body the marks of the Lord Jesus." Was not Martin Luther an extremist: "Here I stand; I cannot do otherwise, so help me God." And John Bunyan: "I will stay in jail to the end of my days before I make a butchery of my conscience." And Abraham Lincoln: "This nation cannot survive half slave and half free." And Thomas Jefferson: "We hold these truths to be self-evident, that all men are created equal . . ." So the question is not whether we will be extremists, but what kind of extremists we will be. Will we be extremists for hate or for love? Will we be extremists for the preservation of injustice or for the extension of justice? In that dramatic scene on Calvary's hill three men were crucified for the same crime—the crime of extremism. Two were extremists for immorality, and thus fell below their environment. The other, Jesus Christ, was an extremist for love, truth and goodness, and thereby rose above his environment. Perhaps the South, the nation and the world are in dire need of creative extremists.

Martin Luther King, 1932–1968. American minister.
From a letter written in the Birmingham jail.
Why We Can't Wait.

FORGIVENESS

And so throughout eternity
I forgive you, you forgive me;
As our dear Redeemer said,
This is the Wine, this is the Bread.

William Blake, 1757–1827. English poet, artist, mystic.

Forgiving love is a possibility only for those who know that they are not good, who feel themselves in need of divine mercy, who live in a dimension deeper and higher than that of moral idealism, feel themselves as well as their fellow men convicted of sin by a holy God and know that the differences between the good man and the bad man are insignificant in his sight. When life is lived in this dimension the chasms which divide men are bridged not directly, not by resolving the conflicts on the historical levels, but by the sense of an ultimate unity in, and common dependence upon, the realm of transcendence. For this reason the religious ideal of forgiveness is more profound and more difficult than the rational virtue of tolerance.

Reinhold Niebuhr, 1892–1973.
American theologian, educator, author.
Interpretation of Christian Ethics.

It is not easy to step from a higher position to a lower, and be one with that position in the act of forgiveness. It is much easier to act as judge and keep one's own invulnerable position. God takes no position, and who is man to say that he speaks and acts for God? And they who judge do it in order to escape the thrusts of Reality. Perhaps they climb the citadel of judgment in order to denounce that which in themselves is a need, a desire, a frustration, or a fear. How much more profitable it would be to deal with the evil within themselves honestly. One knows only of a few instances where the judged became the forgiver, for usually pressure begets pressure. Where this forgiveness is possible, God surely is at work.*

L. M. N.

And the scribes and the Pharisees bring a woman taken in adultery; and having set her in the midst, they say unto him, "Teacher, this woman hath been taken in adultery, in the very act. Now in the law Moses commanded us to stone such: what then sayest thou of her?"

And this they said, trying him, that they might have whereof to accuse him.

But Jesus stooped down, and with his finger wrote on the ground. But when they continued asking him, he lifted up himself, and said unto them, "He that is without sin among you, let him first cast a stone at her." And again he stooped down, and with his fingers wrote on the ground. And they, when they heard it, went out one by one, beginning from the eldest, even unto the last: and Jesus was left alone, and the woman, where she was, in the midst. And Jesus lifted up himself, and said unto her, "Woman, where are they? did no man condemn thee?" And she said, "No man, Master." And Jesus said, "Neither do I condemn thee: go thy way; from henceforth sin no more."

John 8:3–11.
New Testament.

IN INFLUENCE AND ACTION

Influence

We can influence and direct others as we desire their good, but only when they are convinced, with the shrewd sense that all creatures have, that our motives are clean, our statements true, that we do seek their good, and not our advancement and elevation as their essential benefactors. All of us are individual spirits created to evolve into a common union. If we have made ourselves to grow, so that we are advanced some stages beyond the average intensity of individualism, we can directly influence those who wish to grow, and who are feeling the natural need to grow, in that direction. The spirit and character which is already advanced in constant creativeness, in wide compassion and unceasing illumination, knowing what life means and how to attain that meaning—such a spirit not only influences those among whom it is—but its influence spreads radioactively, telepathically, and the limits of its force cannot be set, because the source on which it is drawing is itself illimitable. Being, therefore, is all, and doing merely the symptom and sign of being, as body is the appearance of spirit.*

Anonymous.

Perfectly to have given up one's own is to be merged with God, and then anyone who will touch the man must first touch God, for he is wholly within God and God is around him, as my cap is around my head, and to touch me one must first touch my clothing.

Similarly, when I drink, the drink must first pass over my tongue and there be tasted; but if my tongue is covered with a bitter coating, then however sweet the wine, it will taste bitter, because of the coating through which it reaches me. This is how it is with the person who, having given up all that is his own, is coated with God, so that no creature can touch him without first touching God, and whatever reaches him must reach him through God. Thus it gets its flavor and becomes divine.

Meister Johannes Eckhart, 1260–1327. German scholar, mystic.
Meister Eckhart. Trans. R. Blakney.

The religious man is not the attractive personality. He does not draw men to himself. He is the transparent personality: a window to something beyond himself. He does not make admirers. He does not dazzle men with a fascinating individuality. He challenges them to a supreme loyalty.

Gregory Vlastos, 1909–. Canadian professor of philosophy.
The Religious Person in the World Today.

Action

What the mystic will do with his life after he has *seen,* after he has been *organized and fortified* and has been *made a lover,* we need not stop to ask. It will depend on what is specifically there to be done in his day and generation. But we can take it for settled that he will be a hundred-horsepower person in his world.

Rufus M. Jones, 1863–1948. American philosopher, author.

. . . the more we become conscious of ourselves through self-knowledge, and act accordingly, the more the layer of the personal unconscious that is superimposed on the collective unconscious will be diminished. In this way there arises a consciousness which is no longer imprisoned in the petty, over-sensitive, personal world of the ego, but participates freely in the wider world of objective interests. This widened consciousness is no longer that touchy, egotistical bundle of personal wishes, fears, hopes, and ambitions which always has to be compensated or corrected by unconscious counter-tendencies; instead, it is a function of relationship to the world of objects, bringing the individual into absolute, binding, and indissoluble communion with the world at large. The complications arising at this stage are no longer egotistic wish-conflicts, but difficulties that concern others as much as oneself . . .

Carl G. Jung, M.D., 1875–1961. Swiss psychiatrist.
Two Essays on Analytical Psychology. Trans. R. F. C. Hull.

The winter of 1930–31 was one of the darkest which the city of Tokyo has experienced. The whole nation was in the throes of a financial slump. The poor were in a pitiful plight.

Disregarding precedent, the mayor turned to Kagawa, urged him to become head of the city's Social Welfare Bureau and help him and the city to cut their way through the crisis. The salary would be $9,000 a year and an automobile for his own use.

The mayor's action caused a sensation. It raised a row in the City Council—because of the appointee's views on political and social questions. The conservatives and reactionaries attacked him because of his socialistic views. The socialists and radicals attacked him because of his religious idealism. Within the Bureau itself he was called an idealist, an impractical dreamer, and intrigue against him was rife. . . .

The mayor's offer of a salary Kagawa absolutely refused. With the money he could have supported for an entire year the three social settlements which he personally conducted in Kobe, Osaka, and Tokyo. These institutions desperately needed those funds. . . . But Tokyo was in distress. . . . He would serve only on the condition that there be no salary. He appeared at his office in the stately City Hall in the $1.85 laborer's suit which he wore in the slums. His first official act was to visit the centers of poverty. He secured shelter for those exposed to the cold of winter. He fed the hungry. He preached to the masses.

Tokyo had a modern system of street railways and transportation, but the bulk of its food supplies was still distributed by means of 11,000 house-boats which plied on 218 miles of canals running like arteries into every section of the city. . . .

He found the living conditions among these boatmen to be unspeakably bad. He provided visiting nurses, established dormitories for the children of school age, and places for the parents to sleep. He started eleven new social settlements in as many sections where the need was the greatest.

To Kagawa belongs the credit, not only of initiating the movement for wiping out the slums in six cities of the Empire, but in inducing its chief city to take the second step in solving the problem of poverty by adopting a scheme which guaranteed its own workers protection while unemployed. In the field of social legislation this was a pioneer step not only in Japan, but throughout the Orient.*–**

William Axling, M.D., 1873–1960. American missionary.
Kagawa.

Three Levels of "Action"

Every person has a choice of three levels on which to

live. He can be childish, ego-centric, and soft in mind, fondly imagining that the world revolves around his small desire. The cruelty and injustice from which others suffer cause him no pang: "Why should I go forth to battle in their behalf?" If such a one ventures outside the warm comfortable nest, it is only to dash feverishly over the surface of things. He may seem to be whole-hearted and free; actually he is irresponsible and naive. That is the lowest level.

Against this shallow innocence those on the second level energetically rebel. Some go fascist; others go communist or Pharisee. For the sake of future order or brotherhood, let there be violence now. That the Kingdom of Heaven may come according to my specifications, away with anybody who chooses a method different from that of my party.

Doesn't the end justify the means? These second-levelers make an impressive show. But peace they can find neither within nor without, and they are almost wrecking the world. Like all adolescents, they are not really sure of themselves. As a result, they make an issue of their maturity; or overemphatically protest their realism; or solemnly look down upon everybody else.

On the third level move those athletes of the spirit who are fundamentally effective and aware. The fascists call them "communists"; the communists call them "social fascists"; the Pharisees dismiss them as "sinner." Level number three is always patronized by level number two as though it were only level number one. The communist brushes Kagawa aside as a peddler of religious opium; the sword-fondling nationalist labels Gandhi as a sentimentalist who only turns the other cheek; the half-baked intellectual mutters that Schweitzer is a fool for leaving the popular lecture room to bury himself in Africa. Yet Kagawa, Gandhi, and Schweitzer are more poignantly aware of ultimate reality than inhibited atheists are. They cherish a deeper attachment to native land than arrogant nationalists can feel. They have a wider grasp of philosophy, by being brotherly, than the inhibited intellectuals in their ivory towers ever reach.

Those who have climbed to the second level are preoccupied with their growing pains. The gaiety and gusto of the great souls are literally over their heads. They see no point in sitting at the feet of children. But Kagawa, Gandhi, and Schweitzer do. Put either one in the presence of youngsters and in five minutes they will all be having a jolly and probably hilarious time. Theirs is the gift of making others feel at home because they are themselves at ease with life. Imagine yourself meeting the chubby Japanese in that funny black, unpressed suit he wears in Tokyo; or the half-naked Hindu after evening prayers in an outcaste village; or the stout-bodied Alsatian in full dress emerging from a concert in Paris. At first you might feel embarrassed in the presence of fame. But only for a moment. You would soon be thinking of more important things than the impression you were making. Before long they would be sharing with you a sense of power that is overcoming the world. And you yourself would be laughing with them.

These three have humor not because they have escaped but because they have embraced the sufferings of the underprivileged and the tasks of social change. They are free and spontaneous because they are conscripts of a terrible compassion. They are not insensitive to evil. Indeed, they can tell you far more about it than can those who are of as well as in the world. But the evil has no power to crush or sour them. They see *through* the intervening ugliness to something just and lovely beyond.

What they see does not strike them dumb. They are amazingly articulate. Kagawa bubbles over untiringly through microphones, newspapers, magazines, and books. Gandhi addresses vast crowds, issues innumerable articles, and writes one of the most self-revealing autobiographies. Schweitzer forcefully lectures, preaches, and interprets civilization to itself and himself to the world.

Do their hands produce so much because their hearts are serene? Or is their tranquillity the result of their creativity? Neither is the final cause of the other. But these qualities are the reward of that most important of all human acts—commitment. These three live for and by something infinitely higher than themselves.

Not every moment, but oftener than we, they breathe and dream in union with the deepest law of human life. It is a law that Jesus proclaimed again and again and embodied all the time: If any man tries to defend himself he will be lost, but if he throws all of himself into the cause of the Family of God he will find his soul.

Allan A. Hunter, 1893–. American minister, author.
Three Trumpets Sound.

For long generations our people had offered their "blood, toil, sweat and tears." This process had eaten its way deep into the body and soul of India, poisoning every aspect of our corporate life. . . . And then Gandhi came. He was like a powerful current of fresh air that made us stretch ourselves and take deep breaths; like a beam of light that pierced the darkness and removed the scales from our eyes; like a whirlwind that upset many things, but most of all the working of people's minds. He did not descend from the top; he seemed to emerge from the millions of India, speaking their language and incessantly drawing attention to them and their appalling condition. Get off the backs of these peasants and workers, he told us, all you who live by their exploitation; get rid of the system that produces this poverty and misery. . . .

The essence of his teaching was fearlessness and truth and action allied to these, always keeping the welfare of the masses in view. . . . The dominant impulse in India under British rule was that of fear. . . . It was against this all-pervading fear that Gandhi's quiet and determined voice was raised: Be not afraid.

Was it so simple as all that? Not quite. And yet . . . suddenly, as it were, that black pall of fear was lifted from the people's shoulders—not wholly, of course, but to an amazing degree. . . . A sea change was visible as the need for falsehood and furtive behavior lessened. It was a psychological change—almost as if some expert in psychoanalytical method had probed deep into the patient's past, found out the origins of his complexes, exposed them to his view, and thus rid him of that burden. . . .

Gandhi for the first time entered the Congress organization and immediately brought about a complete change in its constitution. . . . A new technique of action was evolved which, though perfectly peaceful, yet involved nonsubmission to what was considered wrong, and as a consequence, a willing acceptance of the pain and suffering involved in this. . . . The call of action was twofold. There was of course the action involved in challenging and resisting foreign rules; there was also the action which led us to fight our own social evils. Apart from the fundamental objective of the Congress—the freedom of India—and the method of peaceful action, the principal planks of the Congress were national unity, which involved the solution of the minority problems, and the raising of the depressed classes and the ending of the curse of untouchability. . . .

Gandhi influenced millions of people in India in varying degrees; some changed the whole texture of their lives, others were only partly affected, or the effect wore off, and yet not quite, for some part of it could not be wholly shaken off. . . . Some might well say almost in the words of Alcibiades: "Yes, I have heard Pericles and all the other great orators, and very eloquent I thought they were; but they never affected me like that; they never turned my whole soul upside down and left me feeling as if I were the lowest of the low; but this latter day Maryas (meaning Socrates), has often left me in such a state of mind that I've felt I simply couldn't go on living the way I did. . . . I've been bitten by something much more poisonous than a snake; in fact, mine is the most painful kind of bite there is. I've been bitten in the heart, or the mind, or whatever you like to call it. . . ."[1] *–**

Jawaharlal Nehru, 1889–1964. Indian statesman
The Discovery of India.

Freedom in Action

Freedom does not come from a series of emancipations from external restrictions. Those we never quite escape. No matter what our independence, we are only exchanging one tyranny for another. Freed from the interference of domineering parents, a young man may be left the slave of his friends, of his ambition, slave of his own desire to be free. No one who has lived in one community for any length of time can fail to notice the pathetic subservience of the average man to public opinion; his dread lest he should lose that which he never quite had—the esteem of those around him. There is only one way of escape from this dread which follows most men from adolescence to old age. It is the sense of belonging wholly to a transcendent value. So

[1]From *The Five Dialogues of Plato*. Everyman's Library (E. P. Dutton and Co.).

long as one loves oneself, one will fear the things which have power to hurt that self. Release comes only with the self-transcendence of love.

There are two kinds of security: One, when the future is guaranteed; the other, when the present is right. Men have often looked to religion for that first kind of assurance: that it will protect their health, their reputation, their worldly goods, their families, their friends, and will reserve them a comfortable corner in the world to come. It is the other kind of security that is the effortless possession of the committed man. It does not rest on credulity, but on the simple willingness to do the right, and follow it, so far as one can see it. In the hour of danger one can only ask oneself: "What else could I have done? It was the only right thing that I could see. Of course I shall stand the consequences, and would do it again, if I had the chance. For the rest, I can only trust to the same power of good that compelled me, and is now constraining others to the same work." This is the sense of religious freedom and religious security: Freedom, because one knows that one's own personality is ultimately unimportant; security, because one knows that the kingdom of love is the only thing worth living for, worth suffering for, if need be, worth dying for.*

Gregory Vlastos, 1909–. Canadian professor of philosophy.
The Religious Person in the World Today.

His going on foot in England had nothing to do with the Negro slave trade, except in that remote sense in which all evil is interrelated. Nor was it a personal asceticism; nor due to those good Quaker reasons, so soothing to hear, about a "stop in his mind" or "a leading." No, it was plainly and simply because he would not by one penny support the stagecoaches. The stagecoaches, concentrating on transport of passengers, were only about ten years old. In order to compete with the waggons, which carried both goods and passengers at first, the coaches had to aim at speed. . . . Woolman, an expert in horses, observed these vehicles on the road. He saw them reharnessed at the inns. He saw the postilion boys—young, so as to be light—lifted stiff from the leader, staggering into the inn, white-faced and sick, for poor food and insufficient rest. And his heart burned again for the world's cruelty. He watched the horses, too, foaming at the mouth, red in the eyes, breathing hard, being led to their stalls for just the minimum of food and rest that would enable them to keep up the killing pace, under the whip, when their turn came round again. And this was summer weather, conditions were at their best. How would things be in the winter, when snow drifted in the hollows, and ice made roads slippery, and the bitter night wind met that unprotected boy upon the leader?

"As my journey hath been without a horse," says Woolman, "I have had several offers of being assisted on my way in these stagecoaches, but have not been in them, nor have I had freedom to send letters by these posts in the present way of their riding, the stages being so fixed and one boy so dependent on another as to time, and going at great speed, that in long cold winter nights the poor boys suffer much. I heard in America of the way of these posts, and cautioned Friends in the General Meeting of Ministers and Elders at Philadelphia, and in the Yearly Meeting of Ministers and Elders in London, not to send letters to me on any common occasion by post. And though on this account I may be likely not to hear so often from my family left behind . . . yet for righteousness sake I am content. . . . Stage-coaches frequently go upwards of one hundred miles in twenty-four hours; and I have heard Friends say in several places that it is common for horses to be killed with hard driving, and that many others are driven till they grow blind. Post-boys pursue their business, each one to his stage, all night through the winter. Some boys who ride long stages suffer greatly in winter nights, and at several places I have heard of their being frozen to death. So great is the hurry in the spirit of this world that in aiming to do business quickly, and to gain wealth, the creation at this day doth loudly groan."

Here again that ounce of action which Woolman supplied spoke more loudly and was longer remembered than any of his words.*

Janet Whitney, 1894–. English writer.
John Woolman: American Quaker.

WITHIN THE BELOVED COMMUNITY

And his mother and his brothers came. And they stood outside the house and sent word in to him to come outside to them. There was a crowd sitting around him when they told him,

"Your mother and your brothers are outside asking for you."

He answered,

"Who are my mother and my brothers?"

And looking around at the people sitting about him, he said,

"Here are my mother and my brothers! Whoever does the will of God is my brother and sister and mother."

Mark 3:31–35.
New Testament. Trans. E. J. Goodspeed.

The New Community

I want you to form the nucleus of a new community which shall start a new life amongst us—a life in which the only riches is integrity of character. So that each one may fulfill his own nature and deep desires to the utmost, but wherein tho', the ultimate satisfaction and joy is in the completeness of us all as one. Let us be good all together, instead of just in the privacy of our chambers, let us know that the intrinsic part of all of us is the best part, the believing part, the passionate, generous part. We can all come croppers, but what does it matter? We can laugh at each other, and dislike each other, but the good remains and we know it. And the new community shall be established upon the known, eternal good part in us. This present community consists, as far as it is a framed thing, in a myriad of contrivances for preventing us from being let down by the meanness in ourselves or in our neighbours. But it is like a motor car that is so encumbered with non-skid, non-puncture, non-burst, non-this and non-that contrivances, that it simply can't go any more. I hold this the most sacred duty—the gathering together of a number of people who shall so agree to live by the *best* they know, that they shall be *free* to live by the best they know. The ideal, the religion, must now be *lived, practised*. . . .

After the War, the soul of the people will be so maimed and so injured that it is horrible to think of. And this shall be the new hope: that there shall be a life wherein the struggle shall not be for money or for power, but for individual freedom and common effort towards good. That is surely the richest thing to have now—the feeling that one is working, that one is part of a great, good effort or of a great effort towards goodness. It is no good plastering and tinkering with this community. Every strong soul must put off its connection with this society, its vanity and chiefly its fear, and go naked with its fellows, weaponless, armourless, without shield or spear, but only with naked hands and open eyes. Not self-sacrifice, but fulfilment, the flesh and the spirit in league together, not in arms against one another. And each man shall know that he is part of the greater body, each man shall submit that his own soul is not supreme even to himself. "To be or not to be" is no longer the question. The question now is how shall we fulfil our declaration, "God is." For all our life is now based on the assumption that God is not—or except on rare occasions.

. . . We must go very, very carefully at first. The great serpent to destroy is the will to Power: the desire for one man to have some dominion over his fellow-men. Let us have no personal influence, if possible—no personal magnetism, as they used to call it, nor persuasion—no "Follow me"—but only "Behold." And a man shall not come to save his own soul. Let his soul go to hell. He shall come because he knows that his own soul is not the be-all and the end-all, but that all souls of all things do but compose the body of God, and that God indeed shall *BE*.

I do hope that we shall all of us be able to agree, that we have a common way, a common interest, not a private way and a private interest only.*

D. H. Lawrence, 1885–1940. English novelist, poet, essayist.
From a letter[2] to Lady Ottoline Morrell, February, 1915.

The Third Order as a "Vital Cell"

The formation of the Third Order of Franciscans is one of the most important events in the spiritual life of the Middle Ages. It was an attempt to carry the gospel of love and the Franciscan way of life into the domain of home and everyday life. It was a vital spontaneous growth rather than a planned event. Whole villages or cities like that for instance of Cannara or Poggibons, or even Florence, came thronging round Francis. The very crowd of applicants for

[2]*The Letters of D. H. Lawrence*, edited by Aldous Huxley.

his two Orders threatened to defeat his purpose. The members of this Third Order were not asked to give up houses or lands or home or family. They were only asked to penetrate their lives with a passion for Christ, to live with joy and enthusiasm, and to make life a radiant affair.

Whoever was free at heart from *slavery to things* and eager for love and peace and truth was thereby a candidate for this Order. The pure in heart, the meek, the humble, the poor in spirit, were in it and of it. Those who labored and were heavy laden were members of it. Those who caught Francis' spirit of passionate love and devotion belonged to it, even before it was technically founded. It was thus a movement rather than an organization. From the very first and all through its history it was a vital cell within the larger life of the Church, an *ecclesiola* in *Ecclesia.* It was throughout a nursery of saints. It brought forth more than eighty canonized or beatified saints. The list of martyrs among them is an extraordinary one, with St. Joan of Arc at the top of the list. This movement profoundly affected every walk and department of life, but above everything else, it sanctified the home and it produced lives of beauty in a dark world. It gave reality—the reality of experience—to religion and it restored joy and radiance to a world that had largely lost them.

One of the most important aspects of this Third Order was its attempt to follow Christ as a band of "peace-makers." It brought a new Truce of God to a world forever at war. Its members were forbidden to bear arms in offensive warfare and until the Rule was altered by Pope Nicholas V they might not bear arms at all. And they were allowed, in case they were vassals, to refuse military service to their suzerains. They had caught the spirit which Francis showed to the Soldan as Housman has put it in his Little Plays. "I would show the Christ, Soldan. Or if by that name thou know Him not, then by His other name, which is Love, wherein also dwell Joy and Peace."

Hardly less important was the cultivation of the group spirit by this Third Order. It formed a vital movement among artisans and working men, which developed into one of the powerful forces that finally led to the disintegration of the feudal system.

There is a charming legend in the Little Flowers which catches the beauty of this group spirit. The story says that once St. Louis, King of France, clad as a poor pilgrim, knocked at the door of a Franciscan convent and asked for Brother Giles. A hint from the keeper of the convent, or, as other accounts say, a Divine revelation, gave Giles the secret. He ran to meet his guest. They embraced and knelt together. Then, without having broken the silence, Louis arose from his knees and went on his journey. When Giles came back to his cell the brothers reproached him for not having said anything to his royal visitor. With simplicity Giles answered: "I read his heart, and he read mine."

Such then, or something like it, was the Third Order of St. Francis.*–**

Rufus M. Jones, 1863–1948. American philosopher, author.
Inward Light (December, 1941).

Characteristic of the "Beloved Community"

"See how these Christians love one another" might well have been a spontaneous exclamation in the days of the apostles. The Holy Fellowship, the Blessed Community has always astonished those who stood without it. The sharing of physical goods in the primitive church is only an outcropping of a profoundly deeper sharing of a Life, the base and center of which is obscured to those who are still oriented about self, rather than about God. To others, tragic to say, the very existence of such a Fellowship within a common Life and Love is unknown and unguessed. In its place, psychological and humanistic views of the essential sociality and gregariousness of man seek to provide a social theory of church membership. The precious word *Fellowship* becomes identified with a purely horizontal relation of man to man, not with that horizontal-vertical relationship of man to man *in God.*

It appeared in vivid form among the early Friends. The early days of the Evangelical movement showed the same bondedness in love. The disclosure of God normally brings the disclosure of the Fellowship. We don't create it deliberately; we find it and we find ourselves increasingly within it as we find ourselves increasingly within Him. . . .

In the Fellowship cultural and educational and national and racial differences are leveled. Unlettered men are at ease with the truly humble scholar who lives in the Life, and the scholar listens with joy and openness to God's dealing with the workingman. We find men with chilly theologies but with glowing hearts. We overleap the boundaries of church membership and find Lutherans and Roman Catholics, Jews and Christians, within the Fellowship. We re-read the poets and the saints, and the Fellowship is enlarged. With urgent hunger we read the Scriptures, with no thought of pious exercise, but in order to find more friends for the soul. We brush past our historical learning in the Scriptures, to seize upon those writers who lived in the Center, in the Life and in the Power. Particularly does devotional literature become illuminated. Time telescopes and vanishes, centuries and creeds are overleaped. The incident of death puts no boundaries to the Blessed Community, wherein men live and love and work and pray in that Life and Power which gave forth the Scriptures. And we wonder and grieve at the overwhelmingly heady preoccupation of religious people with problems, unless they have first come into the Fellowship of the Light.

The final grounds of holy Fellowship are in God. Persons in the Fellowship are related to one another through Him, as all mountains go down into the same earth. They get at one another through Him.

The relation of each to all, through God, is real, objective, existential. It is an eternal relationship which is shared in by every stick and stone and bird and beast and saint and sinner of the universe. On all, the wooing love of God falls urgently, persuadingly. But he who, having willed, yields to the loving urgency of that Life which knocks at his heart, is entered and possessed and transformed and transfigured. The scales fall from his eyes when he is given to eat of the tree of knowledge, the fruit of which is indeed for the healing of the nations.

This community of life and love is far deeper than current views based upon modern logic would suppose. Logic finds, beneath every system of thought, some basic assumptions or postulates from which all other items of belief are derived. It is said that those who share in a system of thought are those who hold basic assumptions in common. But these assumptions are of the intellect, subsequent products, efforts to capture and clarify and make intelligible to ourselves and to others some fragment of that immediacy of experience in God. Theological quarrels arise out of differences in assumptions. But Holy Fellowship, freely tolerant of these important yet more superficial clarifications, lives in the Center and rejoices in the unity of His love.

And this Fellowship is deeper than democracy, conceived as an ideal of group living. It is a theocracy wherein God rules and guides and directs His listening children. The center of authority is not in man, not in the group, but in the creative God Himself. Nor do all members share equally in spiritual discernment, but upon some falls more clearly the revealing light of His guiding will. "Weighty Friends," with delicate attunement both to heaven and to earth, bulk large in practical decisions. It would be a mistake indeed to suppose that Holy Fellowship is chained fast to one political system, or bound up inextricably with the fortunes of any one temporal structure of society. It is certainly true that some temporal systems are more favorable than are others to the flowering of the Fellowship. But within all groups and nations and creeds it springs up, smiling at differences, for, existing in time, it is rooted in the Eternal One.*

Thomas R. Kelly, 1893–1941. American philosopher, educator.
A Testament of Devotion.

The Rebuilding of "Modern" Society

Our social frame, our material and mental background, should be rebuilt. But society is not plastic. Its form cannot be changed in an instant. Nevertheless . . . each individual has the power to modify his way of life, to create around him an environment slightly different from that of the unthinking crowd. He is capable of isolating himself in some measure, of imposing upon himself certain physiological and mental disciplines, certain work, certain habits, of acquiring the mastery of his body and mind. But if he stands alone, he cannot indefinitely resist his material, mental, and economic environment. In order to combat this environment victoriously, he must associate with others having the same purpose. Revolutions often start with small groups in which the new tendencies ferment and grow.

The dissenting groups would not need to be very numerous to bring about profound changes in modern society. It is a well-established fact that discipline gives great strength to men. None of the dogmas of modern society are immutable . . . Other modes of existence and of thought are possible. Culture without comfort, beauty without luxury, machines without enslaving factories, science without the worship of matter, would restore to man his intelligence, his moral sense, his virility, and lead him to the summit of his development.***

Alexis Carrel, 1873–1944. French surgeon, biologist.
Man the Unknown.

Slowly, through all the universe, that temple of God is being built wherever, in any world, a soul, by free-willed obedience, catches the fire of God's likeness. When, in your hard fight, in your tiresome drudgery, or in your terrible temptation, you catch the purpose of your being, and give yourself to God, and so give him the chance to give himself to you, your life, a living stone, is taken up and set into the growing wall. . . . Wherever souls are being tried and ripened, in whatever commonplace and homely ways, there God is hewing out the pillars for his temple.*

Phillips Brooks, 1835–1893, American clergyman.

Unto what is the kingdom of God like? And whereunto shall I liken it? It is like unto leaven, which a woman took and hid in three measures of meal, till it was all leavened. It is like a grain of mustard seed, which, when it is sown upon the earth, though it be less than all the seeds that are upon the earth, yet when it is sown, groweth up, and becometh greater than all the herbs, and putteth out great branches; so that the birds of the heaven can lodge under the shadow thereof.

Again, the kingdom of heaven is like unto a treasure hidden in the field; which a man found, and hid; and in his joy he goeth and selleth all that he hath, and buyeth that field.

If any man hath ears to hear, let him hear.

And take heed how ye hear: for whosoever hath, to him shall be given; and whosoever hath not, from him shall be taken away even that which he thinketh he hath.**[3]

Jesus of Nazareth.

---

[3]Chosen from Luke 13:18–20; Matthew 13:43–44; Luke 8:18–19.

Appendix

The Object of Devotion

Men must be ruled by God or they will be ruled by tyrants.

WILLIAM PENN

I am in every religion as a thread through a string of pearls.

BHAGAVAD-GITA

And ye shall seek me, and find me when ye shall search for me with all your heart.

JEREMIAH

It is not as important what a person's beginning idea of God is, as *that* it is, and that it develops sufficiently to awaken the devotion necessary to penetrate those levels of consciousness wherein lie the major obstacles to the perception and experience of a supra-personal reality.

We have seen that there are several fields of knowledge[1] which point toward the existence of a transcendent and immanent reality. An approach to such a conviction as we have said before, can be made through the postulates of reason; the processes of history; the implications of science; the mystical insights into nature and art; the exploration of dreams; through the lives of those who seem to some as personal manifestations of God in history. The material assembled here gives only the barest hint of what has been glimpsed by means of these various approaches. Obviously each selection presents only a small portion of the author's

[1]See Introduction pp. 203–205.

full insight. It is hoped that what has been included will help deepen and extend the reader's own sense of ultimate reality—of the meaning and purpose in the universe.

For some readers these statements on the Object of Devotion may seem meaningless and confusing. Such reactions need not keep the sincere seeker from following the Way, for as Henry Nelson Wieman writes, "People who live this Way have very diverse ideas of God, and some seem to have scarcely any idea of God at all." Those who are conditioned against all ideas of God as such may use whatever seems worthful to them, whether it be "Truth," "Love," "Simplicity," "Wisdom," or any attribute that speaks to them of permanency and value. Such value can provide the opening wedge to devotion.

There were four major advices discovered in our research concerning the Object of Devotion. (1) That no idea, nor yet all ideas of God, can approximate the actual Reality which men seek—that ideas are mere fragments of a Whole, mere clues to the infinite nature of the Good. That in this area more than in any other the words used to express ideas should be considered as symbols only and kept distinct from the actual reality which they attempt to describe. (2) That no idea should be held or clung to as final, but rather that one should be ready to have his particular idea of God "smashed to bits . . . in order to, in an instant, find God . . . for God is the destroyer of gods." (3) That some ideas, particularly of anthropomorphic implication, block expanding cosmology and thus handicap a growing perception of God. (4) That those who progress beyond conviction through purgation to real Illumination and beyond, dismiss all ideas of God as such, for their experience transcends any rational concept. As Meister Eckhart wrote: "To tell the truth, the intellect is no more content with (the idea of) God than it would be with a stone or a tree. It can never rest until it gets to the core of the matter, crashing through to that which is beyond the idea of God and truth, until it reaches the *in principio,* the beginning of beginnings, the origin or source of all goodness and truth." And as a modern philosopher expresses it: "No matter how true an idea of God religion may hand on, the true idea may constitute a wall which keeps God out, if it is adopted as an idea simply—that is to say, as a repetition of other men's insights, as a universal idea. God, who is truly said to explain man to himself, must explain me to myself. What I require to find in a god is that 'This is what I have wanted; this is what I have been meaning all the time; the world as I now see it is a world in which I as a primitive, various, infinitely discontented will, can completely live and breathe.' This is what the mystic is trying to make plain—that the idea, as a universal, is not sufficient for any man to live by.

"Hence the chief burden of his revelation (as if of the idea's own never-resting conscience) is that religion must exist as experience and not as idea only. There is nothing in sensation which physical science cannot exhaust, except the experience of having sensations: in the same way, there is nothing in the mystic experience not expressible in idea, except the experiencing itself. This is the chief part of the mystic knowledge which cannot be otherwise known, namely that the mystic experience is possible. Monotonously and age after age, men rediscover and reannounce this invariant truth, as if they were calling on men to exist, to live, to save their souls. And what is it to save one's soul, if not to be original in this sense (and in what follows from it)? From this point of view the reiteration of the mystic is justified."[2]

All those who seek Thee tempt Thee,
And those who find would bind Thee
To gesture and to form.

But I would comprehend Thee
As the wide Earth enfolds Thee.
Thou groweth with my maturity,
Thou art in calm and storm.

I ask of Thee no vanity
To evidence and prove Thee.
Thou wert in aeons old.

Perform no miracles for me,
But justify Thy laws to me—

---

[2]*The Meaning of God in Human Experience,* by William Ernest Hocking, pp. 450–451.

Which, as the years pass by me,
All soundlessly unfold.

Rainer Maria Rilke, 1875–1926. German poet.
Rainer Maria Rilke Poems. Trans. Jessie Lemont.

Some Modern Ideas of God

God as the Completed Ideal Harmony

The order of the world is no accident. There is nothing actual which could be actual without some measure of order. The religious insight is the grasp of this truth: that the order of the world, the depth of reality of the world, the value of the world in its whole and in its parts, the beauty of the world, the zest of life, the peace of life, and the mastery of evil, are all bound together—not accidentally, but by reason of this truth: that the universe exhibits a creativity with infinite freedom, and a realm of forms with infinite possibilities; but that this creativity and these forms are together impotent to achieve actuality apart from the completed ideal harmony, which is God. . . .

The limitation of God is his goodness. He gains his depth of actuality by his harmony of valuation. It is not true that God is in all respects infinite. If He were, He would be evil as well as good. Also this unlimited fusion of evil with good would mean mere nothingness. He is something decided and is thereby limited.

He is complete in the sense that his vision determines every possibility of value. Such a complete vision coordinates and adjusts every detail. Thus his knowledge of the relationships of particular modes of value is not added to, or disturbed, by the realization in the actual world of what is already conceptually realized in his ideal world. This ideal world of conceptual harmonization is merely a description of God himself. Thus the nature of God is the complete conceptual realization of the realm of ideal forms. . . . God is the one systematic, complete fact, which is the antecedent ground conditioning every creative act.

The depths of his existence lie beyond the vulgarities of praise or of power. He gives to suffering its swift insight into values which can issue from it. He is the ideal companion who transmutes what has been lost into a living fact within his own nature. He is the mirror which discloses to every creature its own greatness.

The kingdom of heaven is not the isolation of good from evil. It is the overcoming of evil by good. This transmutation of evil into good enters into the actual world by reason of the inclusion of the nature of God, which includes the ideal vision of each actual evil so met with a novel consequent as to issue in the restoration of goodness.

God has in his nature the knowledge of evil, of pain, and of degradation, but it is there as overcome with what is good. . . . Every event on its finer side introduces God into the world. Through it his ideal vision is given a base of actual fact to which He provides the ideal consequent, as a factor saving the world from self-destruction of evil. The power by which God sustains the world is the power of himself as the ideal. He adds himself to the actual ground from which every creative act takes its rise. The world lives by its incarnation of God in itself.

God is that function in the world by reason of which our purposes are directed to ends which in our own consciousness are impartial as to our own interests. He is that element in life in virtue of which judgment stretches beyond facts of existence to values of existence. He is that element in virtue of which our purposes extend beyond values for ourselves to values for others. He is that element in virtue of which the attainment of such a value for others transforms itself into value for ourselves.

He is the binding element in the world. The consciousness which is individual in us, is universal in him; the love which is partial in us is all-embracing in him. Apart from him there could be no world, because there could be no adjustment of individuality. His purpose in the world is quality of attainment. His purpose is always embodied in the particular ideals relevant to the actual state of the world. Thus all attainment is immortal in that it fashions the actual ideals which are God in the world as it is now. Every act leaves the world with a deeper or a fainter impress of God. He then passes into his next relation to the world with enlarged, or diminished, presentation of ideal values.

He is not the world, but the valuation of the world. In abstraction from the course of events, this valuation is a necessary metaphysical function. Apart from it, there could be no definite determination of limitation required for attainment. But in the actual world, He confronts what is actual in it with what is possible for it. Thus He solves all indeterminations.

The passage of time is the journey of the world towards the gathering of new ideas into actual fact. This adventure is upwards and downwards. Whatever ceases to ascend, fails to preserve itself and enters upon its inevitable path of decay.*

Alfred North Whitehead, 1861–1947.
English philosopher, mathematician.
Religion in the Making.

Goa as Benevolent Power

I do dimly perceive that whilst everything around me is ever-changing, ever-dying, there is underlying all that change a Living Power that is changeless, that holds all together, that creates, dissolves, and re-creates. That informing Power or Spirit is God; and since nothing else that I see merely through the senses can or will persist, He alone is.

And is this power benevolent or malevolent? I see it as purely benevolent. For I can see that in the midst of death, life persists; in the midst of untruth, truth persists; in the midst of darkness, light persists. Hence I gather that God is Life, Truth, Light. He is Love. He is the supreme Good.

But He is no God who merely satisfies the intellect, if He ever does. God, to be God, must rule the heart and transform it. He must express Himself in every smallest act of His votary. This can only be done through a definite realization more real than the five senses can ever produce. Sense perceptions can be, and often are, false and deceptive, however real they may appear to us. Where there is realization outside the senses it is infallible. It is proved, not by extraneous evidence, but in the transformed conduct and character of those who have felt the real presence of God within.

Such testimony is to be found in the experiences of an unbroken line of prophets and sages in all countries and climes. To reject this evidence is to deny oneself.

This realization is preceded by an immovable faith. He who would in his own person test the fact of God's presence can do so by a living faith. Exercise of faith will be the safest where there is a clear determination summarily to reject all that is contrary to Truth and Love.*

Mohandas K. Gandhi, 1869–1948. Hindu statesman, mystic.
Quoted in *Gandhi's Ideas* by C. F. Andrews.

God as Verb—as Be-ing

It has sometimes been argued that anthropomorphic symbols for "God" are important and even necessary because the fundamental powers of the cosmos otherwise are seen as impersonal. One of the insights characteristic of the rising woman consciousness is that this kind of dichotomizing between cosmic power and the personal need not be. That is, it is not necessary to anthropomorphize or to reify transcendence in order to relate to this personally. In fact, the process is demonic in some of its consequences. . . . [It] has been characteristic of patriarchal consciousness making "the Other" [the] repository of the contents of the lost self. Since women are now beginning to recognize in ourselves the victims of such dichotomizing processes, the insight extends to other manifestations of the pathological splitting off of reality into falsely conceived opposites. Why indeed must "God" be a noun? Why not a verb—the most active and dynamic of all? Hasn't the naming of "God" as a noun been an act of murdering that dynamic Verb? And isn't the Verb infinitely more personal than a mere static noun? The anthropomorphic symbols for God may be intended to convey personality, but they fail to convey that God is Be-ing. Women now who are experiencing the shock of nonbeing and the surge of self-affirmation against this are inclined to perceive transcendence as the Verb in which we participate—live, move, and have our being.

This Verb—the Verb of Verbs—is intransitive. It need not be conceived as having an object that limits its dynamism. That which it is over against is nonbeing. Women in the process of liberation are enabled to perceive this because our liberation consists in refusing to be "the Other" and asserting instead "I am"—without making another "the Other." Unlike Sartre's "us versus a third" (the closest approximation to love possible in his world) the new sisterhood is saying "us versus nonbeing." When Sartre wrote that "man [sic] fundamentally *is* the desire to be God," he was saying that the most radical passion of human life is to be a God who does not and cannot exist. The ontological hope of which I am speaking is neither this self-deification nor the simplistic reified images often lurking behind such terms as "Creator," "Lord," "Judge," that Sartre rightly rejects. It transcends these because its experiential basis is courageous *participation* in being. This ontological hope also has little in common with the self-enclosed "ontological arguments" of Anselm or Descartes. It enables us to break out of this prison of subjectivity because it implies commitment together.*

Mary Daly, contemporary theologian.
Beyond God the Father.

God as the Spirit in Which Truth Has Its Shrine

We recognize that the type of knowledge after which physics is striving is much too narrow and specialised to constitute a complete understanding of the environment of the human spirit. A great many aspects of our ordinary life and activity take us outside the outlook of physics. For the most part no controversy arises as to the admissibility and importance of these aspects; we take their validity for granted and adapt our life to them without any deep self-questioning. It is therefore somewhat of an anomaly that among the many extra-physical aspects of experience religion alone should be singled out as specially in need of reconciliation with the knowledge contained in science. Why should anyone suppose that all that matters to human nature can be assessed with a measuring rod or expressed in terms of the intersections of world-lines? If defence is needed, the defence of religious outlook must, I think, take the same form as the defence of an aesthetic outlook. The sanction seems to lie in an inner feeling of growth or achievement found in the exercise of the aesthetic faculty and equally in the exercise of the religious faculty. It is akin to the inner feeling of the scientist which persuades him that through the exercise of another faculty of the mind, namely its reasoning power, we reach something after which the human spirit is bound to strive.

It is by looking into our own nature that we first discover the failure of the physical universe to be co-extensive with our experience of reality. The "something to which truth matters" must surely have a place in reality whatever definition of reality we may adopt. In our own nature, or through the contact of our consciousness with a nature transcending ours, there are other things that claim the same kind of recognition—a sense of beauty, of morality, and finally at the root of all spiritual religion an experience which we describe as the presence of God. In suggesting that these things constitute a spiritual world I am not trying to substantialise them or objectivise them—to make them out other than we find them to be in our experience of them. But I would say that when from the human heart, perplexed with the mystery of existence, the cry goes up, "What is it all about?" it is no true answer to look only at that part of experience which comes to us through certain sensory organs and reply: "It is about atoms and chaos; it is about a universe of fiery globes rolling on to impending doom; it is about tensors and non-commutative algebra." Rather it is about a spirit in which truth has its shrine, with potentialities of self-fulfilment in its response to beauty and right. Shall I not also add that even as light and colour and sound come into our minds at the prompting of a world beyond, so these other stirrings of consciousness come from something which, whether we describe it as beyond or deep within ourselves, is greater than our own personality?

Sir Arthur Eddington, 1882–1944.
English physicist, astronomer.
New Pathways in Science.

God as Pervading All Reality

If God pervades all reality, He must pervade material reality. If God is not in the material world, He is unreal or half-real. Traditional theology is confused and confusing on this point. On the one hand, it assures us that God made the heavens and the earth. On the other hand, it defines God as a purely spiritual being, and thus politely banishes Him from the world that He has made. Thus many Christians are atheists in their conception of the material world and in their dealings with it.

Consider that all-important basis of our common life today: the Machine. Our own period of world-history began with the Industrial Revolution; any social revolutions, past or pending, would be unthinkable in this period without that mechanical revolution which increased man's power over nature a hundredfold or more. What is the religious meaning of the machine? Many Christians distrust it on principle. They look upon it as inhuman, unnatural, not to say diabolical, and godless. It figures in many sermons as a Frankenstein's monster that enslaves man. This is not only atheism, but nonsense as well. Only man can enslave man. Man can be enslaved through the machine (as he can also be liberated through the machine); never by the machine.

But there is nothing inhuman or unhuman about the machine. Only man can make it. A machine is as distinctively and brilliantly and expressively human as a violin sonata or a theorem in Euclid. It is not just a bit of matter. It is matter transformed in the likeness of a human thought. Indeed it is a human thought, projected from men's brain in the external world, given body, so it can carry on an independent existence. And it is not only man who expresses himself through the machine. It is God. For with the one exception of speech, the machine is the greatest instrument of human interdependence yet discovered. If God be "the power that makes us one," the order of reality that forces us out of exclusive isolation into creative unity with one another, then the machine is surely a divine agency.

One cannot overestimate the importance of this point. For it means that the command to love is written in the material structure of our everyday life. Mutuality is not just a shiny ideal that catches the eye of a few idealists. It is the demand of the historic process. It is not merely a moral obligation, which can be set aside because of more urgent practical necessities. It is the most urgently practical need of our life. It is a moral obligation precisely because it is also a material necessity. For it is obvious that the machine is not a tool for individual production but for co-operative production; that it is essentially a public utility. It is created by co-operative scientific thinking. It can function only by linking together immense numbers of men as workers, managers, consumers. Take this public utility and make it the property of one man, or a few men, who will use it for their private profit, and what happens? You are trying, once again, to do the impossible. You try to turn an agency of co-operation into an agency of individual profit. You will not work it according to its own nature. So it will not work at all. And so you get closed factories, unemployed millions, and people suffering and dying for lack of those very things that men and factories could produce for the use of all, but cannot produce for the profit of a few. And common folk look at it all, and shake their heads, and say, "It is madness." That is just what it is. But the madness is not in the machine. The machine is one of the most compellingly rational of human discoveries. The madness is in those who would use a rational thing to further the irrational ends of exploitation and domination. It is the madness of trying to use an instrument of God for the purposes of the devil.

And what will God do? What can He do? He cannot change His nature to make up for our stupidity, and make unworkable things workable for our sake. The prophets discovered this long ago. They found that, if men will not know willingly the God of love, they will know unwillingly the God of wrath. There are not two gods. The God of wrath is the God of love vindicating Himself in the death of those who will not live in love. It is the laws of health that destroy those who disobey them. There are no laws of disease other than the laws of health. It is the laws of logic that condemn those who ignore them to nonsense and self-contradiction. The identical forms that show up the crookedness of illogical thinking prove the straightness of logical thinking. It is God, not the devil, who rules the world through the terror and desolation of unemployment and concentration camps and pogroms and air-raids, in Germany, in Spain, in China, in Poland. The initiative lies with God, and the judgment lies with God. The power of love perennially present in the structure of human life, now more urgent than ever in the co-operative nature of the machine, is the power of God. It is pressing down upon human divisiveness and pride, crushing us in so far as we will not obey, destroying the old order that will not yield to the new.*

Gregory Vlastos, 1909–. Canadian professor of philosophy.
Christian Faith and Democracy.

God as Other Mind—as Eternal Substance

I shall always be more certain that God is, than what he is: it is the age-long problem of religion to bring to light the deeper characteristics of this fundamental experience. But the starting point of this development is no mere That Which, without predicates. Substance is known as Subject: reality from the beginning is known as God. The idea of God is not an attribute which in the course of experience I come to attach to my original whole-idea: the unity of my world which makes it from the beginning a whole, knowable in simplicity, is the unity of other Selfhood.

God then is immediately known, and permanently known, as the Other Mind which in creating Nature is also creating me. Of this knowledge nothing can despoil us; this knowledge has never been wanting to the self-knowing mind of man.

We may find our thought of God following in arrear of the best conception we have of ourselves; but it is only because we know that whatever selfhood we have is an involution of the selfhood of the Whole, and that our external relations to our fellows do but follow and reproduce in their own more distant fashion the relation of God to us which from his view is internal. Hence the remark that "Man is never long content to worship gods of moral character greatly inferior to his own" may be accepted, with its sting drawn, because of what we know of our relation to the Whole of which we are natural parts.

The conception of God as Law has its right in destroying the *poverty* of my thought of personality. I confess that this word "person" has for me a harsh and rigid sound, smacking of the Roman Code. I do not love the word personality. I want whatever is accidental and arbitrary and atomic and limited and case-hardened about that conception to be persistently beaten and broken by whatever of God I can see in the living law and order of this Universe until it also has all such totality and warmth.

But I see that personality is a stronger idea than law; and has promise of mutuality and intercourse that laws, even if living, cannot afford. I see further that personality *can include law*, as law cannot include personality. And I see, finally, that this deepening conception of personality is not more an ideal than an experience. For God is not falsely judged in experience *to be both one and the other*. The negation of any one such attribute by the other is only for the enlargement of the first, not for its destruction. Until I can perfectly conceive personality, God must be for me alternately person and law; with the knowledge that these two attributes of one being are not, in truth, inconsistent, and that their mode of union is also something that I shall verify in some moment of present knowledge, as by anticipation of an ultimate attainment. Not only is God to be found in experience, but whatever attributes are genuinely predicated of him are to be found there also.

God is the Eternal Substance, and is known as such; God is also the Eternal Order of things: but God is That Which does whatever Substance is found to do. If it is the knowledge of God that first gives us our human comradeship and its varied and satisfying responsiveness, the God who is the bearer of that responsiveness is not himself without response. These comrades are in a measure God's organs of response, even as Nature is God's announcement of his presence and individuality: but God has also a responsiveness of his own, and herein lies the immediate experience of the personality of God. The relations between man and God have, in the course of religious history, become more deeply personal and passionate, with the deepening sense of evil and spiritual distress. The soul finds at length its divine companion. But as religion enters into these deeper and more fertile strata of the knowledge of God, it becomes evident that the development of religion falls increasingly upon the shoulders of individual men, whose experience of God and its cognitive content becomes authoritative for others. We find that religion becomes universal at the same time that it becomes most peculiarly personal, and takes its impetus and name from individual founders and prophets. Buddhism and Christianity and Islam are religions of redemption and of universal propagandism; and it is they, chiefly, that willingly refer their character and revelation of God to one person.*

William Ernest Hocking, 1873–1966. American philosopher.
The Meaning of God in Human Experience.

God as Immanent and Transcendent

It is foolish to seek for God outside of oneself. This will result either in idolatry or in scepticism. To seek God within oneself is better, but there is danger lest this will result in egomania, in becoming an opponent of order or a nihilist.

Therefore, he who truly seeks God should discover the unchangeable laws which operate outside of himself and recognize within himself a profound and mysterious purpose. Through being cognizant of a power which pervades both within and without, cognizant also of a world of growth which is common to both, recognizing, moreover, the immutability of the moral order and recognizing the fact that God as life fills both the inner and the outer, that He is the creator of absolute values, the preserver and unfolder of all things—thus and thus only will one be able to cease going astray.

Toyohiko Kagawa, 1888–1960.
Japanese social reformer, Christian minister.
As quoted in *Kagawa* by William Axling.

God's Imprint in the Psyche as the "Self"—the Mid-point of Personality[3]

The remarkable capacity of the human soul for change is expressed in the transcendent function . . . [which, through] a long and continuous series of transformations, has as [its] goal the attainment of the mid-point of the personality. . . .

It may not be immediately apparent what is meant by a "mid-point of the personality." I will therefore try to outline this problem in a few words. If we picture the conscious mind, with the ego as its centre, as being opposed to the unconscious, and if we now add to our mental picture the process of assimilating the unconscious, we can think of this assimilation as a kind of approximation of conscious

[3]The reader should consider these brief extracts as giving only the barest clues to the author's total observations concerning that "irrational," "powerfully alive," "indefinable existent" rooted in the psyche which he terms the Self. The reader is referred to the author's text, Part Two, on "Individuation"—Chaps. III and IV. He is also referred to Part I of *Psychology and Alchemy,* Coll. Works, Vol. 12 (in which Dr. Jung refers to the God-image or archetype as the imprint of God in the psyche. In other writings he differentiates between the God-image (or "Self") as experienced in the Soul of man, and the Godhead—seeming to allow for an immanent and a transcendent aspect of God).—Ed.

and unconscious, where the centre of the total personality no longer coincides with the ego, but with a point midway between the conscious and the unconscious. This would be the point of new equilibrium, a new centering of the total personality, a virtual centre which, on account of its focal position between conscious and unconscious, ensures for the personality a new and more solid foundation. I freely admit that visualizations of this kind are no more than the clumsy attempts of the unskilled mind to give expression to inexpressible, and well-nigh indescribable, psychological facts. I could say the same thing in the words of St. Paul: "Yet not I live, but Christ liveth in me." Or I might invoke Lao-tzu and appropriate his concept of Tao, the Middle Way and creative centre of all things. In all these the same thing is meant. Speaking as a psychologist with a scientific conscience, I must say at once that these things are psychic factors of undeniable power; they are not the inventions of an idle mind, but definite psychic events obeying definite laws and having their legitimate causes and effects, which can be found among the most widely differing peoples and races today, as thousands of years ago. I have no theory as to what constitutes the nature of these processes. One would first have to know what constitutes the nature of the psyche. I am content simply to state the facts.*–**

Carl G. Jung.

The following extracts from Chapter IV of the author's text describe the advanced stages of the individuation process wherein the ego finds it possible "to disengage itself from the entanglements with collectivity and the collective unconscious."

One of the phases of this disentanglement relates to the emergence of what Dr. Jung terms the "mana-personality,"[4] which the ego must assimilate and relate to (rather than identify with), if there is to be progression toward the final goal. See pp. 150 and 161 of this anthology.—Ed.

---

[4]The mana-personality Dr. Jung describes as a "being of superior wisdom, on one side, and a being of superior will on the other"—placing one "in uncomfortable kinship with the gods." Christ (in the Temptations), Paul, and others after them wrestled with this power which can become daemonic or divine, according to how it is confronted and related to. See the author's text pp. 225–238.—Ed.

. . . the dissolution of the mana-personality through conscious assimilation of its contents leads us, by a natural route, back to ourselves as an actual, living something, poised between two world-pictures and their darkly discerned potencies. This "something" is strange to us and yet so near, wholly ourselves and yet unknowable, a virtual centre of so mysterious a constitution that it can claim anything—kinship with beasts and gods, with crystals and with stars—without moving us to wonder, without even exciting our disapprobation. This "something" claims all that and more, and having nothing in our hands that could fairly be opposed to these claims, it is surely wiser to listen to this voice.

I have called this centre the *self*. Intellectually the self is no more than a psychological concept, a construct that serves to express an unknowable essence which we cannot grasp as such, since by definition it transcends our powers of comprehension. It might equally well be called the "God within us." The beginnings of our whole psychic life seem to be inextricably rooted in this point, and all our highest and ultimate purposes seem to be striving towards it. This paradox is unavoidable, as always, when we try to define something that lies beyond the bourn of our understanding.

. . . the self has as much to do with the ego as the sun with the earth. They are not interchangeable. Nor does it imply a deification of man or a dethronement of God. What is beyond our understanding is in any case beyond its reach. When, therefore, we make use of the concept of a God we are simply formulating a definite psychological fact, namely the independence and sovereignty of certain psychic contents which express themselves by their power to thwart our will, to obsess our consciousness and to influence our mood and actions. We may be outraged at the idea of an inexplicable mood, a nervous disorder, or an uncontrollable vice being, so to speak, a manifestation of God. But it would be an irreparable loss for religious experience if such things, perhaps even evil things, were artificially segregated from the sum of autonomous psychic contents. . . . What seems evil, or at least meaningless and valueless to contemporary experience and knowledge, might on a higher level of experience and knowledge appear as the source of the best—everything depending, naturally, on the use one makes of one's seven devils. To explain them as meaningless robs the personality of its proper shadow, and with this it loses its form. . . . it remains a two-dimensional phantom, a more or less well brought-up child.

The conception of God as an autonomous psychic content makes God into a moral problem—and that, admittedly, is very uncomfortable. But if this problem does not exist, God is not real, for nowhere can he touch our lives. He is then either an historical and intellectual bogey or a philosophical sentimentality.

If we leave the idea of "divinity" quite out of account and speak only of "autonomous contents," we maintain a position that is intellectually and empirically correct, but we silence a note which, psychologically, should not be missing. By using the concept of a divine being we give apt expression to the peculiar way in which we experience the workings of these autonomous contents. . . . by affixing the attribute "divine" to [them] . . . we are admitting their relatively superior force. And it is this superior force which has at all times constrained men to ponder the inconceivable, and even to impose the greatest suffering upon themselves in order to give these workings their due. It is a force as real as hunger and the fear of death.

The self could be characterized as a kind of compensation for the conflict between inside and outside. This formulation would not be unfitting, since the self has somewhat the character of a result, of a goal attained, something that has come to pass very gradually and is experienced with much travail. So too the self is our life's goal, for it is the completest expression of that fateful combination we call individuality, the full flowering not only of the single individual, but of the group, in which each adds his portion to the whole.*–**

Carl G. Jung, M.D., 1875–1961. Swiss psychiatrist.
Two Essays on Analytical Psychology. Trans. R. F. C. Hull.

God as a Paradox

Although the God-concept is a spiritual principle *par excellence,* the collective metaphysical need nevertheless insists that it is at the same time a conception of the First Cause, from which proceed all those instinctual forces that are opposed to the spiritual principle. God would thus be not only the essence of spiritual light, appearing as the latest flower on the tree of evolution, not only the spiritual goal of salvation in which all creation culminates, not only the end and aim, but also the darkest, nethermost cause of Nature's blackest deeps. This is a tremendous paradox which obviously reflects a profound psychological truth. For it asserts the essential contradictoriness of one and the same being, a being whose innermost nature is a tension of opposites. Science calls this "being" energy, for energy is like a living balance between opposites. For this reason the God-concept, in itself impossibly paradoxical, may be so satisfying to human needs that no logic however justified can stand against it. Indeed the subtlest cogitation could scarcely have found a more suitable formula for this fundamental fact of inner experience.

Carl G. Jung, M.D., 1875–1961. Swiss psychiatrist.
On Psychic Energy and Other Central Concepts in Analytical Psychology. Trans. R. F. C. Hull.

God as Mystery and Meaning

A genuine Christian faith must move between those who claim to know so much about the natural world that it ceases to point to any mystery beyond itself, and those who claim to know so much about the mystery of the "unseen" world that all reverence for its secret and hidden character is dissipated. A genuine faith must recognize the fact that it is through a dark glass that we see; though by faith we do penetrate sufficiently to the heart of the mystery not to be overwhelmed by it. A genuine faith resolves the mystery of life by the mystery of God. It recognizes that no aspect of life or existence explains itself, even after all known causes and consequences have been traced. All known existence points beyond itself. To realize that it points beyond itself to God is to assert that the mystery of life does not dissolve life into meaninglessness. Faith in God is faith in some ultimate unity of life, in some final comprehensive purpose which holds all the various, and frequently contradictory, realms of coherence and meaning together. A genuine faith does not mark this mysterious source and end of existence as merely an X, or as an unknown quantity. The Christian faith, at least, is a faith in revelation. It believes that God has made Himself known. It believes that He has spoken through the prophets and finally in His Son. It accepts the revelation in Christ as the ultimate clue to the mystery of God's nature and purpose in the .world, particularly the mystery of the relation of His justice to His mercy. But these clues to the mystery do not eliminate the periphery of mystery. God remains *deus absconditus.*

Reinhold Niebuhr, 1892–1973.
American theologian, educator, author.
Discerning the Signs of the Times.

God as Revealed in Jesus Christ

The approach of Faith, this appreciation of the nature of God as He has been unveiled in the ethical processes of history, especially in the Person of Christ, and in His expanding conquest of the world must always be one of the great factors of spiritual religion.

Once at least there shone through the thin veil of matter a personal Life which brought another kind of world than this world of naturāl law and utilitarian aims full into light. There broke through a revelation of Purpose in the Universe so far beyond the vague trend of purpose dimly felt in slowly evolving life that it is possible here to catch an illuminating vision of what the goal of the long drama may be—the unveiling of sons of God. Here the discovery can be made that the deepest Reality toward which Reason points, and which the mystical experience *feels,* is no vague Something Beyond, but a living, loving Someone, dealing with us as Person with person. In Him there comes to focus in a Life that we can love and appreciate a personal character which impresses us as being absolutely good and as being in its inexhaustible depth of love and Grace worthy to be taken as the revelation of the true nature of the God whom all human hearts long for. And finally through this personal revelation of God in Christ there has come to us a clear insight that pain and suffering and tragedy can be taken up into a self-chosen Life and absorbed without spoiling its immense joy, and that precisely through suffering-love, joyously accepted, a Person expressing in the world the heart of God may become the moral and spiritual Saviour of others.

Nowhere else in the universe—above us or within us—has the moral significance of life come so full into sight, or the reality of actual divine fellowship, whether in our aspirations or in our failures, been raised to such a pitch of practical certainty as in the personal life and death and resurrection and steady historical triumph of Jesus Christ. He shows the moral supremacy, even in this imperfect empirical world, of the perfectly good will, and He impresses those who see Him—see Him, I mean, with eyes that can penetrate through the temporal to the eternal and find His real nature—as being the supreme personal unveiling of God, strong enough in His infinite Grace and divine self-giving to convince us of the eternal co-operation of God with our struggling humanity, and to settle our Faith in the essential Saviourhood of God.

He who sees *that* in Christ has found a real way to God and has discovered a genuine way of salvation. It is the way of Faith, but Faith is no airy and unsubstantial road, no capricious leap. There is no kind of aimful living conceivable that does not involve faith in something trans-subjective—, faith in something not given in present empirical experience. Even in our most elementary life-adjustments there is something operative in us which far underlies our conscious perceiving and the logic of our conclusions. We are moved, not alone by what we clearly picture and coldly analyse, but by deep-lying instincts which defy analysis, by background and foreground fringes of consciousness, by immanent and penetrative intelligence which cannot be brought to definite focus, by the vast reservoirs of accumulated wisdom through which we *feel* the way to go though we can pictorially envisage no "spotted trees" that mark the trail.

This religious and saving Faith, through which the soul discovers God and makes the supreme life-adjustment to Him, is profoundly moral and, in the best sense of the word, rational. It does not begin with an assumption, blind or otherwise, as to Christ's metaphysical nature, it does not depend upon the adoption of systematically formulated doctrines; it becomes operative through the discovery of a personal Life, historically lived—and continued through the centuries as a transforming Spirit—rich enough in its experience to exhibit the infinite significance of life, inwardly deep enough in its spiritual resources to reveal the character of God, and strong enough in sympathy, in tenderness, in patience, and in self-giving love to beget forever trust and confidence and love on the part of all who thus find Him.

The God whom we learn to know in Christ—the God historically revealed—is no vague first Cause, no abstract Reality, no all-negating Absolute. He is a concrete Person, whose traits of character are intensely moral and spiritual. His will is no fateful swing of mechanical law; it is a morally good will which works patiently and forever toward a harmonized world, a Kingdom of God. The central trait of His character is Love. He does not *become* Father. He is not reconciled to us by persuasive offerings and sacrifices. He is inherently and by essential disposition Father and the God of all Grace. He is not remote and absentee—making a world "in the beginning," and leaving it to run by law, or only occasionally interrupting its normal processes—He is immanent Spirit, working always, the God of beauty and organizing purpose. He is Life and Light and Truth, an Immanuel God who can and does show Himself in a personal Incarnation, and so exhibits the course and goal of the race.*

Rufus M. Jones, 1863–1948. American philosopher, author.
Spiritual Reformers of the 16th and 17th Centuries.

He is the Way.
Follow Him through the Land of Unlikeness;
You will see rare beasts, and have unique adventures.

He is the Truth.
Seek Him in the Kingdom of Anxiety;
You will come to a great city that has expected your
return for years.

He is the Life.
Love Him in the World of the Flesh;
And at your marriage all its occasions shall
dance for joy.

W. H. Auden, 1907–1973. English poet.
For the Time Being.—"A Christmas Oratorio."

Some Generalized Mystic Ideas of God

It is striking to note the remarkable similarity in the ideas of the Object of Devotion as expressed by the great mystics in all religions. Their ideas lose specific content, and launch into greater and greater abstractions regarding their beloved. Their experience of God seems so much greater than any conceptual knowledge of Him that they are forced to leave all ideas as such, and can only express the weight of their new knowledge through such generalizations as "the ground of the soul," "the deepest abyss," "the inner motive force," "That which is," "the inner Voice," and "the inner Light." They seem to agree with Olier, who writes: "It is better to make a complete and perfect sacrifice of metaphysical speculation, and simply to adore the unknown mystery of God's grace. You cannot believe how profitable is intellectual silence in regard to these things, and how well it holds the soul in freedom, humility and simplicity."—Ed.

Neo-platonic Expression

Those divinely possessed and inspired have at least the knowledge that they hold some greater thing within them, though they cannot tell what it is; from the movements that stir them and the utterances that come from them they perceive the power that moves them: in the same way, it must be, we stand towards the Supreme when we hold intellect pure; we know the Divine Mind within, that which gives Being and all else of that order; but we know, too, that it is none of these, but a nobler principle than anything we know as Being—fuller and greater; above reason, mind and feeling—conferring these powers.

Plotinus, 204–270. Greek philosopher, mystic.

Judaic Expression

O Lord, thou hast searched me, and known me.
  Thou knowest my downsitting and mine uprising,
  Thou understandest my thought afar off.
Thou searchest out my path and my lying down,

And art acquainted with all my ways.
For there is not a word in my tongue,
But, lo, O Lord, thou knowest it altogether.
Thou hast beset me behind and before,
And laid thine hand upon me.
Such knowledge is too wonderful for me;
It is high, I cannot attain unto it.
Whither shall I go from thy spirit?
Or whither shall I flee from thy presence?
If I ascend up into heaven, thou art there:
If I make my bed in Sheol, behold, thou art there.
If I take the wings of the morning,
And dwell in the uttermost parts of the sea;
Even there shall thy hand lead me,
And thy right hand shall hold me.
If I say, Surely the darkness shall overwhelm me,
And the light about me shall be night;
Even the darkness hideth not from thee,
But the night shineth as the day:
The darkness and the light are both alike to thee.
Search me, O God, and know my heart,
Try me, and know my thoughts;
And see if there be any way of wickedness in me,
And lead me in the way everlasting.

Psalm 139.
Old Testament.

Christian Mystic Expressions

Thou calledst, and shoutedst, and burstest, my deafness. Thou flashedst, shonest, and scatteredst my blindness. Thou breathedst odours, and I drew in breath and pant for Thee. Thou touchedst me, and I burned for Thy peace. For Thou hast created us for Thyself, and our heart is restless until it find rest in Thee.

Not with doubting, but with assured consciousness, do I love Thee, Lord. Thou hast stricken my heart with Thy word, and I loved Thee. Yea also heaven, and earth, and all that therein is, behold, on every side they bid me love Thee. But what do I love, when I love Thee? not beauty of bodies, nor the fair harmony of time, nor the brightness of the light, so gladsome to our eyes, nor sweet melodies of varied songs, nor the fragrant smell of flowers, and ointments, and spices, not manna and honey, not limbs acceptable to embracements of flesh. None of these I love, when I love my God; and yet I love a kind of light, and melody, and fragrance, and meat, and embracement, when I love my God, the light, melody, fragrance, meat, embracement of my inner man: where there shineth unto my soul, what space cannot contain, and there soundeth, what time beareth not away, and there smelleth, what breathing disperseth not, and there tasteth, what eating diminisheth not, and there clingeth, what satiety divorceth not. This is it which I love, when I love my God.

And what is this? I asked the earth, and it answered me, "I am not He"; and whatsoever are in it, confessed the same. I asked the sea and the deeps, and the living creeping things, and they answered, "We are not thy God, seek above us." I asked the moving air; and the air with his inhabitants answered, "I am not God." I asked the heavens, sun, moon, stars, "Nor (say they) are we the God whom thou seekest." And I replied unto all the things which encompass the door of my flesh, "Ye have told me of my God, that ye are not He; tell me something of Him." And they cried out with a loud voice, "He made us." (The invisible things of God speak to all; but they only, understand, who compare the voice received from without, with the truth within.)

What then do I love, when I love my God? By my very soul will I ascend to Him. I will pass beyond that power whereby I am united to my body. I will pass beyond this power of mine which is called memory, desirous to arrive at Thee, and to cleave unto Thee.

How then do I seek Thee, O Lord? For when I seek Thee, by God, I seek a happy life. I will seek Thee, that my soul may live. For my body liveth by my soul; and my soul by Thee. Nor is it I alone, or some few besides, but we all would fain be happy; a happy life is joy in the truth: for this is a joying in Thee, Who art the Truth, O God my light, health of my countenance, my God. Happy then will man be, when, no distraction interposing, he shall joy in that only Truth, by Whom all things are true.

Too late loved I Thee, O Thou Beauty of ancient days, yet ever new! Behold, Thou wert within, and I abroad, and there I searched for Thee. Thou wert with me, but I was not with Thee. When I shall with my whole self cleave to Thee, I shall no where have sorrow, or labour; and my life shall wholly live, as wholly full of Thee.*–**

Saint Augustine, 354–430. Latin church father.
Confessions. Trans. E. B. Pusey.

Oh, who will give me a voice that I may cry aloud to the whole world that God, the all highest, is in the deepest abyss within us and is waiting for us to return to Him. Oh, my God, how does it happen in this poor old world, that Thou art so great and yet nobody finds Thee, that Thou callest so loudly and nobody hears Thee, that Thou art so near and nobody feels Thee, that Thou givest Thyself to everybody and nobody knows Thy name! Men flee from Thee and say they cannot find Thee; they turn their backs and say they cannot see Thee; they stop their ears and say they cannot hear Thee!

Hans Denck, 1495–1527. German mystic, spiritual reformer.
On the Law of God.

How inexhaustible God's resources, wisdom, and knowledge are! How unfathomable his decisions are, and how untraceable his ways!

Who has ever known the Lord's thoughts, or advised him?

Or who advanced anything to him, for which he will have to be repaid?

For from him everything comes; through him everything exists; and in him everything ends! Glory to him forever!

Saint Paul, first century Christian Apostle.
New Testament (Rom. 11:33–36). Trans. E. J. Goodspeed.

For silence is not God, nor speaking is not God; fasting is not God, nor eating is not God; loneliness is not God; nor company is not God; nor yet any of all the other two such contraries. He is hid between them, and may not be found by any work of thy soul, but all only by love of thine heart. He may not be known by reason, He may not be gotten by thought, nor concluded by understanding; but He may be loved and chosen with the true lovely will of thine heart. . . . Such a blind shot with the sharp dart of longing love may never fail of the prick, the which is God.[4]

But now thou askest me and sayest, "How shall I think on Himself, and what is He?" and to this I cannot answer thee but this: "I wot not."

For thou hast brought me with thy question into that same darkness, and into that same cloud of unknowing, that I would thou wert in thyself. For of all other creatures and their works, yea, and of the works of God's self, may a man through grace have full head of knowing, and well he can think of them: but of God Himself can no man think. And therefore I would leave all that thing that I can think, and choose to my love that thing that I cannot think. For why; He may well be loved, but not thought. By love may He be gotten and holden; but by thought never. And therefore, although it be good sometime to think of the kindness and the worthiness of God in special, and although it be a light and a part of contemplation: nevertheless yet in this work it shall be cast down and covered with a cloud of forgetting. And thou shalt step above it stalwartly but listily, with a devout and a pleasing stirring of love, and try for to pierce that darkness above thee. And smite upon that thick cloud of unknowing with a sharp dart of longing love; and go not thence for anything that befalleth.

Unknown English mystic, fourteenth century.
The Cloud of Unknowing. Ed. Dom Justin McCann.

He who does not love does not know God; for God is love. . . .

God is love, and he that dwelleth in love, dwelleth in God and God in him.

Saint John.
New Testament (I John 4:8, 16).

Taoist Expression

There is a primal essence that is all-inclusive and undifferentiated and which existed before there was any appearance of heaven and earth. How tranquil and empty it is! How self-sufficing and changeless! How omnipresent and infinite! Yet this tranquil emptiness becomes the Mother of

[4]*The Epistle of Discretion.*

all. Who knows its name? I can only characterize it and call it *Tao*. Though it is quite inadequate, I will even call it the Great. But how boundless is its Greatness! It stretches away into the far distances (like a circle) only to return again.

Tao is eternal but is unnamable. Its simplicity, though considered as of the humblest, is most independent. Nothing in the world is able to bring it into subjection.

Great *Tao* is all pervading! It is available everywhere, on the right hand and on the left. Everything is dependent upon it for existence and it never fails them.

Tao is invisible but permeates everywhere; no matter how one uses it or how much, it is never exhausted.

To common people *Tao*'s principle of simplicity and humility seems weak and insipid; they desire and seek music and dainties. Indeed, *Tao* has no taste! When looked at, there is nothing to be prized; when listened for, it can scarcely be heard; but its satisfactions are inexhaustible.

Tao acts without assertion, yet all things proceed in conformity with it.

The superior man, as soon as he listens to *Tao*, earnestly practices *Tao;* an average man, hearing of *Tao*, sometimes remembers it and sometimes forgets it; and inferior man, hearing of *Tao*, ridicules it. If it were not thus ridiculed, it would not be worth following as *Tao*.*

Laotzu, sixth century B.C. Chinese philosopher.
Laotzu's Tao and Wu-Wei.
Trans. by Bhikshu Wai-dau and D. Goddard.

Hindu Expression

Formless, that self-luminous Being exists within and without, higher than the highest. From Him issue life, and mind and senses—ether, air, water, fire, and the earth. . . . He is the innermost Self in all beings. He who knows him hidden in the shrine of his heart cuts the knot of ignorance even in this life. Self-luminous, ever present in the hearts of all, is the great Being. He is the refuge of all. In Him exists all that moves and breathes. Adorable is He, He is the supreme goal. He is beyond the known, and beyond the knowable. He is self-luminous, subtler than the subtlest; in Him exist all the worlds and those that live therein. He is that imperishable *Brahman*. He is the life-principle; He is the speech and the mind; He is the truth; He is immortal. He is to be realized. Attain Him, O friend.

The Upanishads (Mundaka),
The "Old Testament" of Hindu Scriptures.
Trans. Swami Prabhavananda.

From a Modern Mystic

Think of the world you carry within you, and call this thinking what you will; whether it be remembering your own childhood or yearning towards your own future—only be attentive to that which rises up in you and set it above everything that you observe about you. What happens in your innermost being is worthy of your whole love; you must somehow keep working at it and not lose too much time and too much courage in explaining your position to people. . . .

And if it worries you and makes you afraid to think of your childhood and of the simplicity and quiet that goes with it, because you cannot believe any more in God, who appears everywhere in it, then ask yourself whether you really have lost God? Is it not, rather, that you have never possessed him? For when should that have been? Do you believe that a child can hold him, him whom men bear only with effort and whose weight crushes the old? Do you believe that any one who really had him could lose him like a little stone, or do you not think rather that whoever had him could only be lost by him? . . .

Why do you not think of him as the coming one, imminent from all eternity, the future one, the final fruit of a tree whose leaves we are? What keeps you from projecting his birth into coming ages and living your life like a painful and beautiful day in the history of a great gestation? Do you not see, how everything that happens is always beginning again, and could it not be his beginning, since beginning in itself is always so beautiful? If he is the most perfect, must not the lesser be before him, so that he can select himself out of fullness and overflow?—Must he not be the last, in order to include everything in himself, and what sense would we have if he, whom we long for, had already been?

As the bees bring in the honey, so do we fetch the sweetest out of everything and build him. Even with the trivial, with the insignificant (if it but happens out of love) do we begin, with work and with rest after it, with a silence or with a small lonely joy, with everything that we do alone, without supporters and participants, we begin him whom we shall not live to know, even as our forebears could not live to know us. And yet they, who are long gone, are in us, as predisposition, as a charge upon our destiny, as blood that stirs, and as gesture that rises up out of the depths of time.

Is there anything that can take from you the hope of thus some day being in him, the farthest, the ultimate?

Celebrate Christmas in this devout feeling, that perhaps he needs this very fear of living from you in order to begin; these very days of your transition are perhaps the time when everything in you is working at him, as you have already once, as a child breathlessly worked at him. Be patient and without unwillingness and think that the least we can do is to make his becoming not harder than the earth makes it for the spring when it wants to come. . . .*

Rainer Maria Rilke, 1875–1926. German poet.
Letters to a Young Poet. Trans. M. D. Herter Norton.

Recommended Reading

Psychology

Adler, Gerhard, *Studies in Analytical Psychology* (Putnam, 1966).

Bertine, Eleanor, *Human Relationships* (McKay, 1958).

Castillejo, Irene de, *Knowing Woman* (Putnam, 1973).

Cheng Man-Ch'ing and Robert W. Smith, *Tai Chi* (Tuttle, 1967).

Delza, Sophia, *Mind and Body in Harmony* (New Directions, 1961).

Fromm, Erich, *The Art of Loving* (paperback, Bantam, 1963).

Hannah, Barbara, *Striving Toward Wholeness* (Putnam, 1971).

Harding, M. Esther, *Woman's Mysteries* (Putnam, 1972); *Psychic Energy* (Pantheon, 1963); *Journey Into Self* (Longmans, Green, 1956); *The Way of All Woman* (Putnam, 1970).

Hillman, James, *Insearch* (Scribner, 1967).

Horney, Karen, *Neurosis and Human Growth* (Norton, 1950).

Howes, Elizabeth and Moon, Sheila, *Man the Choicemaker* (Westminster, 1973).

Jacobi, Jolande, *Psychological Reflections* (from writings of C. G. Jung; paperback, Harper, 1961); *The Psychology of Jung* (Yale, repr., 1963).

Jaffe, Aniela, *The Myth of Meaning* (Putnam, 1971).

Jung, Carl G., *Modern Man in Search of a Soul* (paperback, Harvest, 1964); *Two Essays on Analytical Psychology,* Vol. 7, Coll. Works; *The Development of Personality,* Vol. 17, Coll. Works (Princeton, repr., 1964); *The Secret of the Golden Flower* (Kegan Paul, repr., 1962); *The Undiscovered Self,* Vol. 10, Coll. Works, *Civilization in Transition,* Vol. 10, Coll. Works (Princeton, repr., 1970); *Symbols of Transformation* (Princeton, repr. 1967); *Psychology and Religion: West and East* (Princeton, repr. 1969); *Psychology and Alchemy,* Vol. 12, Coll. Works (Princeton, repr. 1968); *Memories, Dreams, Reflections* (Pantheon, 1963); *Man and His Symbols* (Doubleday, repr. 1969); *Psyche and Symbol,* edited by Violet de Laszlo (Doubleday, 1958).

Kunkel, Fritz, *How Character Develops* (Scribner, 1940); *In*

Search of Maturity (Scribner, 1943); *Creation Continues* (paperback, Word, 1973).

Macmurray, John, *Reason and Emotion* (paperback, Humanities 1973).

Martin, P. W. *Experiment in Depth* (Routledge, Kegan Paul, 1955).

May, Rollo, *Man's Search for Himself* (Signet, 1967).

Neumann, Erich, *The Origins and History of Consciousness* (paperback, Harper, 1962); *Art and the Creative Unconscious* (Pantheon, 1959); *Depth Psychology and a New Ethic* (Putnam, 1969).

O'Connor, Elizabeth, *Our Many Selves* (Harper and Row, 1971).

Progoff, Ira, *Death and Rebirth of Psychology* (paperback, McGraw Hill, 1973); *Jung's Psychology and Its Social Meaning* (paperback, Doubleday, 1973).

Raynolds, Robert, *The Choice to Love* (Harper, 1959).

Rogers, Carl, *Client-Centered Therapy* (Houghton, 1951).

Sibbald, Luella, *The Man With the Water Pitcher* (Guild for Psychological Studies, 1972).

Whitmont, Edward C., *The Symbolic Quest* (Putnam, 1969).

Wickes, Frances G., *The Inner World of Man* (Holt, 1948); *The Inner World of Choice* (Harper, 1963).

White, Victor, *God and the Unconscious* (Henry Regnery Co. 1953).

Religion

Austin, Mary, *Experiences Facing Death* (Bobbs-Merrill, 1931).

Berdyaev, Nicolas, *Freedom and the Spirit,* O. F. Clark, tr. (Bles, 1935).

The Bhagavad-Gita, The Song of God, trans. by Swami Prabhavananda and Christopher Isherwood (Harper, 1944).

The Bible, Revised Standard Version (Nelson, 1946).

Buber, Martin, *Tales of the Hasidim, The Later Masters* (Schocken, 1948); *The Eclipse of God* (paperback, Harper, 1957); *To Hallow This Life,* ed. Jacob Trapp (Harper, 1958); *Between Man and Man* (paperback, Macmillan, 1968); *I and Thou* (paperback repr. Scribner, 1970).

Chapman, Dom John, *Spiritual Letters,* ed. R. Huddleston (Sheed, 1954).

Chaudhuri, Haridas, *Integral Yoga* (paperback, Quest, 1974).

The Cloud of Unknowing, trans. and intro. by Ira Progoff (Julian, 1957).

Daly, Mary, *Beyond God the Father* (Beacon, 1973).

Eckhart, Meister, *Meister Eckhart,* a modern trans. by Raymond B. Blakney, ed. (Harper, 1941).

Eranos Yearbook, Vol. 2, *The Mysteries* (Routledge & Kegan Paul 1955).

Fenelon, François, *Fénelon's Letters to Men and Women* (Newman, 1957); *Letters and Reflections,* ed. by T. S. Kepler (World, 1955).

Fleg, Edmond, *The Jewish Anthology,* trans. by Maurice Samuel Behrman (Greenwood).

Gregg, Richard B., *The Power of Non-Violence* (rev. ed. Schocken, 1958); *Self Beyond Yourself* (Lippincott, 1956).

Herrigel, Eugen, *Zen in the Art of Archery* (Pantheon, 1953).

Herschel, Abraham, *Who Is Man?* pub.

Hocking, William E., *Human Nature and Its Remaking* (rev. ed. Yale, 1923); *The Meaning of Immortality in Human Experience* (Greenwood, 1957); *The Meaning of God in Human Experience* (Yale, 1912).

Howes, Elizabeth, *Intersection and Beyond* (Guild for Psychological Studies, 1971).

Howes, Elizabeth and Moon, Sheila, *Man the Choicemaker* (Westminster, 1973).

Huxley, Aldous, *The Perennial Philosophy* (Harper, 1945).

James, William, *Varieties of Religious Experience* (paperback, Mentor 1958).

Johnston, William, *The Still Point* (paperback, Perennial, 1971).

Jones, Rufus, *Spiritual Reformers of the 16th and 17th Centuries* (Macmillan, 1914).

Kazantzakis, Nikos, *The Saviours of God* (Simon & Schuster, 1960); *Report to Greco* (paperback, Bantam, 1966).

Kelly, Thomas R., *A Testament of Devotion* (Harper, 1941).

Kelsey, Morton T., *Dreams: The Dark Speech of the Spirit* (Doubleday, 1968).

Kierkegaard, Sören, *Purity of Heart* (paperback, Harper, 1956).

Lao-tzu, *Way of Life, An American Version of the Tao Teh King* by Witter Bynner (Putnam, 1941).

Lewis, C. S., *The Screwtape Letters* (Bles, 1942).

May, Rollo, *Existence* (Basic Books, 1958).

Merton, Thomas, *The Sign of Jonas* (Doubleday, 1973); *Zen and the Birds of Appetite* (New Directions, 1968); *No Man Is An Island* (paperback, Image, 1967); *New Seeds of Contemplation* (New Directions, 1961); *Asian Journal.*

Moon, Sheila, *Joseph's Son* (Golden Quill Press, 1972).

Otto, Rudolph, *The Idea of the Holy* (paperback, Oxford, 1967).

Pelgrin, Mark, *And A Time To Die* (Guild for Psychological Studies, 1961).

Radin, Paul, *Primitive Man as Philosopher* (Dover repr. 1957).

Reps, Paul, ed., *Zen Flesh, Zen Bones* (Tuttle, 1967).

Sanford, John, *God's Forgotten Language* (Lippincott, 1968).

Sharman, Henry Burton, *The Records of the Life of Jesus* (Harper, 1917).

Steere, Douglas V., *Work and Contemplation* (Harper, 1957); *On Listening to Another* (Harper, 1955).

Suzuki, Diasetz T., *Introduction to Zen Buddhism, Zen Buddhism* (paperback, Doubleday, 1956).

Teilhard de Chardin, *Hymn of the Universe* (Harper, 1965); *The Divine Milieu* (paperback, Harper, 1968).

Tillich, Paul, *The Courage To Be* (Yale, 1952); *The Shaking of the Foundations* (paperback, Scribner, 1967); *The New Being* (Scribner, 1955).

Underhill, Evelyn, *Mysticism* (Dutton, 1948).

Watts, Alan W., *Myth and Ritual in Christianity* (Vanguard 1948).

Weil, Simone, *Waiting on God* (Harper and Row).

Mythology

Campbell, Joseph, *The Hero With a Thousand Faces* (paperback, Meridian, 1967); *Masks of God* (Viking, 1959).

Castaneda, Carlos, *Journey to Ixtlan* (Simon & Schuster, 1972).

Hamilton, Edith, *Mythology* (paperback, Mentor, 1959).

Jung, Carl G. and Kerenyi, C., *Essays on a Science of Mythology* (paperback, Harper, 1963).

Kerenyi, C., *Gods of the Greeks* (Thames and Hudson, 1951).

Larousse *Encyclopedia of Mythology* (Paul Hamlyn, 1966).

Moon, Sheila, *A Magic Dwells* (Wesleyan, 1970).

Neumann, Erich, *Amor and Psyche* (paperback, Harper).

Niehardt, John, *Black Elk Speaks* (Univ. of Nebraska Press, 1961).

von Franz, Marie-Louise, *The Golden Ass of Apuleius* (Spring Publications, 1970); *The Feminine in Fairy Tales* (Spring Publications, 1972).

Waters, Frank, *The Hopi* (Viking, 1963).

Zimmer, Heinrich, *Myth and Symbols in Indian Art and Civilization* (paperback, Harper, 1962).

Novelists, Poets, Critics, Playwrights, Painters

Here we suggest the writings of:

Conrad Aiken, Brother Antoninus, Sholem Asch, W. H. Auden, Mary Austin, William Blake, Charlotte Brontë, Florence Cane, Aaron Copland, e e cummings, Dante Alighieri, Emily Dickinson, Feodor Dostoevski, T. S. Eliot, Robert Frost, Christopher Fry, Brewster Ghiselen, Kahlil Gibran, Harold Goddard, J. W. von Goethe, Dag Hammarskjöld, Hermann Hesse, Josephine Johnson, Nikos Kazantzakis, D. H. Lawrence, Denise Levertov, C. S. Lewis, Archibald MacLeish, Thomas Mann, Jacques Maritain, Herman Melville, Sheila Moon, Charles Morgan, John Middleton Murray, Alan Paton, Charles Péguy, Herbert Read, Mary Renault, Rainer Maria Rilke, Theodore Roethke, Romain Rolland, Nancy W. Ross, J. D. Salinger, May Sarton, G. B. Shaw, Edith Sitwell, Dylan Thomas, J.R.R. Tolkien, Leo Tolstoi, Mary Webb, Patrick White, Charles Williams, W. B. Yeats.

Scientists, Naturalists

Here we suggest the writings of:

Sally Carrigher, Rachel Carson, Theodore Dobzhansky, Loren Eiseley, Joseph Wood Krutch, G. Rachel Levy, John Muir, Wolfgang Pauli, Donald Culross Peattie, Michael Polanyi, P. Teilhard de Chardin, Henry David Thoreau, Shafica Karagulla.

INDEX

Index of Authors

Index of Subject Matter